Green Garden Salad, page 29

Curried Seafood Bake,
page 116

Green Vegetable Medley,
page 40

Tournedos
in Wine Sauce,
page 48

Macaroni Bolognese, page 135

Elegant Stuffed Chicken Quarters, page 82,
Sautéed Cherry Tomatoes, page 37, and
Pan-fried Potatoes, page 35

Sesame Thins, page 160

GOOD HOUSEKEEPING'S
RECIPES FOR 1981

HEARST BOOKS
New York

Good Housekeeping Staff

Editor in Chief
John Mack Carter

Food Director
Mildred Ying

Associate Director
Susan Deborah Goldsmith

Associates
Ellen H. Connelly, Joyce A. Kenneally

Assistants
Pamela Madison Berger, Diane Simone Dixon,
Normajean Sarle, Victoria Scocozza

Editorial Coordination: Eleanore W. Karsten

Design: Sonja E. Douglas

How-to line illustrations: Marilyn MacGregor

Spot engravings from the facsimile editions of an
1895 issue of the Montgomery Ward & Co.
catalogue, copyright 1969, and *Food and Drink,*
copyright 1980, both by Dover Publications, Inc.,
New York City.

10 9 8 7 6 5 4 3 2 1

Printed in the U.S.A.

Contents

Foreword

Creating new recipes for America's cooks is a way of life at *Good Housekeeping*. Every year we develop and test more than 500 recipes in the Good Housekeeping Institute kitchens for publication in our magazine. Each of these recipes is tried again and again by the home economists on our staff to make completely certain that it is clear and concise, that it omits no steps or essential information, and—most important—that any cook who follows it will produce an appetizing, nutritious, and delicious dish.

Our concern for creating clear and reliable recipes has led us to take great care in writing our recipes. All the ingredients are listed in the order in which they are used, and the time required to complete the recipe and the number of servings produced are given at the beginning to save you time and help you plan each meal. In addition, the steps are numbered for easy reference, and you'll find that you never have to turn a page to complete a recipe.

This volume is designed to answer the continuing requests that we receive from readers of *Good Housekeeping* magazine for a more permanent record of the recipes that we create each year. You will find here all the prized favorites that first appeared in the magazine in each month's specially featured recipe section, as well as the recipes that appeared in "Favorites from Our Dining Room," "30-Minute Entrées and Desserts," and "Susan, Our Beginning Cook." But, for greater convenience in making recipe selections, we have rearranged the recipes in this compendium in food categories—from appetizers and salads through main dishes and desserts.

I am particularly proud that this complete collection of 1981 recipes continues more strongly than ever the *Good House-keeping* tradition that began in 1885 of developing original recipes. I also want to give special thanks to Debby Goldsmith and Ellen Connelly for their invaluable assistance on this project.

—Mildred Ying
Director, Food Department, Good Housekeeping Magazine

Appetizers and Soups

Artichokes with Lemon Butter

TIME: about 45 minutes—SERVINGS: 2

2 large artichokes

2 cups water

4 tablespoons butter or margarine

1 tablespoon chopped parsley

1 teaspoon lemon juice

1/4 teaspoon Worcestershire

1. With sharp knife, cut off stems and 1 inch straight across top of each artichoke. Pull off any small, loose, or discolored leaves from around bottom of artichokes. With kitchen shears, carefully trim thorny tips of leaves; discard tips.

2. Gently spread artichoke leaves apart and remove leaves from center to expose fuzzy and prickly portions (choke). With spoon, carefully scrape out choke from center of artichokes. Discard chokes. Rinse artichokes well under running cold water.

3. Place artichokes on stem end in 4-quart saucepan; add water; over high heat, heat to boiling. Reduce heat to low; cover and simmer artichokes 30 minutes or until a leaf can be pulled off easily.

4. Meanwhile, prepare lemon butter: In 1-quart saucepan over medium heat, melt butter or margarine; stir in parsley, lemon juice, and Worcestershire. Keep warm.

5. Serve artichokes with lemon butter in small bowls to dip leaves in.

Sausage-stuffed Mushrooms

TIME: about 1 hour—SERVINGS: 15

1 1/2 pounds medium mushrooms (about 30)

1/2 pound pork sausage meat

1/2 cup shredded mozzarella cheese

1/4 cup seasoned bread crumbs

parsley, for garnish (optional)

1. Remove stems from mushrooms; chop stems. Set mushrooms and stems aside.

2. In 10-inch skillet over medium heat, cook sausage until well browned. With slotted spoon, remove sausage to paper towels to drain. Spoon off all but 2 tablespoons drippings from skillet.

3. In hot drippings over medium heat, cook mushroom stems until tender, about 10 minutes, stirring frequently. Remove skillet from heat; stir in sausage, cheese, and crumbs.

4. Preheat oven to 450° F. Fill mushroom caps with sausage mixture. Place stuffed mushrooms in 15 1/2" by 10 1/2" jelly-roll pan. Bake 15 minutes. Makes about 30 appetizers.

Avocado and Shrimp in Butter Sauce

TIME: about 30 minutes—SERVINGS: 6

³/₄ pound large shrimp

2 cups water

¹/₂ cup dry white wine

2 teaspoons white-wine vinegar

1 medium green onion, cut into 1-inch pieces

1 small garlic clove, cut in half

¹/₂ cup butter

1 ripe avocado, at room temperature

sliced green onion, for garnish

1. Shell and devein shrimp, but leave tail part of shell on. In 2-quart saucepan over high heat, heat water to boiling. Add shrimp; heat to boiling. Reduce heat to medium; cook shrimp 2 to 3 minutes until shrimp are tender and pink. Drain; keep warm.

2. In same saucepan, combine wine, vinegar, green onion, and garlic. Over high heat, heat to boiling. Boil about 5 minutes or until liquid is reduced to about 2 tablespoons. Discard green onion and garlic. Reduce heat to medium; add butter, 2 tablespoons at a time, beating constantly with wire whisk until butter is melted and mixture is thickened. Keep butter sauce warm. (Do not use margarine, or sauce will not be thick.)

3. To serve, peel avocado and remove seed; cut avocado into twelve wedges. On each of six warm small plates, spoon some butter sauce; arrange two avocado wedges, and a few shrimp. Garnish with sliced green onion; serve immediately.

Spanakopitas

TIME: about 2¹/₄ hours—SERVINGS: 20

2 tablespoons olive oil

1 small onion, diced

1 10-ounce package frozen chopped spinach, thawed and squeezed dry

1 egg

¹/₃ cup grated Parmesan cheese

¹/₈ teaspoon pepper

about ¹/₃ pound phyllo (also called strudel leaves, available in Greek pastry shops and most supermarket frozen-food sections)

¹/₂ cup butter or margarine, melted

1. In 2-quart saucepan over medium heat, in hot oil, cook onion until tender, stirring occasionally. Remove from heat; stir in spinach, egg, cheese, and pepper.

2. With knife, cut phyllo lengthwise into 2-inch-wide strips. Place strips on waxed paper, then cover with slightly damp towel.

3. Brush top of one strip of phyllo with melted butter; place 1 teaspoonful spinach mixture at short end of strip.

4. Fold one corner of strip diagonally over filling so the short edge meets the long edge, forming a right angle.

5. Continue folding over at right angles until you reach the end of the strip, to form a triangular-shape package. Repeat with remaining phyllo strips and spinach filling.

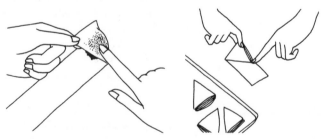

6. Preheat oven to 425° F. Place packages, seam side down, in 15¹/₂″ by 10¹/₂″ jelly-roll pan; brush with butter. Bake triangles 15 minutes or until golden brown. Serve hot. Makes 42 appetizers.

Party Shrimp Canapés

TIME: about 40 minutes—SERVINGS: 10

10 slices white bread

2 tablespoons butter or margarine

¹/₂ teaspoon thyme leaves

¹/₂ 8-ounce package frozen shelled and deveined shrimp, cooked and minced

1. Preheat broiler if manufacturer directs. Cut crusts from bread slices. With 2-inch fluted round cookie cutter, cut some circles from bread slices. Cut remaining bread into 1¹/₂-inch triangles and 2″ by 1″ pieces to make 20 cutouts in all. In blender, blend bread trimmings to make ¹/₂ cup crumbs.

½ cup shredded Swiss cheese (2 ounces)

⅓ cup mayonnaise

¼ teaspoon salt

fresh dill, radish slices, parsley sprigs, and capers, for garnish

2. In 1-quart saucepan, melt butter with thyme. With pastry brush, brush cutouts with butter mixture; place on cookie sheet; broil 2 minutes or just until golden.

3. Mix shrimp, bread crumbs, cheese, mayonnaise, and salt; spread some on each cutout.

4. About 7 to 9 inches from source of heat (or at 450° F.), broil canapés 10 minutes or until hot. Garnish canapés with dill, radish slices, parsley sprigs, or capers. Makes 20 canapés.

TO DO AHEAD: Early in day, prepare as above in steps 1 through 3. Cover and refrigerate. About 20 minutes before serving, broil and garnish as above.

Crab Strudel

TIME: about 1½ hours—SERVINGS: 12

butter or margarine

1 tablespoon minced green onion

3 tablespoons all-purpose flour

¼ teaspoon salt

⅛ teaspoon pepper

1⅓ cups milk

2 6-ounce packages frozen Alaska King or Snow crabmeat, thawed and drained

3 tablespoons cooking or dry sherry

about ⅓ pound phyllo (also called strudel leaves, available in Greek pastry shops and most supermarket frozen-food sections)

¼ cup dried bread crumbs

radish roses, for garnish

parsley sprigs, for garnish

1. In 2-quart saucepan over medium heat, in 4 tablespoons hot butter or margarine, cook green onion until tender, stirring occasionally. Stir in flour, salt, and pepper until blended; cook 1 minute. Gradually stir milk into flour mixture; cook, stirring constantly, until thickened and smooth. Stir in crabmeat and sherry; remove saucepan from heat.

2. In small saucepan over low heat, melt 4 tablespoons butter or margarine.

3. On waxed paper, overlap a few sheets of phyllo to make a 16″ by 12″ rectangle, brushing each sheet of phyllo with some melted butter or margarine. Sprinkle with 1 tablespoon bread crumbs. Continue layering, brushing each sheet of phyllo with some butter or margarine and sprinkling every other layer with 1 tablespoon bread crumbs.

4. Preheat oven to 375° F. Starting along a short side of phyllo, evenly spoon crabmeat mixture to cover about half of rectangle. From crabmeat-mixture side, roll phyllo jelly-roll fashion.

5. Place roll, seam side down, on cookie sheet; brush with remaining butter or margarine. Bake 40 minutes or until golden. For easier slicing, cool strudel about 15 minutes on cookie sheet on wire rack.

6. To serve, cut strudel into 1-inch-thick slices. Arrange a slice of strudel on a small plate; garnish with a radish rose and some parsley sprigs.

Sour-Cream-and-Cabbage Pie

TIME: about 1 hour—SERVINGS: 12

¼ cup salad oil

6 cups finely shredded cabbage (about 1 pound)

¼ pound medium mushrooms, sliced

1 medium onion, diced

1 teaspoon salt

1 teaspoon sugar

⅛ teaspoon pepper

piecrust mix for two 9-inch piecrusts

½ cup sour cream

1 pint cherry tomatoes

small lettuce leaves

1. In 5-quart Dutch oven over medium heat, in hot salad oil, cook cabbage, mushrooms, onion, salt, sugar, and pepper until vegetables are tender, about 20 minutes, stirring occasionally. Keep warm.

2. Preheat oven to 425° F. Prepare piecrust mix as label directs. Roll half of pastry into circle to line a 12-inch pizza pan. Cut remaining pastry into four equal portions. With hands, roll each into an 18-inch-long strand; gently twist each two strands together to make a rope. Moisten edge of pastry in pizza pan with water; top with pastry rope, pressing gently in place. Bake piecrust 10 minutes or until lightly browned.

3. Stir sour cream into cabbage mixture; spoon mixture into piecrust. Bake 10 minutes longer or until crust is golden brown and pie is hot.

4. Meanwhile, cut each cherry tomato into five wedges but not all the way through, to resemble a flower.

5. To serve, cut pie into twelve wedges. Garnish each serving with a lettuce leaf and one or two cherry-tomato flowers.

French-fried Cheese Bites
TIME: about 30 minutes—SERVINGS: 15

1 pound Port du Salut or Fontina cheese

2 eggs

1/4 cup water

1 cup dried bread crumbs

salad oil

salt

1. Cut cheese into 1-inch cubes. In pie plate with fork, beat eggs with water. Place bread crumbs on waxed paper. Dip cheese cubes in egg mixture, then into bread crumbs to coat evenly. Repeat until each cheese cube is coated twice with both egg and crumbs.

2. In 3-quart saucepan over medium heat, heat about 3/4 inch salad oil to 325° F. on deep-fat thermometer (or, heat oil in electric skillet set at 325° F.). Fry cheese cubes, a few at a time, about 1 minute or until golden brown. With slotted spoon, remove fried cheese to paper-towel-lined oven-safe plate; keep warm in 200° F. oven while you fry more batches. Cheese flavor varies; when all the cubes are fried, if needed, lightly sprinkle cheese cubes with salt. Serve immediately while they are soft and creamy inside. Makes about 30 appetizers.

Gingered Melon Wedges
TIME: about 2 hours—SERVINGS: 8

1 large honeydew melon

2 tablespoons confectioners' sugar

1/2 teaspoon ground ginger

1. Cut melon in half lengthwise and remove seeds; slice each half into 4 wedges. Slash the pulp of wedges criss-cross into bite-size pieces, then cut pulp loose from rind, leaving pulp in place.

2. In cup, combine sugar and ginger; sprinkle over melon. Cover melon and refrigerate.

Jumbo-Shrimp Appetizer
TIME: about 40 minutes—SERVINGS: 2

4 jumbo shrimp

1 cup water

1 tablespoon cooking or dry sherry

1/4 teaspoon salt

1/3 cup chili sauce

1 1/2 teaspoons prepared horseradish

1 teaspoon lemon juice

2 drops hot-pepper sauce

lettuce leaves

1. Shell and devein shrimp but leave tail part of the shell on. In 1-quart saucepan, heat water, sherry, and salt to boiling. Add shrimp; heat to boiling. Reduce heat to medium; cook shrimp 2 to 3 minutes, until shrimp are tender and pink. Drain shrimp; refrigerate about 20 minutes or until ready to serve.

2. Meanwhile, prepare sauce: In small bowl, mix chili sauce, horseradish, lemon juice, and hot-pepper sauce; cover and refrigerate.

3. To serve, line two wine glasses (or small plates) with lettuce leaves; spoon sauce on leaves; arrange two shrimp on rim of each glass.

Chilled Lemony Mushrooms
TIME: about 2 hours or start early in day—SERVINGS: 8

1 pound medium mushrooms

1 medium lemon

1/4 cup salad oil

2 tablespoons water

1 1/2 teaspoons soy sauce

1/4 teaspoon salt

1/4 teaspoon sugar

1/4 teaspoon rubbed sage

2 small heads Bibb lettuce

1. Rinse mushrooms under running cold water; trim tough stem ends and slice mushrooms. Cut six very thin slices and squeeze 2 teaspoons juice from lemon; set aside.

2. In 3-quart saucepan over medium-high heat, in hot salad oil, cook mushrooms, stirring frequently, until mushrooms are coated with oil. Stir in water, soy sauce, salt, sugar, sage, lemon slices, and lemon juice; heat to boiling. Reduce heat to medium; continue cooking 3 minutes longer or until mushrooms are tender, stirring often. Spoon mushroom mixture into bowl; cover and refrigerate until well chilled.

3. To serve, cut each head of Bibb lettuce into four wedges. Arrange lettuce and mushrooms on eight small plates.

Salmon Pâté

TIME: about 2¹/₄ hours or start day ahead—SERVINGS: 12

1 15¹/₂- or 16-ounce can salmon, drained

1 8-ounce package cream cheese, softened

2 tablespoons chopped green onions

1 tablespoon lemon juice

¹/₂ teaspoon salt

¹/₈ teaspoon pepper

¹/₈ teaspoon dill weed

2 tablespoons capers

assorted crackers

1. In blender at medium speed or in food processor with knife blade attached, blend first 7 ingredients until smooth. Spoon mixture into small bowl; stir in capers.

2. Cover bowl and refrigerate mixture until well chilled, about 2 hours. Serve with assorted crackers. Makes about 2¹/₂ cups pâté.

Salmon-Sole Mousse

TIME: about 4¹/₂ hours or start day ahead—SERVINGS: 10

¹/₄ cup cooking or dry sherry

water

1 16-ounce package frozen sole fillets

1 envelope unflavored gelatin

¹/₂ teaspoon salt

1 7³/₄-ounce can salmon, drained

¹/₂ bunch watercress

1 cup heavy or whipping cream

Caper Mayonnaise (see Index)

1. In 10-inch skillet over medium heat, heat sherry and about ¹/₂ inch water to boiling. Add frozen sole fillets; cover and cook 15 minutes or until fish flakes easily when tested with a fork. With pancake turner, remove sole to plate; set aside. Reserve ¹/₂ cup poaching liquid; discard remaining liquid.

2. In small saucepan, evenly sprinkle gelatin over ¹/₄ cup cold water; let stand 1 minute to soften; stir in reserved poaching liquid. Over medium heat, cook, stirring constantly, until gelatin is completely dissolved.

3. In blender at medium speed or in food processor with knife blade attached, blend sole with any liquid in plate, gelatin mixture, and salt until sole is very smooth. Pour into large bowl; cover and refrigerate until chilled and almost set, about 45 minutes.

4. Meanwhile, in medium bowl, finely flake salmon. Mince enough watercress to make ¹/₃ cup; place in small bowl. Reserve remaining watercress for garnish.

5. In small bowl with mixer at medium speed, beat heavy or whipping cream until stiff peaks form. Fold whipped cream into sole mixture until blended. Fold ¹/₂ cup sole mixture into salmon. Fold another ¹/₂ cup sole mixture into watercress. Spoon half of remaining sole mixture into 9″ by 5″ loaf pan; top with salmon mixture, then watercress mixture. Spoon remaining sole mixture on top. Cover and refrigerate until set, at least 3 hours.

6. Prepare Caper Mayonnaise.

7. To serve, unmold mousse onto cutting board; cut into ten slices. For each serving, spoon some Caper Mayonnaise onto a small plate; place a slice of mousse on top. Garnish with watercress leaves.

Deviled-Ham Pinwheels

TIME: about 30 minutes or start early in day—SERVINGS: 15

1 4¹/₂-ounce can deviled ham

1 tablespoon grated orange peel

1 tablespoon prepared mustard

2 teaspoons prepared horseradish

1 1-pound loaf unsliced white bread (8 inches long), crust removed

1. In bowl, mix first 4 ingredients.

2. Cut bread lengthwise into five ¹/₄-inch-thick slices. With rolling pin lightly flatten each slice. Spread about 2 tablespoons ham mixture over surface of each slice. From short side, roll each slice jelly-roll fashion; cut evenly crosswise to make six sandwiches. Makes 30 appetizers.

Tomato Boats

TIME: about 2 hours or start early in day—SERVINGS: 8

2 large tomatoes

1 small eggplant (¹/₂ pound)

1 small onion

1 small green pepper

1 small zucchini

¹/₄ cup salad oil

1¹/₂ teaspoons salt

1 teaspoon oregano leaves

³/₄ teaspoon sugar

Crusty Bread Flowers (right)

spinach leaves, for garnish

1. Cut each tomato into four wedges. With spoon, scoop out pulp from tomato wedges, leaving a ¹/₄-inch-thick shell; cover and refrigerate tomato shells. Chop tomato pulp.

2. Cut eggplant into ¹/₂-inch cubes. Dice onion and green pepper. Cut zucchini crosswise into ¹/₄-inch-thick slices; cut slices into thin strips.

3. In 4-quart saucepan over medium heat, in hot salad oil, cook eggplant, onion, and chopped tomato pulp until vegetables are tender, about 20 minutes, stirring occasionally. Stir in green pepper, zucchini, salt, oregano, and sugar; cook 5 minutes or until green pepper and zucchini are tender-crisp, stirring occasionally. Spoon mixture into medium bowl; cover and refrigerate until mixture is chilled.

4. Meanwhile, prepare Crusty Bread Flowers.

5. To serve, fill each tomato shell with some eggplant mixture. Garnish each serving with spinach leaves and Crusty Bread Flowers.

Crusty Bread Flowers: Preheat broiler if manufacturer directs. In small bowl, stir *4 teaspoons butter* or margarine, softened, *1 teaspoon sesame seeds*, and *¹/₄ teaspoon garlic powder* until mixed. With 1¹/₂-inch flower-shaped cookie or canapé cutter, cut *4 thin slices white bread* into 16 flowers. (Reserve trimmings for bread crumbs another day.) Spread one side of bread flowers with butter mixture; arrange bread, butter side up, on cookie sheet. Broil about 3 minutes to toast. Remove from oven; set aside.

Pâté in Aspic

TIME: about 6 hours or start day ahead—SERVINGS: 8

butter or margarine

¹/₂ pound chicken livers

¹/₄ pound mushrooms, sliced

2 tablespoons minced green onions

¹/₈ teaspoon dill weed

salt

¹/₈ teaspoon hot-pepper sauce

cooking or dry sherry

3 cups water

3 chicken-flavor bouillon cubes or envelopes

¹/₈ teaspoon pepper

2 envelopes unflavored gelatin

2 small cucumbers

1 small carrot

1 lemon

1. In 10-inch skillet over medium-high heat, in 2 tablespoons hot butter or margarine, cook chicken livers, mushrooms, green onions, dill weed, and ¹/₄ teaspoon salt until chicken livers are lightly browned but still pink inside, about 5 minutes, stirring frequently. Stir in hot-pepper sauce and ¹/₄ cup sherry; cover and simmer 5 minutes to blend flavors.

2. In food processor with knife blade attached or in blender at medium speed, blend chicken-liver mixture and 4 tablespoons butter or margarine until smooth, stopping blender occasionally and scraping sides with rubber spatula. (Mixture will be thin.) Pour mixture into small bowl; cover and refrigerate 2¹/₂ hours or until firm.

3. Prepare aspic: In 2-quart saucepan, mix water, chicken-flavor bouillon, pepper, ¹/₃ cup sherry, and ¹/₄ teaspoon salt; sprinkle gelatin evenly over chicken-broth mixture. Over medium heat, heat mixture, stirring constantly, until gelatin is completely dissolved.

4. For ease in handling, arrange eight 6-ounce custard cups in 15¹/₂″ by 10¹/₂″ jelly-roll pan. Pour about 1 teaspoonful gelatin mixture into each cup; refrigerate until set, about 10 minutes.

5. Thinly slice 1 cucumber and the carrot. With vegetable peeler, shave some peel from lemon; cut into eight 2″ by ¹/₈″ strips. In bottom of each custard cup on aspic, arrange a few cucumber slices, a carrot slice, and a strip of lemon peel to make an attractive design; cover with ¹/₈-inch layer of gelatin mixture; refrigerate until set, about 10 minutes.

6. With two spoons, shape chicken-liver mixture into eight balls, using about 1 rounded tablespoon mixture for each ball. Place a chicken-liver ball in center of each custard cup. Pour remaining gelatin mixture over pâté to cover. Refrigerate until set, about 2 hours.

7. To serve, unmold each onto a small plate. Thinly slice remaining cucumber. Garnish aspic with cucumber slices.

Toasted Almonds

TIME: about 45 minutes or start up to 2 weeks ahead

YIELD: about 3³/₄ cups

¼ cup water

³/₄ teaspoon salt

4 4¹/₂-ounce cans blanched whole almonds

Preheat oven to 400° F. In cup with spoon, mix water and salt until salt is dissolved. In 15¹/₂" by 10¹/₂" jelly-roll pan, mix almonds with water mixture. Spread almonds in single layer. Bake 20 minutes or until lightly browned, stirring occasionally. Cool almonds in pan on wire rack. Store in tightly covered container to use within two weeks.

Chili Dip with Fresh Vegetables

TIME: about 2 hours or start early in day—YIELD: 2¹/₂ cups

1 medium bunch celery

3 medium zucchini

1 bunch broccoli

1 pound large mushrooms

1 28-ounce can tomatoes, drained

1 small onion

¼ cup lightly packed parsley

¼ cup canned green chilies

1 medium garlic clove

1 tablespoon white vinegar

1 teaspoon oregano leaves

¹/₂ teaspoon salt

1. Separate celery into stalks and cut zucchini into sticks. Cut broccoli into flowerets and cut each mushroom in half. Wrap vegetables separately in plastic wrap; refrigerate.

2. Prepare dip: In blender at low speed, blend remaining ingredients until smooth. Pour dip into small bowl; cover; refrigerate.

3. About 15 minutes before serving, in a basket lined with foil, place dip; surround with vegetables.

Spicy Cheddar-Beer Dip

TIME: about 20 minutes or start day ahead—YIELD: about 2 cups

1 10-ounce package extra-sharp Cheddar cheese, shredded (2¹/₂ cups)

¹/₂ cup beer

¼ cup mayonnaise

1 teaspoon caraway seeds

1 teaspoon Worcestershire

¼ teaspoon salt

¼ teaspoon ground red pepper

In blender at medium speed or in food processor with knife blade attached, blend all ingredients until smooth. Cover and refrigerate if not serving right away.

SERVING SUGGESTIONS: Serve with unsalted crackers and assorted vegetables, such as sliced zucchini or cucumbers, celery and carrot sticks, or sliced radishes.

Tomato-Curry Bisque

TIME: about 1 hour—SERVINGS: 12

3 large green onions, thinly sliced

1 tablespoon salad oil

2 medium carrots, diced

2 celery stalks, diced

2 teaspoons curry powder

1 46-ounce can tomato juice

1 10³/₄-ounce can condensed beef consommé

1 cup water

¹/₂ teaspoon Worcestershire

1. Reserve 1 tablespoon green onion for garnish; set aside. In 4-quart saucepan over medium heat, in hot salad oil, cook green onions, carrots, celery, and curry powder until vegetables are tender, stirring occasionally. Stir in tomato juice and remaining ingredients; over high heat, heat to boiling. Reduce heat to low; cover and simmer 20 minutes to blend flavors, stirring occasionally.

2. In blender at medium speed, blend one quarter of soup mixture at a time until smooth; pour into large bowl. Return soup to saucepan; heat through.

3. To serve, garnish soup with reserved green onion. Makes about 8¹/₂ cups.

Onion Soup

TIME: about 45 minutes—SERVINGS: 5

6 tablespoons butter or margarine

6 large onions, thinly sliced (about 6 cups)

3 10½-ounce cans condensed beef broth

3 cups water

1 teaspoon sugar

½ teaspoon Worcestershire

¼ teaspoon salt

5 1-inch-thick slices French or Italian bread

¾ pound Swiss or Gruyère cheese, thinly sliced

1. In 4-quart saucepan over medium heat, melt butter or margarine; add onions; cook until onions are tender and golden, stirring occasionally. Stir in undiluted beef broth, water, sugar, Worcestershire, and salt; over high heat, heat to boiling. Reduce heat to low; cover and simmer 15 minutes.

2. Meanwhile, preheat broiler if manufacturer directs. Place bread slices on cookie sheet; toast bread in broiler until browned on both sides. Arrange cheese slices on toast; broil until cheese is melted.

3. Ladle soup into five 16-ounce soup bowls. Place a cheese-topped bread slice on soup in each bowl. Serve immediately as a main dish. Makes about 9 cups.

Cheese-Vegetable Chowder

TIME: about 30 minutes—SERVINGS: 4

3 cups diced cabbage

4 tablespoons butter or margarine

1 medium carrot, shredded

1 medium onion, diced

4 cups milk

¼ teaspoon pepper

1 chicken-flavor bouillon cube or envelope

1 8-ounce package pasteurized process cheese spread or cheese food, diced (1 cup)

salt

crackers

1. In 4-quart saucepan over medium heat, cook first 4 ingredients until vegetables are tender, stirring occasionally. Stir in milk, pepper, and bouillon; heat to boiling. Remove saucepan from heat; stir in cheese until melted. Add salt to taste.

2. Serve chowder as a main dish with crackers. Makes about 6 cups.

Velvety Pumpkin Bisque

TIME: about 30 minutes—SERVINGS: 10

2 tablespoons butter or margarine

1 tablespoon minced green onion

1 16-ounce can pumpkin

1 cup water

2 teaspoons brown sugar

½ teaspoon salt

⅛ teaspoon white pepper

⅛ teaspoon ground cinnamon

2 chicken-flavor bouillon cubes or envelopes

2 cups half-and-half

1 lemon, thinly sliced, for garnish

minced parsley, for garnish

1. In 2-quart saucepan over medium heat, in hot butter or margarine, cook green onion until tender, stirring occasionally. Stir in pumpkin, water, brown sugar, salt, pepper, cinnamon, and bouillon until blended and mixture begins to boil; cook 5 minutes to blend flavors. Stir in half-and-half; heat through.

2. To serve, ladle soup into soup bowls; garnish each serving with a lemon slice and some minced parsley. Makes about 5 cups.

Succotash Chowder

TIME: about 1 hour—SERVINGS: 16

6 tablespoons butter or margarine

2 medium celery stalks, minced

1 medium onion, minced

1 large green pepper, diced

¹/₂ cup all-purpose flour

2 cups water

1 13³/₄- or 14¹/₂-ounce can chicken broth

1 7¹/₂- to 8¹/₄-ounce can tomatoes

1 16- or 17-ounce can whole-kernel corn

1 16- or 17-ounce can lima beans

2 cups half-and-half

1 tablespoon chopped parsley, for garnish

1. In 5-quart Dutch oven or saucepot over medium heat, melt butter or margarine; add celery, onion, and green pepper, and cook until vegetables are tender, stirring occasionally. Stir in flour until blended. Gradually stir in water and chicken broth; cook, stirring frequently, until thickened, about 10 minutes.

2. Drain tomato liquid into soup mixture. Chop tomatoes; add tomatoes, corn with its liquid, lima beans with their liquid, and half-and-half. Cook over medium heat until mixture is heated through, stirring occasionally. Sprinkle with parsley. Makes about 12 cups.

Cream-of-Squash Soup

TIME: about 45 minutes—SERVINGS: 6

1 medium butternut squash (about 2 pounds)

water

2 cups half-and-half

1¹/₄ teaspoons salt

¹/₈ teaspoon pepper

1 chicken-flavor bouillon cube or envelope

watercress sprigs, for garnish

1. Peel and cut butternut squash into 1-inch chunks. In 3-quart saucepan over high heat, heat squash and 1 inch water to boiling. Reduce heat to low; cover and simmer 10 minutes or until squash is very tender. Drain.

2. In blender at medium speed, blend squash until very smooth.

3. In 3-quart saucepan over medium heat, heat squash, half-and-half, salt, pepper, and bouillon until hot, stirring occasionally. Spoon soup into soup bowls; garnish each with a watercress sprig. Makes about 4 cups.

Frankfurter Chowder

TIME: about 30 minutes—SERVINGS: 4

3 tablespoons butter or margarine

2 medium onions, thinly sliced

4 medium potatoes, peeled and cut into bite-size pieces

1 cup water

¹/₂ teaspoon salt

¹/₄ teaspoon cracked pepper

1¹/₂ cups milk

1 16-ounce package frankfurters, cut into ¹/₂-inch diagonal slices

1. In 3-quart saucepan over medium heat, melt butter or margarine; add onions and cook until tender, stirring occasionally. Add potatoes, water, salt, and cracked pepper; over high heat, heat to boiling. Reduce heat to low; cover and simmer 15 minutes or until potatoes are fork-tender.

2. Add milk and frankfurters; cook over medium-low heat until mixture is heated through, stirring occasionally. Serve as a main dish. Makes about 6 cups.

Ham-and-Bean Vegetable Soup

TIME: about 4 hours—SERVINGS: 10

1 16-ounce package dry pea (navy) beans

water

2 tablespoons salad oil

4 medium onions, sliced

5 teaspoons salt

1/2 teaspoon pepper

1 pound cooked ham, cut into bite-size pieces

2 green peppers, cut into 1/2-inch pieces

1/2 small head green cabbage, coarsely shredded (about 2 cups)

1 teaspoon thyme leaves

1 20-ounce bag frozen mixed vegetables

1 10-ounce bag spinach

1. Rinse beans in running cold water and discard any stones or shriveled beans. In 8-quart Dutch oven or saucepot over high heat, heat beans and 8 cups water to boiling; cook 3 minutes. Remove Dutch oven from heat; cover and let mixture stand 1 hour. Drain and rinse beans; set aside.

2. In same Dutch oven over medium heat, in hot salad oil, cook onions until tender, stirring occasionally. Return beans to Dutch oven; add salt, pepper, and 9 cups water; over high heat, heat to boiling. Reduce heat to low; cover and simmer 1 1/4 hours or until beans are almost tender.

3. To bean mixture add ham, peppers, cabbage, and thyme; over high heat, heat to boiling. Reduce heat to low; cover and simmer 30 minutes longer or until vegetables and beans are tender. Add frozen mixed vegetables and spinach; over medium heat, cook until frozen vegetables are tender. Serve as a main dish. Makes about 20 cups.

Hearty Clam-Lima Chowder

TIME: about 30 minutes—SERVINGS: 6

2 6 1/2-ounce cans minced clams

water

3 tablespoons butter or margarine

1 medium onion, minced

2 tablespoons all-purpose flour

3 cups milk

1 10-ounce package frozen baby lima beans

1 1/2 teaspoons salt

1/4 teaspoon celery salt

1/4 teaspoon pepper

1 12-ounce can vacuum-packed corn

1. Drain and reserve liquid from clams. Add enough water to clam liquid to make 2 cups; set clams and liquid mixture aside.

2. In 3-quart saucepan over medium heat, melt butter or margarine; add onion and cook until tender, stirring occasionally. Stir in flour until blended. Gradually stir in clam-liquid mixture and cook until mixture is slightly thickened, stirring.

3. Stir in milk, frozen lima beans, salt, celery salt, and pepper; over high heat, heat to boiling. Reduce heat to low; cover; simmer 5 minutes. Add corn and reserved clams; heat through. Serve as a main dish. Makes about 8 cups.

Fish-and-Clam Chowder

TIME: about 30 minutes—SERVINGS: 5

1 16-ounce package frozen flounder, cod, or haddock fillets

2 tablespoons salad oil

1 medium green pepper, cut into thin strips

1 small onion, diced

1 small garlic clove, minced

1 16-ounce can tomatoes

1 8-ounce bottle clam juice

1/4 teaspoon basil

1/8 teaspoon pepper

1 10-ounce can whole baby clams

1. Remove frozen fish fillets from freezer; let stand at room temperature 10 minutes to thaw slightly; then cut fish into bite-size chunks.

2. Meanwhile, in 4-quart saucepan over medium heat, in hot salad oil, cook green pepper, onion, and garlic until vegetables are tender, stirring occasionally.

3. To vegetables in saucepan, add tomatoes with their liquid, clam juice, basil, pepper, and fish chunks; over high heat, heat to boiling. Reduce heat to low; cover and simmer 10 minutes. Add clams with their liquid; cook until clams are heated through and fish flakes easily when tested with a fork. Serve as a main dish. Makes about 6 cups.

Oyster Soup en Croûte

TIME: about 1 hour—SERVINGS: 12

Pastry (right)

4 tablespoons butter or margarine

4 green onions, minced (¼ cup)

2 tablespoons all-purpose flour

3 8-ounce bottles clam juice

2 8-ounce containers shucked oysters

2 cups half-and-half

1½ cups water

1 tablespoon cooking or dry sherry

½ teaspoon salt

⅛ teaspoon pepper

1 egg

1. Prepare Pastry.

2. On lightly floured surface with floured rolling pin, roll pastry, one half at a time, ⅛ inch thick. From each pastry half, cut out six pastry circles (twelve in all), ½ inch larger than top of custard cup. (You will need twelve 6-ounce custard cups for this recipe.) Reroll trimmings ⅛ inch thick. With floured, ½-inch flower-shaped canapé cutter, cut as many pastry flowers as possible. Cover pastry circles and flowers with plastic wrap; set aside.

3. In 3-quart saucepan over medium heat, melt butter or margarine; add green onions and cook until tender, stirring occasionally. Stir in flour until blended; cook 1 minute, stirring constantly. Stir in clam juice, oysters with their liquid, half-and-half, water, sherry, salt, and pepper; over high heat, heat to boiling.

4. For easier handling, arrange custard cups in 15½″ by 10½″ jelly-roll pan; ladle hot soup into cups.

5. Preheat oven to 400° F. In small bowl with fork, beat egg slightly. Moisten edges of custard cups with water. Firmly press a pastry circle on top of each custard cup; brush pastry circles with egg. Press some pastry flowers onto each pastry circle; brush flowers with egg. Bake 20 to 25 minutes, until pastry is golden.

Pastry: In medium bowl, stir *2 cups all-purpose flour* and *½ teaspoon salt*. With pastry blender or two knives used scissor fashion, cut *¾ cup shortening* into flour until mixture resembles coarse crumbs. Sprinkle *5 tablespoons cold water*, a tablespoon at a time, into mixture, mixing with fork after each addition until pastry is just moist enough to hold together. With hands, shape pastry into a ball.

Garden Borscht

TIME: about 2 hours or start early in day—SERVINGS: 10

2 tablespoons salad oil

2 medium celery stalks, thinly sliced

2 medium carrots, thinly sliced

1 medium onion, diced

1½ pounds beets, peeled and coarsely shredded

2 medium tomatoes, diced

1 6-ounce can tomato paste

2 beef-flavor bouillon cubes

8 cups water

¼ cup cider vinegar

3 tablespoons sugar

1 tablespoon salt

1 8-ounce container sour cream (1 cup)

1. In 8-quart Dutch oven or saucepot over medium heat, in hot salad oil, cook celery, carrots, and onion until tender, stirring frequently. Add beets and remaining ingredients except sour cream; over high heat, heat to boiling. Reduce heat to low; cover and simmer about 50 minutes or until vegetables are very tender, stirring occasionally. Skim off fat from liquid in Dutch oven.

2. Serve borscht hot or refrigerate to serve cold later. Top each serving with some sour cream. Makes about 10 cups.

Chilled Cucumber Soup

TIME: about 4 hours—SERVINGS: 6

4 tablespoons butter or margarine

4 cups chopped peeled cucumbers

1 cup chopped green onions

1/4 cup all-purpose flour

4 cups chicken broth

salt

pepper

1/2 cup half-and-half

cucumber slices, for garnish

1. In 12-inch skillet over medium-high heat, in butter, cook cucumbers and onions. Blend flour well into the pan juices.

2. Gradually add broth, stirring; cook until mixture thickens and begins to boil. Add salt and pepper to taste.

3. Cover; simmer over low heat 10 minutes, stirring occasionally. Refrigerate until chilled.

4. In covered blender at medium speed, blend some of mixture until smooth.

5. Strain blended mixture through sieve into bowl; discard seeds. Repeat with rest of mixture.

6. Stir in half-and-half. Pour into chilled individual bowls; garnish with cucumber slices. Makes about 5 1/2 cups.

Carrot-Yogurt Soup

TIME: about 2 1/2 hours or start early in day—SERVINGS: 5

2 tablespoons butter or margarine

5 medium carrots, thinly sliced (about 2 1/4 cups)

1 small onion, diced

1 1/2 teaspoons brown sugar

1 teaspoon salt

1/8 teaspoon pepper

1/8 teaspoon ground cinnamon

3 1/2 cups water

1/2 8-ounce container plain yogurt

1 tablespoon chopped mint or parsley, for garnish

1. In 3-quart saucepan over medium heat, melt butter or margarine. Add carrots, onion, brown sugar, salt, pepper, and cinnamon; cook until onion is tender, stirring occasionally. Add water; over high heat, heat to boiling. Reduce heat to low; cover and simmer 10 minutes or until carrots are tender.

2. In blender at medium speed, blend half of carrot mixture at a time until smooth; pour into large bowl. Stir in yogurt. Cover and refrigerate 2 hours or until chilled. Sprinkle with chopped mint. Makes about 3 3/4 cups.

Strawberry-Rhubarb Soup

TIME: about 3 hours—SERVINGS: 4

1 pint strawberries

1 pound rhubarb

1 1/4 cups orange juice

about 1/2 cup sugar

1/4 cup chopped orange sections

1. Hull and slice strawberries and set aside four of the best slices.

2. Trim rhubarb, discarding any tough fibers. Cut stalks into bite-size chunks.

3. In 3-quart saucepan over medium heat, heat fruit and orange juice to boiling. Simmer about 10 minutes.

4. Remove pan from heat. Stir in sugar to taste. Allow to cool.

5. In covered blender at low speed, blend soup, half at a time.

6. Pour soup into a bowl, and fold in orange sections. Refrigerate, covered.

7. Serve soup in chilled bowls, each garnished with a strawberry slice. Makes about 4 1/4 cups.

Salads and Vegetables

Artichoke-and-Mushroom Salad

TIME: about 1¹/₂ hours or start early in day—SERVINGS: 8

2 9-ounce packages frozen artichoke hearts

1 pound medium mushrooms

2 4-ounce jars pimento, drained

¹/₂ cup salad oil

3 tablespoons cider vinegar

1 tablespoon lemon juice

1 tablespoon prepared mustard

¹/₂ teaspoon salt

¹/₈ teaspoon pepper

lettuce leaves

1. Prepare frozen artichoke hearts as labels direct, but prepare both packages together and omit salt; drain. Meanwhile, thinly slice mushrooms; cut pimento into thin strips.

2. In large bowl with fork or wire whisk, mix salad oil, vinegar, lemon juice, mustard, salt, and pepper. Add artichoke hearts, mushrooms, and pimento; toss gently to coat with dressing. Cover and refrigerate at least 1 hour, stirring occasionally.

3. To serve, line chilled platter with lettuce leaves; spoon vegetables and dressing onto lettuce.

Greek-style Tomato Salad

TIME: about 2¹/₂ hours or start early in day—SERVINGS: 8

6 medium tomatoes, sliced

¹/₄ pound feta cheese, crumbled

1 small onion, thinly sliced

1 3¹/₂-ounce can pitted ripe olives, drained and sliced

¹/₂ cup olive or salad oil

¹/₃ cup red-wine vinegar

2 tablespoons minced parsley

4 teaspoons sugar

¹/₂ teaspoon basil

¹/₄ teaspoon salt

¹/₄ teaspoon cracked pepper

lettuce leaves

1. Place tomato slices, feta cheese, onion, and olives in 13″ by 9″ baking dish; set aside.

2. In small bowl with fork, mix olive oil, vinegar, parsley, sugar, basil, salt, and pepper. Pour dressing over tomato mixture; with rubber spatula, gently lift tomato slices to coat with dressing. Cover baking dish and refrigerate at least 2 hours to blend flavors.

3. To serve, line chilled large platter with lettuce leaves. Arrange tomato mixture on lettuce.

Caesar Salad

TIME: about 30 minutes—SERVINGS: 6

Garlic Croutons (right)

2 medium heads romaine lettuce or the equivalent in iceberg or leaf lettuce

1/3 cup olive or salad oil

1/3 cup grated Parmesan cheese

2 tablespoons lemon juice

1/4 teaspoon salt

1/8 teaspoon cracked pepper

1 2-ounce can anchovy fillets, drained

1 egg

1. Prepare the Garlic Croutons; set aside. Wash romaine under running cold water; drain thoroughly in colander or French lettuce basket; pat dry with paper towels.

2. Into chilled large salad bowl, tear the romaine into bite-size pieces.

3. Add olive oil and toss gently until the romaine leaves are thoroughly coated.

4. Add Parmesan cheese, lemon juice, salt, cracked pepper, anchovies, and uncooked egg; toss again gently to mix well.

5. Garnish salad with Garlic Croutons. Serve salad immediately.

Garlic Croutons: Trim crusts from *3 white bread slices;* cut slices into *1/2*-inch cubes. In 10-inch skillet over medium heat, heat *1/4 cup salad oil;* add *1 small garlic clove* and cook until golden, about 2 minutes; discard garlic. Add bread cubes; cook, stirring frequently, until the cubes are crisp and golden. Drain well on paper towels.

Cold Vegetable Salad with Zucchini Dressing

TIME: about 2 hours or start early in day—SERVINGS: 8

4 medium potatoes

water

1 bunch broccoli

4 hard-cooked eggs

1 16-ounce can sliced beets, drained

3/4 cup olive or salad oil

1/3 cup red-wine vinegar

2 tablespoons chopped parsley

1 tablespoon prepared mustard

1 teaspoon sugar

1/2 teaspoon salt

1/2 teaspoon coarsely ground black pepper

1 small zucchini, shredded (about 3/4 cup)

1/2 medium green pepper, minced

1. Cook potatoes: In 3-quart saucepan over high heat, heat unpeeled potatoes and enough water to cover to boiling. Reduce heat to medium-low; cover and cook 25 to 30 minutes, until potatoes are fork-tender; drain. Cool potatoes slightly, until easy to handle. Peel and cut potatoes into 1/4-inch-thick slices.

2. Cut broccoli into 2" by 1" pieces. In 12-inch skillet over high heat, in 1 inch boiling water, heat broccoli to boiling. Reduce heat to low; cover and simmer about 5 minutes or until broccoli is tender-crisp; drain.

3. Cut each hard-cooked egg in half. Arrange eggs, potatoes, broccoli, and beets in separate piles on chilled large platter. Cover and refrigerate at least 1 hour.

4. Meanwhile, in small bowl with fork, mix olive oil, vinegar, parsley, mustard, sugar, salt, and pepper until well blended. Stir in zucchini and green pepper; cover and refrigerate.

5. To serve, stir zucchini dressing to mix. Pour over vegetables and eggs.

All-Season Salad with Feta Dressing

TIME: about 25 minutes—SERVINGS: 8 to 10

1 small head chicory

1 small head leaf lettuce

1 small head Boston lettuce

1 6-ounce package radishes, thinly sliced

1/4 pound feta cheese

1/3 cup olive or salad oil

1/4 cup white-wine vinegar

1 tablespoon sugar

1/4 teaspoon oregano leaves

1/8 teaspoon cracked pepper

1. Into large bowl, tear chicory and lettuce into bite-size pieces. Add radish slices.

2. In small bowl, crumble cheese into pieces the size of rice; with fork, stir in oil and remaining ingredients. Pour dressing over lettuce; toss to mix.

Cabbage Salad

TIME: about 3 hours or start day ahead—SERVINGS: 16

½ cup cider vinegar

½ cup salad or olive oil

2 tablespoons brown sugar

2 teaspoons salt

1 teaspoon dry mustard

1 teaspoon ground cinnamon

¼ teaspoon ground allspice

¼ teaspoon ground ginger

1 large head cabbage (about 3 pounds), shredded

2 medium green peppers, thinly sliced

1 small onion, grated

1 6-ounce package radishes, thinly sliced

1. In large bowl, mix first 8 ingredients. Add cabbage and remaining ingredients; toss gently to mix well.

2. Cover and refrigerate at least 2 hours to blend flavors, tossing occasionally.

Boston-Lettuce Salad

TIME: about 30 minutes—SERVINGS: 6

2 medium heads Boston lettuce

⅓ cup mayonnaise

⅓ cup milk

2 tablespoons chopped watercress

2 tablespoons catchup

1 teaspoon sugar

¼ teaspoon salt

⅛ teaspoon pepper

1. Rinse Boston lettuce heads under running cold water; remove and discard any wilted outer leaves. Drain well. Cut each head into wedges. Arrange lettuce wedges in salad bowl.

2. In small bowl, mix mayonnaise with remaining ingredients. Spoon dressing mixture over lettuce wedges.

Danish Cucumber Salad

TIME: about 5 hours or start early in day—SERVINGS: 8

4 medium cucumbers

salt

½ cup white vinegar

¼ cup sugar

2 tablespoons chopped fresh dill

¼ teaspoon white pepper

1. Cut cucumbers into paper-thin slices. In large bowl, mix cucumbers with 2 teaspoons salt. Let stand at room temperature 1 hour.

2. Drain liquid from cucumbers. Stir in vinegar, sugar, dill, pepper, and 1 teaspoon salt until well mixed. Cover and refrigerate at least 3 hours.

Orange-and-Avocado Salad

TIME: about 30 minutes—SERVINGS: 8

¼ cup orange juice

3 tablespoons lemon juice

3 tablespoons olive or salad oil

2 teaspoons sugar

1 teaspoon salt

4 large oranges, peeled and cut into sections

2 medium avocados, sliced

1 medium head romaine lettuce

1 large head Boston lettuce

1. In large bowl, mix orange juice, lemon juice, olive oil, sugar, and salt. Gently stir in oranges and avocados.

2. Into fruit mixture, tear lettuce into bite-size pieces. Gently toss to mix well.

Cranberry-Pineapple Salad Mold
TIME: about 4$1/2$ hours or start day ahead—SERVINGS: 16

1 envelope unflavored gelatin

water

1 6-ounce package cherry-flavor gelatin

1 6-ounce package lemon- or lime-flavor gelatin

1 12-ounce package fresh or frozen cranberries

2 medium celery stalks

1 15$1/4$- to 20-ounce can pineapple chunks

1 cup sugar

1. In 4-quart saucepan, evenly sprinkle unflavored gelatin over 2 cups water; cook over medium heat until gelatin is completely dissolved, stirring frequently. Remove saucepan from heat; stir in cherry-flavor and lemon-flavor gelatins until gelatin is completely dissolved. Stir in 3 cups cold water. Refrigerate until mixture mounds slightly when dropped from a spoon, about 1 hour.

2. Meanwhile, coarsely chop cranberries and mince celery; place in medium bowl. Drain pineapple; add pineapple chunks and sugar to cranberries, stirring until sugar is completely dissolved.

3. Fold fruit mixture into thickened gelatin. Pour into 10-inch Bundt pan or 12-cup mold. Cover and refrigerate until set, at least 3 hours.

4. To serve, unmold gelatin onto chilled platter.

Crunchy Radish Salad
TIME: about 2 hours or start early in day—SERVINGS: 6

4 6-ounce packages radishes, thinly sliced

1$1/2$ teaspoons salt

2 tablespoons minced green onions

$1/4$ cup salad oil

lettuce leaves

1. In medium bowl, toss radishes and salt until well mixed; cover and let stand 1 hour.

2. Tipping bowl over sink, press radishes with hand to drain liquid. Stir in green onions.

3. In small saucepan over high heat, heat salad oil until very hot and it begins to smoke. Slowly and evenly pour hot oil over radish mixture; toss with fork to mix well. Cover bowl and refrigerate 45 minutes or until salad is well chilled.

4. To serve, line chilled plate with lettuce leaves. Arrange radish mixture on lettuce.

Julienne of Vegetables Rémoulade
TIME: about 2$1/2$ hours—SERVINGS: 6

4 large zucchini (about 3 pounds)

4 medium carrots

1 medium green pepper

$1/4$ medium head red cabbage

salt

$3/4$ cup mayonnaise

1 tablespoon minced parsley

1 tablespoon prepared mustard

1 teaspoon capers, minced

$1/2$ teaspoon tarragon

lettuce leaves

1. Cut zucchini, carrots, and green pepper into matchstick-thin strips. Finely shred cabbage to make about 1$1/2$ cups.

2. In large bowl, toss zucchini, carrots, green pepper, and $3/4$ teaspoon salt until well mixed. In small bowl, toss red cabbage and $1/4$ teaspoon salt until well mixed. Cover bowls and let stand 1 hour.

3. Drain vegetables: Tip bowls, one at a time, over sink, pressing vegetables with hand to drain as much liquid as possible.

4. Add red cabbage, mayonnaise, parsley, mustard, capers, and tarragon to vegetables in large bowl; toss gently to coat with dressing. Cover and refrigerate at least 1 hour.

5. To serve, line platter with lettuce leaves; arrange salad on lettuce.

Green Garden Salad

TIME: about 20 minutes—SERVINGS: 12

3/4 cup frozen peas

1 small head romaine lettuce

1 small head Boston lettuce

1 small head red-leaf lettuce

2 green onions, thinly sliced

1 small cucumber, thinly sliced

1 celery stalk, thinly sliced

1/2 small bunch watercress

1/4 cup salad oil

3 tablespoons white-wine vinegar

1 tablespoon sugar

1 tablespoon chopped parsley

1/2 teaspoon garlic salt

1/2 teaspoon salt

1/4 teaspoon oregano leaves

1/8 teaspoon seasoned pepper

1. In small bowl, place frozen peas; cover with boiling water and let stand 5 minutes to "cook" peas.

2. Meanwhile, into large bowl, tear lettuce into bite-size pieces. Drain peas and add to lettuce in bowl with green onions, cucumber, celery, and watercress.

3. Prepare dressing: In small bowl with fork, mix salad oil and remaining ingredients.

4. Toss salad gently with dressing to coat.

Cucumbers with Dilled Yogurt Dressing

TIME: about 15 minutes—SERVINGS: 6

1 8-ounce container plain yogurt

1 teaspoon lemon juice

1/4 teaspoon dill weed

1/4 teaspoon salt

2 medium cucumbers, thinly sliced

In medium bowl, mix yogurt, lemon juice, dill, and salt. Add cucumbers; with rubber spatula, gently toss to mix well.

Cranberry-Wine Mold

TIME: about 4 1/2 hours or start day ahead—SERVINGS: 16

4 packages unflavored gelatin

1 cup water

3 cups cranberry-juice cocktail or red grape juice

1 1/2 cups dry red wine

1/2 cup packed light-brown sugar

red and green grapes, for garnish

1. In 1-quart saucepan, evenly sprinkle gelatin over water; let stand 1 minute to soften. Cook over medium heat until gelatin is completely dissolved, stirring frequently.

2. Pour gelatin mixture into large bowl with cranberry juice, red wine, and brown sugar. Stir mixture until sugar is completely dissolved. Pour mixture into 6-cup mold. Cover and refrigerate until set, about 4 hours.

3. To serve, unmold gelatin onto chilled platter. Garnish with grapes.

Best Coleslaw

TIME: about 1 1/2 hours or start early in day—SERVINGS: 8

1 cup mayonnaise

2 tablespoons milk

2 tablespoons cider vinegar

1 1/2 teaspoons sugar

1/2 teaspoon salt

1/8 teaspoon pepper

1 medium head cabbage, shredded (8 cups, lightly packed)

1 large carrot, shredded

In large bowl, mix mayonnaise, milk, cider vinegar, sugar, salt, and pepper. Add cabbage and carrot, and toss gently until well coated. Cover and refrigerate for about 1 hour to blend flavors.

Perfect Potato Salad

TIME: about 1 hour or start early in day—SERVINGS: 6

6 medium potatoes (2 pounds)
water
1/2 cup mayonnaise
1 1/4 teaspoons salt
2 teaspoons cider vinegar
2 teaspoons minced onion
1 teaspoon prepared mustard
1/8 teaspoon coarsely ground black pepper
about 1/4 cup milk
2 large celery stalks, thinly sliced (1 cup)
lettuce leaves

1. In 4-quart saucepan over high heat, heat unpeeled potatoes and enough water to cover to boiling. Reduce heat to medium-low; cover and cook 25 to 30 minutes until potatoes are fork-tender. Drain. Cool potatoes slightly until easy to handle. Peel and cut potatoes into bite-size chunks.

2. In large bowl with rubber spatula, mix mayonnaise, salt, vinegar, onion, mustard, pepper, and 1/4 cup milk. Stir in potatoes and celery, adding milk if needed until desired consistency.

3. Serve potato salad immediately on lettuce leaves. Or, cover and refrigerate salad to serve later.

Parslied Potato Salad

TIME: about 3 hours or start day ahead—SERVINGS: 12

15 medium potatoes (5 pounds)
water
3/4 cup salad oil
1/3 cup cider vinegar
1/4 cup minced parsley
1 tablespoon prepared mustard
2 1/4 teaspoons salt
1 teaspoon minced green onion
1/4 teaspoon cracked pepper

1. In 6-quart saucepot over high heat, heat unpeeled potatoes and enough water to cover to boiling. Reduce heat to medium-low; cover and cook 25 to 30 minutes until potatoes are fork-tender.

2. Meanwhile, in large bowl with fork, mix salad oil, vinegar, parsley, mustard, salt, green onion, and pepper.

3. When potatoes are done, drain; cool potatoes until easy to handle. Peel; cut potatoes into thin slices. Add potatoes to salad dressing; with rubber spatula, toss gently until well coated. Cover and refrigerate at least 2 hours to blend flavors, tossing occasionally.

Lemon-buttered Asparagus

TIME: about 30 minutes—SERVINGS: 6

2 1/2 pounds asparagus
3 tablespoons butter or margarine
1 tablespoon lemon juice
3/4 teaspoon salt

1. Prepare asparagus: Hold base of each stalk firmly and bend stalk (end will break off at spot where it becomes tough); discard tough ends; with sharp knife, remove scales. If you like, trim rough end of each asparagus stalk even.

2. In 12-inch skillet over medium heat, melt butter or margarine. Add asparagus, lemon juice, and salt; cover and cook until asparagus is tender-crisp, about 5 minutes, turning asparagus occasionally.

Asparagus Mimosa

TIME: about 30 minutes—SERVINGS: 12

1 egg
4 10-ounce packages frozen asparagus spears
1/2 teaspoon salt
water
1/2 cup butter or margarine
2 tablespoons lemon juice
1/4 teaspoon tarragon leaves
1/4 teaspoon cracked pepper
1/4 teaspoon prepared mustard

1. Hard-cook egg. Peel egg and coarsely chop; set aside.

2. Meanwhile, in 12-inch skillet over high heat, heat frozen asparagus, salt, and 1/2 inch water to boiling, gently separating asparagus spears with fork. Reduce heat to low; cover and simmer 5 minutes or until asparagus is fork-tender. Drain, leaving asparagus in skillet.

3. To asparagus in skillet, add butter or margarine, lemon juice, tarragon, pepper, and mustard; over medium heat, heat until butter melts, stirring occasionally.

4. To serve, arrange asparagus on warm platter. Pour butter sauce over asparagus; sprinkle with chopped egg.

Sesame Green Beans

TIME: about 30 minutes—SERVINGS: 6

1½ pounds green beans
2 teaspoons sesame seeds
water
3 tablespoons soy sauce
2 tablespoons salad oil

1. Trim ends from green beans. If green beans are very long, cut in half.

2. In small saucepan over medium heat, cook sesame seeds until golden brown, stirring and shaking saucepan frequently. Remove saucepan from heat.

3. Meanwhile, in 3-quart saucepan over medium heat, in 1 inch boiling water, heat green beans to boiling. Reduce heat to low; cover and simmer 10 minutes or until beans are tender-crisp, stirring occasionally. Drain.

4. Return green beans to saucepan; stir in soy sauce and salad oil. Over low heat, cook green beans about 10 minutes longer to blend flavors, stirring frequently. Sprinkle beans with sesame seeds. Serve beans warm, or cover and refrigerate to serve cold later.

Broccoli Puffs

TIME: about 1½ hours—SERVINGS: 10

4 slices bacon
4 eggs
2 cups milk
1¾ cups all-purpose flour
¾ teaspoon salt
1 10-ounce package frozen chopped broccoli, thawed and patted dry

1. In 10-inch skillet over medium-low heat, cook bacon until browned; remove to paper towels to drain. Crumble bacon. Reserve 2 tablespoons bacon drippings.

2. Preheat oven to 375° F. Grease ten 6-ounce custard cups; set in jelly-roll pan for easier handling. In large bowl with wire whisk or fork, beat eggs until foamy. Beat in milk, flour, salt, bacon, and reserved drippings until smooth. Stir in chopped broccoli.

3. Fill each custard cup three-quarters full with egg mixture. Bake 45 minutes or until golden and toothpick inserted in center comes out clean. Serve immediately (puffs will fall upon standing).

Broccoli Timbales

TIME: about 1 hour—SERVINGS: 6

1 10-ounce package frozen chopped broccoli, thawed and squeezed dry
3 tablespoons butter or margarine
1 small onion, minced
2 tablespoons all-purpose flour
2 cups half-and-half
4 eggs
1 envelope chicken-flavor bouillon
1 teaspoon salt
⅛ teaspoon pepper
boiling water

1. Finely chop broccoli; set aside.

2. Preheat oven to 350° F. In 1-quart saucepan over medium heat, in hot butter or margarine, cook onion until tender, stirring occasionally. Stir in flour until blended; cook 1 minute, stirring frequently. Gradually stir in 1 cup half-and-half; cook, stirring constantly, until slightly thickened. Remove saucepan from heat.

3. Grease six 6-ounce custard cups. In medium bowl with wire whisk or fork, mix eggs, bouillon, salt, pepper, and remaining half-and-half. Stir in onion mixture and broccoli. Ladle egg mixture into custard cups; set cups in 13" by 9" baking pan; place pan on oven rack. Pour boiling water in pan to come halfway up side of cups. Bake 35 minutes or until knife inserted in center of mixture comes out clean.

4. To serve, invert custard cups onto warm platter.

Sautéed Cabbage and Spinach

TIME: about 30 minutes—SERVINGS: 8

1 medium head green cabbage (about 2 pounds)
2 tablespoons salad oil
1¼ teaspoons salt
½ teaspoon sugar
½ 10-ounce bag spinach

With sharp knife, core and coarsely shred cabbage. In 5-quart Dutch oven over high heat, heat salad oil until hot; add cabbage, salt, and sugar, and cook, stirring frequently, until cabbage is tender-crisp, about 5 minutes. Add spinach; cook 1 minute longer, stirring constantly.

Sautéed Caraway Cabbage

TIME: 15 minutes—SERVINGS: 6

1 **small head green cabbage**

3 **tablespoons salad oil**

1 **teaspoon caraway seeds**

1 **teaspoon salt**

1. With knife, coarsely shred cabbage.

2. In 5-quart Dutch oven over high heat, in hot salad oil, cook cabbage, caraway seeds, and salt, stirring quickly and frequently until cabbage is tender-crisp, about 10 minutes.

Sautéed Red Cabbage

TIME: about 45 minutes—SERVINGS: 8

1 **large head red cabbage (about 3 pounds)**

1/4 **cup salad oil**

1 **medium onion, diced**

1 3/4 **teaspoons salt**

1/4 **teaspoon pepper**

2 **tablespoons wine vinegar**

1 1/2 **teaspoons brown sugar**

1. Discard any tough outer leaves from cabbage. Reserve 6 large leaves from cabbage; set aside. Finely shred enough cabbage to make 1/4 cup; set aside. Coarsely shred remaining cabbage.

2. In 5-quart saucepot or Dutch oven over high heat, in hot salad oil, cook coarsely shredded cabbage, onion, salt, and pepper until vegetables are tender-crisp, about 10 minutes, stirring frequently. Remove saucepot from heat; add vinegar and brown sugar; toss to mix well.

3. To serve, line platter with reserved cabbage leaves. Spoon cabbage mixture on leaves; garnish with finely shredded cabbage.

Minted Carrots

TIME: about 45 minutes—SERVINGS: 6

2 **15- to 16-ounce cans small whole carrots, drained**

1/4 **cup mint jelly**

2 **tablespoons butter or margarine, cut into small pieces**

1 **tablespoon brown sugar**

1/2 **teaspoon salt**

1. Prepare outdoor grill for barbecuing.

2. Meanwhile, on double thickness of heavy-duty foil, mix all ingredients. Wrap carrot mixture in foil, being careful that seam of foil is folded several times to seal in juices.

3. Place foil packet on grill over medium heat; cook 10 minutes or until heated through, turning packet occasionally with tongs.

TO COOK ON TOP OF RANGE: About 15 minutes before serving, in 2-quart saucepan, combine all ingredients. Over medium heat, cook until carrots are heated through, stirring occasionally.

Sugared Carrots

TIME: about 1 1/2 hours—SERVINGS: 12

4 **16-ounce bags carrots**

water

4 **tablespoons butter or margarine**

3 **tablespoons brown sugar**

1 1/4 **teaspoons salt**

1/8 **teaspoon pepper**

1. Cut each carrot crosswise in half; cut each half lengthwise into thin slices; then cut slices into matchstick-thin strips.

2. In 5-quart saucepot over high heat, in 1 inch boiling water, heat carrots to boiling. Reduce heat to low; cover and simmer about 10 minutes or until carrots are tender, stirring occasionally. Drain well, leaving carrots in saucepot.

3. To carrots in saucepot, add butter or margarine, brown sugar, salt, and pepper; over medium heat, heat until butter and sugar are melted, gently stirring occasionally.

Silver-Dollar Corn Cakes

TIME: about 30 minutes—SERVINGS: 6

about 3 medium ears corn, husked

1 cup pancake mix

1 tablespoon sugar

¹/₄ teaspoon salt

salad oil

confectioners' sugar

1. With sharp knife, cut kernels from corn to make about 1¹/₂ cups kernels.

2. In medium bowl, prepare pancake mix as label directs. Stir in sugar, salt, and corn.

3. Heat griddle or 12-inch skillet over medium heat; lightly brush with salad oil. Drop batter by heaping tablespoonfuls onto griddle, making several corn cakes at a time. Cook until tops are slightly set and undersides are golden. With pancake turner, turn corn cakes and cook until undersides are golden; place on warm platter; keep warm. Repeat with remaining batter, brushing griddle with more salad oil if necessary.

4. To serve, sprinkle corn cakes lightly with confectioners' sugar.

Cucumbers au Gratin

TIME: about 45 minutes—SERVINGS: 8

6 large cucumbers (about 4 pounds)

water

salt

3 tablespoons butter or margarine

3 tablespoons all-purpose flour

¹/₄ teaspoon pepper

¹/₄ teaspoon caraway seeds

2 cups milk

1 4-ounce package shredded sharp Cheddar cheese

1. Peel cucumbers. Cut each cucumber lengthwise in half; remove seeds; then cut each half crosswise in half.

2. In 12-inch skillet over high heat, in 1 inch boiling water, heat cucumbers and ¹/₂ teaspoon salt to boiling. Reduce heat to low; cover and simmer about 10 minutes or until cucumbers are tender, stirring occasionally.

3. Meanwhile, in 2-quart saucepan over medium heat, melt butter or margarine; stir in flour, pepper, caraway seeds, and 1 teaspoon salt until smooth. Gradually stir in milk; cook, stirring constantly, until thickened and smooth. Stir in half of Cheddar cheese until melted. Remove saucepan from heat.

4. Preheat broiler if manufacturer directs. Drain cucumbers well. In 12″ by 8″ baking dish, arrange half of cucumber pieces; top with half of sauce mixture. Repeat. Sprinkle top with remaining cheese. About 7 to 9 inches from source of heat (or at 450° F.), broil cucumber mixture 3 minutes or until cheese is melted and golden brown.

Sweet-and-Sour Cucumbers

TIME: about 25 minutes—SERVINGS: 4

3 large cucumbers (about 2 pounds)

¹/₃ cup water

1 tablespoon all-purpose flour

2 tablespoons tarragon vinegar

4 teaspoons sugar

1¹/₂ teaspoons salt

¹/₈ teaspoon pepper

1. With vegetable peeler, peel cucumbers, leaving ¹/₂-inch-wide strips of green peel for attractive color. Cut cucumbers crosswise into ¹/₂-inch-thick slices; set aside.

2. In 3-quart saucepan, mix water and remaining ingredients. Add cucumbers; over high heat, heat to boiling. Reduce heat to low; cover and simmer 10 minutes or until cucumbers are tender and sauce is slightly thickened, stirring mixture occasionally.

Szechwan Eggplant

TIME: about 1 hour—SERVINGS: 8

2 **medium eggplants (about 1 pound each)**
salad oil
1³/₄ **cups water**
2 **tablespoons soy sauce**
1 **tablespoon sugar**
1 **tablespoon cornstarch**
1 **tablespoon minced peeled ginger root or**
   1¹/₄ **teaspoons ground ginger**
1 **teaspoon hot-pepper sauce**
¹/₄ **teaspoon salt**
1 **chicken-flavor bouillon cube**
1 **green onion, finely chopped**

1. Cut eggplants lengthwise into ¹/₂-inch-thick slices; cut each slice lengthwise in half.

2. In 12-inch skillet over medium-high heat, in ¹/₄ cup hot salad oil, cook eggplant, a few slices at a time, until browned on both sides; remove slices as they brown to paper towels to drain, adding more oil if needed.

3. In same skillet, mix water and remaining ingredients. Cook over medium heat, stirring constantly, until mixture boils and slightly thickens. Return eggplant to skillet; heat through.

Sautéed Herbed Mushrooms

TIME: about 30 minutes—SERVINGS: 6

4 **tablespoons butter or margarine**
2 **pounds medium mushrooms**
¹/₂ **teaspoon salt**
¹/₄ **teaspoon thyme leaves**
¹/₈ **teaspoon pepper**

In 5-quart Dutch oven or 12-inch skillet over medium-high heat, melt butter or margarine. Add mushrooms, salt, thyme, and pepper; cook, stirring frequently, until mushrooms are tender, about 10 minutes.

Pickled Onions

TIME: about 45 minutes—SERVINGS: 6

2 **16-ounce jars tiny whole white onions,**
   drained
¹/₂ **cup packed light-brown sugar**
¹/₄ **cup cider vinegar**
1 **teaspoon salt**
¹/₈ **teaspoon ground cloves**

1. Prepare outdoor grill for barbecuing.

2. Meanwhile, on double thickness of heavy-duty foil, mix all ingredients. Wrap onion mixture in foil, being careful that seam of foil is folded several times to seal in juices.

3. Place foil packet on grill over medium heat; cook 10 to 15 minutes until onions are heated through, turning packet occasionally with tongs.

TO COOK ON TOP OF RANGE: About 15 minutes before serving, in 2-quart saucepan, combine all ingredients. Over medium heat, heat to boiling. Reduce heat to low; simmer 5 minutes to blend flavors, stirring occasionally.

Apple-Juice-Batter Onion Rings

TIME: about 45 minutes—SERVINGS: 8

1¹/₄ **cups all-purpose flour**
1 **cup apple juice**
1 **teaspoon salt**
³/₄ **teaspoon double-acting baking powder**
¹/₈ **teaspoon pepper**
1 **egg**
salad oil
2 **large onions (about 1¹/₄ pounds)**

1. Prepare batter: In medium bowl with wire whisk or fork, mix first 6 ingredients and 1 tablespoon salad oil just until flour is moistened.

2. In 12-inch skillet over medium heat, heat ³/₄ inch salad oil to 350° F. on deep-fat thermometer (or, heat oil in electric skillet set at 350° F.). While oil is heating, cut onions into ¹/₄-inch-thick slices; separate slices into rings.

3. Dip onion rings, a few at a time, into batter, and fry in hot oil about 3 minutes or until golden. With tongs, remove onion rings to paper-towel-lined jelly-roll pan to drain. Keep warm in 200° F. oven while you fry more batches. Serve immediately.

Stir-fried Sugar Snap Peas

TIME: about 15 minutes—SERVINGS: 4

1 pound Sugar Snap peas
1 tablespoon salad oil
1/2 teaspoon salt

1. Remove stem ends and strings along both sides of pods of Sugar Snap peas (do not shell). Rinse with cold water.

2. In 3-quart saucepan over medium heat, heat salad oil until very hot; add Sugar Snap peas and salt; cook until tender-crisp, about 3 to 5 minutes, stirring quickly and frequently.

Pan-fried Potatoes

TIME: about 30 minutes—SERVINGS: 4

4 medium potatoes
3 tablespoons butter or margarine
1 teaspoon salt

Cut potatoes into 1/4-inch-thick slices. In 12-inch skillet, melt butter or margarine over medium heat; add potato slices, and cook, turning occasionally, 20 minutes or until tender. Sprinkle with salt.

Potatoes Anna

TIME: about 1 1/2 hours—SERVINGS: 4

2 tablespoons butter or margarine
1 teaspoon salt
3 large potatoes, peeled

1. In 1-quart saucepan over low heat, melt butter or margarine; add salt. Preheat oven to 425° F.

2. With knife, slice potatoes about 1/4 inch thick.

3. In greased 8-inch pie plate, arrange potato slices, overlapping them; drizzle butter mixture on top. Cover plate tightly with foil; bake 20 minutes.

4. Uncover and bake about 55 minutes more or until potatoes are very tender and crusty.

5. Let stand at room temperature 5 minutes. With metal spatula, carefully loosen potatoes from pie plate. Place inverted serving plate over potatoes; holding both plates, invert and unmold. Cut into wedges.

Cheesy Potatoes in Foil

TIME: about 1 1/4 hours—SERVINGS: 6

4 large potatoes (2 pounds), unpeeled and cut into 1/4-inch slices
1 medium onion, minced
4 tablespoons butter or margarine, cut into small pieces
1 teaspoon salt
1/4 teaspoon pepper
1/4 teaspoon caraway seeds
1 4-ounce package shredded sharp Cheddar cheese

1. Prepare outdoor grill for barbecuing.

2. Meanwhile, wrap all ingredients except Cheddar cheese in double thickness of heavy-duty foil, being careful seam of foil is folded several times to seal in juices.

3. Place foil packet on grill over medium heat; cook 35 minutes or until potatoes are tender, turning packet often with tongs. Remove packet from heat; sprinkle potato mixture with Cheddar cheese.

TO COOK ON TOP OF RANGE: About 30 minutes before serving, spray 12-inch skillet with *vegetable cooking spray* as label directs; place skillet over medium heat. In skillet, melt butter or margarine; add potatoes, onion, salt, pepper, and caraway seeds. Cover and cook potato mixture until potatoes are tender and browned, about 15 minutes, turning potatoes occasionally with pancake turner. Remove skillet from heat; sprinkle potato mixture with Cheddar cheese; cover skillet until cheese melts.

Roasted Potato Fans

TIME: about 1¹/₄ hours—SERVINGS: 6

6 **medium potatoes (2 pounds)**

6 **tablespoons butter or margarine**

¹/₂ **teaspoon salt**

¹/₄ **teaspoon basil**

¹/₄ **teaspoon marjoram leaves**

¹/₈ **teaspoon pepper**

1. Peel potatoes. Cut each potato crosswise into ¹/₄-inch-thick slices, being careful to cut each slice only three-quarters of the way through potato.

2. In 13″ by 9″ baking pan in 400° F. oven, melt butter or margarine. Arrange potatoes, cut side up, in pan; brush with melted butter; sprinkle with salt, basil, marjoram, and pepper. Bake 1 hour or until potatoes are golden and slices are fanned out, occasionally brushing potatoes with butter in pan.

Party Potato Casserole

TIME: about 2 hours—SERVINGS: 10

8 **medium potatoes (2¹/₂ pounds)**

water

1 **8-ounce container sour cream (1 cup)**

2 **tablespoons milk**

butter or margarine, softened

salt

pepper

1 **12-ounce package frozen cooked squash, thawed**

1 **egg**

1 **10-ounce package frozen chopped spinach, thawed and drained**

2 **teaspoons grated onion**

¹/₄ **cup shredded Cheddar cheese**

1. In 5-quart saucepot or Dutch oven over high heat, heat potatoes and enough water to cover to boiling. Reduce heat to medium-low; cover and cook potatoes 30 minutes or until fork-tender; drain. Cool potatoes slightly; peel potatoes.

2. In large bowl with mixer at low speed, beat potatoes, sour cream, milk, 2 tablespoons butter or margarine, ¹/₂ teaspoon salt, and ¹/₈ teaspoon pepper until smooth and fluffy. Set aside.

3. Preheat oven to 350° F. In small bowl, mix thawed frozen squash with 1 tablespoon butter or margarine and ¹/₈ teaspoon salt; set aside.

4. In second small bowl, beat egg slightly; add thawed frozen spinach, grated onion, 1 tablespoon butter or margarine, and ¹/₈ teaspoon salt; mix well; set aside.

5. In 2-quart deep glass casserole or glass soufflé dish, evenly spread one third of mashed potatoes; top with squash mixture in an even layer, then with another one third of potatoes, then with spinach mixture, then with remaining potatoes.

6. Bake casserole 40 minutes or until heated through. Remove from oven; sprinkle Cheddar cheese over top of potatoes and let stand a few minutes, until cheese melts.

Brown-Butter Potatoes and Rutabagas

TIME: about 1 hour—SERVINGS: 16

15 **medium potatoes (5 pounds)**

2 **medium rutabagas (3 pounds)**

water

2 **teaspoons salt**

1 **teaspoon sugar**

¹/₄ **teaspoon pepper**

³/₄ **cup butter or margarine**

1 **cup hot milk**

parsley sprigs, for garnish (optional)

1. Peel potatoes and rutabagas; cut each into 1-inch chunks. In 8-quart Dutch oven or saucepot over high heat, heat potatoes, rutabagas, and enough water just to cover vegetables to boiling. Reduce heat to medium-low; cover and cook about 15 minutes or until potatoes and rutabagas are fork-tender. Drain.

2. In large bowl with mixer at low speed, beat potatoes, rutabagas, salt, sugar, pepper, and ¹/₂ cup butter or margarine until fluffy. Beating at medium speed, gradually add milk; continue beating 2 minutes or until mixture is smooth. Keep warm.

3. To serve, in 1-quart saucepan over medium-low heat, melt ¹/₄ cup butter or margarine; continue cooking until butter turns golden brown, stirring occasionally. Immediately remove saucepan from heat. (If butter gets too dark, it will have a bitter taste.) Spoon mashed-potato mixture into large bowl; pour browned butter over mixture. If you like, garnish with parsley sprigs.

Pan-roasted Sweet-Potato Chunks

TIME: about 45 minutes—SERVINGS: 12

6 medium sweet potatoes (3 pounds)

3 tablespoons butter or margarine

1. Peel sweet potatoes; cut into 1-inch chunks.

2. In 12-inch skillet over medium-low heat, melt butter or margarine. Add half of sweet potato chunks. Cover skillet; cook 20 minutes or until sweet potatoes are tender and browned on all sides, turning potatoes occasionally. With pancake turner, remove potatoes to bowl; keep warm. Repeat with remaining potatoes, but do not add additional butter or margarine.

Honeyed Pumpkin

TIME: about 45 minutes—SERVINGS: 4

1 4-pound pumpkin

4 cups water

1 teaspoon salt

2 tablespoons butter or margarine

2 tablespoons honey

1/2 teaspoon ground allspice (optional)

1. With sharp knife, cut pumpkin into quarters. Remove seeds and stringy portions.

2. In 4-quart saucepan over high heat, heat pumpkin, water, and salt to boiling; reduce heat to low; cover and simmer 25 to 30 minutes, until the pumpkin is fork-tender.

3. Drain pumpkin. Cool slightly and scoop flesh from peel into same saucepan. With potato masher or slotted spoon, mash pumpkin; drain well.

4. Over low heat, heat pumpkin about 3 minutes, shaking pan occasionally to evaporate excess liquid. Stir in butter, honey, and allspice; mix well.

Summer-Squash Medley

TIME: about 15 minutes—SERVINGS: 6

1 pound small zucchini

1 pound small yellow straightneck squash

water

salt

1/2 cup chopped parsley

4 tablespoons butter or margarine

2 tablespoons lemon juice

1/4 teaspoon pepper

1. Cut zucchini and straightneck squash into strips about 2 inches long.

2. In 3-quart saucepan over medium heat, in 1 inch boiling water, heat zucchini, squash, and 2 teaspoons salt to boiling. Reduce heat to low; cover and simmer 3 minutes or until vegetables are tender-crisp; drain.

3. Return vegetables to saucepan; over low heat, stir in 1 teaspoon salt, chopped parsley, butter, lemon juice, and pepper until butter is melted.

Sautéed Cherry Tomatoes

TIME: about 10 minutes—SERVINGS: 4

2 tablespoons butter or margarine

1 pint cherry tomatoes

In 3-quart saucepan over high heat, melt butter or margarine; add cherry tomatoes. Cook 4 or 5 minutes, just until tomatoes are heated through and skins start to wrinkle, stirring frequently.

Stir-fried Vegetables

TIME: 15 to 30 minutes—SERVINGS: 6

1½ **pounds asparagus or 1 bunch broccoli or 3 medium zucchini (about 8 ounces each)**

2 **tablespoons salad oil**

salt

1. Prepare the vegetables: ASPARAGUS: Remove tough end: Hold stalk at base, bend until it snaps. With small knife, remove scales, then rinse to wash away all grit. Cut stalks into uniform pieces so they will cook evenly. BROCCOLI: Cut flowerets from stalk; cut into same-size segments. Cut off woody end of stalk; peel stalk to remove tough outer skin. Slice stalk into thin strips that will cook in same time as flowerets. ZUCCHINI: Scrub gently under running water to remove hidden grit. Slice off stem and blossom end of each zucchini and discard. Slice zucchini into ¼-inch-thick slices.

2. Heat about 2 tablespoons of salad oil over medium-high heat in 10-inch skillet or 4-quart saucepan (or in a wok if you have one) until very hot. Add vegetable. Cook, stirring quickly and frequently until the vegetable is coated with oil. Add salt to taste and continue cooking until tender-crisp, about 3 minutes for asparagus, 5 minutes for zucchini, 10 minutes for broccoli, keeping heat medium-high and stirring the vegetables frequently. For firmer vegetables such as broccoli, which take a little longer to cook, add a little water—about 2 tablespoons to ¼ cup—while cooking, and cover pan for the last minute or two of cooking time.

NOTE: Using these directions you can stir-fry many other vegetables—cauliflower, celery, carrots, etc. For quick, even cooking, cut them into small, equal-size pieces. Gauge cooking time by the vegetable's firmness of texture—the firmer it is, the longer it will take to cook through. If you like, for a little extra flavor, add a sprinkling of ground black pepper, soy sauce, or sesame seeds.

Stir-fried Vegetable Mix

TIME: about 25 minutes—SERVINGS: 6

3 **tablespoons salad oil**

2 **medium carrots, cut in matchstick-thin strips**

1 **medium onion, thinly sliced**

1 **small bunch broccoli, cut in 2″ by ½″ pieces**

¾ **teaspoon salt**

½ **teaspoon sugar**

1 **4-ounce can whole mushrooms**

1. In 12-inch skillet over high heat, in hot oil, cook carrots, onion, and broccoli, stirring quickly and frequently, about 3 to 4 minutes.

2. Add salt, sugar, and mushrooms with their liquid; cover and cook 5 to 6 minutes, until vegetables are tender-crisp, stirring occasionally.

Savory Italian Vegetables

TIME: about 1 hour—SERVINGS: 6

2 medium zucchini (about 8 ounces each), cut into ¼-inch slices

1 small eggplant (about 1 pound), cut into ½-inch cubes

1 large green pepper, cut into thin strips

1 medium onion, thinly sliced

1 pint cherry tomatoes

½ cup water

4 tablespoons butter or margarine, cut into small pieces

1 3-ounce jar pimento-stuffed olives, drained and each cut in half

1 teaspoon salt

1 teaspoon sugar

½ teaspoon basil

¼ teaspoon pepper

1. Prepare outdoor grill for barbecuing.

2. Meanwhile, on double thickness of heavy-duty foil, mix all ingredients. Wrap vegetable mixture in foil, being careful that seam of foil is folded several times to seal in juices.

3. Place foil packet on grill over medium heat; cook 25 minutes or until vegetables are tender, turning packet occasionally with tongs.

TO COOK ON TOP OF RANGE: About 30 minutes before serving, in covered 12-inch skillet over medium heat, cook all ingredients until vegetables are tender, about 10 minutes, stirring occasionally.

Curried Vegetables

TIME: about 45 minutes—SERVINGS: 12

water

1 pound green beans, each cut in half

salad oil

1 medium eggplant (1 pound), cut into 1½-inch chunks

3 medium onions, quartered

2 medium green peppers, cut into ½-inch-wide strips

2 large carrots, thinly sliced

1 tablespoon curry powder

2¼ teaspoons salt

2 medium tomatoes, cut into wedges

1. In 5-quart Dutch oven or saucepot over high heat, in 1 inch boiling water, heat green beans to boiling. Reduce heat to low; cover and simmer 10 minutes or until beans are tender-crisp, stirring occasionally. With slotted spoon, remove beans from Dutch oven to large bowl; discard water.

2. In same Dutch oven over medium-high heat, in ¼ cup hot salad oil, cook eggplant until tender and browned on all sides, stirring frequently; remove eggplant to bowl with beans.

3. In 3 more tablespoons hot salad oil, cook onions, green peppers, and carrots until tender-crisp, stirring frequently. Stir in curry powder; cook 1 minute. Return beans and eggplant to Dutch oven; stir in salt and 1½ cups water. Over high heat, heat to boiling. Reduce heat to low; cover and simmer 10 minutes to blend flavors. Add tomatoes; heat through.

4. Serve vegetables warm, or cover and refrigerate to serve cold later.

Celebration Vegetable Platter

TIME: about 1 hour or start early in day—SERVINGS: 12

1 6-ounce bag radishes

¼ pound medium mushrooms

2 medium zucchini (about 1 pound)

1 10-ounce bag spinach

2 15-ounce cans white asparagus, drained

1 16-ounce can sliced beets, drained

½ cup pimento-stuffed olives, sliced

¼ cup red-wine vinegar

3 tablespoons salad oil

¾ teaspoon basil

½ teaspoon sugar

¼ teaspoon salt

⅛ teaspoon pepper

1. Cut radishes into roses. Slice mushrooms. Cut each zucchini crosswise into 3 pieces; cut each piece lengthwise into thin slices; then cut each slice into matchstick-thin strips. Line large platter with spinach leaves. Arrange radishes, mushrooms, zucchini, asparagus, beets, and olives on spinach; cover and refrigerate.

2. In small bowl, mix vinegar and remaining ingredients. Cover and refrigerate. Pour salad dressing over vegetables just before serving.

Green-Vegetable Medley

TIME: about 45 minutes or start early in day—SERVINGS: 16

3 large bunches broccoli

5 medium zucchini

1 bunch green onions

salad oil

salt

²/₃ cup water

1 teaspoon basil

¹/₈ teaspoon pepper

1 tablespoon soy sauce

lettuce leaves

1. Cut broccoli into 2″ by 1″ pieces. Cut zucchini into ¹/₂-inch-thick slices. Cut each green onion into 2-inch pieces; if root-end pieces of green onions are too thick, cut each lengthwise in half.

2. In 8-quart Dutch oven over medium heat, in ¹/₃ cup hot salad oil, cook green onions until tender, about 3 minutes, stirring frequently. With rubber spatula, stir in broccoli and 1¹/₄ teaspoons salt until broccoli is coated with oil. Add water; cover Dutch oven and cook broccoli 5 to 8 minutes, until tender-crisp, stirring occasionally. Remove vegetables and liquid to large bowl.

3. In same Dutch oven over medium heat, in ¹/₄ cup hot salad oil, cook zucchini, basil, pepper, and 1 teaspoon salt until zucchini is tender-crisp, stirring occasionally. Return broccoli mixture to Dutch oven; add soy sauce; toss to mix well.

4. Line large platter with lettuce leaves. Spoon vegetables onto lettuce-leaf-lined platter. Serve hot or refrigerate to serve cold later.

Tangy Winter Vegetables

TIME: about 3 hours or start day ahead—SERVINGS: 12

¹/₂ cup salad oil

1 16-ounce bag carrots, cut into ¹/₂-inch-thick slices

2 medium onions, each cut into quarters

salt

pepper

4 10-ounce containers Brussels sprouts, each cut in half

¹/₂ cup water

2 tablespoons white-wine vinegar

³/₄ teaspoon sugar

¹/₂ teaspoon basil

1. In 8-quart Dutch oven over medium-high heat, in hot salad oil, cook carrots, onions, ³/₄ teaspoon salt, and ¹/₈ teaspoon pepper until vegetables are tender, about 10 minutes, stirring frequently. With slotted spoon, remove carrot mixture to large bowl.

2. To oil remaining in Dutch oven over high heat, add Brussels sprouts, 2 teaspoons salt, and ¹/₈ teaspoon pepper. Stir until Brussels sprouts are coated with oil. Add water; heat to boiling. Reduce heat to medium; cover Dutch oven and cook Brussels sprouts about 10 minutes or until tender-crisp, stirring occasionally. Remove Brussels sprouts and liquid to bowl with carrot mixture.

3. Add vinegar, sugar, and basil to vegetables in bowl; with rubber spatula, toss gently to mix well. Cover and refrigerate vegetable mixture at least 2 hours to blend flavors, tossing occasionally.

Country Vegetables

TIME: about 1 hour or start day ahead—SERVINGS: 10

salad oil

4 large carrots, thinly sliced diagonally

salt

¹/₂ pound Chinese pea pods or 1 6-ounce package frozen Chinese pea pods, thawed

1 pound medium mushrooms, each cut in half

1 pint cherry tomatoes

1 small bunch broccoli, cut into 2″ by 1″ pieces

1 small head cauliflower, separated into flowerets

1 medium onion, quartered

¹/₂ cup water

2 tablespoons soy sauce

1. In 8-quart Dutch oven over medium-high heat, in 2 tablespoons hot salad oil, cook carrots and ¹/₄ teaspoon salt until carrots are tender-crisp, about 3 to 5 minutes, stirring often. With slotted spoon, remove carrots to large bowl. In 1 more tablespoon hot oil, cook pea pods and ¹/₄ teaspoon salt 1 or 2 minutes, stirring. Remove to bowl.

2. In 3 more tablespoons hot oil, stir mushrooms and ¹/₄ teaspoon salt until mushrooms are coated. Cover; cook 3 to 5 minutes, stirring occasionally. Remove to bowl. In 1 more tablespoon hot oil, cook tomatoes until heated through, about 1 minute, stirring. Remove to bowl. In 2 more tablespoons hot oil, stir broccoli, cauliflower, and onion until well coated; add water and ¹/₂ teaspoon salt; cover and cook 5 to 10 minutes, until tender-crisp, stirring occasionally.

3. Remove Dutch oven from heat. Return all vegetables to Dutch oven; add soy sauce; mix well; spoon vegetables onto large platter. Serve hot or refrigerate to serve cold later.

Gingery Apple Rings

TIME: about 30 minutes—SERVINGS: 6

1 large lemon

6 tablespoons butter or margarine

1/4 cup packed brown sugar

2 tablespoons water

2 teaspoons minced peeled ginger root or
1/2 teaspoon ground ginger

1/8 teaspoon salt

4 medium Golden Delicious apples, cored
and cut into 1/2-inch rings

1. Grate 1 tablespoon peel and squeeze 2 tablespoons juice from lemon.

2. In 12-inch skillet over medium heat, heat lemon peel, lemon juice, butter or margarine, brown sugar, water, ginger, and salt until butter is melted and sugar is dissolved. Add apples; cook about 10 minutes or until apples are tender, gently turning apple rings occasionally with pancake turner.

Pan-fried Apple Wedges

TIME: about 15 minutes—SERVINGS: 4

2 red cooking apples, cored

2 tablespoons butter or margarine

1/2 cup apple jelly

1. Cut apples into 1/2-inch-thick wedges.

2. In 12-inch skillet over medium heat, in hot butter or margarine, cook apple wedges about 5 to 7 minutes until apples are tender-crisp; with pancake turner, turn wedges once during cooking.

3. Stir in apple jelly; heat through. Serve with baked ham or with breakfast pancakes.

Baked Bananas

TIME: about 25 minutes—SERVINGS: 4

3 tablespoons butter or margarine

4 slightly unripe medium bananas, peeled

salt

1. Preheat oven to 450° F. In oven, in pie plate or baking dish, melt butter.

2. Remove plate from oven and roll bananas in melted butter; sprinkle lightly with salt.

3. Bake 10 to 12 minutes or until bananas are fork-tender. Serve hot as a vegetable.

Gingered Peaches

TIME: about 10 minutes—SERVINGS: 6

1 29- to 30-ounce can sliced cling peaches

1 tablespoon slivered preserved ginger

In 2-quart saucepan over medium heat, stir peaches with their liquid and the ginger. Cook until peaches are heated through, stirring occasionally.

Grilled Curried Fruit

TIME: about 45 minutes—SERVINGS: 6

1 16- or 17-ounce can pear halves, drained

1 16- or 17-ounce can cling peach halves,
drained

1 8 1/4-ounce can sliced pineapple, drained,
each slice cut in half

1/2 cup packed brown sugar

2 tablespoons butter or margarine, cut
into small pieces

4 teaspoons mild curry powder

1. Prepare outdoor grill for barbecuing.

2. Meanwhile, on double thickness of heavy-duty foil, mix all ingredients. Wrap mixture in foil, being careful that seam of foil is folded several times to seal in juices.

3. Place foil packet on grill over medium heat; cook 15 to 20 minutes until mixture is hot, turning packet occasionally with tongs. Just before serving, stir fruit to mix well. Serve with barbecued poultry, ham, steak, or lamb.

TO COOK ON TOP OF RANGE: About 20 minutes ahead, in 3-quart saucepan over medium heat, heat all ingredients to boiling, stirring often. Reduce heat to low; simmer 5 minutes to blend flavors.

Stuffed Whole Cabbage

TIME: about 2¹/₄ hours—SERVINGS: 6

1 **large head green cabbage (about 4 to 4¹/₂ pounds)**

water

1 **16-ounce package pork-sausage meat**

¹/₂ **pound medium mushrooms, thinly sliced**

1 **medium onion, diced**

2 **cups cooked rice**

¹/₂ **pound Port du Salut or Bel Paese cheese, coarsely shredded**

1 **16-ounce can tomatoes**

1 **6-ounce can tomato paste**

1 **tablespoon brown sugar**

1 **teaspoon Worcestershire**

¹/₂ **teaspoon salt**

¹/₄ **teaspoon pepper**

¹/₄ **teaspoon basil**

1. Discard any tough outer leaves from cabbage; then carefully remove 3 large leaves; set aside. With sharp knife, carefully cut out stem and center of cabbage, leaving a 1-inch-thick shell. Dice cut-out cabbage; reserve. Discard stem.

2. In 4-quart saucepan over high heat, heat 2 inches water to boiling. Add cabbage shell; heat to boiling. Reduce heat to low; cover and simmer 20 minutes. Remove cabbage; drain. Discard water.

3. Meanwhile, in 5-quart Dutch oven or saucepot over medium heat, cook pork-sausage meat until browned. With slotted spoon, spoon about three quarters sausage meat into large bowl and remaining into small bowl; set aside. In drippings remaining in Dutch oven over medium heat, cook mushrooms, onion, and 1 cup diced cabbage until vegetables are tender, stirring occasionally. Add vegetables to sausage in large bowl; stir in rice and cheese.

4. Fill cabbage with rice mixture. Arrange reserved cabbage leaves over opening in cabbage to completely cover rice mixture. With string, tie cabbage securely to hold leaves in place.

5. In same 5-quart Dutch oven, mix remaining sausage meat, remaining diced cabbage, tomatoes with their liquid, and remaining ingredients, stirring to break up tomatoes. Place stuffed cabbage, stem end up, in sauce. Over high heat, heat to boiling. Reduce heat to low; cover and simmer until cabbage is fork-tender, about 1¹/₄ hours, occasionally basting cabbage with sauce.

6. To serve, place cabbage, stem end down, on warm deep platter; remove string. Spoon sauce around cabbage; cut cabbage into wedges.

Meat-sauced Eggplant-and-Cheese Casseroles

TIME: about 2¹/₂ hours—SERVINGS: 12

salad oil

1¹/₂ **pounds beef for stew, diced**

1 **small onion, diced**

1 **medium garlic clove, minced**

9 **medium tomatoes (about 3 pounds), peeled and cut into chunks**

1 **6-ounce can tomato paste**

2 **tablespoons sugar**

¹/₂ **teaspoon basil**

¹/₂ **teaspoon crushed red pepper**

salt

²/₃ **cup all-purpose flour**

3 **large eggplants (about 1¹/₂ pounds each), cut crosswise into ¹/₂-inch slices**

1 **16-ounce package mozzarella cheese, shredded (4 cups)**

1. Prepare meat sauce: In 5-quart Dutch oven over high heat, in 2 tablespoons hot salad oil, cook beef for stew, onion, and garlic until juices from meat evaporate and meat is browned, stirring frequently. Add tomatoes, tomato paste, sugar, basil, crushed red pepper, and 3¹/₂ teaspoons salt; heat to boiling. Reduce heat to low; cover and simmer 40 minutes or until meat is tender, stirring occasionally.

2. Meanwhile, prepare eggplant: On waxed paper, mix flour with ¹/₂ teaspoon salt. Coat eggplant with flour mixture. In 12-inch skillet over medium heat, in ¹/₄ cup hot salad oil, cook eggplant, a few slices at a time, until browned on both sides, adding more oil as needed. Remove eggplant slices as they brown to paper towels to drain.

3. Preheat oven to 350° F. Set aside 1 cup cheese. Into each of three 8″ by 8″ baking dishes, spoon ³/₄ cup meat sauce. Arrange half of eggplant slices on meat sauce in pans; sprinkle with remaining 3 cups cheese; top with remaining eggplant, then remaining sauce. Sprinkle with reserved 1 cup cheese.

4. Cover one baking dish with foil; bake 30 minutes or until hot and bubbly; serve immediately (4 main-dish servings). Freeze remaining two baking dishes to serve later.

TO FREEZE AND SERVE UP TO 1 MONTH LATER: Wrap unbaked baking dishes of meat-sauced eggplant tightly with foil; label and freeze. To serve, about 2 hours before serving, preheat oven to 350° F. Bake wrapped, frozen dish about 1³/₄ hours or until hot and bubbly.

Baked Eggplant Casseroles

TIME: about 35 minutes—SERVINGS: 4

¹/₄ cup all-purpose flour

¹/₄ teaspoon salt

¹/₈ teaspoon pepper

1 medium eggplant (1 pound)

salad oil

1 15- to 15¹/₂-ounce jar spaghetti sauce

¹/₂ 15- to 16-ounce container ricotta cheese (1 cup)

¹/₂ 8-ounce package mozzarella cheese, coarsely shredded

1. On waxed paper, combine flour, salt, and pepper. Cut eggplant into ¹/₄-inch-thick slices; dip eggplant slices into flour mixture to coat.

2. Preheat oven to 350° F. In 12-inch skillet over medium-high heat, in ¹/₄ cup hot salad oil, cook eggplant, a few slices at a time, until tender and browned on both sides, removing slices to plate as they brown and adding more oil as needed.

3. Into four 16-ounce oven-safe shallow casseroles or ramekins, spoon half of spaghetti sauce; arrange half of eggplant slices on sauce. Top with ricotta cheese, remaining eggplant slices, then mozzarella cheese and remaining spaghetti sauce. Bake 20 minutes or until cheese melts and mixture is hot and bubbly.

Eggplant Parmigiana

TIME: about 1 hour—SERVINGS: 6

³/₄ cup all-purpose flour

2 teaspoons salt

¹/₃ cup milk

1 large eggplant, cut into ¹/₄-inch slices (about 2 pounds)

salad oil

1 15-ounce can tomato sauce

¹/₂ cup grated Parmesan cheese

1 8-ounce package mozzarella cheese, shredded

1. On sheet of waxed paper, combine flour and salt; pour milk into small bowl. Dip eggplant in milk; coat with flour.

2. In 12-inch skillet over medium-high heat; in 2 tablespoons oil, cook eggplant, a few slices at a time, until golden, adding more oil as needed. Remove from skillet; drain.

3. Preheat oven to 350° F. In greased 12″ by 8″ baking dish, arrange half of eggplant slices; spoon half of tomato sauce over eggplant; sprinkle with half Parmesan and then top with half mozzarella; repeat. Bake, uncovered, 25 minutes or until heated through.

Stuffed Eggplant

TIME: about 35 minutes—SERVINGS: 4

2 medium eggplants (about ³/₄ pound each)

water

salt

3 tablespoons olive or salad oil

1 medium onion, thinly sliced

1 medium green pepper, cut into thin strips

1 large garlic clove, minced

1 large tomato, cut into bite-size pieces

1 small zucchini, thinly sliced

1 teaspoon sugar

¹/₂ teaspoon basil

¹/₄ teaspoon cracked pepper

1 15¹/₄- to 20-ounce can red kidney beans, drained

1 4-ounce package shredded mozzarella cheese

1. With knife, cut each eggplant lengthwise in half. Cut out center of eggplant, leaving a ¹/₂-inch shell. Cut eggplant centers into bite-size pieces; set aside.

2. In 12-inch skillet, mix ¹/₂ inch water and 1 teaspoon salt. Arrange eggplant shells, cut side up, in water; over high heat, heat to boiling. Reduce heat to low; cover and simmer about 5 minutes or until eggplant shells are just fork-tender. (Do not cook any longer, or shells will collapse when filled.) Drain eggplant shells well; place in jelly-roll pan; set aside.

3. Meanwhile, in 3-quart saucepan over medium heat, in hot olive oil, cook onion, green pepper, and garlic until vegetables are tender-crisp, stirring occasionally. Add cut-up eggplant, tomato, zucchini, sugar, basil, pepper, and 1¹/₂ teaspoons salt. Reduce heat to medium-low; cover and simmer 15 minutes or until vegetables are tender, stirring occasionally. Stir in kidney beans; heat through.

4. Preheat oven to 400° F. Spoon vegetable mixture into eggplant shells; top with cheese. Bake stuffed eggplant 10 minutes or until cheese is melted and mixture is hot.

Crab-filled Jumbo Mushrooms

TIME: about 1 hour—SERVINGS: 4

1 6-ounce package
long-grain-and-wild-rice mix

8 jumbo mushrooms (1 pound)

butter or margarine

2 green onions, minced (about ¼ cup)

1 tablespoon all-purpose flour

⅛ teaspoon pepper

¾ cup milk

2 cups white-bread cubes (4 slices)

1 tablespoon cooking or dry sherry

1 6-ounce package frozen Alaska King or
Snow crabmeat, thawed, drained, and
flaked

½ 4-ounce package shredded Cheddar
cheese (½ cup)

½ 8-ounce package mozzarella cheese,
cut into 8 slices

1 tablespoon minced parsley

1. Prepare rice as label directs; keep warm.

2. Meanwhile, remove stems from mushrooms; dice and reserve stems.

3. In 12-inch skillet over medium heat, melt 2 tablespoons butter or margarine; add mushroom caps and cook 5 minutes, turning caps once. With slotted spoon, remove caps to 8″ by 8″ baking pan.

4. In same skillet over medium heat, melt 2 more tablespoons butter or margarine; add green onions and reserved diced mushroom stems, and cook until tender, stirring occasionally. Stir in flour and pepper until blended. Gradually stir in milk and cook, stirring constantly, until mixture is slightly thickened and smooth. Stir in bread cubes, sherry, crab, and Cheddar cheese. Remove saucepan from heat.

5. Preheat oven to 425° F. Spoon some crab filling into each mushroom cap, shaping filling into a high mound. Bake 10 minutes or until hot. Top each mushroom with a slice of mozzarella cheese and bake about 3 minutes longer or until cheese is melted.

6. To serve, spoon rice mixture onto warm platter; arrange mushrooms on rice; sprinkle mushrooms with parsley.

Super-quick Stuffed Peppers

TIME: about 30 minutes—SERVINGS: 6

¾ pound ground beef

1 small onion, diced

1 15¼- to 20-ounce can red kidney beans,
drained

1 8-ounce can tomato sauce

½ teaspoon sugar

¼ teaspoon thyme leaves

⅛ teaspoon pepper

salt

3 large green peppers

water

1 tablespoon cornstarch

2 tablespoons shredded Cheddar cheese

1. In 3-quart saucepan over medium-high heat, cook ground beef and onion until meat is browned and onion is tender, about 10 minutes, stirring occasionally. Stir in kidney beans, tomato sauce, sugar, thyme, pepper, and 1 teaspoon salt; heat to boiling. Reduce heat to low; cover and simmer 10 minutes to blend flavors.

2. Meanwhile, cut green peppers lengthwise in half; discard seeds. Place pepper halves in 12-inch skillet; add about ½ inch water and 1 teaspoon salt; over high heat, heat to boiling. Reduce heat to low; cover and simmer 5 minutes or until tender-crisp. Drain.

3. In cup, mix cornstarch and ½ cup water; gradually stir into meat mixture; cook over medium heat, stirring, until mixture is slightly thickened.

4. To serve, place peppers, cut side up, on warm platter. Spoon meat mixture into green peppers; sprinkle with shredded Cheddar cheese.

Stuffed Acorn Squash

TIME: about 1 hour—SERVINGS: 4

2 medium acorn squash (2 pounds)

½ cup brown rice

1 16-ounce package pork-sausage meat

1 egg

1 3-ounce can sliced mushrooms, drained

1 tablespoon maple syrup or maple-flavor
syrup

½ teaspoon salt

1. Preheat oven to 350° F. Cut each acorn squash lengthwise in half; discard seeds. Place squash halves, cut side down, in 12″ by 8″ baking dish; bake 45 minutes. Meanwhile, prepare rice as label directs.

2. In 10-inch skillet over medium heat, cook pork-sausage meat until browned. With slotted spoon, remove meat (discard drippings) to medium bowl; toss with egg, mushrooms, syrup, cooked brown rice.

3. Turn squash halves, cut side up, in baking dish; sprinkle with salt. Spoon meat mixture into squash halves. Cover with foil and bake 15 minutes or until squash are tender.

Spaghetti Squash with Spicy Meat Sauce

TIME: about 1 hour—SERVINGS: 4

1 2½-pound spaghetti squash

water

1 beef top round steak, cut ½ inch thick (about 1 pound)

2 tablespoons salad oil

1 small onion, diced

1 small garlic clove, minced

¾ teaspoon chili powder

4 medium tomatoes (about 1½ pounds), diced (4 cups)

2 teaspoons sugar

¾ teaspoon salt

1. Cut spaghetti squash lengthwise in half; discard seeds. In 12-inch skillet over high heat, in 1 inch boiling water, place squash, cut side up; heat to boiling. Reduce heat to low; cover and simmer 40 minutes or until squash is fork-tender.

2. Meanwhile, dice beef top round steak. In 3-quart saucepan over high heat, in hot salad oil, cook beef, onion, and garlic until juices from meat evaporate and meat is browned, stirring frequently. Stir in chili powder; cook 1 minute. Add tomatoes, sugar, and salt; heat to boiling, stirring to loosen brown bits on bottom of pan. Reduce heat to low; cover and simmer 30 minutes or until meat is tender and sauce is slightly thickened, stirring occasionally.

3. When squash is done, remove from skillet; drain. With two forks, lift up pulp of squash to form spaghetti-like strands. Spoon meat sauce over squash; serve as spaghetti.

Beef-stuffed Zucchini

TIME: about 40 minutes—SERVINGS: 6

3 medium zucchini (about 8 ounces each)

1 pound ground beef

1 small onion, diced

salad oil

¼ teaspoon oregano leaves

¼ teaspoon pepper

1 15-ounce can tomato sauce

1 4-ounce package shredded mozzarella cheese

salt

¼ cup water

1 teaspoon sugar

1. Cut each zucchini lengthwise in half. Scoop out center of zucchini, leaving a ¼-inch-thick shell. Dice scooped-out zucchini. Set zucchini shells aside.

2. In 12-inch skillet over medium-high heat, cook ground beef, onion, and diced zucchini until meat is browned and onion and zucchini are tender, stirring occasionally and adding salad oil if necessary. Stir in oregano, pepper, half of tomato sauce, half of cheese, and ¾ teaspoon salt; remove skillet from heat.

3. Into each zucchini shell, spoon some meat mixture; set aside. In same skillet, stir water, sugar, remaining tomato sauce, and ¼ teaspoon salt. Arrange stuffed zucchini in sauce in skillet; over high heat, heat to boiling. Reduce heat to low; cover and simmer until zucchini is fork-tender, about 10 minutes, stirring occasionally. Sprinkle remaining cheese over stuffed zucchini. Cover skillet and cook about 2 minutes longer or until cheese is melted.

Zucchini "Lasagna"

TIME: about 1½ hours—SERVINGS: 6

½ pound ground beef

⅓ cup chopped onion

1 15-ounce can tomato sauce

½ teaspoon salt

½ teaspoon oregano leaves

¼ teaspoon basil

⅛ teaspoon pepper

4 medium zucchini

1 8-ounce container creamed cottage cheese (1 cup)

1 egg

2 tablespoons all-purpose flour

¼ pound mozzarella cheese, shredded

1. In 10-inch skillet over medium-high heat, cook ground beef and onion until onion is tender, about 10 minutes, stirring occasionally. Spoon off fat. Add tomato sauce, salt, oregano, basil, and pepper; heat to boiling. Reduce heat to low, and simmer 5 minutes to blend flavors, stirring occasionally.

2. Preheat oven to 375° F. Meanwhile, with sharp knife, slice zucchini lengthwise into ¼-inch-thick slices. In small bowl, combine cottage cheese with egg until well mixed.

3. In bottom of 12″ by 8″ baking dish, arrange half of zucchini in a layer and sprinkle with a tablespoon flour. Top with cottage-cheese mixture and half of meat mixture. Repeat with remaining zucchini and flour; sprinkle with mozzarella cheese and then remaining meat mixture.

4. Bake, uncovered, 40 minutes, until hot and bubbly and zucchini is fork-tender. Let stand 10 minutes for easier cutting.

Country Vegetable-Beef Casserole

TIME: about 2 hours—SERVINGS: 8

1/3 cup salad oil

3 medium red or green peppers, cut into bite-size pieces

2 medium onions, sliced

2 medium zucchini, cut into 1/2-inch-thick slices

1/2 pound ground beef

1 2-pound butternut squash, peeled, cut into 1/2-inch pieces

1 16-ounce can tomatoes

1 15 1/2- to 20-ounce can garbanzo beans, drained

1 10-ounce package frozen baby lima beans

1 6-ounce can tomato paste

1/2 cup water

3 3/4 teaspoons salt

2 1/2 teaspoons brown sugar

1/4 teaspoon pepper

1. In 12-inch skillet over medium heat, in hot salad oil, cook peppers, onions, and zucchini until lightly browned, stirring often. Remove to 4 1/2-quart casserole.

2. In drippings remaining in skillet over high heat, cook ground beef until well browned. Add squash and remaining ingredients; heat to boiling.

3. Spoon meat mixture into casserole; mix well. Bake casserole, covered, in 350° F. oven 1 hour or until hot and bubbly and vegetables are fork-tender.

Meat, Poultry, and Seafood

Barbecued Steak

TIME: about 1 hour—SERVINGS: 4

barbecue sauce (see Index)

unseasoned meat tenderizer

1 beef top round steak or 1 beef chuck blade steak, cut 1¼ inches thick

1 tablespoon minced parsley (optional)

1 teaspoon grated lemon peel (optional)

1. Prepare outdoor grill for barbecuing.

2. Meanwhile, prepare one of the barbecue sauces listed in the Index.

3. Following the label directions on meat tenderizer, prepare steak. Place steak on grill over medium heat; grill about 20 minutes for rare or until of desired doneness, turning steak occasionally; during the last 10 minutes of cooking, brush steak with barbecue sauce. Garnish steak with parsley and lemon peel if you like.

TO BROIL STEAK IN OVEN: About 45 minutes before serving, preheat broiler if manufacturer directs. Meanwhile, prepare one of the barbecue sauces listed in the Index. Prepare steak with meat tenderizer as label directs. Place steak on rack in broiling pan. Broil steak about 20 minutes for rare or until of desired doneness; turn steak once, and during last 10 minutes of cooking, brush with sauce. Garnish as above.

Broiled Chuck Steak with Sautéed Vegetables

TIME: about 40 minutes—SERVINGS· 6

½ cup chili sauce

2 tablespoons prepared mustard

1 tablespoon red-wine vinegar

2 teaspoons Worcestershire

1 teaspoon sugar

salt

oregano leaves

1 beef chuck 7-bone steak (center cut), cut 1¼ inches thick (about 3½ pounds)

unseasoned meat tenderizer

2 tablespoons salad oil

4 large green peppers, cut into ½-inch-wide strips

4 large onions, sliced

¼ teaspoon cracked pepper

1 medium tomato, cut into thin wedges

1. Preheat broiler if manufacturer directs. In small bowl, combine chili sauce, mustard, vinegar, Worcestershire, sugar, 1 teaspoon salt, and ¼ teaspoon oregano; set aside.

2. Place beef chuck 7-bone steak on rack in broiling pan. Sprinkle steak with meat tenderizer as label directs. Broil steak 10 minutes; brush half of chili-sauce mixture on steak; broil 5 minutes longer. Turn steak; broil 10 minutes. Brush steak with remaining sauce; broil 5 minutes longer for rare or until of desired doneness.

3. Meanwhile, in 5-quart Dutch oven or saucepot over medium heat, in hot salad oil, cook green peppers, onions, pepper, 1 teaspoon salt, and ½ teaspoon oregano until vegetables are tender, stirring frequently. Add tomato wedges; heat through. Arrange steak and vegetables on warm platter.

Pan-fried Steaks with Wine Sauce

TIME: about 20 minutes—SERVINGS: 2

2 beef top loin or rib eye steaks, each cut
 ³/₄ inch thick

salt

pepper

1 medium green onion, minced

1 tablespoon butter or margarine

¹/₄ cup cooking or dry red wine

parsley sprigs, for garnish

1. Trim several pieces of fat from edge of steaks. In 12-inch skillet over medium heat, heat fat until lightly browned; using spoon, press and rub fat over bottom of skillet to grease it well; discard fat. Add steaks to skillet; over medium-high heat, cook about 8 minutes for rare, turning steaks once. (If medium or well-done meat is preferred, cook 2 to 3 minutes longer.) Remove steaks to warm platter; lightly sprinkle with salt and pepper; keep warm.

2. Pour off all but 2 tablespoons drippings from pan. Add green onion and butter; cook over medium heat until onion is tender, stirring occasionally. Stir in wine, scraping to loosen brown bits from bottom of skillet; cook 1 minute. Pour sauce over steaks; garnish with parsley.

Cubed Steaks with Caper Sauce

TIME: about 20 minutes—SERVINGS: 4

butter or margarine

4 beef cubed steaks (about 1 pound)

1 medium onion, thinly sliced

¹/₃ cup water

1 tablespoon capers

1 tablespoon prepared mustard

parsley sprigs, for garnish

1. In 12-inch skillet over medium heat, in 2 tablespoons hot butter or margarine, cook two beef cubed steaks at a time until browned on both sides and tender, about 5 minutes. Remove steaks to platter; keep warm.

2. In drippings remaining in skillet over medium heat, melt 2 tablespoons butter or margarine; add onion; cook until tender, stirring occasionally. Stir in water, capers, and mustard; cook until mixture boils and thickens slightly, stirring constantly. Pour caper sauce over steaks. Garnish with parsley sprigs.

Tournedos in Wine Sauce

TIME: about 1 hour—SERVINGS: 6

6 thin slices French bread

1¹/₂ pounds medium mushrooms

6 tablespoons butter or margarine

seasoned salt

seasoned pepper

6 beef loin tenderloin steaks, each cut 1¹/₄
 inches thick

¹/₄ cup water

¹/₄ cup port wine

watercress sprigs, for garnish

1. Preheat broiler if manufacturer directs. Place bread on cookie sheet. Broil 3 minutes or until golden on both sides, turning once.

2. If you like, flute mushrooms.

3. In 12-inch skillet over medium-high heat, in 4 tablespoons hot butter or margarine, cook mushrooms, ¹/₄ teaspoon seasoned salt, and ¹/₈ teaspoon seasoned pepper until mushrooms are tender, stirring often. Place mushrooms on one end of warm platter; keep warm.

4. Sprinkle steaks with 1 teaspoon seasoned salt and ¹/₄ teaspoon seasoned pepper. In same skillet over medium-high heat, in 2 more tablespoons hot butter or margarine, cook steaks until undersides of steaks are browned, about 5 minutes; turn steaks and cook about 5 minutes longer for rare or until of desired doneness. Arrange toast and steaks on platter with mushrooms; keep warm.

5. Reduce heat to medium. To drippings in skillet, add water and port, stirring to loosen brown bits in skillet; heat to boiling. Pour sauce over steaks. Garnish with watercress.

Cheese-filled Teriyaki Steaks

TIME: about 3½ hours—SERVINGS: 4

4 beef cubed steaks (about 1 pound)

3 tablespoons soy sauce

2 tablespoons brown sugar

2 tablespoons cooking or dry sherry

1 tablespoon salad oil

½ teaspoon ground ginger

¼ teaspoon garlic powder

1 4-ounce package shredded mozzarella cheese

1. With meat mallet or dull edge of French knife, pound each beef cubed steak to about ⅛-inch thickness. In 13″ by 9″ baking dish, mix soy sauce, brown sugar, sherry, salad oil, ginger, and garlic powder; add cubed steaks, turning to coat with marinade. Cover and refrigerate at least 2 hours, turning steaks occasionally.

2. About 45 minutes before serving, prepare outdoor grill for barbecuing.

3. Remove steaks from marinade; reserve marinade. Arrange cheese on two steaks; top with remaining steaks. Skewer each stack together with toothpicks.

4. Place cheese-filled steaks on grill over medium heat; cook about 10 minutes for rare or until of desired doneness, turning steaks occasionally and basting frequently with marinade. Discard toothpicks.

TO BROIL IN OVEN: About 3½ hours before serving, pound and marinate meat as above. About 30 minutes before serving, preheat broiler if manufacturer directs. Arrange cheese on steaks and skewer closed as above. Place steaks on rack in broiling pan; broil about 10 minutes for rare or until of desired doneness, turning once, and basting occasionally with marinade.

Tangy Steak and Vegetables

TIME: about 30 minutes—SERVINGS: 4

1 beef top round steak, cut ¾ inch thick (about 1 pound)

2 tablespoons soy sauce

2 tablespoons cooking or dry sherry

1 tablespoon chili sauce

1 teaspoon cornstarch

⅛ teaspoon ground ginger

salad oil

2 green peppers, each cut into bite-size pieces

1 medium onion, quartered

1 large carrot, thinly sliced diagonally

½ teaspoon salt

1. Cut beef top round steak lengthwise in half. Then, with knife held in slanting position, almost parallel to the cutting surface, slice across width of each half into ⅛-inch-thick slices. In medium bowl, mix meat slices, soy sauce, sherry, chili sauce, cornstarch, and ginger; set aside.

2. In 5-quart Dutch oven over high heat, in 3 tablespoons hot salad oil, cook peppers, onion, carrot, and salt until vegetables are tender-crisp, about 3 to 5 minutes, stirring frequently. With slotted spoon, remove vegetables to small bowl; set aside.

3. In same Dutch oven over high heat, in 2 more tablespoons hot salad oil, cook meat mixture until meat is browned, about 2 minutes, stirring frequently. Return vegetables to Dutch oven. Cook over high heat until heated through.

Barbecued Hamburgers

TIME: about 45 minutes—SERVINGS: 4

barbecue sauce (see Index)

1 pound ground beef

1. Prepare outdoor grill for barbecuing.

2. Meanwhile, prepare one of the barbecue sauces listed in the Index.

3. Make four patties from ground beef. Place patties on grill over medium heat; grill about 10 minutes for medium or until of desired doneness, turning patties occasionally with pancake turner; during last 5 minutes of cooking, brush patties with barbecue sauce.

TO BROIL HAMBURGERS IN OVEN: About 30 minutes before serving, preheat broiler if manufacturer directs. Meanwhile, prepare one of the barbecue sauces listed in the Index, and make beef patties. Place patties on rack in broiling pan; broil 3 minutes; brush with some sauce; broil 1 minute. Turn patties with pancake turner; broil about 5 minutes or until of desired doneness, brushing patties occasionally with remaining sauce.

Hamburgers Rémoulade

TIME: about 25 minutes—SERVINGS: 6

1½ **pounds ground beef**

1 **slice white bread**

½ **cup mayonnaise**

1½ **teaspoons chopped parsley**

1½ **teaspoons cider vinegar**

1½ **teaspoons prepared mustard**

¼ **teaspoon sugar**

⅛ **teaspoon salt**

⅛ **teaspoon tarragon**

1. Preheat broiler if manufacturer directs. Shape ground beef into six ½-inch-thick oval patties. Place patties on rack in broiling pan. Broil patties 10 minutes for medium, turning once. (If well-done hamburgers are desired, cook 2 to 3 minutes longer.)

2. Meanwhile, into small bowl, tear bread into small pieces; add remaining ingredients; mix well.

3. When patties are done, spread mayonnaise mixture over patties; broil 1 minute longer or until topping is hot and bubbly.

Saucy Beef-Bean Burgers

TIME: about 1 hour—SERVINGS: 6

salad oil

1 **medium onion, chopped**

1 **garlic clove, minced**

1 **15½- to 20-ounce can garbanzo beans, drained**

3 **slices white bread**

¾ **pound ground beef**

1 **egg**

½ **teaspoon thyme leaves**

¼ **teaspoon pepper**

salt

1 **28-ounce can tomatoes**

2 **tablespoons brown sugar**

1 **cup thinly sliced dill pickles**

1. In 12-inch skillet over medium heat, in 2 tablespoons hot salad oil, cook onion and garlic until tender, stirring occasionally. Remove from heat.

2. In large bowl with back of spoon, mash garbanzo beans. Into bean mixture, tear bread into small pieces; add onion mixture, ground beef, egg, thyme, pepper, and 1 teaspoon salt. Shape mixture into twelve ½-inch-thick round patties.

3. In same skillet over medium-high heat, in 2 more tablespoons hot oil, cook patties, half at a time, until browned on both sides, removing them to plate as they brown. Pour off any remaining oil in skillet.

4. Return patties to skillet; add tomatoes with their liquid, brown sugar, and 1½ teaspoons salt, stirring to break up tomatoes; over medium heat, heat to boiling. Reduce heat to low; cover and simmer 15 minutes, stirring occasionally. Stir in pickles; cook 5 minutes longer.

Teriyaki Beef Kabobs

TIME: about 4 hours or start early in day—SERVINGS: 8

1 **2-pound beef top round steak, cut about 1 inch thick**

¼ **cup packed light brown sugar**

¼ **cup soy sauce**

2 **tablespoons lemon juice**

1 **tablespoon salad oil**

¼ **teaspoon ground ginger**

1 **garlic clove, minced**

1 **small pineapple, cut into 1-inch chunks**

1. Trim any excess fat from steak, and cut meat into 1-inch chunks.

2. Prepare marinade: Combine brown sugar, soy sauce, lemon juice, oil, ginger, and garlic; stir in beef chunks. Cover and refrigerate at least 3 hours, stirring meat often.

3. About 30 minutes before serving, preheat broiler if manufacturer directs. Thread meat and pineapple chunks alternately on 12-inch metal skewers. (Pineapple quickly tenderizes meat, so thread skewers just before broiling; if done earlier, meat becomes mushy.)

4. Broil 15 minutes for rare or until of desired doneness, basting occasionally with marinade and turning once. To check doneness, make slit in center of meat.

Company Shrimp-and-Sirloin Kabobs

TIME: about 4½ hours—SERVINGS: 6

1 beef loin sirloin steak, boneless, cut 1 inch thick (about 1¼ pounds)

¼ cup steak sauce

⅛ teaspoon hot-pepper sauce

1 small garlic clove, minced

cooking or dry sherry

salad oil

salt

½ pound large shrimp

sugar

2 small zucchini (about 6 ounces each)

1 bunch green onions

½ 10-ounce bag spinach

4 teaspoons lemon juice

1. Cut beef loin sirloin steak into 1¼-inch chunks. In medium bowl, toss steak, steak sauce, hot-pepper sauce, garlic, ¼ cup sherry, 1 tablespoon salad oil, and 1 teaspoon salt; cover and refrigerate about 3 hours, tossing occasionally.

2. Shell and devein shrimp, leaving tail and last segment of shell on. In another medium bowl, toss shrimp with 3 tablespoons salad oil, 1 tablespoon sherry, ½ teaspoon salt, and ¼ teaspoon sugar. Cover and refrigerate about 3 hours, tossing occasionally.

3. About 1 hour before serving, prepare outdoor grill for barbecuing.

4. Meanwhile, cut each zucchini crosswise into six chunks. Cut off and discard roots from each green onion. Starting from root end, cut two 2½-inch pieces from each green onion (save green tops for use in salad another day). Finely shred spinach; place in large bowl; cover and refrigerate. In cup, mix lemon juice, 2 tablespoons salad oil, 1 teaspoon sugar, and ⅛ teaspoon salt; set lemon dressing aside.

5. On six long skewers (about 18 inches long) alternately thread meat, shrimp, zucchini, and green onions; reserve meat marinade. Place skewers on grill over medium heat; cook about 10 minutes for rare or until meat is of desired doneness, turning skewers frequently and brushing with meat marinade often.

6. To serve, toss spinach with lemon dressing. Place spinach salad on platter; arrange kabobs on top of spinach. Serve each kabob with some spinach salad.

TO BROIL IN OVEN: About 4 hours before serving, marinate steak and shrimp as above in steps 1 and 2. About 1 hour before serving, prepare zucchini, green onions, spinach, and lemon dressing as in step 4 above, then preheat broiler if manufacturer directs. On six all-metal skewers, alternately thread meat, shrimp, zucchini, and green onions; reserve meat marinade. Place skewers on rack in broiling pan; broil 10 minutes for rare or until meat is of desired doneness, turning skewers and brushing with meat marinade occasionally. Serve kabobs as in step 6.

Saucy Short Ribs

TIME: about 3½ hours—SERVINGS: 8

2 tablespoons salad oil

4 pounds beef chuck short ribs

2 pounds small white onions

2 medium garlic cloves

1 8-ounce can whole-berry cranberry sauce

4 large celery stalks, cut into 2-inch pieces

1 cup water

¾ cup catchup

1 tablespoon prepared horseradish

1¼ teaspoons salt

¼ teaspoon pepper

1. In 5-quart Dutch oven over medium-high heat, in hot salad oil, cook beef chuck short ribs, a few at a time, until well browned on all sides, removing ribs as they brown.

2. Reduce heat to medium; add onions and garlic to drippings in Dutch oven, and cook until lightly browned, stirring mixture occasionally. Spoon off fat from Dutch oven. Return ribs to Dutch oven; stir in cranberry sauce and remaining ingredients.

3. Cover Dutch oven and bake in 350° F. oven 2½ hours, stirring occasionally, until meat is fork-tender. Skim off fat from sauce.

Tenderloin en Croûte

TIME: about 2 hours—SERVINGS: 6

1 medium eggplant (about 1¹/₂ pounds)

salad oil

salt

2 tablespoons butter or margarine

1 2- to 2¹/₂-pound beef loin tenderloin roast, well trimmed and tied with string

1 medium onion, minced

¹/₄ cup dried bread crumbs

coarsely ground black pepper

piecrust mix for two 9-inch piecrusts

1 egg, slightly beaten

¹/₂ cup water

1 tablespoon capers

¹/₂ cup heavy or whipping cream

¹/₄ cup dry vermouth

2 teaspoons all-purpose flour

2 teaspoons prepared mustard

1 teaspoon meat-extract paste

¹/₄ teaspoon sugar

watercress sprigs, for garnish

1. Slice eggplant lengthwise into ¹/₄-inch-thick slices. In 12-inch skillet over medium heat, in 3 tablespoons hot salad oil, cook eggplant, a few slices at a time, until tender and browned on both sides, adding more oil as needed. Remove eggplant slices as they brown to paper towels to drain. Sprinkle eggplant slices lightly with salt.

2. In same skillet over medium-high heat, in hot butter or margarine, cook beef loin tenderloin roast until well browned on all sides, about 5 minutes. Remove meat to plate; set aside.

3. In drippings in skillet over medium heat, cook onion until tender, stirring occasionally. Remove skillet from heat; stir in bread crumbs, ¹/₂ teaspoon salt, and ¹/₄ teaspoon pepper; set aside.

4. Prepare piecrust mix as label directs. On lightly floured surface with floured rolling pin, roll pastry into a 15″ by 15″ square. With knife, cut 2-inch strip of pastry from one edge; reserve for decorating the crust.

5. Preheat oven to 425° F. With kitchen shears, cut string from roast. Pat onion mixture on top of roast; wrap with eggplant slices. Center eggplant-wrapped roast, crumb side down, lengthwise on pastry. Bring one long side of pastry up over roast; brush with some beaten egg. Bring other long side up, overlapping edges, pressing lightly to seal. Fold up both ends; brush with egg to seal. Place pastry-wrapped roast, seam side down, in 15¹/₂″ by 10¹/₂″ jelly-roll pan. Brush pastry crust with egg.

6. With canapé cutter or knife, cut reserved pastry to make an attractive design; arrange on top of pastry crust; brush with egg. Bake 30 to 35 minutes, until meat thermometer reaches 140° F. With two pancake turners, carefully transfer roast to warm platter. Let stand 10 minutes for easier slicing.

7. Meanwhile, prepare caper sauce: In blender at medium speed or in food processor with knife blade attached, blend water and capers until capers are pureed. In same skillet, mix caper mixture, heavy or whipping cream, vermouth, flour, mustard, meat-extract paste, sugar, and ¹/₄ teaspoon pepper until smooth; over medium heat, heat until sauce is slightly thickened, stirring frequently.

8. To serve, garnish platter with watercress. Cut roast into 1-inch-thick slices. Pass caper sauce to serve with roast.

Favorite Rib Eye Roast

TIME: about 1³/₄ hours—SERVINGS: 16

1 medium garlic clove

¹/₂ cup prepared mustard

2 tablespoons soy sauce

2 tablespoons olive or salad oil

¹/₂ teaspoon coarsely ground black pepper

¹/₄ teaspoon ground ginger

1 4-pound beef rib eye roast or rib roast

2 tablespoons minced parsley

1. Into small bowl with garlic press, press garlic. Stir in mustard and next 4 ingredients. Place beef rib eye roast or rib roast on rack in open roasting pan. With pastry brush, brush half of mustard mixture over top of roast. Insert meat thermometer into center of thickest part of roast. Roast in 350° F. oven until meat thermometer reaches 140° F. for rare (about 20 minutes per pound) or until of desired doneness.

2. About 10 minutes before roast is done, brush roast with remaining mustard mixture.

3. To serve, evenly press parsley on mustard mixture on roast. Place roast on warm large platter.

Country Pot Roast with Winter Vegetables

TIME: about 3¹/₂ hours—SERVINGS: 12 to 14

2 tablespoons salad oil

1 4- to 4¹/₂-pound beef chuck cross rib pot roast, boneless

1 medium onion, diced

1 small garlic clove, minced

1 10³/₄-ounce can condensed cream of mushroom soup

1 cup cooking or dry red wine

¹/₂ cup water

1 teaspoon salt

¹/₂ teaspoon pepper

¹/₂ teaspoon sugar

6 medium potatoes (about 2 pounds)

2 large acorn squash (about 1 pound each)

2 10-ounce packages frozen Brussels sprouts

1. In 8-quart Dutch oven over medium-high heat, in hot salad oil, cook beef chuck cross rib pot roast until well browned on all sides; remove meat to plate; set aside.

2. In same Dutch oven in drippings over medium heat, cook onion and garlic until tender, stirring occasionally. Stir in undiluted cream of mushroom soup, wine, water, salt, pepper, and sugar. Return meat to Dutch oven; over high heat, heat to boiling. Reduce heat to low; cover and simmer about 2¹/₂ hours, stirring occasionally.

3. About 1 hour before meat is done, peel potatoes; cut into bite-size chunks. Cut each acorn squash in half; remove seeds; cut into bite-size chunks. Add potatoes and squash to meat mixture; over high heat, heat to boiling. Reduce heat to low; cover and simmer 30 minutes. Add Brussels sprouts; cook 15 minutes longer or until meat and vegetables are fork-tender.

4. To serve, remove meat to warm deep platter; arrange vegetables around meat. Skim off fat from liquid in Dutch oven. Serve liquid with meat and vegetables.

Apple-glazed Beef Brisket

TIME: about 5 hours or start early in day—SERVINGS: 10 to 12

1 4- to 4¹/₂-pound beef brisket

1 small onion, cut into quarters

1 garlic clove, cut in half

10 whole cloves

water

1 10-ounce jar apple jelly

¹/₃ cup cooking or dry white wine

3 tablespoons minced green onions

3 tablespoons prepared mustard

1¹/₂ teaspoons salt

³/₄ teaspoon curry powder

¹/₂ teaspoon cracked pepper

1. In 8-quart Dutch oven or saucepot over high heat, heat beef brisket, onion, garlic, cloves, and enough water to cover meat to boiling. Reduce heat to low; cover and simmer 2¹/₂ to 3 hours, until meat is fork-tender. (If starting early in the day, remove meat to platter; cover and refrigerate.)

2. About 1 hour before serving, prepare outdoor grill for barbecuing.

3. Meanwhile, in small metal-handled saucepan, mix apple jelly, white wine, green onions, mustard, salt, curry powder, and cracked pepper.

4. Heat mixture on grill until jelly is melted, stirring occasionally. Place cooked brisket on grill over medium heat; cook 30 minutes or until heated through, brushing with jelly mixture and turning meat occasionally. Serve remaining jelly mixture with meat.

TO BAKE IN OVEN: Early in day or day ahead, precook beef brisket as above. About 1 hour before serving, preheat oven to 325° F. Prepare jelly mixture as above over medium heat. Place beef brisket in 13″ by 9″ baking pan; bake 45 minutes or until meat is heated through, brushing occasionally with some jelly mixture. Serve as above.

Herbed Roast Beef

TIME: about 2¹/₂ hours—SERVINGS: 16

1 4-pound beef top round roast

³/₄ teaspoon basil

³/₄ teaspoon marjoram leaves

¹/₂ teaspoon cracked pepper

³/₄ teaspoon salt

1. Rub beef top round roast with basil, marjoram, and pepper. Place meat on rack in open roasting pan. Insert meat thermometer into center of meat. Roast in 325° F. oven 1³/₄ to 2 hours, until meat thermometer reaches 140° F. for rare, or until of desired doneness (25 minutes per pound).

2. Place meat on cutting board; sprinkle with salt; let stand 10 minutes for easier slicing. If you like, serve with pan juices.

Country Pot Roast

TIME: about 5 hours—SERVINGS: 20

2 garlic cloves

1 5-pound beef chuck cross rib pot roast, boneless, or bottom rump round roast

¼ cup all-purpose flour

¼ cup salad oil

1 cup tomato juice

2 medium carrots, sliced

2 medium onions, cut up

1 cup thinly sliced celery

1 tablespoon salt

1 teaspoon oregano leaves

¼ teaspoon pepper

celery leaves or parsley sprigs, for garnish

1. Crush garlic; rub onto roast. On waxed paper, coat meat with flour.

2. In 8-quart Dutch oven over high heat, in hot salad oil, cook pot roast until browned on all sides.

3. Add tomato juice and remaining ingredients except celery leaves; heat to boiling. Reduce heat to low.

4. Cover Dutch oven and simmer for 4 hours or until the meat is fork-tender, turning it occasionally. Transfer the meat to a warm platter.

5. Fill blender three-fourths full with liquid and vegetables; cover; blend at high speed; pour into large bowl; repeat until all is blended.

6. Return the blended mixture to the Dutch oven; heat to boiling. Garnish the roast with celery leaves and serve with the hot gravy.

Beef Bourguignon with Chestnuts

TIME: about 3 hours—SERVINGS: 10

salad oil

2½ pounds beef for stew, cut into 1½-inch chunks

1½ pounds mushrooms, each cut in half or quarters

6 slices bacon, diced

1 pound small white onions

2 medium carrots, diced

1 medium celery stalk, diced

1 cup cooking or dry red wine

2 teaspoons sugar

1 teaspoon salt

¼ teaspoon pepper

1 beef-flavor bouillon cube or envelope

water

1 pound chestnuts

2 tablespoons all-purpose flour

1 tablespoon minced parsley, for garnish

1. In 5-quart Dutch oven over medium-high heat, in 2 tablespoons hot salad oil, cook beef for stew, half at a time, until well browned on all sides. With slotted spoon, remove meat to plate; set aside. In drippings remaining in Dutch oven (add 1 tablespoon salad oil if necessary) over medium heat, cook mushrooms 5 minutes; with slotted spoon, remove mushrooms to medium bowl; set aside.

2. In same Dutch oven over medium heat, cook bacon, onions, carrots, and celery until bacon and vegetables are browned, stirring frequently. Stir in wine, sugar, salt, pepper, bouillon, and 1¼ cups water. Return meat to Dutch oven; over high heat, heat to boiling. Reduce heat to low; cover and simmer 1½ hours or until meat is almost tender, stirring occasionally.

3. Meanwhile, in 2-quart saucepan over high heat, heat chestnuts and enough water to cover to boiling. Reduce heat to medium; cover and cook 15 minutes. Remove saucepan from heat. Immediately, with slotted spoon, remove four chestnuts from water. With kitchen shears, carefully cut each chestnut on flat side through shell. With fingers, peel off shell and skin, keeping chestnuts whole if possible. Repeat with remaining chestnuts. (Chestnuts will be difficult to peel when cool.)

4. When meat is ready, stir mushrooms and chestnuts into meat mixture. Continue cooking until meat is fork-tender, about 15 minutes.

5. To serve, skim off fat from liquid in Dutch oven. In cup with fork, stir flour and ¼ cup water until blended. Gradually stir flour mixture into beef mixture in Dutch oven; cook over medium heat, stirring, until mixture is thickened. Spoon meat mixture into warm bowl; sprinkle with parsley.

Spicy Bean-and-Short-Rib Stew

TIME: about 4$^1/_2$ hours—SERVINGS: 8

1 16-ounce package dry pink beans

water

3 tablespoons salad oil

3 pounds beef chuck short ribs, cut into serving pieces

2 tablespoons chili powder

5 teaspoons sugar

4 teaspoons salt

$^1/_2$ teaspoon pepper

1 pound small white onions

1 cup tomato juice

$^1/_4$ cup cider vinegar

1 tablespoon chopped parsley, for garnish

1. Rinse beans in running cold water and discard any stones or shriveled beans. In 8-quart Dutch oven or saucepot over high heat, heat beans and 8 cups water to boiling; cook 3 minutes. Remove Dutch oven from heat; cover and let stand 1 hour. Drain and rinse beans; set aside.

2. In same Dutch oven over medium-high heat, in hot salad oil, cook beef short ribs, a few pieces at a time, until browned on all sides, removing short ribs to large bowl as they brown. Spoon off fat remaining in Dutch oven.

3. Return beans and short ribs to Dutch oven; add chili powder, sugar, salt, pepper, and 6 cups water; over high heat, heat to boiling. Reduce heat to low; cover and simmer 2 hours, stirring mixture occasionally.

4. Skim off fat from liquid in Dutch oven. Stir in white onions, tomato juice, and cider vinegar; over high heat, heat to boiling. Reduce heat to low; cover and simmer 1 hour longer or until beans, meat, and onions are tender, stirring occasionally. Serve stew in warm deep platter; sprinkle with parsley.

Beef and Green Beans in Mustard Sauce

TIME: about 45 minutes—SERVINGS: 4

water

1$^1/_2$ pounds green beans

salt

1 beef top round steak, cut $^3/_4$ inch thick (about 1 pound)

$^1/_4$ cup prepared mustard

2 teaspoons cornstarch

$^1/_4$ teaspoon pepper

2 tablespoons salad oil

1 small onion, minced

lettuce leaves

1. In 3-quart saucepan over high heat, in 1 inch boiling water, heat green beans and $^1/_2$ teaspoon salt to boiling. Reduce heat to low; cover and simmer 10 minutes or until the beans are tender-crisp. Drain.

2. Meanwhile, cut beef top round steak into 1-inch chunks; set aside.

3. In small bowl, stir mustard, cornstarch, pepper, 1 cup water, and 1 teaspoon salt until blended; set aside. In 10-inch skillet over medium-low heat, in hot salad oil, cook onion until very tender, stirring occasionally. Increase heat to medium-high; add beef chunks; cook until beef chunks are browned on outside and delicate pink inside, stirring frequently. Gradually stir mustard mixture into beef mixture in skillet; cook over medium heat until slightly thickened, stirring constantly. With slotted spoon, remove beef to medium bowl; keep warm, leaving sauce in skillet.

4. Reduce heat to low; add green beans to sauce remaining in skillet; heat through, tossing to coat beans. Arrange green beans on half of large platter. Line other half of platter with lettuce leaves; top with beef mixture.

Beef Paprika

TIME: about 2 hours—SERVINGS: 8

2 tablespoons salad oil

1 garlic clove, cut in half

2 pounds beef for stew, cut into 1$^1/_2$-inch chunks

4 medium onions, sliced

1 tablespoon paprika

$^1/_2$ cup water

1 6-ounce can tomato paste

1 teaspoon salt

1 teaspoon sugar

$^1/_2$ teaspoon pepper

$^3/_4$ cup milk

2 tablespoons all-purpose flour

1. In 5-quart Dutch oven over medium-high heat, in hot salad oil, cook garlic 1 minute; discard. Add beef and onions; cook until meat is lightly browned and onions are tender, stirring frequently. Stir in paprika; cook 1 minute. Add water, tomato paste, salt, sugar, and pepper; over high heat, heat to boiling. Reduce heat to low; cover and simmer 1$^1/_2$ hours or until meat is fork-tender, stirring occasionally.

2. When meat is done, skim off fat from liquid in Dutch oven. In cup, mix milk and flour until blended. Gradually stir flour mixture into liquid in Dutch oven; cook over medium heat until slightly thickened, stirring.

Country Beef and Beans

TIME: about 4½ hours—SERVINGS: 8

1 cup dry pea (navy) beans

1 cup dry red kidney beans

water

2 tablespoons salad oil

4 beef shank cross-cuts, each cut about 1 inch thick (about 3 pounds)

2 medium onions, sliced

2 teaspoons salt

½ teaspoon thyme leaves

⅛ teaspoon crushed red pepper

½ pint cherry tomatoes, each cut in half

1. Rinse beans in running cold water and discard any stones or shriveled beans. In 8-quart Dutch oven over high heat, heat beans and 8 cups water to boiling; cook 3 minutes. Remove Dutch oven from heat; cover, and let stand 1 hour. Drain and rinse beans; set aside.

2. In same Dutch oven over medium-high heat, in hot salad oil, cook beef shank cross-cuts until well browned on both sides, removing shanks to plate as they brown; set aside. Reduce heat to medium. To drippings remaining in Dutch oven, add onions and cook until tender, stirring occasionally.

3. Return shanks to Dutch oven. Add salt, thyme, crushed red pepper, and 4 cups water; over high heat, heat to boiling. Reduce heat to low; cover and simmer 1 hour. Add beans; over high heat, heat to boiling. Reduce heat to low; cover and simmer 1½ hours longer or until meat and beans are tender, stirring occasionally. Skim off fat from liquid in Dutch oven. Add cherry tomatoes; heat through.

Chunky Beef-and-Bean Stew

TIME: about 3½ hours—SERVINGS: 4

½ 16-ounce package dry pinto beans (about 1 cup)

water

2 tablespoons salad oil

¾ pound beef for stew, cut into 1-inch chunks

1 large onion, diced

2 large carrots, cut into 1-inch chunks

2 medium celery stalks, cut into 1-inch chunks

2 medium turnips, cut into bite-size chunks

2 teaspoons salt

½ teaspoon thyme leaves

¼ teaspoon pepper

1. Rinse beans in running cold water and discard any stones or shriveled beans. In 5-quart Dutch oven over high heat, heat beans and 4 cups water to boiling; cook 3 minutes. Remove Dutch oven from heat; cover and let stand 1 hour. Drain and rinse beans; set aside.

2. In same Dutch oven over medium-high heat, in hot oil, cook beef for stew until well browned on all sides. With slotted spoon, remove meat to small bowl; set aside.

3. In drippings remaining in Dutch oven over medium heat, cook onion until tender, stirring occasionally. Add meat, beans, carrots, remaining ingredients, and 3 cups water; over high heat, heat to boiling. Reduce heat to low; cover and simmer 1½ hours or until meat and beans are tender, stirring occasionally.

Beef in Beer

TIME: about 2¾ hours—SERVINGS: 8

4 slices bacon, cut into 1-inch pieces

3 large onions (1½ pounds), sliced

3 pounds beef for stew, cut into 2-inch chunks

salad oil

2 tablespoons all-purpose flour

1 12-ounce can or bottle beer

1 cup water

1 beef-flavor bouillon cube or envelope

1 small bay leaf

2 teaspoons sugar

¾ teaspoon salt

¼ teaspoon thyme leaves

⅛ teaspoon pepper

2 tablespoons red-wine vinegar

1. In 12-inch skillet over medium heat, cook bacon until browned; with slotted spoon, remove bacon to 3-quart casserole. In drippings remaining in skillet, cook onions until tender and lightly browned, stirring frequently. With slotted spoon, remove to casserole.

2. In drippings remaining in skillet over medium-high heat, cook beef for stew, a few pieces at a time, until well browned (adding some salad oil if necessary), removing pieces to casserole as they brown.

3. In same skillet over medium heat, into an additional 2 tablespoons hot salad oil, stir flour; cook, stirring constantly, until flour is dark brown. Gradually stir in beer and remaining ingredients except vinegar; cook until sauce is slightly thickened.

4. Pour sauce into casserole; mix well. Bake, covered, in 350° F. oven 1¾ hours or until meat is fork-tender. Spoon off fat from sauce in casserole. Stir in wine vinegar.

Beef-and-Rice Supper

TIME: about 2 hours—SERVINGS: 4

2 tablespoons salad oil

³/₄ pound beef for stew, cut into ³/₄-inch chunks

1 medium onion, chopped

1 small garlic clove, minced

1 16-ounce can stewed tomatoes

4 cups water

1 tablespoon salt

1 tablespoon Worcestershire sauce

1 teaspoon sugar

¹/₂ teaspoon pepper

¹/₄ teaspoon basil

4 medium carrots, cut into 2-inch chunks

1¹/₂ cups regular long-grain rice

1. In 5-quart Dutch oven or saucepot over medium-high heat, in hot oil, cook beef until well browned on all sides. With slotted spoon, remove meat to small bowl; set aside.

2. In drippings in Dutch oven over medium heat, cook onion and garlic until onion is tender, stirring occasionally. Add meat, stewed tomatoes with their liquid, and next 6 ingredients; over high heat, heat to boiling. Reduce heat to low; cover and simmer 1 hour, stirring occasionally.

3. Skim off fat from liquid in Dutch oven. Add carrots; over high heat, heat to boiling. Reduce heat to low; cover and simmer 10 minutes. Stir in rice; over high heat, heat to boiling. Reduce heat to low; cover and simmer 20 minutes or until rice is cooked and meat is tender, stirring occasionally.

Burgundy Baked Steak Strips

TIME: about 2 hours—SERVINGS: 8

1 2-pound beef top round steak, cut about 1 inch thick

¹/₄ cup all-purpose flour

salad oil

1 envelope beef-flavor bouillon

1 cup water

1 tablespoon salt

¹/₂ teaspoon pepper

1 pound small white onions, each cut in half

6 medium potatoes, cut into chunks

1¹/₂ cups red Burgundy wine

1. On waxed paper, coat round steak with 2 tablespoons flour. On cutting board, with meat mallet or dull edge of French knife, pound flour into meat. Cut meat into 4″ by ¹/₂″ strips.

2. In 12-inch skillet over medium-high heat, in 2 tablespoons hot salad oil, cook meat, several pieces at a time, until well browned on all sides, removing pieces as they brown to 3-quart casserole; add more oil if needed.

3. Meanwhile, in small bowl with wire whisk, stir bouillon, water, salt, pepper, and remaining 2 tablespoons flour; pour into drippings in skillet and heat to boiling. Pour mixture over beef in casserole. Add onions, potatoes, and Burgundy. Cover and bake in 350° F. oven about 1¹/₂ hours or until meat and potatoes are tender.

Beef-and-Vegetable Salad

TIME: about 1 hour—SERVINGS: 4

3 medium potatoes (1 pound)

water

¹/₃ cup salad oil

¹/₄ cup cider vinegar

1 tablespoon prepared mustard

1¹/₂ teaspoons salt

¹/₄ teaspoon basil

¹/₄ teaspoon cracked pepper

1 green onion, minced

1 pound cooked beef top round roast

1 10-ounce bag spinach

1 6-ounce package radishes

1. In 3-quart saucepan over high heat, heat unpeeled potatoes and enough water to cover to boiling. Reduce heat to medium-low; cover and cook 25 to 30 minutes, until potatoes are fork-tender.

2. Meanwhile, in large bowl with fork, mix salad oil, vinegar, mustard, salt, basil, pepper, and green onion.

3. Cut beef top round roast into bite-size thin slices (about 3 cups); add to dressing in bowl; set aside.

4. When potatoes are done, drain. Cool potatoes slightly until easy to handle. Peel and cut potatoes into bite-size chunks. Tear spinach into bite-size pieces. Thinly slice radishes. Add potatoes, spinach, and radishes to bowl with meat; toss gently to coat with dressing.

Beef-and-Oyster Pie

TIME: about 2 hours—SERVINGS: 10

1 beef kidney (about 1 pound)

1/4 cup all-purpose flour

2 pounds beef for stew, cut into 1-inch chunks

salad oil

1 garlic clove, cut in half

4 medium carrots, cut into 1-inch chunks

1 large onion, chopped

1 12-ounce can or bottle beer

2 tablespoons steak sauce

1/2 teaspoon salt

1/4 teaspoon pepper

water

1 8-ounce container shucked oysters

piecrust mix for one 9-inch piecrust

1 egg yolk

1. Rinse kidney. With knife, remove membranes and hard white parts from kidney; cut kidney into 1-inch chunks. On waxed paper, coat kidney chunks with 1 tablespoon flour; place in small bowl. Coat beef for stew with remaining flour; place on plate.

2. In 5-quart Dutch oven over medium-high heat, in 1/4 cup hot salad oil, cook garlic until golden; discard garlic. In same Dutch oven, cook kidney until well browned. With slotted spoon, remove kidney to bowl; set aside.

3. In oil remaining in Dutch oven, cook beef for stew until well browned. With slotted spoon, remove beef for stew to plate. In drippings remaining in Dutch oven (add 2 tablespoons salad oil if necessary) over medium heat, cook carrots and onion until lightly browned, stirring frequently. Return beef for stew to Dutch oven; stir in beer, steak sauce, salt, pepper, and 1/2 cup water; over high heat, heat to boiling. Reduce heat to low; cover and simmer 1 1/2 hours or until beef is fork-tender.

4. When beef is tender, stir kidney and oysters with their liquid into beef mixture; spoon into 2 1/2-quart round casserole.

5. Prepare piecrust mix as label directs. Preheat oven to 400° F. On lightly floured surface with lightly floured rolling pin, roll dough into a circle about 1 1/2 inches larger all around than top of casserole. Place pastry loosely over meat mixture. With kitchen shears, trim pastry edge, leaving 1-inch overhang. Fold overhang under and press gently all around casserole rim to make a high stand-up edge. With tip of knife, cut several slits in pastry top. In cup with fork, mix egg yolk with 1 teaspoon water. Brush crust with egg-yolk mixture. If you like, reroll scraps and use a cookie cutter to cut out shapes to decorate top of pie; brush cut-outs with yolk mixture. Bake pie 20 minutes or until crust is golden and mixture is heated through.

Monday Pie

TIME: 40 minutes—SERVINGS: 4

2 cups cubed cooked beef top round roast

1 10 1/4-ounce can beef gravy

1 16-ounce can small whole potatoes, drained

1 16-ounce can green beans, drained

1/4 cup cooking or dry red wine

1 medium tomato, chopped

1 3.75-ounce package refrigerated tender flaky buttermilk biscuits

1. Preheat oven to 375° F. In shallow 2-quart casserole, mix first six ingredients. Bake 10 minutes.

2. Remove casserole from oven. Pat each biscuit to flatten slightly; arrange on top of mixture. Bake 20 minutes or until biscuits are browned.

Rice-and-Ground-Beef Bake

TIME: about 1¼ hours—SERVINGS: 12

2 cups regular long-grain rice

1 pound ground beef

1 medium onion, diced

1 28-ounce can tomatoes

1 6-ounce can tomato paste

1 teaspoon salt

1 teaspoon sugar

½ teaspoon oregano leaves

¼ teaspoon pepper

1 15- or 16-ounce container ricotta cheese (2 cups)

¼ cup minced parsley

¼ cup water

1 egg

1 8-ounce package mozzarella cheese, shredded

1. Prepare rice as label directs.

2. Meanwhile, in 10-inch skillet over medium-high heat, cook ground beef and onion until all pan juices evaporate and beef is browned, stirring occasionally. Add tomatoes, their liquid, and next 5 ingredients; over high heat, heat to boiling. Reduce heat to low; cover; simmer 5 minutes to blend flavors, stirring occasionally.

3. Preheat oven to 375° F. In medium bowl, combine ricotta cheese, parsley, water, and egg. In 13″ by 9″ baking dish, spoon one third of meat sauce. Sprinkle sauce with half of cooked rice; top with half of ricotta mixture, then with one third meat sauce and half of mozzarella cheese. Repeat layering with remaining rice, ricotta, meat sauce, and mozzarella cheese. Cover baking dish with foil, and bake 30 minutes or until hot and bubbly.

Beef-and-Cabbage Picnic Pie

TIME: about 2 hours—SERVINGS: 12

3 cups all-purpose flour

1 cup butter or margarine, softened

1 16-ounce container sour cream (2 cups)

¼ cup salad oil

10 cups diced cabbage

2 teaspoons sugar

2 large onions, diced

½ pound mushrooms, sliced

salt

2 pounds ground beef

¼ teaspoon pepper

¼ cup dried bread crumbs

1 egg, slightly beaten

1. Into large bowl, measure flour. With pastry blender or two knives used scissor fashion, cut butter or margarine and 1 cup sour cream into flour until mixture resembles coarse crumbs. With hands, shape pastry into a ball; wrap with plastic wrap and refrigerate.

2. In 8-quart Dutch oven or saucepot over medium heat, in hot salad oil, cook cabbage, sugar, half of onions, half of mushrooms, and 1½ teaspoons salt until vegetables are tender, about 20 minutes, stirring occasionally. Remove Dutch oven from heat; stir in half of remaining sour cream.

3. Meanwhile, in 12-inch skillet over medium-high heat, cook ground beef, pepper, remaining onion and mushrooms, and 1½ teaspoons salt until all pan juices evaporate and meat is well browned, stirring occasionally. Spoon excess fat from meat mixture. Stir in remaining sour cream.

4. Preheat oven to 400° F. On lightly floured surface, with lightly floured rolling pin, roll half of pastry into an 18″ by 13″ rectangle. Gently press pastry into bottom and up sides of 15½″ by 10½″ jelly-roll pan; sprinkle with bread crumbs.

5. Spoon cabbage mixture into pastry-lined pan; top with ground-beef mixture. Roll remaining pastry into 16½″ by 11½″ rectangle; place over filling. Tuck overhang under; press around edges to seal. With tip of knife, lightly mark pastry to form a decorative design; cut a few slashes in pastry for air to escape during baking. Brush top of pie with beaten egg. Bake 50 minutes or until crust is golden brown and pie is hot. Cut into 12 pieces. Serve pie hot or cover and refrigerate to serve cold later.

TO FREEZE AND SERVE UP TO 1 MONTH LATER: Prepare and bake pie as above; cool. Wrap tightly with foil; label and freeze. To serve, about 1 hour before serving, unwrap pie; loosely cover with foil; bake about 1 hour or until hot.

Skillet Beef and Vegetables

TIME: about 1 hour—SERVINGS: 6

1 pound ground beef

1 large onion, diced

1 pound green beans, each cut crosswise in half

3 medium tomatoes (about 1 pound), chopped

2 medium carrots, diced

1 medium celery stalk, diced

$^1/_4$ cup water

$1^1/_2$ teaspoons salt

$1^1/_4$ teaspoons sugar

$^1/_2$ teaspoon pepper

1 8-ounce package mozzarella cheese, shredded

1. In 12-inch skillet over medium-high heat, cook ground beef and onion until juices from meat evaporate and meat is browned, stirring occasionally. Add green beans and remaining ingredients except cheese. Over high heat, heat to boiling. Reduce heat to low; cover and simmer 30 minutes or until beans are tender, stirring occasionally. Spoon off fat from skillet.

2. Stir half of cheese into meat mixture; sprinkle remaining cheese on top. Cover and cook 2 to 3 minutes longer, until cheese melts.

Tasty Twin Meat Loaves

TIME: about $1^1/_2$ hours—SERVINGS: 12

3 tablespoons salad oil

1 medium onion, minced

1 small green pepper, minced

3 pounds ground beef

$2^1/_2$ cups soft bread crumbs (5 slices white bread)

$^1/_2$ cup milk

3 tablespoons prepared horseradish

1 tablespoon salt

$1^1/_2$ teaspoons dry mustard

3 eggs

$^3/_4$ cup catchup

1. In 4-quart saucepan over medium heat, in hot salad oil, cook onion and green pepper until tender, stirring occasionally. Remove from heat. Stir in ground beef, bread crumbs, milk, horseradish, salt, mustard, eggs, and $^1/_2$ cup catchup; mix well.

2. Preheat oven to 350° F. Shape meat mixture into two 8″ by 4$^1/_2$″ loaves; place in 13″ by 9″ baking dish; brush tops of loaves with remaining catchup. Bake 1 hour.

Easy Chili

TIME: about 30 minutes—SERVINGS: 4

2 tablespoons salad oil

1 medium green pepper, diced

1 small onion, diced

2 teaspoons chili powder

2 16-ounce cans stewed tomatoes

1 $15^1/_4$- to 20-ounce can red kidney beans

4 cups diced cooked meat loaf

$^3/_4$ cup water

$^1/_2$ teaspoon salt

$^1/_2$ teaspoon sugar

$^1/_4$ teaspoon pepper

1. In 4-quart saucepan over medium heat, in hot salad oil, cook green pepper and onion until tender, stirring occasionally. Stir in chili powder; cook 1 minute.

2. Stir in stewed tomatoes, beans with their liquid, and remaining ingredients; over high heat, heat to boiling. Reduce heat to low; cover and simmer 10 minutes to blend flavors, stirring occasionally.

Dill-sauced Meat Bites

TIME: about 15 minutes—SERVINGS: 4

2 tablespoons butter or margarine

1 tablespoon all-purpose flour

¹/₄ teaspoon salt

¹/₂ cup milk

¹/₂ cup water

4 1-inch-thick slices cooked meat loaf (1 pound), cut into bite-size chunks

¹/₄ teaspoon dill weed

1. In 2-quart saucepan over medium heat, melt butter or margarine; stir in flour and salt until blended. Gradually stir in milk and water; cook, stirring constantly, until mixture is slightly thickened and smooth.

2. Gently stir in meat-loaf chunks; heat through. Spoon meat and sauce into warm bowl; sprinkle with dill.

Meat-Loaf Tostados

TIME: about 30 minutes—SERVINGS: 2

3 tablespoons salad oil

4 6-inch packaged corn tortillas

2 ¹/₄-inch-thick slices cooked meat loaf

¹/₂ 16-ounce can refried beans (³/₄ cup)

1¹/₂ cups lightly packed shredded lettuce

1 small tomato, thinly sliced

¹/₂ 4-ounce package shredded Cheddar cheese (¹/₂ cup)

bottled mild taco sauce

1. In 10-inch skillet over medium heat, in hot salad oil, fry 1 tortilla at a time, a few seconds on each side until soft and blistered and lightly browned. Remove tortilla to paper towels to drain; keep warm.

2. In oil remaining in skillet over medium heat, cook meat-loaf slices until browned on both sides. In small saucepan over low heat, heat refried beans.

3. For each serving, on dinner plate, overlap 2 tortillas slightly; spread with half of refried beans; top with half of shredded lettuce, 1 meat-loaf slice, half of tomato slices, then sprinkle with half of cheese. Serve tostados with taco sauce.

Autumn Beef-Barley Dinner

TIME: about 3 hours—SERVINGS: 8

3 tablespoons salad oil

2 pounds beef for stew, cut into 1-inch chunks

2 large onions, diced

6 cups water

¹/₂ cup medium barley

2³/₄ teaspoons salt

1 teaspoon oregano leaves

¹/₂ teaspoon pepper

2 10-ounce containers Brussels sprouts

2 medium tomatoes, each cut into 8 wedges

1. In 12-inch skillet over medium-high heat, in hot salad oil, cook beef for stew, half at a time, until browned on all sides, removing pieces to 4-quart casserole as they brown. In drippings remaining in skillet over medium heat, cook onions until tender, stirring occasionally. Add water; over high heat, heat to boiling, stirring to loosen brown bits.

2. Pour onion mixture over beef in casserole; stir in barley, salt, oregano, and pepper. Cover casserole and bake in 350° F. oven 1¹/₂ hours, stirring occasionally.

3. Stir in Brussels sprouts (if Brussels sprouts are very large, cut each in half). Bake casserole 30 minutes. Add tomato wedges; continue baking 10 minutes longer or until meat and vegetables are fork-tender.

Oxtail-Ragout Casserole

TIME: about 4 hours—SERVINGS: 4

2 tablespoons salad oil

3 pounds oxtails, cut into 1-inch pieces

1 medium onion, sliced

1 28-ounce can tomatoes

1 16-ounce bag carrots, cut into 1½-inch chunks

4 medium turnips (1 pound), cut into 1-inch chunks

4 medium celery stalks, cut into 1-inch pieces

3 cups water

2 teaspoons salt

¾ teaspoon sugar

½ teaspoon thyme leaves

¼ teaspoon pepper

1. In 8-quart Dutch oven over medium-high heat, in hot salad oil, cook oxtails, a few pieces at a time, until browned on all sides, removing pieces to 3-quart casserole as they brown. In drippings remaining in Dutch oven over medium heat, cook onion until tender, stirring occasionally.

2. Add tomatoes with their liquid and remaining ingredients; over high heat, heat to boiling. Pour tomato mixture over oxtails in casserole. Cover casserole and bake in 325° F. oven 3 hours or until oxtails are fork-tender, stirring occasionally. Skim off fat from casserole.

Corn-Pone Casserole

TIME: about 1¼ hours—SERVINGS: 6

1 pound ground beef

1 medium onion, diced

4 teaspoons chili powder

1 28-ounce can tomatoes

1½ teaspoons sugar

1½ teaspoons salt

¼ teaspoon cracked pepper

1 16- to 20-ounce can red kidney beans, drained

1 12- to 15-ounce package corn-muffin mix

parsley sprigs, for garnish

1. In 4-quart saucepan over high heat, cook beef and onion until all pan juices evaporate and meat is browned, stirring occasionally. Stir in chili powder; cook 1 minute. Stir in tomatoes with their liquid, sugar, salt, and pepper; over high heat, heat to boiling. Reduce heat to low; cover; simmer 30 minutes, stirring often. Stir in beans. Spoon mixture into 12″ by 8″ baking dish.

2. Preheat oven to 400° F. Prepare corn-muffin-mix batter as label directs. With back of spoon, spread corn-muffin batter evenly over top of meat mixture in casserole. Bake casserole, uncovered, 15 to 20 minutes, until golden and toothpick inserted into corn bread comes out clean. Garnish casserole with parsley.

Beef-and-Cabbage Casserole

TIME: about 1¾ hours—SERVINGS: 6

1 pound ground beef

2 medium onions, diced

1 medium cabbage (about 2 pounds), coarsely shredded

2 medium carrots, thinly sliced

2½ teaspoons salt

¼ teaspoon pepper

¾ cup regular long-grain rice

1 13¾- or 14½-ounce can beef broth

½ cup water

1. In 5-quart saucepot or Dutch oven over high heat, cook ground beef and onions until pan juices evaporate and meat is well browned, stirring occasionally. Remove saucepot from heat. Add cabbage, carrots, salt, and pepper; toss to mix well.

2. Pour rice into 3-quart casserole; spoon ground-beef mixture on top of rice; pour beef broth and water over mixture. Cover casserole; bake in 350° F. oven 1 hour.

3. To serve, stir ground-beef mixture with rice to mix well.

Family-style Corned Beef

TIME: about 4^1/$_2$ hours—SERVINGS: 10 to 12

1 5- to 6-pound package corned-beef brisket

1 medium onion, quartered

1 bay leaf

^{1}/$_2$ teaspoon peppercorns

water

Simmered Vegetables (optional; right)

1. Prepare corned-beef brisket as label directs, or in 8-quart Dutch oven or saucepot over high heat, heat corned beef, onion, bay leaf, peppercorns, and enough water to cover meat to boiling. Reduce heat to low; cover and simmer 3 to 3^1/$_2$ hours, until meat is fork-tender.

2. Remove corned beef from Dutch oven; keep warm. The cooking liquid from corned beef is quite flavorful; if you like, use the cooking liquid to prepare Simmered Vegetables.

3. To serve, slice corned beef and arrange on warm large platter with vegetables.

Simmered Vegetables: To corned-beef cooking liquid in Dutch oven (taste corned-beef cooking liquid; if too salty, discard some of the liquid and replace with fresh water to desired salt level), add *1 small rutabaga,* cut into wedges, *one 16-ounce bag carrots, 6 to 8 small red potatoes;* over high heat, heat to boiling. Reduce heat to low; cover and simmer 15 minutes. Add *1 small head cabbage,* cut into wedges; cook 15 minutes longer or until all vegetables are tender.

German-style Potato Salad with Corned Beef

TIME: about 1 hour—SERVINGS: 6

6 medium potatoes (2 pounds)

water

2^1/$_2$ cups cubed cooked corned beef

6 slices bacon, diced

1 large onion, diced

^{1}/$_2$ cup diced dill pickles

^{1}/$_2$ cup salad oil

^{1}/$_2$ cup red-wine vinegar

2 tablespoons prepared mustard

1 tablespoon prepared horseradish

^{1}/$_2$ teaspoon salt

1 envelope beef-flavor bouillon

1. In 3-quart saucepan over high heat, heat unpeeled potatoes and enough water to cover to boiling. Reduce heat to medium-low; cover and cook 25 to 30 minutes, until potatoes are fork-tender. Drain. Cool potatoes slightly until easy to handle. Peel and slice potatoes; place in large bowl with corned beef.

2. Meanwhile, in 10-inch skillet over medium heat, cook bacon and onion until bacon is browned and onion is tender, stirring occasionally. Stir in pickles, remaining ingredients, and ^{1}/$_2$ cup water. Remove skillet from heat.

3. Pour bacon mixture into bowl with potatoes; toss gently to mix well.

Corned-Beef Hash and Eggs

TIME: about 45 minutes—SERVINGS: 4

vegetable cooking spray

4 tablespoons butter or margarine

3 medium potatoes (1 pound), peeled and diced

1 small green pepper, diced

1 small onion, minced

1^1/$_4$ cups diced cooked corned beef

^{3}/$_4$ cup milk

^{1}/$_2$ teaspoon salt

^{1}/$_8$ teaspoon pepper

4 eggs

1. Spray 10-inch skillet with vegetable cooking spray as label directs, or use skillet with nonstick finish; place skillet over medium heat. In skillet, melt butter or margarine; add potatoes, green pepper, and onion. Cook until potatoes are browned and tender, stirring occasionally. Stir in corned beef, milk, salt, and pepper; heat through.

2. With spoon, make 4 deep indentations in corned-beef mixture. One at a time, break eggs into saucer and slip into indentations. Reduce heat to low; cover skillet and cook about 10 minutes or until eggs are of desired firmness.

Corned-Beef-and-Pear Salad

TIME: about 20 minutes—SERVINGS: 2

2 tablespoons salad oil

1 tablespoon red-wine vinegar

$^1/_2$ teaspoon salt

$^1/_2$ teaspoon sugar

1 cup julienne strips cooked corned beef

1 large pear, cut into bite-size chunks

lettuce leaves

2 tablespoons California walnuts

1. In medium bowl, combine salad oil, vinegar, salt, and sugar. Add corned beef and pear to dressing in bowl; toss to mix well.

2. Line two large wine goblets or salad bowls with lettuce. Spoon corned-beef mixture onto lettuce in goblets; sprinkle with walnuts. Serve as a main dish.

Veal Scallops

TIME: about 45 minutes—SERVINGS: 4

6 veal cutlets, each cut about $^1/_4$ inch thick (about 1 pound)

3 tablespoons all-purpose flour

$^3/_4$ teaspoon salt

pepper

butter or margarine

salad oil

1 small onion, minced

$^3/_4$ cup water

$^1/_4$ cup cooking or dry sherry

2 teaspoons minced parsley

$^3/_4$ teaspoon instant chicken-flavor bouillon

1. On cutting board with meat mallet or dull edge of French knife, pound veal cutlets to $^1/_8$-inch thickness. Cut each cutlet into two or three pieces. On waxed paper, combine flour, salt, and $^1/_4$ teaspoon pepper. Coat veal-cutlet pieces with flour mixture.

2. In 12-inch skillet over medium-low heat, heat 2 tablespoons butter or margarine and 2 tablespoons salad oil until hot; add onion; cook until very tender, stirring occasionally. With slotted spoon, remove onion to small bowl, leaving butter mixture in skillet.

3. Increase heat to medium-high. In butter mixture remaining in skillet, cook half of veal-cutlet pieces at a time, until browned on both sides, about 1 minute, adding more salad oil and butter or margarine if necessary. Remove veal to warm platter; keep warm.

4. Reduce heat to medium. Return onions to skillet; add water, sherry, parsley, bouillon, and $^1/_8$ teaspoon pepper, scraping to loosen brown bits from bottom of skillet. Cook until mixture boils. Pour sauce over cutlets.

Calves' Liver Bonne Femme

TIME: about 1 hour—SERVINGS: 4

$^1/_2$ pound small white onions

water

4 slices calves' liver, each cut $^1/_2$ inch thick (about 1 pound)

2 tablespoons all-purpose flour

1 teaspoon salt

$^1/_8$ teaspoon pepper

ground ginger

6 slices bacon

1 tablespoon honey

1 medium tomato, cut into 8 wedges

parsley sprigs, for garnish

1. In 2-quart saucepan over high heat, heat onions and 1 inch water to boiling. Reduce heat to medium-low; cover and cook 10 to 15 minutes, until onions are fork-tender. Drain onions; set aside. Trim any membrane from calves' liver. On sheet of waxed paper, mix flour, salt, pepper, and $^1/_8$ teaspoon ginger; use to coat liver slices.

2. In 12-inch skillet over medium-low heat, cook bacon until browned. With slotted spoon, remove bacon to paper towels to drain.

3. Pour off all but 2 tablespoons bacon drippings from skillet. In drippings remaining in skillet, over medium-high heat, cook onions until well browned, shaking skillet frequently. With slotted spoon, remove onions to small bowl; set aside. Meanwhile, in cup, mix honey, $^1/_2$ cup water, and $^1/_8$ teaspoon ginger; set aside.

4. In drippings remaining in skillet, over medium heat, cook liver slices about 4 minutes, turning once, until crisp and browned on outside and delicate pink inside (medium done). (Don't overcook, or liver will be tough.) Remove liver to warm large platter; keep warm.

5. Return onions to skillet; add honey mixture, stirring to scrape brown bits from bottom of skillet. Add tomato wedges; heat through. Arrange vegetables on platter with liver. Place bacon slices on liver. Garnish platter with parsley sprigs.

Barbecued Pork Spareribs

TIME: about 2 hours—SERVINGS: 4

barbecue sauce (see Index)

4 pounds pork spareribs

water, for outdoor open grill and oven
    methods

TO COOK ON OUTDOOR COVERED GRILL: 1. Prepare outdoor covered
charcoal grill, using indirect-heat method with drip pan, as manufacturer
directs. Or, follow manufacturer's directions if using covered gas or electric
grill.

2. Meanwhile, prepare one of the barbecue sauces listed in Index.

3. Place pork spareribs, cut into two-rib portions, on grill over drip pan.
Cover grill; cook 1½ hours or until ribs are fork-tender, turning ribs
occasionally and adding briquettes to each side of drip pan at the end of 1
hour, as manufacturer directs. During last 10 minutes of cooking, brush ribs
with barbecue sauce.

TO COOK ON OUTDOOR OPEN GRILL: 1. Precook spareribs: In 8-quart Dutch
oven or saucepot, cover spareribs with water; over high heat, heat to
boiling. Reduce heat to low; cover and simmer 1 hour or until spareribs are
fork-tender. (If starting early in day, remove ribs to platter; cover and
refrigerate.)

2. About 1 hour before serving, prepare outdoor grill for barbecuing.
Meanwhile, prepare one of the barbecue sauces listed in Index.

3. Place cooked spareribs on grill over medium heat; cook 20 minutes or
until heated through, brushing occasionally with sauce and turning ribs
often.

TO BROIL IN OVEN: 1. Precook spareribs as above in "To cook on outdoor
open grill."

2. About 35 minutes before serving, preheat broiler if manufacturer
directs. Prepare one of the barbecue sauces listed in Index.

3. Arrange spareribs, meat side down, on rack in broiling pan. About 7 to
9 inches from source of heat (or at 450° F.), broil ribs 20 minutes or until
heated through, occasionally brushing with sauce and turning ribs once.

Pork Chops with Sour-Cream Sauce

TIME: about 40 minutes—SERVINGS: 4

4 pork loin blade, rib, or sirloin chops,
    each cut ¾ inch thick

1 tablespoon all-purpose flour

1 tablespoon salad oil

1 medium onion, diced

¾ cup water

1 teaspoon salt

⅛ teaspoon pepper

½ 8-ounce container sour cream

2 teaspoons catchup

1. Coat pork chops with flour. In 12-inch skillet over medium-high heat, in
hot salad oil, cook pork chops and onion until meat is well browned on
both sides.

2. Add water, salt, and pepper; heat to boiling. Reduce heat to low; cover
and simmer 25 minutes or until pork chops are fork-tender. Skim off fat
from liquid; stir in sour cream and catchup; heat through (do not boil).

Pork Loin Chops with Prune Stuffing

TIME: about 2 hours—SERVINGS: 6

2 tablespoons butter or margarine

1 small onion, diced

1¹/₂ cups whole-wheat bread cubes (about 3 slices)

1¹/₂ cups pitted prunes, coarsely chopped

¹/₄ teaspoon sage leaves

water

salt

pepper

6 pork loin rib chops, each cut about 1 inch thick

2 chicken-flavor bouillon cubes or envelopes

¹/₄ cup milk

1 tablespoon all-purpose flour

1. In 12-inch skillet over medium heat, in hot butter or margarine, cook onion until tender, stirring occasionally. Remove skillet from heat. Add whole-wheat bread cubes, prunes, sage, ¹/₃ cup water, 1 teaspoon salt, and ¹/₄ teaspoon pepper; mix well.

2. With sharp knife, trim several pieces of fat from edge of pork loin rib chops; reserve fat. Cut each pork chop, from fat side, horizontally almost to the bone to form pocket. Spoon some prune mixture firmly into each pocket; close pockets with toothpicks. Lightly sprinkle pork chops on both sides with salt and pepper.

3. In same skillet over medium-high heat, heat reserved fat until lightly browned; using spoon, press and rub fat over bottom of skillet to grease it well; discard fat. Add three chops to skillet; over high heat, cook until well browned on both sides, removing chops from skillet as they brown. Repeat with remaining chops.

4. Return chops to skillet; add bouillon and 1 cup water; over high heat, heat to boiling. Reduce heat to low; cover and simmer 1¹/₂ hours or until pork chops are fork-tender, turning chops once. Remove pork chops to large platter; discard toothpicks. Keep pork chops warm.

5. Skim off fat from liquid in skillet. In cup, mix milk and flour until blended. Gradually stir flour mixture into liquid in skillet. Cook over medium heat, stirring constantly, until gravy is slightly thickened. Pour gravy over chops.

Pork Chops with Creamy Mustard Sauce

TIME: about 1¹/₂ hours—SERVINGS: 4

1 medium carrot

2 tablespoons salad oil

4 pork loin blade, rib, loin, or sirloin chops, each cut ³/₄ inch thick

1 small onion, minced

2 tablespoons cooking or dry white wine

2 tablespoons prepared mustard

³/₄ teaspoon salt

¹/₄ teaspoon pepper

¹/₄ teaspoon thyme leaves

water

¹/₂ cup milk

2 teaspoons all-purpose flour

1. With sharp knife, cut 1-inch piece off large end of carrot and reserve. Shred remaining carrot; set aside.

2. In 10-inch skillet over medium-high heat, in hot salad oil, cook two pork chops at a time until well browned on both sides; remove pork chops from skillet as they brown.

3. In drippings remaining in skillet over medium heat, cook shredded carrot and onion until onion is tender, stirring occasionally. Stir in wine, mustard, salt, pepper, thyme, and 1 cup water. Return pork chops to skillet; over high heat, heat to boiling. Reduce heat to low; cover and simmer 45 minutes to 1 hour until pork chops are fork-tender, turning pork chops once.

4. Meanwhile, cut reserved piece of carrot lengthwise into thin slices; then cut slices into matchstick-thin strips. In 1-quart saucepan over high heat, heat ¹/₂ cup water to boiling. Add carrot strips; cook 3 minutes or until carrots are tender. Drain carrot strips; discard water. Set carrot strips aside for garnish.

5. Skim off fat from liquid in skillet. In cup, stir milk and flour until blended. Gradually stir flour mixture into liquid in skillet; cook mixture over medium heat until sauce is slightly thickened, stirring constantly. Arrange pork chops with sauce on warm platter. Garnish pork chops with carrot strips.

Pork Kabobs Laredo

TIME: about 5½ hours or start early in day—SERVINGS: 6

1½ **pounds pork shoulder blade (Boston) roast, boneless**

salad oil

1 **medium onion, diced**

1 **garlic clove, minced**

2 **4-ounce cans diced green chilies, drained**

1 **8-ounce can tomatoes**

1 **6-ounce can tomato paste**

½ **cup water**

⅓ **cup orange juice**

1 **tablespoon brown sugar**

¼ **teaspoon crushed red pepper**

salt

2 **medium green peppers**

3 **large nectarines**

1 **pound large mushrooms**

1. Trim excess fat from pork shoulder blade roast; cut pork into 1½-inch chunks. In 2-quart saucepan over medium heat, in 2 tablespoons hot salad oil, cook onion and garlic until tender. Add green chilies, tomatoes with their liquid, tomato paste, water, orange juice, brown sugar, crushed red pepper, and 1 teaspoon salt; heat to boiling. Reduce heat to low; simmer 5 minutes.

2. Spoon half of tomato mixture into medium bowl; stir in ½ teaspoon salt; refrigerate until chilled. Add pork; mix well; cover and refrigerate at least 4 hours or overnight, stirring occasionally. Spoon remaining tomato mixture into small bowl; cover and refrigerate.

3. About 1 hour before serving, prepare outdoor grill for barbecuing. Meanwhile, cut green peppers into 2-inch pieces; cut each nectarine into four wedges. On six long skewers (about 18 inches), thread pork alternately with green peppers, nectarines, and mushrooms (if mushrooms are too large, cut into halves or quarters); reserve tomato mixture marinade from pork. Spoon tomato mixture from small bowl into small metal-handled saucepan.

4. Place skewers on grill over medium heat; cook about 30 minutes or until pork is tender, turning skewers frequently and brushing pork and vegetables occasionally with tomato marinade in medium bowl.

5. Meanwhile, heat tomato mixture in saucepan on grill to serve with pork.

TO BROIL IN OVEN: Early in day or day ahead, prepare pork and tomato mixtures as above. About 1 hour before serving, preheat broiler if manufacturer directs. Cut green peppers and nectarines as above. On six all-metal skewers, thread pork alternately with green peppers, nectarines, and mushrooms. Place skewers on rack in broiling pan. About 7 to 9 inches from source of heat (or at 450° F.), broil 30 to 40 minutes, turning skewers frequently and brushing with marinade as above. Spoon tomato mixture from small bowl into 1-quart saucepan; cook over medium-low heat on top of range until hot, stirring occasionally. Serve as above.

Maple-glazed Pork Tenderloins

TIME: about 5¼ hours or start early in day—SERVINGS: 6

2½ **teaspoons salt**

¼ **teaspoon pepper**

2 **pork loin tenderloins, whole (about ¾ pound each)**

6 **bacon slices**

½ **cup maple-flavor syrup**

1. With hands, rub salt and pepper into pork tenderloins. Place tenderloins in medium bowl; cover and refrigerate at least 4 hours.

2. About 1 hour before serving, prepare outdoor grill for barbecuing.

3. Place two tenderloins with thick ends pointing away from each other and thin ends overlapping slightly to make a long piece of even thickness. Wrap bacon slices around tenderloins; secure with small metal skewers.

4. Into small metal-handled saucepan, measure maple-flavor syrup.

5. Place pork tenderloins on grill over medium heat; cook 25 to 30 minutes, until pork is lightly browned and tender, brushing frequently with maple-flavor syrup and turning meat occasionally. (Internal temperature of meat should be 170° F. on meat thermometer.) Remove metal skewers from tenderloins.

TO BROIL IN OVEN: Early in day, prepare tenderloins as above in steps 1 and 3. About 45 minutes before serving, preheat broiler if manufacturer directs. Place tenderloins on rack in broiling pan. About 7 to 9 inches from source of heat (or at 450° F.), broil 30 to 40 minutes, until pork is lightly browned and tender, brushing frequently with maple-flavor syrup and turning occasionally. (Internal temperature of meat should be 170° F. on meat thermometer.) To serve, remove skewers.

Sherried Pork Tenderloin

TIME: about 30 minutes—SERVINGS: 4

1 pork loin tenderloin, whole (about
³/₄ pound)

2 eggs

¹/₂ cup all-purpose flour

salt

4 tablespoons butter or margarine

2 tablespoons salad oil

³/₄ cup water

2 tablespoons cooking or dry sherry

¹/₈ teaspoon pepper

1 tablespoon chopped parsley

1. With sharp knife, cut pork loin tenderloin crosswise into ¹/₄-inch-thick slices. With meat mallet or dull edge of French knife, pound each pork slice to about ¹/₈-inch thickness.

2. In pie plate with fork, beat eggs. On waxed paper, mix flour and ¹/₂ teaspoon salt. Dip pork slices in egg, then in flour mixture.

3. In 12-inch skillet over medium-high heat, heat butter or margarine and salad oil until hot. Cook pork, several pieces at a time, until lightly browned on both sides, about 3 to 4 minutes, removing pork slices to plate as they brown.

4. Into drippings in skillet, stir water, sherry, pepper, and ¹/₄ teaspoon salt, scraping to loosen brown bits from bottom of skillet; return pork to skillet. Over medium-high heat, heat to boiling; cook about 2 minutes to blend flavors, stirring occasionally. Spoon pork and sauce onto platter; sprinkle with parsley.

Spicy Shredded Pork in Lettuce Cups

TIME: about 30 minutes—SERVINGS: 4

1 1¹/₄-pound pork shoulder blade steak

1 tablespoon cornstarch

2 tablespoons soy sauce

¹/₄ teaspoon salt

¹/₄ teaspoon ground ginger

¹/₄ teaspoon ground red pepper

¹/₄ teaspoon sugar

1 6-ounce package frozen Chinese pea
pods

3 tablespoons salad oil

1 medium onion, thinly sliced

1 medium carrot, cut into 3-inch-long
matchstick-thin strips

1 small garlic clove, minced

4 large Boston or iceberg lettuce leaves

1. Cut pork shoulder blade steak lengthwise in half; discard bone. With knife held in slanting position, almost parallel to the cutting surface, slice across width of each half into ¹/₈-inch-thick slices; cut slices into matchstick-thin strips. In medium bowl, mix pork strips, cornstarch, and next 5 ingredients; set aside.

2. Prepare Chinese pea pods as label directs; drain; set aside.

3. In 10-inch skillet over medium-high heat, in hot salad oil, cook onion, carrot, and garlic until vegetables are tender-crisp, stirring frequently. With slotted spoon, remove vegetables to small bowl. In drippings remaining in skillet over high heat, cook pork mixture until meat is browned and tender, about 5 minutes, stirring frequently. Return vegetable mixture to skillet; add pea pods; heat through. Spoon one-fourth pork mixture onto each lettuce leaf.

Pork Roast with Gravy

TIME: about 4 hours—SERVINGS: 16

1 5- to 6-pound pork shoulder blade
(Boston) roast

salt

pepper

water

3 tablespoons all-purpose flour

1 cup milk

1. Place pork shoulder blade roast, fat side up, on rack in open roasting pan. Sprinkle lightly with salt and pepper. Insert meat thermometer into center of thickest part of roast, being careful that pointed end does not touch fat or bone. Roast in 325° F. oven about 3³/₄ hours, until thermometer reaches 170° F. When roast is done, place on warm platter; let stand 15 minutes for easier carving.

2. Meanwhile, prepare gravy: Pour pan drippings into 2-cup measure or medium bowl (set pan aside); let stand a few seconds until fat separates from meat juices. Skim 3 tablespoons fat from drippings (add *butter* or *margarine if necessary*) into 2-quart saucepan: skim off and discard any remaining fat. Add ¹/₄ cup water to roasting pan; stir until brown bits are loosened; add to meat juices in cup with enough water to make 1 cup.

3. Into fat in saucepan over medium heat, stir flour, 1 teaspoon salt, and ¹/₈ teaspoon pepper; gradually stir in milk and meat-juice mixture; cook, stirring constantly, until gravy is thickened. Serve roast with gravy.

Roast Pork with Parsley-Crumb Crust

TIME: about 6¹/₂ hours—SERVINGS: 28

1 14-pound pork leg (fresh ham), whole

¹/₄ teaspoon pepper

salt

¹/₄ cup prepared mustard

1 teaspoon Worcestershire

¹/₄ teaspoon ground ginger

4 tablespoons butter or margarine

3 slices white bread

¹/₄ cup chopped parsley

water

3 tablespoons all-purpose flour

1 cup milk

1. With knife, remove skin and excess fat from pork leg, leaving only a thin fat covering. Place pork leg, fat side up, on rack in open roasting pan. Rub pork with pepper and 1 teaspoon salt. Insert meat thermometer into center of thickest part of pork, being careful that pointed end of thermometer does not touch fat or bone. Roast in 325° F. oven about 5¹/₂ hours or until thermometer reaches 170° F. (Pork near bone will be slightly pink. If you prefer uniform gray color throughout, roast until thermometer reaches 185° F.) Remove pork leg from oven.

2. In small bowl, mix mustard, Worcestershire, and ginger. In 1-quart saucepan over medium heat, melt butter or margarine; remove saucepan from heat. Into saucepan, tear bread into small pieces. Add chopped parsley; mix well.

3. Skim off 1 tablespoon fat from drippings in roasting pan; add to mustard mixture. With pastry brush, brush mustard mixture onto pork leg. With hands, carefully pat bread-crumb mixture onto pork. Return pork to oven; bake 15 minutes longer or until bread is lightly browned. Place pork on warm large platter or cutting board. Let stand 15 minutes for easier carving.

4. Meanwhile, prepare gravy: Remove rack from roasting pan; pour drippings into 4-cup measure or medium bowl (set pan aside); let stand a few seconds until fat separates from meat juices. Skim 3 tablespoons fat from drippings into 2-quart saucepan; skim off and discard any remaining fat. Add ¹/₄ cup water to roasting pan; stir until brown bits are loosened; add to meat juice in cup with additional water to make 2 cups.

5. Into fat in saucepan over medium heat, stir flour and ¹/₄ teaspoon salt until blended; gradually stir in meat-juice mixture and milk; cook, stirring constantly, until gravy is thickened. Pour gravy into gravy boat.

6. To serve, if you like, wrap small end of pork leg with a clean napkin to conceal shank bone. Serve pork with gravy.

Glazed Pork Roast

TIME: about 3 hours—SERVINGS: 10

1 4¹/₂- to 5-pound pork loin center rib roast

salt

pepper

2 tablespoons apple jelly

water

¹/₃ cup all-purpose flour

¹/₄ teaspoon thyme leaves

1 cup milk

1. Rub pork loin center rib roast with 1 teaspoon salt and ¹/₄ teaspoon pepper. Place roast, fat side up, in open roasting pan. Insert meat thermometer into center of thickest part of roast, being careful pointed end does not touch fat or bone. Roast in 325° F. oven 2 to 2³/₄ hours, until meat thermometer reaches 170° F.

2. When roast is done, place on warm large platter; brush with melted apple jelly; let roast stand 15 minutes for easier carving. Meanwhile, prepare gravy: Pour pan drippings into 2-cup measure or medium bowl (set pan aside); let stand a few seconds until fat separates from meat juices. Skim ¹/₃ cup fat from drippings (add *butter* or margarine if necessary) into 2-quart saucepan; skim off and discard any remaining fat. Add ¹/₄ cup water to roasting pan; stir until brown bits are loosened; add to meat juices in cup with enough water to make 2 cups.

3. Into fat in saucepan over medium heat, stir flour, thyme, 1 teaspoon salt, and ¹/₈ teaspoon pepper; gradually stir in meat-juice mixture and milk, and cook, stirring constantly, until gravy is thickened. Pour into gravy boat. Serve roast with gravy.

Skillet Pork with Vegetables

TIME: about 30 minutes—SERVINGS: 4

3 tablespoons salad oil

1 medium green pepper, cut into ¹/₂-inch-wide strips

1 medium onion, cut into ¹/₄-inch-thick slices

1 medium zucchini (about 8 ounces), cut into ¹/₄-inch-thick slices

1 envelope chicken-flavor bouillon

1 teaspoon salt

³/₄ teaspoon basil

¹/₈ teaspoon pepper

3¹/₂ cups julienne strips cooked pork

2 large tomatoes, cut into wedges

2 tablespoons minced parsley (optional)

In 12-inch skillet over high heat, in hot salad oil, cook green pepper and onion until lightly browned, about 5 minutes, stirring frequently. Add zucchini, bouillon, salt, basil, and pepper, and cook about 3 minutes longer or until vegetables are tender-crisp, stirring frequently. Reduce heat to medium; add pork strips and tomatoes; heat through. If you like, garnish with minced parsley.

Pork-and-Sauerkraut Supper

TIME: about 2³/₄ hours—SERVINGS: 6

2 tablespoons salad oil

6 pork rib or loin chops, each cut ³/₄ inch thick

1 medium onion, diced

1³/₄ cups apple juice

2 16-ounce bags or 2 14- to 16-ounce cans or jars sauerkraut, drained

3 medium potatoes (1 pound), cut into ¹/₄-inch-thick slices

2 red cooking apples, cored and cut into ¹/₂-inch chunks

2 teaspoons brown sugar

¹/₂ teaspoon salt

¹/₈ teaspoon pepper

1. In 12-inch skillet over medium-high heat, in hot salad oil, cook pork chops until browned on both sides. Remove chops to plate.

2. In drippings remaining in skillet over medium heat, cook onion until tender, stirring occasionally. Add ¹/₄ cup apple juice, stirring to loosen brown bits from bottom of skillet.

3. In 13″ by 9″ baking dish, combine onion mixture, sauerkraut, potatoes, apples, brown sugar, and remaining apple juice. Place pork chops on sauerkraut mixture; sprinkle chops with salt and pepper. Cover baking dish with foil and bake in 350° F. oven 2 hours or until meat and potatoes are fork-tender, occasionally basting meat and potatoes with liquid in baking dish.

Pork-and-Zucchini Casserole

TIME: about 1¹/₂ hours—SERVINGS: 6

1 pound ground pork

³/₄ cup chopped onion

¹/₄ cup water

1 10³/₄-ounce can condensed cream of chicken soup

¹/₂ cup cracker meal

2 tablespoons chopped parsley

1 teaspoon salt

¹/₂ teaspoon rubbed sage

¹/₄ teaspoon pepper

2 medium zucchini or yellow straightneck squash, cut into ¹/₄-inch slices (about 1 pound)

¹/₂ 8-ounce package pasteurized process cheese spread, diced

1. Grease a 10″ by 6″ baking dish. In 12-inch skillet over medium-high heat, cook ground pork and onion until lightly browned, stirring occasionally, about 10 minutes; remove from heat. Stir in water, undiluted chicken soup, cracker meal, parsley, salt, sage, and pepper until well mixed.

2. In baking dish, layer about half of squash slices; spoon meat mixture evenly over squash, then arrange remaining squash in three rows on top, leaving space between rows.

3. Cover dish tightly with foil; bake in 350° F. oven 1 hour or until squash is fork-tender. Remove foil and sprinkle cheese between squash slices. Return to oven and bake a few minutes longer to melt cheese.

Deviled Pork Patties

TIME: about 1 hour—SERVINGS: 4

1 pound ground pork

1 cup finely shredded carrots

1 egg

2 tablespoons chili sauce

2 tablespoons prepared mustard

1/2 teaspoon salt

1/4 teaspoon pepper

4 hamburger buns, split

4 lettuce leaves

bread-and-butter pickles

1. Prepare outdoor grill for barbecuing.

2. In medium bowl, mix first 7 ingredients. Make four 1-inch-thick patties.

3. Place patties on grill over medium heat; cook about 20 minutes or until well done, carefully turning patties occasionally. During last 2 to 3 minutes of cooking patties, toast hamburger buns on grill, cut side down, until golden. Serve pork patties in toasted buns with lettuce leaves and pickles.

TO BROIL IN OVEN: About 45 minutes before serving, preheat broiler if manufacturer directs. Prepare pork patties as above. Place patties on rack in broiling pan; broil 20 minutes, turning once. Remove broiling pan from oven; keep patties warm. Arrange buns, cut side up, on cookie sheet. Broil 2 to 3 minutes, until golden. Serve as above.

Pork Rib Bake

TIME: about 1 1/2 hours—SERVINGS: 6

1 20-ounce can sliced pineapple, drained

1 16-ounce bag or 1 14- to 16-ounce can or jar sauerkraut, drained

1/3 cup soy sauce

2 tablespoons brown sugar

4 teaspoons prepared mustard

1 small onion, grated

3 pounds pork loin country-style ribs

1. Reserve 3 pineapple slices for garnish; chop remaining pineapple. In 3-quart casserole, combine chopped pineapple, sauerkraut, soy sauce, sugar, mustard, and onion.

2. Cut pork loin country-style ribs into serving pieces; add to sauerkraut; toss to mix well.

3. Bake casserole, uncovered, in 350° F. oven 1 1/4 hours or until meat is tender. Skim off fat. Slice reserved pineapple slices in half to garnish casserole.

Continental Pork Casserole

TIME: about 1 1/4 hours—SERVINGS: 6

2 tablespoons salad oil

1 1/2 pounds pork pieces, cut into 1-inch chunks

2 large carrots

1 medium onion

1 16-ounce can tomato puree

1 cup water

1/2 cup lightly packed chopped celery leaves

1 tablespoon brown sugar

3 tablespoons cooking or dry red wine

1 teaspoon salt

1/4 teaspoon pepper

1. In 12-inch skillet over medium-high heat, in hot salad oil, cook pork pieces until browned, stirring frequently. With slotted spoon, remove meat to 1 1/2-quart casserole.

2. Meanwhile, cut each carrot crosswise in half; then cut each half lengthwise into thin slices. Thinly slice onion.

3. Preheat oven to 350° F. In drippings remaining in skillet over medium heat, cook carrots and onion until lightly browned, stirring occasionally. Add tomato puree and remaining ingredients; over high heat, heat to boiling, stirring to loosen brown bits from bottom of skillet. Pour sauce into casserole with meat, stirring to mix. Cover casserole and bake 45 minutes or until meat is fork-tender. Skim off fat from sauce in casserole.

Creamy Pork Hash

TIME: about 25 minutes—SERVINGS: 4

2 tablespoons butter or margarine

1 small onion, diced

1 tablespoon all-purpose flour

1 teaspoon salt

3/4 cup milk

2 cups cubed cooked potatoes

2 cups cubed cooked pork

1. In 10-inch skillet over medium heat, in hot butter or margarine, cook onion until tender, stirring occasionally. Stir in flour and salt. Gradually stir in milk; cook, stirring, until slightly thickened.

2. Stir potatoes and pork into sauce mixture. Reduce heat to low; cover skillet and simmer about 10 minutes or until heated through, stirring occasionally.

Glazed Baked Ham

TIME: about 2¼ hours—SERVINGS: 12

1 6- to 7-pound fully cooked smoked butt or shank half ham

½ 10- to 12-ounce jar pineapple preserves

1. Place ham on rack in open roasting pan. Insert meat thermometer into center of ham, being careful that pointed end does not touch fat or bone. Bake ham in 325° F. oven 1¾ to 2 hours, until meat thermometer reaches 140° F.

2. About 35 minutes before ham is done, in 1-quart saucepan over low heat, stir pineapple preserves until melted. During last 30 minutes of baking, with pastry brush, brush ham frequently with melted preserves.

Fruit-sauced Ham Slices

TIME: about 30 minutes—SERVINGS: 6

6 smoked ham boneless center slices, each about ½ inch thick

1 cup pitted dried prunes

1 cup dried apricots

1¾ cups orange juice

¼ cup sugar

1 tablespoon cornstarch

2 tablespoons water

1. Trim piece of fat from ham slice; slash edges of ham slices. In 12-inch skillet over medium-high heat, heat piece of fat until lightly browned, rubbing fat on bottom of skillet to grease it; discard piece of fat. Cook ham slices, a few at a time, until lightly browned on both sides, removing the slices as they brown.

2. Into skillet, stir prunes, apricots, orange juice, and sugar. Return ham to skillet, overlapping slices to fit; spoon some juice over slices; heat to boiling. Reduce heat to low; cover; simmer 20 minutes or until apricots are tender. Place ham slices on warm platter; keep warm.

3. In cup, blend cornstarch and water until smooth; stir into hot mixture in skillet and cook over medium heat, stirring constantly, until mixture is thickened and boils. Serve fruit sauce with ham.

Island Ham and Vegetables

TIME: about 20 minutes—SERVINGS: 4

2 tablespoons salad oil

1 medium onion, sliced

¼ cup cider vinegar

3 tablespoons brown sugar

1 tablespoon cornstarch

2 tablespoons soy sauce

¼ teaspoon ground ginger

¼ teaspoon salt

1 8-ounce can pineapple chunks in pineapple juice

1 6-ounce package frozen Chinese pea pods

2 cups bite-size chunks cooked ham

1 small tomato, cut into wedges

1. In 10-inch skillet over medium heat, in hot oil, cook onion until tender, stirring occasionally.

2. In cup, mix vinegar and next 5 ingredients; stir into skillet. Add pineapple chunks with juice and frozen pea pods; cook, stirring frequently, until mixture boils and thickens slightly. Add diced ham and tomato wedges; heat through.

Ham Rolls with Spinach

TIME: about 1 hour—SERVINGS: 6

3 slices white bread

1 10-ounce package frozen chopped
spinach, thawed and squeezed dry

1 egg

2 teaspoons grated onion

2 6-ounce packages sliced cooked ham

1 tablespoon butter or margarine

1 tablespoon all-purpose flour

1¹/₂ cups milk

¹/₄ cup shredded Cheddar cheese (1 ounce)

1. Preheat oven to 350° F. Into medium bowl, tear bread slices into crumbs; mix well with spinach, egg, and onion. Spread 1 tablespoon spinach mixture on each ham slice; starting with narrow end, roll up jelly-roll fashion. Place ham rolls, seam side down, in one layer, in 1¹/₂-quart shallow baking dish.

2. In 2-quart saucepan over medium heat, melt butter or margarine; stir in flour until blended; cook 1 minute. Gradually stir in milk; cook, stirring constantly, until sauce is slightly thickened and smooth. Stir in cheese until cheese melts. Spoon sauce over ham rolls. Cover dish with foil; bake 25 minutes or until hot and bubbly.

Ham-Spinach Ring

TIME: about 1 hour—SERVINGS: 6

2 tablespoons butter or margarine

2 tablespoons all-purpose flour

1¹/₂ cups milk

2 10-ounce packages frozen chopped
spinach, thawed and squeezed dry

¹/₂ teaspoon salt

3 eggs

1³/₄ cups diced cooked ham

Cheddar-Cheese Sauce (see Index)

1. Preheat oven to 350° F. Grease 5¹/₂-cup ring mold. In 3-quart saucepan over low heat, melt butter or margarine; stir in flour until blended. Gradually stir in milk; cook, stirring constantly, until mixture is thickened and smooth. Stir in spinach, salt, eggs, and 1¹/₂ cups diced ham. Spoon mixture into prepared ring mold.

2. Set ring mold in 13″ by 9″ baking pan; place pan on oven rack. Pour hot water in pan to come halfway up side of mold. Bake 40 minutes or until knife inserted in center of mixture comes out clean. Meanwhile, prepare Cheddar-Cheese Sauce.

3. To serve, with small spatula, loosen edges of mold. Invert mold onto warm platter. Pour cheese sauce over mold. Garnish center of mold with remaining diced ham.

Ham-and-Cheese Salad

TIME: about 20 minutes—SERVINGS: 4

1 10-ounce package frozen peas

boiling water

¹/₂ cup mayonnaise

¹/₄ cup pickle relish

2 tablespoons minced onion

¹/₂ teaspoon salt

2 cups diced cooked ham

³/₄ cup shredded American cheese

¹/₂ cup chopped celery

lettuce leaves

1. In small bowl, place frozen peas; cover with boiling water and let stand 5 minutes to "cook" peas.

2. In medium bowl with fork, stir mayonnaise, relish, onion, and salt until well mixed. Drain peas; add to mayonnaise mixture in bowl with ham, cheese, and celery; toss gently to mix well.

3. Serve mixture on lettuce leaves.

Mediterranean Sausage Bake

TIME: about 1$^1/_2$ hours—SERVINGS: 8

1/2 cup olive or salad oil

1 medium onion, sliced

1 small eggplant (1 pound), cut into
bite-size pieces

2 medium green peppers, cut into bite-size
pieces

1 small garlic clove, minced

2 medium zucchini, cut into 1/2-inch pieces

1 16-ounce can tomatoes

1 teaspoon salt

1 teaspoon sugar

1/2 teaspoon thyme leaves

2$^1/_2$ pounds hot or sweet Italian
sausage links

1/4 cup water

1/4 cup shredded Swiss cheese

2 tablespoons minced parsley

1. In 12-inch skillet over medium heat, in hot olive or salad oil, cook onion until tender-crisp, stirring occasionally. Add eggplant, green peppers, and garlic; cook 10 minutes, stirring frequently. Remove skillet from heat.

2. Preheat oven to 350° F. In 2$^1/_2$-quart casserole, combine vegetable mixture, zucchini, tomatoes with their liquid, salt, sugar, and thyme. Cover casserole and bake 35 minutes or until vegetables are tender.

3. Meanwhile, in same skillet over medium heat, heat sausages and water to boiling. Cover; simmer 5 minutes. Remove cover; continue cooking, turning sausages frequently, until sausages are well browned, about 15 minutes. Remove sausages to paper towels to drain. Slice sausages into 1/2-inch pieces.

4. Remove casserole from oven; stir sausages into vegetable mixture; sprinkle with Swiss cheese. Bake casserole, uncovered, 10 minutes or until heated through. Sprinkle with parsley.

Knackwurst with Sweet-and-Sour Cabbage

TIME: about 30 minutes—SERVINGS: 4

butter or margarine

1 large red cooking apple, cut into
bite-size chunks

1/4 teaspoon ground cinnamon

brown sugar

1 medium cabbage (about 2 pounds),
thinly sliced

1/3 cup cider vinegar

1 teaspoon salt

1/4 teaspoon pepper

1 16-ounce package knackwurst

2 tablespoons maple or maple-flavor syrup

1. In 12-inch skillet over medium-low heat, melt 2 tablespoons butter or margarine; add apple chunks, cinnamon, and 2 teaspoons brown sugar; cook until apple is tender, stirring occasionally. Remove apple mixture to small bowl; set aside.

2. In same skillet over medium heat, melt 2 more tablespoons butter or margarine; add cabbage, vinegar, salt, pepper, and 3 tablespoons brown sugar; cook until cabbage is tender-crisp, stirring frequently. Add apple mixture; heat through.

3. Meanwhile, preheat broiler if manufacturer directs. With sharp knife, cut a few diagonal slashes on each knackwurst; place knackwurst on rack in broiling pan. About 7 to 9 inches from source of heat (or at 450° F.), broil knackwurst 5 to 6 minutes; brush with half of maple syrup. Turn knackwurst; broil 5 to 6 minutes longer; brush with remaining syrup. Arrange cabbage mixture and knackwurst on warm platter.

"Reuben" Casserole

TIME: about 45 minutes—SERVINGS: 8

1 16-ounce bag or 1 14- to 16-ounce can or
jar sauerkraut

1/3 cup bottled Thousand Island dressing

1 12-ounce can luncheon meat, thinly
sliced

1 8-ounce package Swiss or Muenster
cheese slices

about 1/2 8-ounce loaf party rye-bread
slices

1 tablespoon butter or margarine, melted

1. Preheat oven to 400° F. In 13" by 9" baking dish with fork, stir sauerkraut with its liquid and Thousand Island dressing; top with luncheon-meat slices. Bake 15 minutes until bubbly hot.

2. Remove dish from oven. Place cheese slices on top of meat in a single layer; top with bread slices. Lightly brush bread with butter or margarine. Bake, uncovered, 10 minutes longer or until bread is crisp.

Polenta-and-Sausage Casserole

TIME: about 1½ hours—SERVINGS: 8

POLENTA:

1¼ cups enriched regular, quick, or instant farina

4 cups milk

½ teaspoon salt

½ cup butter or margarine

1 cup grated Parmesan cheese

2 eggs

SAUCE:

½ pound sweet Italian sausage links, sliced

½ cup chopped onion

1 garlic clove, crushed

1 16-ounce can tomatoes

1 6-ounce can tomato paste

1 4½-ounce can sliced mushrooms, drained

1 teaspoon salt

½ teaspoon sugar

¼ teaspoon pepper

1. Prepare polenta: In 3-quart saucepan, mix farina, milk, and salt. Cook over medium heat until mixture boils, stirring constantly. Remove from heat; beat in butter or margarine, cheese, and eggs. Pour mixture evenly into 13″ by 9″ baking dish; set aside.

2. Preheat oven to 375° F. Prepare sauce: In 10-inch skillet over medium heat, cook sausages until browned; spoon off fat. Add onion and garlic; cook until onion is tender, stirring frequently. Stir in tomatoes with their liquid and remaining ingredients; heat to boiling.

3. Spoon mixture evenly over polenta. Bake, uncovered, 30 minutes or until hot.

Franks-in-Rolls Casserole

TIME: about 1 hour—SERVINGS: 8

1 16-ounce package frankfurters

8 frankfurter rolls, split

4 eggs

5 cups milk

¼ cup finely chopped dill pickle

3 tablespoons prepared mustard

½ teaspoon salt

1. Preheat oven to 350° F. Grease a 13″ by 9″ baking dish. Slash 8 frankfurters in a few places to prevent curling (use any remaining frankfurters another day). Place each frankfurter in a roll and arrange rolls, split sides up, in dish.

2. In medium bowl, with spoon or wire whisk, beat eggs with remaining ingredients until well mixed; slowly pour mixture over frankfurters and rolls in baking dish.

3. Bake, uncovered, 45 minutes or until knife inserted between rolls in center of dish comes out clean.

Saucy Franks and Beans

TIME: about 30 minutes—SERVINGS: 8

1 8-ounce can pineapple slices in pineapple juice

2 16-ounce cans baked beans

1 16-ounce package frankfurters, cut into bite-size pieces

2 tablespoons prepared mustard

⅛ teaspoon ground cloves

1. Into 10-inch skillet, drain juice from pineapple; set pineapple slices aside. Into juice in skillet, stir beans, frankfurters, mustard, and ground cloves; over medium heat, heat to boiling, stirring often.

2. Cut each pineapple slice in half; place on top of bean mixture. Cover skillet; cook 3 to 5 minutes, until pineapple is heated through.

Mushroom-stuffed Lamb Chops

TIME: about 30 minutes—SERVINGS: 4

4 tablespoons butter or margarine

1/2 pound mushrooms, diced

2 tablespoons minced green onions

1/2 teaspoon savory

salt

pepper

1 1/2 cups white-bread cubes (3 slices)

1/4 cup water

4 lamb loin chops, each cut 1 inch thick (about 1 1/2 pounds)

1. In 10-inch skillet over medium heat, melt butter or margarine; add diced mushrooms, minced green onions, savory, 1/4 teaspoon salt, and 1/8 teaspoon pepper; cook until vegetables are tender, stirring occasionally. Remove skillet from heat. Add white-bread cubes and water; mix well.

2. Preheat broiler if manufacturer directs. With knife, cut each lamb chop, from fat side, horizontally almost to bone to form pocket. Spoon some mushroom mixture firmly into each pocket; close pocket with toothpicks. Place chops on rack in broiling pan; sprinkle with salt and pepper. Broil 10 to 15 minutes for medium-rare or until of desired doneness, carefully turning chops once. Discard toothpicks.

Oven-barbecued Lamb Breast

TIME: about 3 1/2 hours—SERVINGS: 3 or 4

1 3-pound lamb breast

3 medium oranges

1/2 cup chili sauce

2 tablespoons honey

1 teaspoon salt

1 teaspoon Worcestershire

1/4 teaspoon cracked black pepper

1. Cut lamb breast into serving-size portions. Grate 1 tablespoon peel and squeeze 1/4 cup juice from 1 orange.

2. In small bowl, mix well orange peel, juice, chili sauce, and remaining ingredients; set aside.

3. Place lamb in open roasting pan; pour chili-sauce mixture over lamb portions.

4. Bake in 325° F. oven 2 1/2 to 3 hours, until fork-tender, basting with sauce occasionally. Meanwhile, slice rest of oranges crosswise.

5. During last 15 minutes of cooking time, add orange slices to lamb to heat through.

Middle-Eastern Lamb Dinner

TIME: about 1 1/2 hours—SERVINGS: 8

1/2 cup olive or salad oil

2 medium onions, sliced

1 small eggplant, cut into bite-size pieces

2 large celery stalks, cut into 1-inch slices

2 medium green peppers, cut into bite-size pieces

2 medium zucchini, cut into 1-inch pieces

1 16-ounce can tomatoes

1 teaspoon sugar

1 teaspoon basil

1/2 teaspoon cracked pepper

salt

1 1/4 cups regular long-grain rice

1/4 teaspoon turmeric

1/3 cup honey

2 teaspoons curry powder

2 teaspoons lime juice

2 pounds lamb cubes for kabobs, cut into 1 1/2-inch cubes

1. Prepare vegetables: In 12-inch skillet over medium heat, in hot olive or salad oil, cook onions until tender-crisp, stirring occasionally. Add eggplant, celery, and green peppers; cook 5 minutes, stirring frequently. Stir in zucchini, tomatoes with their liquid, sugar, basil, cracked pepper, and 2 teaspoons salt, stirring to break up tomatoes. Over high heat, heat mixture to boiling. Reduce heat to medium-low; cover and cook 30 minutes or until vegetables are tender, stirring occasionally.

2. Meanwhile, prepare rice as label directs, but add turmeric to water; keep warm.

3. Preheat broiler if manufacturer directs. In small bowl, combine honey, curry powder, lime juice, and 2 teaspoons salt. Arrange lamb cubes for kabobs on rack in broiling pan. Broil lamb 20 to 25 minutes for rare, or until lamb is of desired doneness, occasionally brushing with honey mixture and turning lamb with tongs.

4. To serve, lightly sprinkle lamb with salt. Arrange vegetables, rice, and lamb on warm large platter.

Curried Lamb

TIME: about 2¹/₂ hours—SERVINGS: 8

2 tablespoons salad oil

1¹/₂ pounds lamb for stew, cut into 1¹/₂-inch chunks

1 large onion, sliced

1 medium garlic clove, crushed

1 tablespoon curry powder

water

1¹/₂ teaspoons salt

1 teaspoon sugar

¹/₄ teaspoon pepper

1 chicken-flavor bouillon cube or envelope

1 medium eggplant, cut into 1¹/₂-inch chunks

¹/₂ pound green beans, each cut in half

¹/₂ pint cherry tomatoes

1. In 12-inch skillet over medium-high heat, in hot salad oil, cook lamb until well browned, removing pieces as they brown; set browned lamb pieces aside.

2. To drippings remaining in skillet, add onion and garlic; cook over medium heat, until onion is tender, stirring occasionally. Stir in curry powder; cook 1 minute. Add ¹/₂ cup water, stirring to loosen brown bits from bottom of skillet.

3. In 2¹/₂-quart casserole, mix lamb, onion mixture, salt, sugar, pepper, bouillon, and 2¹/₂ cups water. Bake casserole, uncovered, in 350° F. oven 1 hour. Stir in eggplant and green beans; bake 45 minutes. Add cherry tomatoes; bake casserole 10 minutes longer or until meat and vegetables are fork-tender. Skim off fat.

Lamb-and-Soybean Stew

TIME: about 4 hours—SERVINGS: 6

1 16-ounce package dry soybeans

water

3 tablespoons salad oil

3 lamb shanks (about 3 pounds)

2 medium onions, quartered

1 medium green pepper, cut into bite-size pieces

1 medium garlic clove, minced

5 teaspoons salt

³/₄ teaspoon thyme leaves

¹/₂ teaspoon pepper

1 medium bunch broccoli, cut into bite-size pieces

1. Rinse soybeans in running cold water and discard any stones or shriveled beans. In 8-quart Dutch oven or saucepot over high heat, heat beans and 8 cups water to boiling; cook 3 minutes. Remove Dutch oven from heat; cover and let stand 1 hour. Drain and rinse beans.

2. In same Dutch oven over medium-high heat, in hot salad oil, cook lamb shanks until browned on all sides. Remove shanks to large bowl; set aside. In oil remaining in Dutch oven, cook onions, green pepper, and garlic until tender, stirring occasionally.

3. Return soybeans and lamb to Dutch oven; add salt, thyme, pepper, and 5 cups water; over high heat, heat to boiling. Reduce heat to low; cover and simmer 2¹/₄ hours, stirring occasionally.

4. Skim off fat from liquid in Dutch oven. Add broccoli; over high heat, heat to boiling. Reduce heat to low; cover; simmer 10 minutes longer or until beans and meat are tender. Serve stew in large soup bowls.

Moussaka

TIME: about 1¹/₂ hours—SERVINGS: 10

salad oil

2 large eggplants, cut into ¹/₄-inch slices

1¹/₂ pounds ground lamb

1 cup chopped onion

1 small garlic clove, minced

1 cup crumbled feta or shredded Muenster cheese

¹/₂ cup dried bread crumbs

¹/₂ cup dry red wine

¹/₄ cup chopped parsley

¹/₄ cup chili sauce

1¹/₂ teaspoons salt

¹/₄ teaspoon pepper

1 egg

Béchamel Sauce (right)

ground nutmeg

1. In 12-inch skillet over medium heat, in ¹/₄ cup hot salad oil, cook eggplant, a few slices at a time, until golden on both sides, adding more salad oil if necessary.

2. In same skillet over medium heat, cook ground lamb, onion, and garlic until meat is browned, about 10 minutes. Spoon excess fat from meat mixture. Stir in feta cheese and remaining ingredients except sauce and nutmeg until well mixed; remove from heat.

3. Prepare Béchamel Sauce.

4. Preheat oven to 350° F. Arrange half of eggplant in 13" by 9" baking dish; spoon meat mixture evenly over eggplant; top with remaining eggplant. Spoon sauce evenly over eggplant and sprinkle lightly with nutmeg. Bake 30 minutes or until hot.

Béchamel Sauce: In 2-quart saucepan over medium heat, melt ¹/₃ cup *butter* or margarine. With wire whisk or fork, beat in ¹/₂ cup all-purpose *flour* and ¹/₂ teaspoon *salt* until blended. Gradually stir in *one 13³/₄-ounce can chicken broth* and *1 cup milk,* and cook, stirring constantly, until mixture is thickened.

Baked Rabbit and Leeks

TIME: about 2³/₄ hours—SERVINGS: 4

2 medium leeks (about ³/₄ pound)

4 slices bacon, diced

all-purpose flour

1 2-pound package frozen rabbit, thawed

salad oil

1 16-ounce package carrots, sliced

¹/₂ pound mushrooms

1 chicken-flavor bouillon cube or envelope

1³/₄ cups water

¹/₂ cup cooking or dry red wine

1 teaspoon salt

1 teaspoon sugar

¹/₄ teaspoon thyme leaves

¹/₈ teaspoon cracked pepper

¹/₂ cup milk

1. Prepare leeks: Cut off roots and trim leaf end of leeks. Cut each leek crosswise in half; then cut root end of each leek lengthwise in half. Rinse leeks well with running cold water to remove all sand. Place leeks in 3-quart casserole; set aside.

2. In 12-inch skillet over medium heat, cook bacon until browned; with slotted spoon, remove bacon to paper towels; drain. Set bacon aside for garnish later.

3. Meanwhile, place 3 tablespoons flour on waxed paper. Dip rabbit pieces into flour to coat lightly.

4. In drippings remaining in skillet, over medium-high heat, cook rabbit, several pieces at a time, until browned on all sides. With slotted spoon, remove rabbit and place on leeks in casserole.

5. In drippings remaining in skillet (add salad oil if necessary), over medium heat, cook carrots and mushrooms (if mushrooms are big, cut each into quarters) until lightly browned, stirring frequently. Stir in bouillon, water, red wine, salt, sugar, thyme, and cracked pepper; heat to boiling. Pour mushroom mixture over rabbit in casserole. Cover casserole and bake in 350° F. oven 1¹/₂ hours or until rabbit is fork-tender.

6. Skim off fat from liquid in casserole. In cup, mix milk and 1 tablespoon flour; gradually stir mixture into hot liquid in casserole. Bake 10 minutes longer or until mixture is slightly thickened. Sprinkle casserole with bacon.

Roast Chicken with Brown-Rice Stuffing

TIME: about 4 hours—SERVINGS: 8

Brown-Rice Stuffing (right)

1 6- to 6¹/₂-pound roasting chicken

salad oil

water

salt

3 tablespoons all-purpose flour

¹/₄ cup sour cream

parsley sprigs, for garnish

1. Prepare Brown-Rice Stuffing.

2. Remove giblets and neck from chicken; reserve for gravy. Rinse chicken with running cold water and drain well. Spoon some of stuffing lightly into neck cavity. (Do not pack stuffing; it expands during cooking.) Fold neck skin over stuffing; fasten neck skin to back with skewer. With chicken breast side up, lift wings up toward neck, then fold under back of chicken so they stay in place.

3. Spoon stuffing lightly into body cavity. (Bake any leftover stuffing in covered, greased small casserole during last 30 minutes of roasting chicken.) Close, by folding skin lightly over opening; skewer closed if necessary. With string, tie legs and tail together.

4. Place chicken, breast side up, on rack in open roasting pan; brush with salad oil. Roast in 325° F. oven 2¹/₂ to 3 hours. Start checking for doneness during last 30 minutes. (If you like, use a meat thermometer. Before placing chicken in oven, insert meat thermometer into thickest part of meat between breast and thigh, being careful that pointed end of thermometer does not touch bone.)

5. While chicken is roasting, prepare giblets and neck to use in gravy: In 1-quart saucepan over high heat, heat giblets, neck, 1 cup water, and ¹/₄ teaspoon salt to boiling. Reduce heat to low; cover and simmer 30 minutes or until giblets are tender. Drain and reserve broth. Pull meat from neck; discard bones; coarsely chop meat and giblets; refrigerate.

6. When chicken turns golden, cover loosely with a "tent" of folded foil. Remove foil during last 30 minutes of roasting time and, with pastry brush, brush chicken generously with pan drippings for attractive sheen. Chicken is done when thickest part of leg feels soft when pinched with fingers protected by paper towels. (If using meat thermometer, chicken is done when thermometer reaches 180° to 185° F.)

7. Place chicken on warm large platter. Prepare gravy: Remove rack from roasting pan; pour drippings into a 2-cup measure (set pan aside); let stand a few seconds, until fat separates from meat juice. Skim 3 tablespoons fat from drippings into 1-quart saucepan; skim off and discard any remaining fat. Add reserved broth to roasting pan; stir until brown bits are loosened; add to meat juice in cup to make 1¹/₂ cups (add water if necessary). Into fat in saucepan over medium heat, stir flour and ¹/₂ teaspoon salt; gradually stir in meat-juice mixture; cook, stirring, until thickened. Stir in sour cream and reserved giblets and neck meat; heat through; do not boil. Pour gravy into gravy boat.

8. To serve, garnish chicken with parsley sprigs. Serve with gravy.

Brown-Rice Stuffing: In 2-quart saucepan, prepare *1 cup brown rice* as label directs. In 1-quart saucepan over medium heat, melt *4 tablespoons butter* or margarine; add *3 celery stalks,* diced, and *1 small onion,* diced; cook until tender, stirring occasionally. When rice is done, add vegetables, *¹/₄ teaspoon salt,* and *¹/₄ teaspoon cracked pepper;* mix well.

Oven-braised Chicken with Vegetables

TIME: about 2 hours—SERVINGS: 4

1 **medium bunch celery**

2 **tablespoons salad oil**

1 **3-pound broiler-fryer**

1/2 **teaspoon paprika**

3/4 **cup water**

1/4 **cup cooking or dry white wine**

1 1/2 **teaspoons salt**

1/2 **teaspoon thyme leaves**

1/4 **teaspoon cracked pepper**

1 **chicken-flavor bouillon cube or envelope**

3 **medium potatoes, unpeeled, cut into quarters**

2 **large carrots, cut into 2-inch pieces**

1/2 **pound small white onions**

1 **9-ounce package frozen whole green beans, thawed**

1/4 **cup milk**

1 **tablespoon all-purpose flour**

1. Remove outer row of celery stalks; trim root end. About 5 to 6 inches from root end, cut tops and leaves from celery. (Use outer stalks, tops, and leaves for salad or soup another day.) Cut celery bunch lengthwise into quarters. With string, tie each quarter to keep stalks from separating; set aside.

2. In 5-quart Dutch oven over medium-high heat, in hot salad oil, cook chicken until browned on all sides. Sprinkle chicken with paprika. Add celery, water, and next 8 ingredients; heat to boiling. Cover Dutch oven and bake in 350° F. oven 1 1/4 hours. Add green beans; continue baking 15 minutes longer or until chicken and vegetables are fork-tender.

3. Remove Dutch oven from oven. Remove string from celery. On warm deep platter, arrange chicken and vegetables; keep warm.

4. Skim off fat from liquid in Dutch oven. In cup, stir milk and flour until blended. Gradually stir mixture into liquid in Dutch oven; cook over medium heat, stirring, until slightly thickened. Pour gravy over chicken and vegetables.

Barbecued Chicken

TIME: about 1 1/4 hours—SERVINGS: 4

barbecue sauce (see Index)

1 **2 1/2- to 3-pound broiler-fryer, cut into quarters**

1. Prepare outdoor grill for barbecuing.

2. Meanwhile, prepare one of the barbecue sauces listed in the Index.

3. Place chicken pieces on grill over medium heat; cook until golden on both sides, about 10 minutes. Then, to avoid charring, stand chicken pieces upright, leaning one against the other. Rearrange pieces from time to time and cook about 25 minutes. Brush chicken pieces with barbecue sauce; cook 5 to 10 minutes longer, until chicken is fork-tender.

TO BROIL IN OVEN: About 1 hour before serving, preheat broiler if manufacturer directs. Prepare one of the barbecue sauces listed in the Index. Rub chicken with some *salad oil*. Place chicken, skin side down, in broiling pan. About 7 to 9 inches from source of heat (or at 450° F.), broil 20 minutes or until golden. Brush generously with some sauce; broil 2 to 3 minutes. Turn chicken pieces skin side up; broil 10 minutes. Then brush with remaining sauce; broil 10 minutes or until fork-tender.

Deviled Chicken Legs

TIME: about 4 1/2 hours or start early in day—SERVINGS: 6

1/2 **cup soy sauce**

3 **tablespoons cooking or dry sherry**

2 **tablespoons prepared mustard**

1/2 **teaspoon hot-pepper sauce**

6 **medium chicken legs (about 3 pounds)**

1 **cup dried bread crumbs**

1 **teaspoon salt**

4 **tablespoons butter or margarine, melted**

1. In 13″ by 9″ baking dish, combine soy sauce, sherry, mustard, and hot-pepper sauce. Add chicken legs to marinade. Cover; refrigerate at least 3 hours, turning chicken occasionally.

2. About 1 hour before serving, preheat broiler if manufacturer directs. On waxed paper, mix bread crumbs with salt. Remove chicken from marinade; discard marinade. Coat chicken with bread-crumb mixture.

3. Place chicken, skin side down, in broiling pan. Drizzle half of melted butter or margarine over chicken. About 7 to 9 inches from source of heat (or at 450° F.), broil chicken 20 minutes or until browned. Turn chicken skin side up and drizzle with remaining butter or margarine; broil 15 to 20 minutes longer, until fork-tender.

Apple Barbecued Chicken

TIME: about 50 minutes—SERVINGS: 8

2 tablespoons salad oil
1 medium onion, minced
1 8- to 8½-ounce jar unsweetened applesauce
1 cup catchup
¼ cup red-wine vinegar
2 tablespoons brown sugar
2 tablespoons Worcestershire
1½ teaspoons chili powder
1 teaspoon salt
¼ teaspoon ground cinnamon
2 2½- to 3-pound broiler-fryers, cut up

1. Preheat broiler if manufacturer directs. In 2-quart saucepan over medium heat, in hot salad oil, cook onion until tender. Remove from heat; stir in applesauce and next 7 ingredients; set aside.

2. Place chicken, skin side down, in large broiling pan. About 7 to 9 inches from source of heat (or at 450° F.), broil chicken 20 minutes or until golden. Brush generously with some sauce; broil 2 to 3 minutes. Turn chicken pieces skin side up; broil 10 minutes. Then brush with remaining sauce; broil 10 minutes longer or until fork-tender.

Chicken-and-Sausage Mixed Grill

TIME: about 1½ hours—SERVINGS: 8

1 pound hot or sweet Italian sausage links
2 tablespoons water
¾ cup catchup
¼ cup packed brown sugar
2 tablespoons lime or lemon juice
2 tablespoons salad oil
1 teaspoon salt
1 teaspoon Worcestershire
¼ teaspoon seasoned pepper
1 2½- to 3-pound broiler-fryer, cut up

1. Prepare outdoor grill for barbecuing.

2. Meanwhile, in 10-inch skillet over medium heat, heat sausages and water to boiling; cover and simmer 10 minutes. Remove sausages to plate; set aside.

3. In small bowl, mix catchup and remaining ingredients except chicken.

4. Place chicken on grill over medium heat; cook until golden on both sides, about 10 minutes. Then, to avoid charring, stand chicken pieces upright, leaning one against the other. Rearrange pieces from time to time and continue cooking about 25 mintues. Brush chicken pieces with some barbecue sauce; cook 5 to 10 minutes longer, until chicken is fork-tender.

5. During last 15 minutes of cooking chicken, place sausages on grill; cook 10 minutes or until browned on all sides. Brush sausages with remaining barbecue sauce; cook 5 minutes longer.

TO BROIL IN OVEN: About 1 hour before serving, cook sausages and prepare barbecue sauce as above in steps 2 and 3. Preheat broiler if manufacturer directs. Rub chicken with some *salad oil*. Place chicken, skin side down, in broiling pan. About 7 to 9 inches from source of heat (or at 450° F.), broil 20 minutes or until golden. Brush generously with some sauce; broil 2 to 3 minutes. Turn chicken pieces skin side up; broil 10 minutes. Then brush with some sauce; broil 10 minutes or until fork-tender. During last 15 minutes of cooking chicken, place sausages in broiling pan with chicken; cook 10 minutes, until browned. Brush sausages with remaining barbecue sauce; cook 5 minutes longer, until sausages are heated through.

Chicken-and-Vegetable Packets

TIME: about 2 hours—SERVINGS: 4

3 **large potatoes, unpeeled and cut into bite-size pieces**

3 **large carrots, diagonally sliced**

1/2 **pound green beans, each cut in half**

3/4 **cup water**

2 **tablespoons butter or margarine, cut into small pieces**

11/4 **teaspoons salt**

1/4 **teaspoon pepper**

1/4 **teaspoon thyme leaves**

1 **envelope chicken-flavor bouillon or 2 teaspoons instant chicken-flavor bouillon**

1 **21/2- to 3-pound broiler-fryer, cut up**

1. Prepare outdoor grill for barbecuing.

2. In large bowl, mix all ingredients except chicken. On double thickness of heavy-duty foil, place one fourth of chicken; top with one fourth of vegetable mixture. Wrap chicken and vegetable mixture in foil, being careful seam of foil is folded several times to seal in juices. Repeat to make three more packets.

3. Place packets on grill over medium heat; cook 45 minutes or until chicken and vegetables are fork-tender, turning packets occasionally with tongs.

TO COOK ON TOP OF RANGE: About 11/4 hours before serving, in 12-inch skillet over medium-high heat, melt 2 tablespoons butter or margarine; add chicken and cook until lightly browned on all sides. Add potatoes, carrots, green beans, water, salt, pepper, thyme, and bouillon; heat to boiling. Reduce heat to low; cover and simmer 40 minutes or until chicken and vegetables are fork-tender. Skim off fat from liquid in skillet.

Elegant Stuffed Chicken Quarters

TIME: about 11/2 hours—SERVINGS: 4

3 **tablespoons butter or margarine**

2 **medium zucchini (1 pound), shredded**

3 **slices white bread**

1 **egg**

1/2 **cup shredded Swiss cheese (2 ounces)**

1/8 **teaspoon pepper**

salt

1 **21/2- to 3-pound broiler-fryer, cut into quarters**

2 **tablespoons honey**

1. Prepare stuffing: In 2-quart saucepan over medium heat, melt butter; add zucchini and cook until tender, about 2 minutes, stirring frequently. Remove from heat. Into saucepan, tear bread into small pieces; stir in egg, cheese, pepper, and 1/2 teaspoon salt.

2. Preheat oven to 400° F. Carefully loosen skin on each chicken quarter by pushing fingers between skin and meat to form a pocket; spoon some stuffing into each pocket. Place chicken in 13″ by 9″ baking pan; bake 50 minutes or until fork-tender.

3. To serve, remove chicken to warm platter; brush with honey and sprinkle lightly with salt.

Fruited Chicken

TIME: about 1 hour—SERVINGS: 4

3 **tablespoons salad oil**

8 **medium chicken thighs (2 to 21/2 pounds)**

4 **medium green peppers, cut into 3/4-inch-wide strips**

1 **medium onion, sliced**

1 **16- to 17-ounce can sliced cling peaches**

1/4 **cup cider vinegar**

2 **tablespoons soy sauce**

2 **tablespoons brown sugar**

1/2 **teaspoon salt**

1/4 **teaspoon pepper**

water

1 **tablespoon cornstarch**

2 **medium tomatoes, cut into wedges**

1. In 12-inch skillet over medium-high heat, in hot salad oil, cook chicken thighs until browned on all sides. Remove chicken to bowl.

2. In drippings remaining in skillet, cook green peppers and onion until tender-crisp, stirring occasionally.

3. Drain peach liquid into skillet; reserve peaches. Return chicken to skillet; stir in vinegar, soy sauce, brown sugar, salt, pepper, and 1/4 cup water; over high heat, heat to boiling. Reduce heat to low; cover; simmer 25 minutes or until chicken is fork-tender.

4. In cup, mix cornstarch and 2 tablespoons water. Gradually stir cornstarch mixture into simmering liquid in skillet and cook, stirring constantly, until slightly thickened and smooth. Add reserved peaches and tomato wedges; heat through.

Crisp Baked Chicken

TIME: about 3 hours—SERVINGS: 4

butter or margarine

1 medium onion, minced

1 small garlic clove, minced

1 8-ounce container plain yogurt

1½ teaspoons ground ginger

1 teaspoon salt

¼ teaspoon pepper

1 2½- to 3-pound broiler-fryer, cut up

3½ cups whole-wheat-flake cereal, crushed

¼ cup regular toasted wheat germ

1. Prepare marinade: In 1-quart saucepan over medium heat, melt 2 tablespoons butter or margarine; add onion and garlic, and cook until tender, stirring occasionally. Spoon onion mixture into a medium bowl; stir in yogurt, ginger, salt, and pepper. Add chicken, turning to coat with marinade. Cover and refrigerate 2 hours, turning occasionally.

2. On waxed paper, mix cereal and wheat germ. Coat chicken with cereal mixture.

3. In 13″ by 9″ baking dish, in 400° F. oven, melt 3 tablespoons butter or margarine. Remove baking dish from oven. Arrange chicken, skin side up, in single layer in butter in baking dish; bake 40 minutes.

Stir-fried Chicken and Peppers

TIME: about 45 minutes—SERVINGS: 4

4 whole medium chicken breasts

¼ cup soy sauce

2 tablespoons cooking or dry sherry

1 tablespoon cornstarch

1 tablespoon apple jelly

1 teaspoon minced peeled ginger root or ¼ teaspoon ground ginger

½ teaspoon crushed red pepper

salad oil

¾ cup California walnuts

⅛ teaspoon sugar

2 medium green peppers, cut into bite-size pieces

⅛ teaspoon salt

1 small bunch green onions, each cut into thirds

1. Remove skin and bones from chicken breasts; cut meat into 1½-inch chunks. In medium bowl, combine chicken, soy sauce, sherry, cornstarch, apple jelly, ginger, and crushed red pepper; set aside.

2. In 1-quart saucepan over medium heat, in 1 tablespoon hot salad oil, cook walnuts until golden, about 5 minutes, stirring frequently. Remove saucepan from heat; sprinkle walnuts with sugar. Spoon walnuts onto paper towels to drain.

3. In wok or 5-quart Dutch oven over medium-high heat, in ⅓ cup hot salad oil, cook green peppers and salt, with slotted spoon stirring quickly and frequently (stir-frying), until peppers are tender-crisp, about 2 minutes. Spoon peppers onto plate, leaving oil in wok.

4. In oil remaining in wok over medium heat, cook green onions until browned but not burned, stirring occasionally, about 5 minutes. With slotted spoon, remove green onions; discard.

5. In same wok over high heat, in remaining oil, cook chicken mixture, stirring quickly and frequently, until chicken is tender, about 5 minutes. Return peppers to wok; heat through.

6. Spoon chicken mixture into warm bowl; sprinkle walnuts over chicken.

Chicken Legs with Rice-Sausage Stuffing

TIME: about 2 hours—SERVINGS: 8

1 cup regular long-grain rice

1 16-ounce package pork-sausage meat

1 large celery stalk, diced

1 small onion, minced

¾ cup milk

¼ teaspoon salt

8 large chicken legs (about 4 pounds)

2 tablespoons soy sauce

honey

watercress sprigs, for garnish

1. Prepare stuffing: Prepare rice as label directs. Meanwhile, in 5-quart Dutch oven or saucepot over medium heat, cook pork-sausage meat until browned, stirring to break up sausage. With slotted spoon, remove sausage to medium bowl. To drippings in Dutch oven, add celery and onion and cook until tender, stirring occasionally. Remove Dutch oven from heat; stir in cooked rice, cooked sausage, milk, and salt.

2. Preheat oven to 400° F. Carefully loosen skin on each chicken leg by pushing fingers between skin and meat to form a pocket; spoon some stuffing into each pocket. Place chicken in large, open roasting pan; brush with soy sauce. Bake 50 minutes or until chicken is fork-tender.

3. To serve, remove chicken to warm platter; brush lightly with honey. Garnish with watercress.

Chicken Italienne

TIME: about 1½ hours—SERVINGS: 6

1 pound sweet Italian sausage links

3 whole large chicken breasts

salt

pepper

½ 8-ounce package mozzarella cheese, cut into 12 strips

1 16-ounce can stewed tomatoes

½ cup water

1 tablespoon brown sugar

1 tablespoon red-wine vinegar

4 medium carrots, cut crosswise into ¼-inch pieces

1 cup lightly packed celery leaves, chopped

1. Remove casing from sausage. In 12-inch skillet over medium heat, cook sausage meat until browned, stirring occasionally to break up meat. With slotted spoon, remove meat to paper towels to drain, leaving drippings in skillet.

2. Cut each chicken breast in half; remove skin and bones. With meat mallet or dull edge of French knife, pound each chicken-breast half to ¼-inch thickness. Sprinkle chicken with ½ teaspoon salt and ¼ teaspoon pepper. Place about 2 tablespoons sausage meat and 2 strips of mozzarella on narrow end of one chicken-breast half. Starting with end with sausage and cheese, roll chicken breast jelly-roll fashion; fasten seam with toothpicks. Repeat with remaining chicken, sausage, and mozzarella.

3. In drippings in skillet over medium-high heat, lightly brown chicken bundles on all sides. Remove bundles to plate; set aside. To drippings in skillet, add stewed tomatoes, water, brown sugar, red-wine vinegar, carrots, celery leaves, ¾ teaspoon salt, and ¼ teaspoon pepper; over high heat, heat to boiling. Reduce heat to low; cover and simmer 30 minutes or until carrots are fork-tender.

4. Skim off fat from liquid in skillet. Add chicken bundles, seam side down; over high heat, heat to boiling. Reduce heat to low; cover; simmer until bundles are tender, about 5 minutes.

5. To serve, discard toothpicks from chicken bundles; arrange, seam side down, on warm deep platter. Pour sauce and vegetables over bundles.

Chicken with Watercress Sauce

TIME: about 1 hour—SERVINGS: 4

2 tablespoons salad oil

1 2½- to 3-pound broiler-fryer, cut into quarters

¾ cup water

2 medium celery stalks, each cut crosswise in half

1 medium onion, cut into quarters

salt

pepper

½ bunch watercress

¾ cup half-and-half

2 tablespoons butter or margarine

2 tablespoons all-purpose flour

⅛ teaspoon sugar

1 tablespoon finely grated lemon peel

1. In 12-inch skillet over medium-high heat, in hot oil, cook chicken until browned on all sides. Add water, celery, onion, ½ teaspoon salt, and ⅛ teaspoon pepper; over high heat, heat to boiling. Reduce heat to low; cover; simmer 35 minutes or until chicken is fork-tender. Remove chicken to warm deep platter; cover; keep warm.

2. Skim fat from broth in skillet; reserve ½ cup broth. (Cover and refrigerate remaining broth and vegetables for soup another day.)

3. Set aside one fourth of watercress for garnish later. Cut off and discard large stems from remaining watercress. In blender at high speed or in food processor with knife blade attached, blend watercress and half-and-half until smooth; set aside.

4. In same skillet over medium heat, melt butter or margarine; stir in flour, sugar, ⅛ teaspoon salt, and ⅛ teaspoon pepper until blended. Gradually stir in reserved chicken broth and pureed watercress mixture, and cook, stirring constantly, until mixture is slightly thickened. Pour sauce around chicken on platter. Garnish with reserved watercress and grated lemon peel.

Chicken-and-Shrimp Stir-fry

TIME: about 45 minutes—SERVINGS: 4

2 whole large chicken breasts (about 1¼ pounds)

¾ pound small shrimp or 1 8-ounce package frozen shelled and deveined shrimp, thawed and drained

1. Remove skin and bones from chicken breasts; cut each breast in half; cut each half lengthwise into thin strips. If using fresh shrimp, shell and devein shrimp. In medium bowl, combine chicken, shrimp, sherry, cornstarch, ginger, and ½ teaspoon salt; set aside. In cup, stir water and bouillon until blended; set aside.

2 tablespoons cooking or dry sherry

4 teaspoons cornstarch

1/4 teaspoon ground ginger

salt

2/3 cup water

1 teaspoon instant chicken-flavor bouillon

salad oil

2 small zucchini (about 1/2 pound), cut diagonally into 1/2-inch slices

1/2 pound medium mushrooms, thickly sliced

1 medium bunch green onions, cut crosswise into 4-inch pieces

2. In 12-inch skillet over medium heat, in 3 tablespoons hot salad oil, cook zucchini, mushrooms, and 1/2 teaspoon salt, stirring quickly and frequently (stir-frying), until zucchini are tender-crisp, about 3 to 5 minutes. Spoon zucchini mixture into small bowl.

3. In same skillet over medium-low heat, in 5 tablespoons hot oil, cook green onions until tender, about 4 minutes, stirring occasionally. Increase heat to high; add chicken mixture and stir-fry until chicken loses its pink color, about 3 to 5 minutes. Stir in bouillon mixture; reduce heat to medium; cover skillet and let mixture simmer 1 to 2 minutes, until chicken and shrimp are tender. Remove cover; stir in zucchini mixture; heat through.

Sweet-and-Sour Chicken

TIME: about 30 minutes—SERVINGS: 4

2 whole medium chicken breasts

1/4 cup cider vinegar

2 tablespoons brown sugar

1 tablespoon cornstarch

2 tablespoons soy sauce

2 tablespoons water

1/2 teaspoon salt

1/4 teaspoon pepper

3 tablespoons salad oil

1 medium onion, sliced

1 10-ounce package frozen peas

1 20-ounce can pineapple chunks in pineapple juice

1. Remove skin and bones from chicken breasts; cut breast meat into 1 1/2-inch chunks. In cup, mix vinegar, brown sugar, cornstarch, soy sauce, water, salt, and pepper.

2. In 12-inch skillet over medium heat, in hot salad oil, cook onion until tender, stirring occasionally. Increase heat to medium-high; add chicken; cook, stirring frequently, until chicken is tender, about 5 minutes.

3. Add frozen peas, pineapple chunks with juice, and cornstarch mixture; cook, stirring frequently, until mixture boils and thickens slightly.

Chicken with Mushroom Linguine

TIME: about 1 hour—SERVINGS: 4

salad oil

1/2 pound mushrooms, thinly sliced

salt

1/3 cup all-purpose flour

1/2 teaspoon pepper

1 2 1/2- to 3-pound broiler-fryer, cut up

water

1 8-ounce package linguine

1/4 cup minced watercress

1/3 cup sour cream

1. In 12-inch skillet over medium-high heat, in 2 tablespoons hot oil, cook mushrooms and 1/2 teaspoon salt until tender, stirring often; remove to small bowl.

2. On waxed paper, mix flour, pepper, and 1 teaspoon salt; use to coat chicken pieces; reserve any remaining mixture. In same skillet over medium-high heat, in 3 more tablespoons hot oil, cook chicken until browned on all sides. Add 2 cups water; heat to boiling. Reduce heat to low; cover; simmer 35 minutes or until chicken is tender.

3. Meanwhile, prepare linguine as label directs; drain; toss with mushrooms and watercress; spoon into deep platter; keep warm.

4. Skim off fat from liquid in skillet. Stir in sour cream. In cup, mix 3 tablespoons water and reserved flour mixture; stir into liquid in skillet; cook over medium heat, stirring often, until slightly thickened. Spoon chicken and sauce onto platter with linguine.

Chicken-Eggplant Bake

TIME: about 2 hours—SERVINGS: 6

salad oil

1 medium onion, diced

1 small garlic clove, minced

1 16-ounce can tomato puree

1 tablespoon brown sugar

1/4 teaspoon oregano leaves

salt

3 whole small chicken breasts

butter or margarine

1/4 cup all-purpose flour

1/4 teaspoon pepper

1 medium eggplant (about 1 pound), cut into 1/4-inch slices

1 8-ounce package mozzarella cheese, thinly sliced

1. In 3-quart saucepan over medium heat, in 2 tablespoons hot oil, cook onion and garlic until tender. Add tomato puree, sugar, oregano, and 1/2 teaspoon salt; over high heat, heat to boiling. Reduce heat to low; cover; simmer 30 minutes.

2. Meanwhile, cut chicken breasts into cutlets: On cutting board, cut each chicken breast in half. Working with one half at a time, place it skin side up. With tip of sharp knife, starting parallel and close to large end of rib bone, cut and scrape meat away from bone and rib cage, gently pulling back meat in one piece as you cut. Discard bones and skin, and cut off white tendon. Holding knife parallel to work surface, slice each piece of boneless chicken breast horizontally in half to make two cutlets.

3. With meat mallet or dull edge of French knife, pound each chicken cutlet to about 1/8-inch thickness. Cut each cutlet into two pieces.

4. In 12-inch skillet over medium-high heat, in 1 tablespoon hot salad oil and 1 tablespoon hot butter or margarine, cook four chicken pieces at a time until chicken loses its pink color, about 1 minute, adding more salad oil and butter or margarine if necessary. Remove chicken pieces to plate; set aside.

5. On waxed paper, mix flour, pepper, and 1/2 teaspoon salt. Coat eggplant slices with mixture. In same skillet over medium heat, in 2 tablespoons hot oil, cook eggplant, a few slices at a time, until tender and browned on both sides, adding more oil if necessary. Drain slices on paper towels.

6. Preheat oven to 350° F. Into 13" by 9" baking dish, spoon one third of tomato sauce; top with one half of chicken pieces; one half of eggplant slices; one half of mozzarella cheese. Repeat, ending with sauce. Bake 25 minutes or until hot and bubbly.

Chicken Cordon Bleu

TIME: about 1 1/4 hours—SERVINGS: 6

6 medium whole chicken breasts, skinned and boned

1 8-ounce package Swiss cheese slices

1 8-ounce package sliced cooked ham

3 tablespoons all-purpose flour

1 teaspoon paprika

6 tablespoons butter or margarine

1/2 cup dry white wine

1 chicken-flavor bouillon cube or envelope or 1 teaspoon chicken-flavor stock base

1 tablespoon cornstarch

1 cup heavy or whipping cream

1. Spread chicken breasts flat; fold cheese and ham slices to fit on top; fold breasts over filling and fasten edges with toothpicks.

2. On waxed paper, mix flour and paprika; use mixture to coat chicken pieces.

3. In 12-inch skillet over medium heat, in hot butter or margarine, cook chicken until browned on all sides. Add wine and bouillon. Reduce heat to low; cover and simmer 30 minutes or until fork-tender; remove the toothpicks.

4. In cup, blend cornstarch and cream until smooth; gradually stir into skillet. Cook, stirring constantly, until thickened; serve over chicken.

Cheese-filled Chicken Cutlets

TIME: about 45 minutes—SERVINGS: 6

3 whole medium chicken breasts

¹/₄ teaspoon salt

all-purpose flour

butter or margarine

1 8-ounce package mozzarella cheese, thinly sliced

¹/₂ pound mushrooms, thinly sliced

¹/₈ teaspoon pepper

¹/₂ cup water

¹/₂ cup milk

¹/₄ cup cooking or dry white wine

1 chicken-flavor bouillon cube or envelope

parsley sprigs, for garnish

1. Cut chicken breasts into cutlets: On cutting board, cut each chicken breast in half. Working with one half at a time, place it skin side up. With tip of sharp knife, starting parallel and close to large end of rib bone, cut and scrape meat away from bone and rib cage, gently pulling back meat in one piece as you cut. Discard bones and skin, and cut off white tendon. Holding knife parallel to work surface, slice each piece of boneless chicken breast horizontally to make two cutlets.

2. With meat mallet or dull edge of French knife, pound each chicken cutlet to about ¹/₈-inch thickness. On waxed paper, mix salt with 3 tablespoons flour. Coat chicken cutlets with flour mixture.

3. In 12-inch skillet over medium heat, melt 3 tablespoons butter or margarine; add cutlets, a few at a time, and cook until lightly browned on both sides, adding more butter or margarine if necessary. Remove cutlets from skillet. Arrange cheese slices on six cutlets; top with remaining cutlets. Skewer cutlets together with toothpicks; set aside.

4. In drippings remaining in skillet over medium heat, melt 2 more tablespoons butter or margarine. Add mushrooms; cook until tender, stirring occasionally.

5. To mushroom mixture, stir in pepper and 1 tablespoon flour until blended. Gradually stir in water, milk, wine, and bouillon; heat to boiling, stirring to loosen brown bits from bottom of skillet. Return cutlets to skillet; heat to boiling. Reduce heat to low; cover and simmer 5 minutes or until cheese is melted. Discard toothpicks. Spoon cutlets and sauce onto large platter; garnish with parsley sprigs.

Chicken Cutlets Paprika

TIME: about 1 hour—SERVINGS: 4

1 medium carrot

1 cup water

2 whole large chicken breasts

3 tablespoons all-purpose flour

salt

salad oil

butter or margarine

1 green onion, thinly sliced

1¹/₂ teaspoons paprika

1 cup half-and-half

1. Prepare garnish: Thinly slice carrot. With ¹/₂-inch flower-shaped canapé cutter, cut carrot slices to resemble flower petals. In 1-quart saucepan over high heat, heat water to boiling. Add carrot flowers; cook about 3 minutes or until carrots are tender. Drain and set aside.

2. Cut chicken breasts into cutlets: On cutting board, cut each chicken breast in half. Working with one half at a time, place it skin side up. With tip of sharp knife, starting parallel and close to large end of rib bone, cut and scrape meat away from bone and rib cage, gently pulling back meat in one piece as you cut. Discard bones and skin, and cut off white tendon. Holding knife parallel to work surface, slice each piece of boneless breast horizontally in half to make two cutlets.

3. With meat mallet or dull edge of French knife, pound each chicken cutlet to about ¹/₈-inch thickness. On waxed paper, mix flour and 1 teaspoon salt. Coat chicken cutlets with flour mixture.

4. In 12-inch skillet over medium-high heat, in 1 tablespoon hot salad oil and 1 tablespoon butter or margarine, cook half of chicken cutlets at a time until lightly browned on both sides, about 1 minute, adding more salad oil and butter or margarine if necessary. Remove chicken cutlets to plate; keep warm.

5. Reduce heat to medium. In drippings in skillet, cook green onion until almost tender, stirring occasionally. Stir in paprika; cook 1 minute. Add half-and-half and ¹/₂ teaspoon salt, scraping to loosen brown bits from bottom of skillet. Cook 3 minutes or until slightly thickened, stirring frequently. Return chicken cutlets to skillet; heat through.

6. To serve, spoon chicken and sauce into warm deep platter and garnish with carrot flowers.

Chicken-Rice Square

TIME: about 1¼ hours—SERVINGS: 6

2 tablespoons butter or margarine

1 small onion, minced

1 garlic clove, minced

2 cups water

salt

1 cup regular long-grain rice

3 eggs

¾ cup heavy or whipping cream

¼ teaspoon ground red pepper

2 10-ounce packages frozen chopped spinach, thawed and squeezed dry

1 5- to 6¾-ounce can chicken, flaked

1 cup shredded Swiss cheese (4 ounces)

1. In 2-quart saucepan over medium heat, melt butter; add onion and garlic; cook until tender, stirring often. Add water and 1 teaspoon salt; over high heat, heat to boiling. Stir in rice; heat to boiling. Reduce heat to low; cover; simmer 20 minutes or until rice is tender and liquid is absorbed.

2. Meanwhile, grease 9″ by 9″ baking pan. In large bowl with fork or wire whisk, beat eggs, heavy cream, ground red pepper, and 1 teaspoon salt. Stir in rice, spinach, chicken, and ¾ cup cheese.

3. Preheat oven to 350° F. Spoon mixture into pan, packing firmly. Sprinkle with remaining cheese. Cover with foil; bake 30 minutes. Remove foil and bake 10 minutes or until hot.

Corn-Batter Chicken

TIME: about 1 hour—SERVINGS: 4

1 cup all-purpose flour

⅔ cup milk

⅓ cup yellow cornmeal

1½ teaspoons double-acting baking powder

1½ teaspoons chili powder

¾ teaspoon salt

1 egg

1 2½- to 3-pound broiler-fryer, cut up

salad oil

1. In pie plate, combine first 7 ingredients. Coat chicken pieces with cornmeal mixture.

2. In 12-inch skillet over medium-high heat, heat ¼ inch salad oil until hot. With pancake turner, carefully place chicken pieces, skin side up, in hot oil. Cook about 5 minutes or until underside of chicken is golden; reduce heat to low; cook about 5 minutes longer. With pancake turner, turn chicken skin side down; cook over medium-high heat about 5 minutes; reduce heat to low; cook about 5 minutes longer or until chicken is fork-tender. Remove chicken pieces, skin side up, to paper towels to drain.

Chicken-and-Peppers Skillet

TIME: about 30 minutes—SERVINGS: 4

2 whole large chicken breasts

3 tablespoons soy sauce

1 tablespoon cooking or dry sherry

2 teaspoons cornstarch

⅛ teaspoon garlic powder

⅛ teaspoon sugar

2 medium green or red peppers

½ pound mushrooms

salad oil

½ cup water

2 pitas (sandwich pocket bread)

1. Cut each chicken breast in half; remove skin and bones. Then, with knife held in slanting position almost parallel to the cutting surface, slice across width of each half into ⅛-inch-thick slices. In medium bowl, mix chicken, soy sauce, sherry, cornstarch, garlic powder, and sugar; set aside.

2. Cut green peppers into ¼-inch-wide strips; thinly slice mushrooms. In 12-inch skillet over medium-high heat, in 2 tablespoons hot salad oil, cook green peppers and mushrooms, stirring quickly and frequently, until vegetables are tender-crisp, about 2 minutes. With slotted spoon, remove vegetables to bowl.

3. In same skillet over high heat, in 3 more tablespoons hot salad oil, cook chicken mixture, stirring quickly and frequently, until chicken is tender, about 5 minutes. Return vegetables to skillet. Add water; heat to boiling, stirring to loosen brown bits from bottom of skillet. Serve pitas with chicken mixture.

Tuna-sauced Chicken

TIME: about 45 minutes—SERVINGS: 6

3 whole large chicken breasts

1 3^1/$_2$-ounce can tuna, packed in oil

^{3}/$_4$ cup mayonnaise

2 tablespoons chopped parsley

2 tablespoons milk

2 tablespoons lemon juice

1 tablespoon diced onion

^{1}/$_4$ teaspoon sugar

salt

pepper

salad oil

1 pint cherry tomatoes, each cut in half

lettuce leaves

4 pitted ripe olives, chopped, for garnish

1. Cut chicken breasts into cutlets: On cutting board, cut each chicken breast in half. Working with one half at a time, place it skin side up. With tip of sharp knife, starting parallel and close to large end of rib bone, cut and scrape meat away from bone and rib cage, gently pulling back meat in one piece as you cut. Discard bones and skin, and cut off white tendon. Holding knife parallel to work surface, slice each piece of boneless chicken breast horizontally in half to make two cutlets.

2. With meat mallet or dull edge of French knife, pound each chicken cutlet to about ^{1}/$_8$-inch thickness. Set chicken aside.

3. Prepare tuna sauce: In blender at high speed or in food processor with knife blade attached, blend tuna with its oil, mayonnaise, parsley, milk, lemon juice, onion, sugar, ^{1}/$_2$ teaspoon salt, and ^{1}/$_4$ teaspoon pepper until smooth. Pour mixture into 1-quart saucepan; over medium heat, heat through (do not boil). Keep warm.

4. In 12-inch skillet over medium-high heat, in 2 tablespoons hot oil, cook 3 chicken cutlets at a time until lightly browned on both sides, about 1 minute, adding more salad oil if necessary. Remove cutlets to plate; keep warm.

5. In same skillet over medium heat, in drippings and 1 tablespoon hot salad oil, cook cherry tomatoes and ^{1}/$_4$ teaspoon salt until tomatoes are tender, stirring frequently.

6. To serve, line large platter with lettuce leaves. Arrange chicken and cherry tomatoes on lettuce. Spoon tuna sauce over chicken; sprinkle with chopped olives.

Chicken in Cucumber Sauce

TIME: about 1^1/$_4$ hours—SERVINGS: 4

2 medium cucumbers

2 tablespoons salad oil

1 2^1/$_2$- to 3-pound broiler-fryer, cut up

1 medium onion, chopped

1 chicken-flavor bouillon cube

^{1}/$_2$ cup water

1^1/$_4$ teaspoons salt

^{1}/$_8$ teaspoon pepper

^{1}/$_3$ cup milk

1 tablespoon all-purpose flour

1. Peel cucumbers, leaving a few ^{1}/$_8$-inch-wide strips of peel. Cut cucumbers lengthwise in half; with tip of spoon, scoop out and discard seeds. Dice one cucumber; cut remaining cucumber crosswise into thin slices; set aside.

2. In 12-inch skillet over medium-high heat, in hot salad oil, cook chicken until well browned on all sides. Remove chicken to bowl; set aside.

3. In drippings remaining in skillet over medium heat, cook diced cucumber and onion until tender, stirring mixture occasionally. Return chicken pieces to skillet; add bouillon, water, salt, and pepper; over high heat, heat to boiling. Reduce heat to low; cover and simmer 35 minutes or until chicken is fork-tender.

4. Skim fat from liquid in skillet. In cup with fork, stir milk with flour until blended. Gradually stir milk mixture into liquid in skillet; cook over medium heat, stirring constantly, until slightly thickened. Add cucumber slices; heat through.

Chicken-Vegetable Fricassee

TIME: about 1 hour—SERVINGS: 4

3 tablespoons salad oil

1 2¹/₂- to 3-pound broiler-fryer, cut up

2 medium onions, sliced

2 large carrots, cut into 1-inch pieces

1 medium rutabaga (about ³/₄ pound), cut into bite-size cubes

¹/₂ cup cooking or dry white wine

1¹/₂ teaspoons salt

¹/₂ teaspoon basil

¹/₄ teaspoon pepper

water

2 medium potatoes, cut into ¹/₄-inch-thick slices

2 tablespoons all-purpose flour

1. In 8-quart Dutch oven over medium heat, in hot oil, cook chicken and onions until chicken is browned on all sides, stirring occasionally.

2. Add carrots, rutabaga, wine, salt, basil, pepper, and 2 cups water; heat to boiling. Reduce heat to low; cover and simmer 20 minutes, stirring occasionally. Add potatoes; over high heat, heat to boiling. Reduce heat to low; cover and simmer 15 minutes or until chicken and vegetables are tender. Skim off fat from liquid.

3. In cup, stir flour and ¹/₄ cup water until blended. Gradually stir mixture into chicken mixture; cook over medium heat, stirring constantly, until slightly thickened.

Curried Chicken with Dumplings

TIME: about 1 hour—SERVINGS: 4

2 tablespoons salad oil

1 2¹/₂- to 3-pound broiler-fryer, cut up

1 pound small white onions

1 tablespoon curry powder

¹/₃ cup dark seedless raisins

1 teaspoon salt

1 teaspoon brown sugar

water

2 tablespoons all-purpose flour

¹/₂ cup plain yogurt

1 cup buttermilk-baking mix

¹/₃ cup milk

1 large red cooking apple, sliced

1. In 12-inch skillet over medium-high heat, in hot salad oil, cook chicken until browned on all sides. Remove chicken to bowl.

2. In drippings remaining in skillet over medium heat, cook onions until browned. Stir in curry powder; cook 1 minute. Return chicken pieces to skillet; add raisins, salt, brown sugar, and 1³/₄ cups water; over high heat, heat mixture to boiling. Reduce heat to low; cover; simmer 25 minutes. Skim off fat from liquid.

3. In cup, stir flour with ¹/₄ cup water; stir into liquid in skillet, and cook over medium heat until slightly thickened, stirring constantly. Stir in yogurt until smooth.

4. In small bowl with fork, stir buttermilk-baking mix and milk just until blended. (Dough will be soft.) Drop dough by tablespoonfuls into simmering liquid in skillet. Add apple slices. Reduce heat to low; cover and cook 15 minutes, until chicken and apple slices are fork-tender and dumplings are set.

Louisiana Chicken Skillet

TIME: about 1¹/₄ hours—SERVINGS: 4

¹/₄ cup salad oil

16 chicken wings (about 3 pounds)

3 tablespoons all-purpose flour

2 medium celery stalks, diced

1 large green pepper, diced

1 medium onion, diced

1 16-ounce can tomatoes

¹/₂ cup water

1 teaspoon salt

¹/₄ to ¹/₂ teaspoon hot-pepper sauce

1 10-ounce package frozen okra or cut green beans

1. In 12-inch skillet over medium-high heat, in hot oil, cook chicken wings, half at a time, until browned on all sides, removing them to bowl as they brown.

2. Into drippings remaining in skillet, stir flour; cook, stirring, until flour is dark brown (mixture will be thick). Add celery, green pepper, and onion; cook over medium heat until vegetables are tender, stirring often.

3. Return wings to skillet; add tomatoes with their liquid, water, salt, and hot-pepper sauce; over high heat, heat to boiling. Reduce heat to low; cover; simmer 20 minutes. Add frozen okra; cook 15 minutes longer or until chicken and okra are tender.

Chicken-and-Corn Stew

TIME: about 1 hour—SERVINGS: 4

2 tablespoons salad oil

1 2¹/₂- to 3-pound broiler-fryer, cut into quarters

1 medium onion, diced

1 small garlic clove, minced

1 16-ounce can tomatoes

2 teaspoons salt

¹/₂ teaspoon sugar

¹/₄ teaspoon fennel seeds

¹/₄ teaspoon pepper

1 12-ounce can vacuum-packed whole-kernel corn

¹/₄ cup water

1 tablespoon all-purpose flour

1. In 12-inch skillet over medium heat, in hot salad oil, cook chicken, onion, and garlic until chicken is browned on all sides, stirring occasionally.

2. Add tomatoes with their liquid and next 4 ingredients, stirring to break up tomatoes; over high heat, heat to boiling. Reduce heat to low; cover and simmer 30 minutes, stirring occasionally. Add corn; over high heat, heat to boiling. Reduce heat to low; cover and simmer 5 minutes or until corn is heated through and chicken is tender. Skim off fat from liquid.

3. In cup, stir water and flour until blended. Gradually stir flour mixture into chicken mixture; cook over medium heat, stirring constantly, until mixture is slightly thickened.

Chicken Florentine

TIME: about 1 hour—SERVINGS: 4

butter or margarine

1 2¹/₂- to 3-pound broiler-fryer, cut up

³/₄ cup water

¹/₄ teaspoon pepper

1 chicken-flavor bouillon cube

2 medium lemons

¹/₂ pound mushrooms, sliced

¹/₂ teaspoon salt

1 10-ounce bag spinach

¹/₂ cup milk

1 tablespoon all-purpose flour

4 teaspoons prepared horseradish

1. In 12-inch skillet over medium-high heat, melt 3 tablespoons butter or margarine; add chicken and cook until browned on all sides. Add water, pepper, and bouillon; heat to boiling. Reduce heat to low; cover; simmer 30 minutes or until fork-tender.

2. Meanwhile, with sharp knife, cut 1 lemon crosswise into thin slices; cut each slice in half; set aside for garnish later. Squeeze remaining lemon to make 1 tablespoon juice. In 4-quart saucepan over medium heat, melt 2 tablespoons butter or margarine; add lemon juice, mushrooms, and salt, and cook until mushrooms are tender, stirring occasionally. With slotted spoon, spoon mushrooms into small bowl. To liquid remaining in saucepan, add spinach and cook over high heat just until wilted, 2 to 3 minutes, stirring occasionally. Stir in mushrooms; keep warm.

3. Skim off fat from liquid in skillet. In cup, mix milk and flour; gradually stir mixture and horseradish into liquid in skillet; cook over medium heat until slightly thickened, stirring constantly.

4. To serve, arrange spinach mixture on platter; top with chicken pieces. Garnish with reserved lemon slices. Pass gravy in bowl to spoon over chicken and spinach.

Chicken-Vegetable Bake

TIME: about 45 minutes—SERVINGS: 4

1 18- or 20-ounce package frozen Italian mixed vegetables

salt

1 2¹/₂- to 3-pound broiler-fryer, cut up

1 teaspoon paprika

¹/₂ teaspoon pepper

1. Preheat oven to 450° F. In 12" by 8" baking dish, combine frozen vegetables with ¹/₂ teaspoon salt.

2. Sprinkle chicken with paprika, pepper, and 1¹/₂ teaspoons salt; arrange skin side up, covering vegetables completely. Bake 40 minutes or until chicken is tender.

Braised Chicken with Julienne Vegetables

TIME: about 40 minutes—SERVINGS: 4

1 teaspoon paprika

salt

1 2¹/₂- to 3-pound broiler-fryer, quartered

salad oil

4 large carrots

4 large celery stalks

¹/₄ teaspoon pepper

¹/₄ teaspoon thyme leaves

1. On waxed paper, mix paprika and ³/₄ teaspoon salt. Rub chicken quarters with paprika mixture.

2. In 12-inch skillet over medium heat, in 3 tablespoons hot salad oil, cook chicken until lightly browned on all sides. Reduce heat to low; cover and simmer 35 minutes or until chicken is fork-tender, turning occasionally.

3. Meanwhile, cut each carrot and celery stalk crosswise in half; cut each half lengthwise into thin slices; then cut slices into matchstick-thin strips. In 4-quart saucepan over medium heat, in 2 tablespoons hot salad oil, cook carrots, celery, pepper, thyme, and ¹/₂ teaspoon salt until vegetables are tender-crisp, stirring occasionally.

4. Spoon vegetables onto warm platter. Skim off fat from liquid in skillet; arrange chicken pieces on top of vegetables; pour liquid in skillet over chicken.

Creamed Chicken and Oysters

TIME: about 35 minutes—SERVINGS: 6

¹/₂ cup butter or margarine

¹/₄ cup all-purpose flour

2 cups milk

3 cups cut-up cooked chicken or turkey

2 8-ounce cans oysters, drained

1 tablespoon cooking or dry sherry

1 teaspoon salt

¹/₄ teaspoon pepper

1 11-ounce package refrigerated
   heat-and-serve buttermilk biscuits

parsley sprigs, for garnish

1. In 10-inch cook-and-serve skillet over medium heat, melt butter or margarine; stir in flour until blended; gradually stir in milk and cook, stirring constantly, until mixture thickens and boils. Stir in chicken, oysters, sherry, salt, and pepper; reduce heat to low and cook 10 minutes, stirring occasionally.

2. Meanwhile, heat biscuits as label directs.

3. To serve, garnish chicken mixture with parsley and serve over biscuits.

Chicken and Peppers

TIME: about 1¹/₄ hours—SERVINGS: 4

2 whole large chicken breasts

2 tablespoons salad oil

2 medium green peppers, cut into bite-size
   pieces

1 large onion, diced

¹/₄ pound mushrooms, sliced

1 8-ounce can tomatoes

¹/₄ cup cooking or dry red wine

1 teaspoon sugar

¹/₂ teaspoon basil

¹/₂ teaspoon salt

¹/₈ teaspoon pepper

1. Remove bones from chicken breasts; cut each breast in half. In 10-inch skillet over medium-high heat, in hot salad oil, cook chicken until lightly browned. Arrange chicken breasts, skin side up, in 10″ by 6″ baking dish.

2. Preheat oven to 350° F. In drippings remaining in skillet, over medium-high heat, cook green peppers, onion, and mushrooms until peppers and onion are tender-crisp and lightly browned, stirring frequently. Add tomatoes with their liquid and remaining ingredients; over high heat, heat to boiling.

3. Pour tomato mixture over chicken breasts. Bake casserole, uncovered, 20 to 30 minutes, until chicken is fork-tender. Skim off fat from liquid in dish.

Chicken Monterey

TIME: about 1¼ hours—SERVINGS: 6

3 whole medium chicken breasts, each cut in half

salt

2 tablespoons salad oil

1 medium green onion, chopped

3 tablespoons all-purpose flour

2 cups milk

1 cup water

3 tablespoons catchup

½ teaspoon rosemary, crushed

¼ teaspoon pepper

1 chicken-flavor bouillon cube or envelope

1 9-ounce package frozen artichoke hearts, thawed

1 9-ounce package frozen whole green beans, thawed

1. Rub chicken breasts with ¾ teaspoon salt.

2. In 12-inch skillet over medium-high heat, in hot salad oil, cook chicken until browned on all sides. Arrange chicken in 3-quart casserole.

3. Spoon off all but 2 tablespoons drippings from skillet. In remaining hot drippings in skillet over medium heat, cook green onion until tender, stirring occasionally. Stir in flour until blended; gradually stir in milk and water until smooth; stir in catchup, rosemary, pepper, bouillon, and ¾ teaspoon salt; cook, stirring constantly, until sauce is slightly thickened.

4. Preheat oven to 350° F. Pour sauce over chicken in casserole. Cover casserole; bake 30 minutes. Stir in artichoke hearts and green beans; bake 20 minutes longer or until chicken is fork-tender. Skim off fat from sauce in casserole.

Louisiana Chicken

TIME: about 1½ hours—SERVINGS: 8

¼ cup salad oil

2 2- to 2½-pound broiler-fryers, cut up

½ cup all-purpose flour

4 medium celery stalks, thinly sliced

3 medium green peppers, cut into thin strips

2 medium onions, diced

2 chicken-flavor bouillon cubes or envelopes

3 cups water

2¼ teaspoons salt

½ teaspoon hot-pepper sauce

1. In 12-inch skillet over medium-high heat, in hot salad oil, cook chicken, a few pieces at a time, until browned on all sides. Remove chicken pieces as they brown to 4- or 5-quart casserole.

2. Into hot drippings in skillet over medium heat, stir flour; cook, stirring constantly, until flour is dark brown. Add celery, green peppers, and onions; cook until vegetables are tender, stirring frequently. Stir in bouillon, water, salt, and hot-pepper sauce; over high heat, heat mixture to boiling.

3. Preheat oven to 350° F. Pour sauce over chicken in casserole. Bake casserole, uncovered, 45 minutes or until chicken is fork-tender, occasionally basting chicken with sauce in casserole. Skim off fat from sauce.

Chicken-Rice Curry

TIME: about 1¼ hours—SERVINGS: 6

2 tablespoons salad oil

1 2½- to 3-pound broiler-fryer, cut up

1 medium onion, chopped

2 tablespoons curry powder

4 cups water

2 teaspoons salt

¼ teaspoon pepper

1 chicken-flavor bouillon cube

1½ cups regular long-grain rice

1 10-ounce package frozen Fordhook lima beans or baby lima beans

1 medium tomato, cut into wedges

1. In 12-inch skillet over medium-high heat, in hot oil, cook chicken until browned on all sides; remove to large bowl; set aside.

2. In drippings in skillet over medium heat, cook onion until tender, stirring occasionally. Stir in curry powder; cook 1 minute.

3. Return chicken to skillet; add water, salt, pepper, and bouillon; over high heat, heat to boiling. Reduce heat to low; cover; simmer 10 minutes, stirring often.

4. Skim off fat from liquid in skillet. Stir in rice; over high heat, heat to boiling. Reduce heat to low; cover; simmer 10 minutes. Add frozen lima beans; over high heat, heat to boiling. Reduce heat to low; cover; simmer 10 minutes longer or until rice is cooked and chicken is tender, stirring occasionally. Add tomato wedges; heat through.

Chicken and Garbanzo Beans

TIME: about 1¹/₂ hours—SERVINGS: 6

¹/₄ cup all-purpose flour

salt

pepper

1 2¹/₂- to 3-pound broiler-fryer, cut up

¹/₄ cup salad oil

2 medium onions, sliced

¹/₂ cup water

¹/₄ cup cooking or dry white wine

¹/₄ teaspoon basil

1 15¹/₂- to 20-ounce can garbanzo beans

1 10-ounce package frozen cut green beans

1. On waxed paper, combine flour, 1 teaspoon salt, and ¹/₄ teaspoon pepper; coat chicken with mixture. In 12-inch skillet over medium-high heat, in hot oil, cook chicken until browned on all sides. Remove chicken to bowl; set aside. Add onions to drippings in skillet; over medium heat, cook until tender.

2. Return chicken to skillet; add water, wine, basil, 1¹/₄ teaspoons salt, and ¹/₈ teaspoon pepper; over high heat, heat to boiling. Reduce heat to low; cover; simmer 30 minutes, stirring occasionally. Add garbanzo beans with their liquid and frozen green beans; over high heat, heat to boiling. Reduce heat to low; cover; simmer 15 minutes or until chicken and vegetables are tender.

Chicken Breasts in Vegetable-Wine Sauce

TIME: about 1¹/₄ hours—SERVINGS: 6

3 medium carrots

4 medium zucchini (about 8 ounces each)

1 bunch green onions

salad oil

salt

savory

pepper

3 whole large chicken breasts, each cut in half

1¹/₄ cups water

¹/₄ cup cooking or dry white wine

¹/₂ cup half-and-half

1 tablespoon all-purpose flour

1. Cut carrots and zucchini crosswise in half; cut each half lengthwise into thin slices; then cut slices into matchstick-thin strips. Cut each green onion lengthwise in half, then crosswise into 3-inch pieces.

2. In 5-quart Dutch oven or saucepot over medium-high heat, in 2 tablespoons hot oil, cook carrots 2 minutes, stirring frequently. Add zucchini, half of green onions, ³/₄ teaspoon salt, ¹/₄ teaspoon savory, and ¹/₈ teaspoon pepper; cook about 3 minutes longer or until tender-crisp, stirring often. With slotted spoon, remove vegetables to large bowl.

3. In same Dutch oven over medium-high heat, in ¹/₄ cup more hot oil, brown chicken breasts on all sides. Add water, wine, 1¹/₂ teaspoons salt, ¹/₂ teaspoon savory, ¹/₈ teaspoon pepper, and remaining green onions. Over high heat, heat to boiling. Reduce heat to low; cover; simmer 20 minutes or until chicken is fork-tender.

4. In cup, stir half-and-half and flour; gradually stir into liquid in skillet. Cook until mixture is slightly thickened, stirring constantly. Stir in vegetables; heat through.

Chicken with Endive

TIME: about 45 minutes—SERVINGS: 4

1 slice white bread

butter or margarine

4 whole medium chicken breasts, skinned and boned

2 tablespoons lemon juice

1 teaspoon salt

water

2 medium Belgian endives, each cut lengthwise in half

2 tablespoons capers

1 tablespoon all-purpose flour

¹/₄ pound Swiss cheese, shredded (1 cup)

1. With hands, tear bread slice into very small pieces. In 12-inch skillet over medium heat, heat 2 tablespoons butter or margarine and bread crumbs until crumbs are golden brown, stirring frequently; spoon buttered crumbs into small bowl; set aside. Wipe skillet clean.

2. Spread chicken breasts open. Arrange breasts in same skillet; add lemon juice, salt, ¹/₂ cup water, and 2 tablespoons butter or margarine; heat to boiling. Reduce heat to low; cover skillet and simmer 10 minutes. Add endives, cut side down; cover and continue cooking 5 minutes longer or until chicken and endives are fork-tender. With slotted spoon, remove chicken breasts to warm platter; top each with a piece of endive, cut side down. Sprinkle breasts and endives with capers; keep warm.

3. In cup with fork, stir flour and 2 tablespoons water until blended. Gradually stir flour mixture into hot liquid remaining in skillet. Over medium heat, cook until mixture is slightly thickened and boils, stirring constantly. Remove skillet from heat; stir in cheese until melted. Pour cheese mixture over chicken; top with buttered crumbs.

Coq au Vin en Croûte

TIME: about 1³/₄ hours—SERVINGS: 4

all-purpose flour

salt

4 tablespoons butter or margarine

¹/₄ cup sour cream

4 slices bacon, diced

1 2¹/₂- to 3-pound broiler-fryer, cut up

¹/₄ pound small white onions

1¹/₄ cups water

¹/₂ cup cooking or dry white wine

¹/₄ teaspoon pepper

1 16-ounce can small whole carrots, drained

¹/₄ pound medium mushrooms, each cut into quarters

1 egg, slightly beaten

1. Into medium bowl, measure ³/₄ cup flour and ¹/₄ teaspoon salt. With pastry blender or two knives used scissor fashion, cut butter or margarine and sour cream into flour until mixture resembles coarse crumbs. With hands, shape pastry into a ball; wrap with plastic wrap and refrigerate.

2. In 12-inch skillet over medium heat, cook bacon until crisp. With slotted spoon, remove bacon to 2-quart casserole. In drippings remaining in skillet over medium heat, cook chicken and onions until browned on all sides. Remove chicken and onions to casserole.

3. Into drippings remaining in skillet over medium heat, stir 2 tablespoons flour until blended. Gradually stir in water, wine, pepper, and 1 teaspoon salt; cook, stirring constantly, until mixture is slightly thickened and brown bits are loosened. Pour mixture into casserole; stir in carrots and mushrooms.

4. Preheat oven to 350° F. On lightly floured surface, with lightly floured rolling pin, roll pastry 1 inch larger than casserole. Cut decorative design in pastry. Fit crust loosely over chicken mixture; tuck overhang under, pressing pastry to casserole so it will not shrink. Brush pastry with beaten egg. Bake casserole 1 hour or until pastry is golden.

Country Chicken Patties

TIME: about 1 hour—SERVINGS: 4

2 whole large chicken breasts

³/₄ cup dried bread crumbs

3 tablespoons mayonnaise

1 tablespoon minced parsley

1 tablespoon cooking or dry sherry

2 teaspoons grated onion

¹/₄ teaspoon pepper

1 egg

water

salt

¹/₄ cup salad oil

1 medium head iceberg lettuce, coarsely shredded

1 cup frozen peas

1. Remove skin and bones from chicken breasts; cut chicken meat into 1-inch chunks. With meat grinder using medium cutting disk or food processor with knife blade attached, coarsely grind chicken meat.

2. In large bowl, mix ground chicken, bread crumbs, mayonnaise, parsley, sherry, onion, pepper, egg, ¹/₄ cup water, and ³/₄ teaspoon salt. With hands, shape chicken mixture by tablespoonfuls into 1¹/₂-inch round patties.

3. In 12-inch skillet over medium-high heat, in hot oil, cook chicken patties, a few at a time, until golden (about 3 minutes on each side). Remove patties to plate as they brown; keep warm.

4. To drippings remaining in skillet over medium-high heat, add shredded lettuce, stirring to coat with drippings. Add ³/₄ cup water and ¹/₂ teaspoon salt; cook 3 minutes, stirring frequently. Add frozen peas; cook 5 minutes or until peas are tender, stirring occasionally. Serve chicken patties on lettuce and peas.

Chicken Livers Marsala

TIME: about 30 minutes—SERVINGS: 4

1 pound chicken livers

1 medium onion

¹/₂ pound medium mushrooms

2 tablespoons butter or margarine

³/₄ teaspoon salt

¹/₈ teaspoon pepper

¹/₂ cup water

1 tablespoon all-purpose flour

2 tablespoons dry Marsala wine

1. Cut each chicken liver in half; remove white membrane. Slice onion and mushrooms.

2. In 12-inch skillet over medium heat, melt butter or margarine; add onion and cook until almost tender, about 5 minutes, stirring occasionally. Add livers, mushrooms, salt, and pepper to onion in skillet; cook until livers are tender but still pink inside, about 5 minutes, stirring often.

3. In cup, mix water, flour, and wine; gradually stir into mixture in skillet; cook, stirring constantly, until mixture is slightly thickened.

Chicken Strudel with Mushroom Sauce

TIME: about 2¹/₂ hours—SERVINGS: 6

1 2¹/₂- to 3-pound broiler-fryer

salt

water

1 8-ounce package Muenster cheese, shredded

2 tablespoons chopped parsley (optional)

pepper

butter or margarine

about ¹/₂ pound phyllo, or 18 strudel leaves (available in Greek pastry shops or most supermarket frozen-food sections)

¹/₂ pound mushrooms, thinly sliced

1 green onion, thinly sliced

2 tablespoons all-purpose flour

¹/₂ cup milk

1 2-ounce jar diced pimento, drained

1. Cook chicken: Rinse chicken, its giblets, and neck in running cold water. Place chicken, breast side down, in 5-quart saucepot or Dutch oven; add giblets, neck, 1 teaspoon salt, and 2 inches water; over high heat, heat to boiling. Reduce heat to low; cover and simmer 35 minutes or until chicken is fork-tender.

2. Remove chicken to large bowl; refrigerate 30 minutes or until easy to handle. Reserve ¹/₂ cup broth. (Save remaining broth for use in soup or gravy another day.) Discard skin and bones; cut chicken meat and giblets into bite-size pieces. In same large bowl, toss chicken pieces with cheese, parsley, and ¹/₄ teaspoon pepper.

3. Grease large cookie sheet. In 1-quart saucepan over low heat, melt ¹/₂ cup butter or margarine. Cut two 24-inch lengths of waxed paper; overlap two lengthwise sides about ¹/₂ inch; fasten with cellophane tape. On waxed paper, place one sheet of phyllo; brush with some melted butter or margarine. Layer two more sheets of phyllo, brushing each sheet with some butter or margarine. Spoon about ²/₃ cup chicken mixture onto center of a narrow end of phyllo. Starting at same narrow end, roll phyllo, jelly-roll fashion; fold ends under to form a "package." Repeat with remaining phyllo and chicken to make six "packages" in all.

4. Preheat oven to 375° F. Place "packages" on cookie sheet, seam side down. Brush each with some melted butter or margarine. Bake 20 to 25 minutes, until golden brown.

5. Meanwhile, in 3-quart saucepan over medium heat, melt 3 tablespoons butter or margarine; add mushrooms and green onion, and cook until vegetables are tender, stirring occasionally. With slotted spoon, spoon vegetables into small bowl. Into liquid remaining in saucepan, stir flour until blended. Gradually stir in milk, reserved chicken broth, ¹/₄ teaspoon salt, and ¹/₈ teaspoon pepper; cook over medium heat until slightly thickened, stirring; stir in mushroom mixture and pimento. Serve mushroom sauce to spoon over each "package."

Cornish Hens with Sweet-and-Sour Sauce

TIME: about 1¹/₂ hours—SERVINGS: 4

2 1¹/₂- to 2-pound fresh or frozen (thawed) Rock Cornish hens

salad oil

¹/₃ cup red-wine vinegar

¹/₃ cup packed light-brown sugar

¹/₄ cup orange juice

3 tablespoons soy sauce

¹/₂ teaspoon salt

¹/₂ teaspoon anise seeds, crushed

1. Prepare outdoor grill for barbecuing. Meanwhile, remove giblets and necks from inside hens; refrigerate to use in soup another day. Rinse hens with running cold water; pat dry with paper towels. With poultry or kitchen shears, cut each hen in half; rub hens with salad oil.

2. In small bowl, mix red-wine vinegar, brown sugar, orange juice, soy sauce, salt, anise, and 1 tablespoon salad oil. With tongs, place hens on grill. Cook over medium heat 30 to 35 minutes, until hens are fork-tender, basting frequently with sauce mixture and turning hens often.

TO BROIL IN OVEN: About 1 hour before serving, preheat broiler if manufacturer directs. Prepare Rock Cornish hens and sauce mixture as above. Place hens, skin side down, in large broiling pan. About 7 to 9 inches from source of heat (or at 450° F.), broil hens 20 minutes or until golden; baste generously with some sauce; broil 2 to 3 minutes. Turn hen pieces skin side up; broil 15 minutes longer or until fork-tender, basting frequently with remaining sauce.

Holiday Cornish Hens

TIME: about 2 hours—SERVINGS: 6

6 1-pound fresh or frozen (thawed) Rock Cornish hens

6 tablespoons butter or margarine

¹/₂ pound mushrooms, sliced

2 celery stalks, diced

1 small onion, diced

¹/₂ pound chicken livers, cut into 1-inch pieces

3 cups white-bread cubes (6 slices)

2 tablespoons cooking or dry sherry

salt

pepper

salad oil

paprika

Gingered Peaches (see Index)

watercress sprigs, for garnish

1. Remove livers from Rock Cornish hens; set aside; refrigerate gizzards, hearts, and necks to use in soup another day. Rinse hens with running cold water; pat dry with paper towels; refrigerate.

2. Prepare stuffing: In 12-inch skillet over medium heat, in hot butter or margarine, cook mushrooms, celery, and onion until vegetables are tender, stirring occasionally. Push vegetables to one side of pan; add chicken livers and Rock Cornish hen livers; cook just until livers lose their pink color. Remove skillet from heat. Stir in bread cubes, sherry, ¹/₄ teaspoon salt, and ¹/₈ teaspoon pepper.

3. Lightly spoon some stuffing into body cavity of each hen. Fold neck skin to back; lift wings up toward neck, then fold under back. With string, tie legs and tail of each hen together. Place hens, breast side up, on rack in open roasting pan.

4. Brush hens with salad oil; lightly sprinkle with salt, pepper, and paprika. Roast hens in 350° F. oven about 1¹/₄ hours, brushing occasionally with drippings in pan. Hens are done when legs can be moved up and down easily, or when two-tined fork is inserted between leg and body cavity and juices that escape are not pink.

5. When hens are done, discard strings. Place hens on warm large platter; keep warm.

6. Prepare Gingered Peaches; arrange on platter with hens. Garnish with watercress sprigs.

Roast Cornish Hens with Spinach Stuffing

TIME: about 2 hours—SERVINGS: 4

butter or margarine

2 celery stalks, diced (1 cup)

1 large green onion, minced (3 tablespoons)

1 10-ounce package frozen chopped spinach, thawed and squeezed dry

1 egg

1¹/₂ cups soft bread crumbs (3 slices white bread)

2 tablespoons milk

salt

cracked pepper

4 1-pound fresh or frozen (thawed) Rock Cornish hens

1 chicken-flavor bouillon cube or envelope

water

2 tablespoons all-purpose flour

1. Prepare spinach stuffing: In 2-quart saucepan over medium heat, cook 4 tablespoons butter or margarine, celery, and green onion until vegetables are tender, stirring often. Remove from heat. Stir in spinach, egg, crumbs, milk, ¹/₄ teaspoon salt, and ¹/₈ teaspoon cracked pepper; set aside.

2. Remove giblets and necks from inside hens; reserve for soup another day. Rinse hens with running cold water; pat dry with paper towels. Lightly spoon some spinach stuffing into body cavity of each hen. Fold neck skin to back; lift wings up toward neck, then fold under back. With string, tie legs and tail of each hen together. Place hens, breast side up, on rack in open roasting pan.

3. In small saucepan over low heat, melt 2 tablespoons butter or margarine. Brush hens generously with butter or margarine; sprinkle lightly with salt. Roast hens in 350° F. oven 1 to 1¹/₂ hours, brushing occasionally with drippings in pan. Hens are done when legs can be moved up and down easily, or when two-tined fork is inserted between leg and body and juices that escape are not pink.

4. When hens are done, discard strings; place hens on warm platter; keep warm. Prepare gravy: Remove rack from roasting pan. Spoon off all but 2 tablespoons fat from pan, leaving pan liquid and brown bits. Add bouillon, 1 cup water, ¹/₄ teaspoon salt, and ¹/₈ teaspoon cracked pepper to pan; over medium heat, heat mixture to boiling, stirring to loosen brown bits. In cup, mix flour and ¹/₄ cup water; gradually stir into liquid in pan; cook over medium heat, stirring, until gravy is thickened. Serve with gravy.

Roast Turkey

TIME: about 5¼ hours—SERVINGS: 12 to 16

1 12- to 14-pound fresh or frozen (thawed)
  ready-to-stuff turkey

salad oil

salt

water

6 medium potatoes

⅓ cup all-purpose flour

parsley sprigs, for garnish

1. Reserve giblets and neck from turkey; set aside. Rinse turkey with running cold water; drain.

2. With turkey breast side up, lift wings up toward neck, then fold under back of turkey so they stay in place. Depending on brand of turkey, with string, tie legs and tail together; or push drumsticks under band of skin; or use stuffing clamp.

3. Place turkey, breast side up, on small rack in open roasting pan. Brush skin with oil. Insert meat thermometer into thickest part of meat between breast and thigh, being careful that pointed end does not touch bone. Roast turkey in 325° F. oven about 4¾ hours. Start checking for doneness last hour of roasting.

4. While turkey is roasting, prepare giblets and neck to use in gravy: In 2-quart saucepan over high heat, heat giblets, neck, ¼ teaspoon salt, and enough water to cover to boiling. Reduce heat to low; cover; simmer 1 hour or until giblets are tender. Drain, reserving broth. Pull meat from neck; discard bones. Coarsely chop neck meat and giblets; refrigerate.

5. About 2 hours after turkey is in oven, prepare pan-roasted potatoes: Peel potatoes; cut each into four to six chunks. In 4-quart saucepan over medium heat, heat 1 inch water and potatoes to boiling. Reduce heat to low; cover; simmer 10 minutes; drain. Arrange potatoes around turkey in pan; turn to coat with drippings in pan. Roast 40 to 60 minutes along with turkey, turning potatoes occasionally, until tender and browned.

6. When turkey turns golden brown, cover loosely with a "tent" of folded foil. Remove foil during last hour of roasting time and brush turkey generously with pan drippings for attractive sheen. Turkey is done when thermometer reaches 180° to 185° F. and thickest part of drumstick feels soft when pressed with finger protected by paper towels.

7. When turkey and potatoes are done, place on warm large platter; keep warm.

8. Prepare gravy: Remove rack from roasting pan; pour pan drippings into 4-cup measure or medium bowl (set pan aside); let stand a few seconds, until fat separates from meat juice. Skim ⅓ cup fat from drippings into 2-quart saucepan (if necessary, add *butter* or margarine to make ⅓ cup); skim off and discard any remaining fat. Add reserved giblet broth to roasting pan; stir until brown bits are loosened; add to meat juice in cup and add enough water to make 4 cups. Into fat in saucepan over medium heat, stir flour and 1½ teaspoons salt until blended; gradually stir in meat-juice mixture; cook, stirring, until thickened. Stir in reserved giblets and neck meat; cook until heated through. Pour gravy into gravy boat.

9. To serve, garnish turkey with parsley sprigs. Pass gravy in gravy boat.

Roast Turkey with Sausage-Cracker Stuffing

TIME: about 6¹/₂ hours—SERVINGS: 16 to 20

1 14- to 16-pound fresh or frozen (thawed)
  ready-to-stuff turkey

water

1 16-ounce package pork-sausage meat

¹/₂ cup butter or margarine

4 large celery stalks, diced

1 large onion, diced

10 cups coarsely broken soda crackers
  (about ³/₄ 16-ounce box)

¹/₂ cup milk

³/₄ teaspoon rosemary

¹/₂ teaspoon pepper

3 eggs

salad oil

Gravy (right)

parsley sprigs, for garnish

1. Remove giblets and neck from turkey. Rinse turkey with running cold water and drain well; cover and refrigerate.

2. Prepare stuffing: In 2-quart saucepan over high heat, heat giblets, neck, and enough water to cover to boiling. Reduce heat to low; cover and simmer 1 hour or until giblets are tender. Drain, reserving broth. Pull meat from neck; discard bones; coarsely chop neck meat and giblets.

3. In 8-quart Dutch oven over medium heat, cook pork-sausage meat until browned. With slotted spoon, remove sausage to medium bowl; set aside. In sausage drippings in Dutch oven over medium heat, melt butter or margarine. Add celery and onion and cook until tender, stirring occasionally. Remove Dutch oven from heat; stir in neck meat, giblets, sausage, crackers, milk, rosemary, pepper, eggs, and ³/₄ cup reserved giblet broth; mix well.

4. Spoon some of stuffing lightly into neck cavity. (Do not pack stuffing; it expands during cooking.) Fold neck skin over stuffing; fasten neck skin to back with one or two skewers. With turkey breast side up, lift wings up toward neck, then fold under back of turkey so they stay in place.

5. Spoon some stuffing lightly into body cavity. (Bake any leftover stuffing in covered, greased small casserole during last 40 minutes of roasting turkey.) Close, by folding skin lightly over opening; skewer if necessary. Depending on brand of turkey, with string, tie legs and tail together; or push drumsticks under band of skin; or use stuffing clamp.

6. Place turkey, breast side up, on rack in open roasting pan; brush skin with salad oil. Insert meat thermometer into thickest part of meat between breast and thigh, being careful that pointed end of thermometer does not touch bone. Roast turkey in 325° F. oven about 5 hours. Start checking for doneness during last hour of roasting.

7. When turkey turns golden brown, cover loosely with a "tent" of folded foil. Remove foil during last hour of roasting time and, with pastry brush, brush turkey generously with pan drippings for attractive sheen. Turkey is done when thermometer reaches 180° to 185° F. and thickest part of drumstick feels soft when pressed with finger protected by paper towels.

8. When turkey is done, place on warm large platter; keep warm. Prepare Gravy.

9. To serve, arrange parsley sprigs around turkey on platter. Pass gravy in gravy boat.

Gravy: Remove rack from roasting pan; pour pan drippings into a 4-cup measure or a medium bowl (set pan aside); let stand a few seconds until fat separates from meat juice. Skim ¹/₃ cup fat from drippings into 2-quart saucepan; skim off and discard any remaining fat. Add remaining reserved giblet broth to roasting pan; stir until brown bits are loosened; add to meat juice in cup and add enough water to make 4 cups.

Into fat in saucepan over medium heat, stir ¹/₃ *cup all-purpose flour* and *1 teaspoon salt* until blended; gradually stir in meat-juice mixture; cook, stirring, until mixture is thickened.

Roast Turkey with Barley Stuffing

TIME: about 5½ hours—SERVINGS: 12 to 14

1½ cups medium barley

1 12-pound fresh or frozen (thawed)
ready-to-stuff turkey

water

1 tablespoon salad oil

2 medium green peppers, diced

2 medium celery stalks, diced

1 large onion, diced

¼ pound mushrooms, chopped

1 tablespoon salt

1 teaspoon ground sage

¼ teaspoon pepper

Pan-Juice Gravy (right)

watercress sprigs, for garnish

1. Prepare barley as label directs; drain.

2. Meanwhile, remove giblets and neck from turkey. Rinse turkey with running cold water and drain well; cover and refrigerate.

3. Prepare stuffing: In 2-quart saucepan over high heat, heat giblets, neck, and enough water to cover to boiling. Reduce heat to low; cover and simmer 1 hour or until giblets are tender. Drain, reserving broth. Pull meat from neck; discard bones; coarsely chop neck meat and giblets.

4. In 4-quart saucepan over medium heat, in hot salad oil, cook green peppers, celery, onion, and mushrooms until tender, stirring occasionally. Remove saucepan from heat; stir in cooked barley, neck meat, giblets, salt, sage, pepper, and ¼ cup reserved giblet broth; mix well.

5. Spoon some of stuffing lightly into neck cavity. Fold neck skin over stuffing; fasten neck skin to back with one or two skewers. With turkey breast side up, lift wings up toward neck, then fold under back of turkey so they stay in place.

6. Spoon remaining stuffing lightly into body cavity. Close, by folding skin lightly over opening; skewer if necessary. Depending on brand of turkey, with string, tie legs and tail together; or push drumsticks under band of skin; or use stuffing clamp.

7. Place turkey, breast side up, on rack in open roasting pan. Insert meat thermometer into thickest part of meat between breast and thigh, being careful that pointed end of thermometer does not touch bone. Roast turkey in 325° F. oven about 4¼ hours. Start checking for doneness during last hour of roasting.

8. When turkey turns golden brown, cover loosely with a "tent" of folded foil. Remove foil during last hour of roasting time and, with pastry brush, brush turkey generously with pan drippings for attractive sheen. Turkey is done when thermometer reaches 180° to 185° F. and thickest part of drumstick feels soft when pressed with finger protected by paper towels.

9. When turkey is done, place on warm large platter; keep warm. Prepare Pan-Juice Gravy.

10. To serve, garnish turkey with watercress sprigs. Pass gravy in gravy boat.

Pan-Juice Gravy: Remove rack from roasting pan. Pour pan drippings into a 2-cup measure or small bowl (set pan aside); let stand a few seconds until fat separates from meat juice. Skim off and discard fat from drippings. Add reserved giblet broth to roasting pan; stir until brown bits are loosened; add to meat juice in cup and add enough *water* to make 2 cups. Pour into 1-quart saucepan. Stir in *1 chicken-flavor bouillon cube* or envelope and *½ teaspoon salt.* Over high heat, heat to boiling.

Roast Turkey with Wild-Rice Stuffing

TIME: about 6½ hours or start early in day—SERVINGS: 12 to 16

Crystallized Fruit, for garnish (opposite)

1 8-ounce package wild rice

water

6 tablespoons butter or margarine

1 pound mushrooms, sliced

2 celery stalks, diced

1. Early in day, prepare Crystallized Fruit.

2. About 6½ hours before serving, prepare stuffing: Rinse wild rice with running cold water. In 2-quart saucepan over high heat, heat 2⅔ cups water to boiling; stir in wild rice. Reduce heat to low; cover and simmer 45 to 50 minutes or until rice is tender and all liquid is absorbed.

3. Meanwhile, in 4-quart saucepan over medium heat, melt butter or margarine; add mushrooms, celery, onion, pepper, and 1¼ teaspoons

1 **medium onion, diced**

1/4 **teaspoon pepper**

salt

1 **cup regular long-grain rice**

1 **12- to 14-pound fresh or frozen (thawed) ready-to-stuff turkey**

salad oil

1/3 **cup all-purpose flour**

lemon leaves, for garnish

salt; cook until vegetables are tender, stirring occasionally. Remove vegetables with any liquid to medium bowl.

4. In same 4-quart saucepan, prepare regular long-grain rice as label directs. When rice is done, stir in wild rice and vegetables.

5. Remove giblets and neck from turkey. Rinse turkey with running cold water and drain well.

6. Spoon some of stuffing lightly into neck cavity. Fold neck skin over stuffing; fasten neck skin to back with one or two skewers. With turkey breast side up, lift wings up toward neck, then fold under back of turkey so they stay in place.

7. Spoon some stuffing lightly into body cavity. (Bake any leftover stuffing in covered, greased small casserole during last 40 minutes of roasting turkey.) Close, by folding skin lightly over opening; skewer if necessary. Depending on brand of turkey, with string, tie legs and tail together; or push drumsticks under band of skin; or use stuffing clamp.

8. Place turkey, breast side up, on rack in open roasting pan. Brush skin with salad oil. Insert meat thermometer into thickest part of meat between breast and thigh, being careful that pointed end of thermometer does not touch bone. Roast turkey in 325° F. oven about 4 3/4 hours. Start checking for doneness during last hour of roasting.

9. While turkey is roasting, prepare giblets and neck to use in gravy: In 3-quart saucepan over high heat, heat giblets, neck, 1/4 teaspoon salt, and enough water to cover to boiling. Reduce heat to low. Cover and simmer 1 hour or until giblets are tender. Drain, reserving broth. Pull meat from neck; discard bones; coarsely chop neck meat and giblets; refrigerate.

10. When turkey turns golden brown, cover loosely with a "tent" of folded foil. Remove foil during last hour of roasting time and, with pastry brush, brush turkey generously with pan drippings for attractive sheen. Turkey is done when thermometer reaches 180° to 185° F. and thickest part of drumstick feels soft when pressed with finger protected by paper towels.

11. When turkey is done, place on warm large platter; keep warm. Prepare gravy: Remove rack from roasting pan. Pour pan drippings into a 4-cup measure or a medium bowl (set pan aside); let stand a few seconds until fat separates from meat juice. Skim 1/3 cup fat from drippings into 2-quart saucepan. Skim off and discard any remaining fat. Add reserved giblet broth to roasting pan; stir until browned bits are loosened; add to meat juice in cup with enough water to make 3 cups.

12. Into fat in saucepan over medium heat, stir flour and 3/4 teaspoon salt until blended. Gradually stir in meat-juice mixture; cook, stirring, until mixture is thickened. Add reserved giblets and neck meat; cook until heated through. Pour gravy into gravy boat.

13. To serve, arrange Crystallized Fruit and lemon leaves around turkey on platter. Serve with gravy.

Crystallized Fruit: Wash and wipe dry *4 small red apples, 4 small pears,* and *1/2 pint kumquats.* With kitchen shears, cut *1 pound seedless green grapes* and *1 pound seedless red grapes* into small bunches.

In pie plate with fork, beat *3 egg whites* slightly. Onto waxed paper measure *2 cups sugar.* Brush fruit with egg white; then coat completely with sugar. Place Crystallized Fruit on rack in 15 1/2" by 10 1/2" jelly-roll pan to dry, about 1 hour. Store Crystallized Fruit, lightly covered with plastic wrap, in refrigerator.

Party Turkey with Radish Mayonnaise

TIME: start early in day or day ahead—SERVINGS: 12 to 16

1 12- to 14-pound fresh or frozen (thawed)
   ready-to-stuff turkey

salad oil

Radish Mayonnaise (see Index)

red cabbage leaves, for garnish

lettuce leaves, for garnish

1. Remove giblets and neck from turkey; reserve for soup another day. Rinse turkey with running cold water; drain well.

2. With turkey breast side up, lift wings up toward neck, then fold under back of turkey so they stay in place. Depending on brand of turkey, with string, tie legs and tail together; or push drumsticks under band of skin; or use stuffing clamp.

3. Place turkey, breast side up, on rack in open roasting pan. Brush skin with salad oil. Insert meat thermometer into thickest part of meat between breast and thigh, being careful that pointed end of thermometer does not touch bone. Roast turkey in 325° F. oven about 3 1/2 hours. Start checking for doneness during last hour of roasting.

4. When turkey turns golden brown, cover loosely with a "tent" of folded foil. Remove foil during last hour of roasting time and, with pastry brush, brush turkey generously with pan drippings for attractive sheen. Turkey is done when thermometer reaches 180° to 185° F. and thickest part of drumstick feels soft when pressed with finger protected by paper towels.

5. Remove turkey from roasting pan; cover and refrigerate until cool. Meanwhile, prepare Radish Mayonnaise.

6. Carve turkey. Arrange sliced turkey on large platter; garnish with red cabbage and lettuce leaves. Cover and refrigerate. Serve sliced cold turkey with Radish Mayonnaise.

Turkey Cordon Bleu

TIME: about 1 hour—SERVINGS: 6

2 medium carrots

1 medium zucchini

butter or margarine

salt

6 fresh or frozen (thawed) turkey cutlets
   (about 1 1/2 pounds)

1 teaspoon paprika

all-purpose flour

1 6-ounce package sliced cooked ham

1 6-ounce package Swiss cheese slices

pepper

3/4 cup water

1/4 cup cooking or dry white wine

1 chicken-flavor bouillon cube or envelope

1 cup half-and-half

1 8-ounce package vermicelli or thin
   spaghetti

1. Cut carrots and zucchini crosswise in half; cut each half lengthwise into thin slices; then cut slices into matchstick-thin strips. In 2-quart saucepan over medium heat, melt 4 tablespoons butter or margarine; add carrots and 1/4 teaspoon salt; cook 3 minutes. Add zucchini and cook 10 minutes longer or until vegetables are tender, stirring occasionally. Remove saucepan from heat; set aside.

2. On cutting board with meat mallet or dull edge of French knife, pound each turkey cutlet into 1/8-inch thickness. On waxed paper, mix paprika, 1/4 cup flour, and 1/2 teaspoon salt. Coat turkey cutlets with flour mixture.

3. In 12-inch skillet over medium-high heat, melt 3 tablespoons butter or margarine; add cutlets, a few at a time, and cook until lightly browned on both sides, adding more butter or margarine if necessary. Remove cutlets from skillet. Top each cutlet with a ham slice, then a cheese slice, folding ham and cheese slices to fit. Fold each cutlet in half; skewer together with a toothpick; set aside.

4. Into drippings remaining in skillet, over medium heat, stir 1 tablespoon flour, 1/4 teaspoon salt, and 1/8 teaspoon pepper. Gradually stir in water, wine, bouillon, and 1/2 cup half-and-half; heat to boiling, stirring to loosen brown bits from bottom of skillet. Return cutlets to skillet; heat to boiling. Reduce heat to low; cover and simmer 5 minutes or until cheese is melted. Remove cutlets to warm larger platter, leaving sauce in skillet. Remove toothpicks from cutlets; keep cutlets and sauce warm.

5. Meanwhile, in 6-quart saucepot, prepare vermicelli as label directs. Drain vermicelli; return to saucepot. Over low heat, heat vermicelli, reserved carrots, zucchini, and 1/2 cup half-and-half until hot, tossing to coat vermicelli well; sprinkle lightly with salt and pepper to taste. Arrange vermicelli mixture on platter with cutlets. Pour sauce over cutlets.

Turkey Cutlets Manhattan

TIME: about 45 minutes—SERVINGS: 6

1 **8-ounce package frozen shrimp, thawed and well drained, or ³/₄ pound shrimp, shelled and deveined**

2 **teaspoons minced green onion**

1 **teaspoon cornstarch**

¹/₈ **teaspoon pepper**

1 **egg white**

cooking or dry sherry

salt

1 **16-ounce package fresh or frozen (thawed) turkey cutlets**

2 **tablespoons all-purpose flour**

3 **tablespoons salad oil**

3 **tablespoons butter or margarine**

1 **large lemon**

¹/₂ **cup water**

1 **tablespoon chopped parsley**

1. Mince shrimp. In medium bowl, mix shrimp, green onion, cornstarch, pepper, egg white, 1 tablespoon sherry, and ¹/₄ teaspoon salt; set aside.

2. On cutting board with meat mallet or dull edge of French knife, pound each turkey cutlet into ¹/₈-inch thickness. Spread some shrimp mixture evenly over one side of each cutlet. On waxed paper, place flour. Dip shrimp-topped turkey cutlets cutlet side down in flour to coat evenly (do not dip shrimp side in flour).

3. In 12-inch skillet over medium-high heat, in hot salad oil and butter or margarine, cook turkey cutlets, a few at a time, until browned on both sides and tender, about 5 minutes. Remove cutlets to warm platter; keep warm.

4. From lemon, grate 1 teaspoon peel and squeeze 1 tablespoon juice. To drippings in skillet over low heat, add lemon peel, lemon juice, water, 2 tablespoons sherry, and ¹/₄ teaspoon salt, stirring to loosen brown bits from bottom of skillet. Stir parsley into sauce; pour over cutlets.

Buffet Turkey Casserole

TIME: about 3¹/₂ hours—SERVINGS: 12

1 **tablespoon salad oil**

1 **2-pound package fresh or frozen (thawed) turkey drumsticks**

4 **cups water**

¹/₂ **cup chopped onion**

2 **parsley sprigs**

¹/₂ **teaspoon pepper**

salt

1 **large carrot, sliced**

1 **large celery stalk, sliced**

1 **16-ounce package narrow noodles**

1 **17-ounce can peas**

1 **4¹/₂-ounce jar sliced mushrooms in cooking juices**

2 **tablespoons chopped pimentos**

¹/₂ **cup all-purpose flour**

1¹/₂ **cups seasoned croutons**

2 **tablespoons butter or margarine, melted**

1. In 12-inch skillet over medium-high heat, in hot salad oil, cook turkey drumsticks until well browned on all sides. Add water, onion, parsley, pepper, and 2 teaspoons salt; heat to boiling. Reduce heat to low; cover and simmer 1¹/₂ hours. Add carrot and celery; cook 30 minutes longer or until turkey is tender.

2. Remove turkey from skillet; cool slightly until easy to handle. Meanwhile, cook noodles as label directs. Remove turkey meat from bones; cut meat into 1-inch pieces. Place turkey and noodles in a 15¹/₂″ by 10¹/₂″ open roasting pan.

3. Preheat oven to 350° F. Drain liquid from peas and mushrooms into small bowl. Add drained vegetables and pimentos to turkey mixture. In cup with fork, gradually stir vegetable liquids into flour and 2 teaspoons salt until well blended; set aside.

4. With slotted spoon, remove vegetables from broth to turkey mixture. Over medium heat, heat broth to boiling. Gradually stir in flour mixture and cook, stirring constantly, until sauce is thickened. Pour sauce over turkey mixture, and gently stir until turkey mixture is well mixed.

5. In small bowl, combine croutons with butter or margarine. Sprinkle croutons over top of mixture. Bake 25 minutes or until hot and bubbly and croutons are lightly browned.

103

Creamed Turkey with Pastry Pillows

TIME: about 1¹/₂ hours—SERVINGS: 20

Easy Pastry Pillows (right)

1 pound hot or sweet Italian sausage links

2 tablespoons water

1 12-pound fresh or frozen (thawed) turkey, roasted

1 cup butter or margarine

2 medium onions, diced

1 pound mushrooms, thinly sliced

1 cup all-purpose flour

1 tablespoon salt

1 teaspoon paprika

³/₄ teaspoon pepper

3 chicken-flavor bouillon cubes or envelopes

3 quarts milk

¹/₂ cup cooking or dry sherry

1 tablespoon minced parsley, for garnish

1. Prepare Easy Pastry Pillows.

2. Meanwhile, in 10-inch skillet over medium heat, heat sausages and water to boiling. Cover; simmer 5 minutes. Remove cover; continue cooking, turning sausages frequently, until sausages are well browned, about 20 minutes. Remove sausages to paper towels to drain. Slice sausages into thin pieces.

3. Cut turkey meat into bite-size chunks; set aside. (Reserve turkey bones for soup another day.)

4. In 8-quart Dutch oven or saucepot over medium heat, melt butter or margarine; add onions and mushrooms and cook until vegetables are tender, stirring occasionally. Stir in flour, salt, paprika, pepper, and bouillon until blended; gradually stir in milk and sherry until smooth; cook, stirring constantly, until sauce is slightly thickened. Add turkey meat and sausage to cream sauce in Dutch oven; heat through.

5. To serve, spoon turkey mixture into large chafing dish. Garnish with parsley. Split each puff pastry horizontally in half. Let each person spoon some creamed turkey over split pastry.

Easy Pastry Pillows: Let *one 17¹/₄-ounce package frozen puff pastry* stand at room temperature 20 minutes. Preheat oven to 350° F. Unfold one sheet of pastry; cut along fold lines to make three 10″ by 3″ rectangles; cut each rectangle crosswise into three pieces. Place pastry pieces on large cookie sheet. Repeat with remaining sheet of pastry. Bake 15 minutes or until puffed and golden. With pancake turner, remove pastries from cookie sheet to wire racks to cool.

Turkey-Orange Salad

TIME: about 30 minutes—SERVINGS: 6

1¹/₂ cups spaghetti twists or elbow macaroni

¹/₄ cup slivered almonds

2 medium cucumbers

4 medium oranges

³/₄ cup mayonnaise

¹/₄ cup milk

¹/₂ teaspoon salt

2¹/₄ cups bite-size chunks cooked turkey

lettuce leaves

1. Prepare spaghetti twists as label directs; drain. Meanwhile, in 10-inch skillet over medium heat, toast almonds until browned, shaking skillet frequently. Remove from heat; set aside.

2. Cut 1 cucumber lengthwise in half; scoop out and discard seeds; dice cucumber. Thinly slice remaining cucumber. Peel oranges. Thinly slice 2 oranges; cut remaining oranges into bite-size pieces.

3. In medium bowl with fork, mix mayonnaise, milk, and salt. Add spaghetti twists, orange pieces, diced cucumber, and turkey; mix well.

4. To serve, line large platter with lettuce. Spoon salad onto lettuce; arrange orange and cucumber slices around salad. Sprinkle with almonds.

Turkey-Custard Cups

TIME: about 30 minutes—SERVINGS: 6

1 tablespoon butter or margarine

1 green onion, minced

1 slice whole-wheat or white bread

1¹/₂ cups diced cooked turkey

¹/₂ 4-ounce package shredded Cheddar cheese (¹/₂ cup)

4 eggs

2 cups milk

¹/₂ teaspoon salt

1. In 1-quart saucepan over medium heat, in hot butter, cook green onion until tender, stirring occasionally.

2. Meanwhile, cut bread into ¹/₄-inch cubes; place bread in six 6-ounce custard cups; sprinkle with diced turkey and shredded cheese. In medium bowl with wire whisk or fork, beat eggs, milk, salt, and green onion; pour mixture into custard cups.

3. Place custard cups in 12-inch skillet; pour water in skillet to come halfway up side of custard cups. Over medium-low heat, heat water to boiling; cover skillet and remove from heat. Let custard stand in covered skillet 15 minutes, until set.

Turkey Florentine

TIME: about 35 minutes—SERVINGS: 6

2 10-ounce packages frozen chopped
   spinach

butter or margarine

3 tablespoons all-purpose flour

salt

2¼ cups milk

3 cups bite-size chunks cooked turkey

1 small onion, minced

½ cup shredded Cheddar cheese

1. In medium bowl, place frozen spinach; cover with boiling water and let stand 10 minutes, stirring occasionally to loosen spinach. Drain spinach well.

2. Meanwhile, in 2-quart saucepan over medium heat, melt 2 tablespoons butter or margarine; stir in flour and ½ teaspoon salt until blended. Gradually stir in milk; cook, stirring constantly, until mixture is slightly thickened. Reserve ¾ cup sauce. Add turkey to remaining sauce; over low heat, heat the turkey mixture through.

3. In 10-inch skillet over medium heat, melt 2 tablespoons butter or margarine; add onion and cook until tender, stirring occasionally. Stir in spinach and reserved sauce; heat mixture through.

4. Preheat broiler if manufacturer directs. Spoon spinach mixture into 10″ by 6″ baking dish or 1½-quart shallow baking dish; top with turkey mixture; sprinkle evenly with cheese. Broil turkey mixture 3 to 5 minutes or until cheese is melted and lightly browned.

Old-fashioned Creamed Turkey with Biscuits

TIME: about 30 minutes—SERVINGS: 6

2 cups all-purpose flour

2 tablespoons sugar

1 tablespoon double-acting baking powder

salt

⅓ cup shortening

⅔ cup milk

1 egg

2 tablespoons butter or margarine

2 medium green peppers, cut into thin
   strips

½ pound mushrooms, sliced

1 small onion, diced

1 10¾-ounce can condensed cream of
   mushroom soup

1 3¼-ounce can pitted ripe olives, drained
   and each cut in half

1 2-ounce jar diced pimento, drained

3 cups bite-size chunks cooked turkey

1 cup water

⅛ teaspoon pepper

1. Prepare biscuits: Preheat oven to 450° F. In medium bowl with fork, mix flour, sugar, baking powder, and 1 teaspoon salt. With pastry blender or two knives used scissor fashion, cut in shortening until mixture resembles coarse crumbs. Add milk; with fork, quickly stir just until mixture forms soft dough and leaves side of bowl.

2. On lightly floured surface with lightly floured hands, knead dough ten times. Pat dough into 6½-inch circle; cut into six wedges. Place wedges on cookie sheet, about 1 inch apart. In cup with fork, beat egg; brush wedges with egg. Bake 12 to 15 minutes until golden.

3. Meanwhile, in 3-quart saucepan over medium heat, melt butter or margarine. Add green peppers, mushrooms, and onion; cook until vegetables are tender, stirring occasionally. Stir in undiluted mushroom soup, remaining ingredients, and ½ teaspoon salt; over high heat, heat to boiling. Reduce heat to low; cover and simmer 10 minutes to blend flavors.

4. To serve, spoon turkey mixture into warm deep platter; arrange biscuit wedges on top.

Chutney-Glazed Barbecued Duckling

TIME: about 2 hours—SERVINGS: 4

1 10- to 12-ounce jar orange marmalade

½ cup chutney

¼ cup packed brown sugar

3 tablespoons cider vinegar

2 teaspoons salt

1 4½- to 5-pound fresh or frozen (thawed) duckling

pepper

TO COOK ON OUTDOOR COVERED GRILL: 1. Prepare outdoor covered charcoal grill, using indirect-heat method with drip pan as manufacturer directs. Follow manufacturer's directions if using covered gas or electric grill.

2. Meanwhile, in small bowl, mix marmalade, chutney (cut chutney if pieces are too large), brown sugar, vinegar, and salt; set glaze aside.

3. Remove giblets and neck from duckling; refrigerate to use in soup another day. Rinse duckling with running cold water; drain well. Pat dry with paper towels. Cut duckling into quarters; trim excess fat and skin on pieces. Sprinkle duckling pieces lightly with pepper.

4. Place duckling pieces on grill over drip pan. Cover grill; roast 1 hour and 25 minutes or until duckling is fork-tender, turning every 15 minutes and adding briquettes to each side of drip pan at the end of 1 hour, as manufacturer directs. During last 10 minutes of roasting, brush duckling with glaze.

TO COOK ON OUTDOOR OPEN GRILL: 1. Prepare outdoor grill for barbecuing.

2. Meanwhile, prepare glaze and duckling as above. Wrap each piece of duckling in double thickness of heavy-duty foil, being careful that seam of foil is folded several times to seal in juices.

3. Place duckling packets on grill, about 4 inches above briquettes, over medium heat; roast 1 hour, turning packets with tongs every 10 to 15 minutes, being sure not to puncture foil (if juices leak out from packets, flame may get too high and char duckling).

4. After cooking duckling 1 hour, remove packets to work surface. Carefully open packets and spoon glaze over duckling. Close foil and roast 15 minutes longer or until duckling is fork-tender.

TO ROAST IN OVEN: 1. Prepare glaze and duckling as above.

2. Place duckling pieces, skin side down, on rack in open roasting pan. Roast in 350° F. oven 1 hour; turn and roast 45 minutes longer or until duckling is fork-tender. Brush with glaze during last 15 minutes of roasting.

Breast of Duckling with Green Peppercorns

TIME: about 40 minutes—SERVINGS: 2

1 4½- to 5-pound fresh or frozen (thawed) duckling

butter or margarine

1 small green onion, minced

2 tablespoons cooking or dry white wine

2 tablespoons water

1 teaspoon green peppercorns

watercress, for garnish

½ 14-ounce jar spiced apples, for garnish

1. Remove breasts from duckling: Remove giblets and neck from duckling; set aside. Rinse duckling with running cold water; pat dry with paper towels. Place duckling, breast side up, on work surface. With sharp knife, working with one side of duckling at a time, insert tip of knife between meat and breastbone, and cut and scrape meat away from bone and rib cage, gently pulling meat back in one piece as you cut. Repeat with other side. Remove and discard skin and any fat on breasts. Reserve remaining duckling, giblets, and neck for use in soup or salad another day.

2. In 7- or 8-inch skillet over medium-high heat, in 2 tablespoons hot butter or margarine, cook duckling breasts until undersides are browned, about 4 minutes; turn breasts and cook about 3 minutes longer for medium-rare or until of desired doneness. Remove breasts to warm platter; slice into thin slices; keep warm.

3. Reduce heat to medium-low. In drippings in skillet and 1 more tablespoon hot butter or margarine, cook green onion until tender. Add wine, water, and green peppercorns, stirring to loosen brown bits on bottom of skillet. Drain any juice from duckling in platter into sauce in skillet. Remove skillet from heat; stir in 1 tablespoon butter or margarine until melted. Pour sauce over duckling breasts. Garnish platter with watercress and spiced apples.

Duckling with Raspberry Sauce

TIME: about 2 hours—SERVINGS: 4

1 4¹/₂- to 5-pound fresh or frozen (thawed)
   duckling

¹/₄ teaspoon pepper

salt

2 10-ounce packages frozen red
   raspberries in quick-thaw pouch, thawed

2 tablespoons brown sugar

1 tablespoon lemon juice

2 teaspoons cornstarch

¹/₂ teaspoon ground cinnamon

watercress sprigs, for garnish

1. Remove giblets and neck from duckling; refrigerate to use in soup another day. Rinse duckling with running cold water; drain well. Pat dry with paper towels.

2. Remove excess fat from inside of body cavity; cut and discard neck skin. Place duckling, breast side up, on work surface; with poultry or kitchen shears, starting at body cavity, cut along one side of breastbone to neck cavity. Spread duckling open; cut in half along one side of backbone. Cut each half crosswise between wing and leg to make two pieces; trim excess fat and skin on pieces. Evenly sprinkle duckling pieces on all sides with pepper and 1¹/₄ teaspoons salt.

3. Place duckling pieces, skin side down, on rack in 13″ by 9″ open roasting pan. Roast in 350° F. oven 1 hour; turn and roast about 45 minutes longer or until thickest part of drumstick feels soft when pinched with fingers protected by paper towels.

4. About 15 minutes before duckling is done, prepare sauce: Into 2-quart saucepan, press 1 package raspberries through medium sieve, straining out seeds but forcing pulp through; discard seeds. Stir in brown sugar, lemon juice, cornstarch, cinnamon, ¹/₂ teaspoon salt, and remaining raspberries. Cook mixture over medium-low heat until sauce is slightly thickened and boils, stirring frequently. Pour raspberry sauce into warm deep platter; arrange duckling on top. Garnish platter with watercress sprigs.

Duckling and Peppers Vinaigrette

TIME: about 2¹/₂ hours—SERVINGS: 4

1 4¹/₂- to 5-pound fresh or frozen (thawed)
   duckling

salt

water

4 medium green peppers, each cut
   lengthwise into 6 strips

4 medium red peppers, each cut
   lengthwise into 6 strips

salad oil

¹/₂ cup red-wine vinegar

1 tablespoon sugar

¹/₄ teaspoon pepper

lettuce leaves

1. Rinse duckling, its giblets, and neck with running cold water. Place duckling, breast side down, in 8-quart Dutch oven or saucepot; add giblets, neck, 1 teaspoon salt, and 2 inches water. Over high heat, heat to boiling. Reduce heat to low; cover and simmer 1 hour or until duckling is fork-tender. Remove duckling to large bowl; refrigerate 30 minutes or until easy to handle.

2. Meanwhile, prepare peppers: Preheat broiler if manufacturer directs. Place peppers in broiling pan; brush lightly with some salad oil. About 5 to 7 inches from source of heat (or at 450° F.), broil peppers 10 minutes or until lightly charred and tender, turning peppers once.

3. While peppers are broiling, prepare vinaigrette dressing: In large bowl with fork or wire whisk, beat vinegar, sugar, pepper, ¹/₃ cup salad oil, and ³/₄ teaspoon salt. Add peppers. With rubber spatula, gently toss until peppers are well coated. Cover and refrigerate 2 hours, stirring occasionally.

4. When duckling is ready, discard skin and bones; cut meat and giblets into bite-size pieces.

5. To serve, line chilled platter with lettuce leaves. With slotted spoon, remove peppers from bowl and arrange peppers and duckling on lettuce. Pour remaining dressing from peppers into small bowl to serve over duckling.

Christmas Goose with Glazed Oranges

TIME: about 4¹/₂ hours—SERVINGS: 8 to 10

Rye-Bread Stuffing (right)

1 10- to 12-pound frozen goose, thawed

1 teaspoon salt

¹/₄ teaspoon pepper

8 small oranges

water

¹/₃ cup light corn syrup

2 tablespoons sugar

Creamy Mushroom Gravy (see Index)

parsley sprigs, for garnish

1. Prepare Rye-Bread Stuffing; set aside.

2. Remove giblets and neck from goose. Refrigerate giblets and neck to use in soup another day. Discard fat from body cavity; rinse goose with running cold water, and drain well. Spoon some stuffing into neck cavity. (Do not pack stuffing; it expands during cooking.) Fold neck skin over stuffing; fasten neck skin to the back with one or two skewers. With goose breast side up, lift wings up toward neck, then fold under back of goose.

3. Spoon stuffing lightly into body cavity. (Bake any leftover stuffing in covered, greased small casserole during last 40 minutes of roasting time.) Fold skin over opening; skewer closed if necessary. With string, tie legs and tail together. With fork, prick skin of goose in several places.

4. Place goose, breast side up, on rack in open roasting pan. Rub goose with salt and pepper. Insert meat thermometer into thickest part of meat between breast and thigh, being careful that pointed end of thermometer does not touch bone. Roast goose in 350° F. oven about 3 hours. Start checking doneness during last 30 minutes.

5. About 1 hour before goose is done, prepare glazed oranges: With knife, carefully remove peel and white membrane from oranges; set aside. Trim off white membrane from a few pieces of peel; then cut peel into long, thin strips to make about ¹/₂ cup, firmly packed. In 10-inch skillet over high heat, heat orange peel and 3 cups water to boiling; cook 15 minutes. Drain; rinse. With 3 cups more water, cook peel 15 minutes again; drain.

6. In same skillet over high heat, heat corn syrup and sugar to boiling and until sugar is dissolved. Add oranges and peel to coat well with corn-syrup mixture. Reduce heat to medium-low, and cook until oranges are heated through, about 10 minutes; keep warm.

7. Prepare Creamy Mushroom Gravy; keep warm.

8. Goose is done when thermometer reaches 190° F. and thickest part of leg feels soft when pinched with fingers protected by paper towels.

9. To serve, remove skewers and strings; place goose on warm large platter; garnish with parsley sprigs and glazed oranges. With pastry brush, brush goose with corn-syrup mixture remaining in skillet. Serve goose with mushroom gravy.

Rye-Bread Stuffing: In 5-quart Dutch oven or saucepot over medium heat, melt ¹/₂ cup butter or margarine. Add 2 celery stalks, diced, and 1 medium onion, diced; cook until vegetables are tender, stirring frequently. Remove Dutch oven from heat; stir in 10 cups rye-bread cubes, 1¹/₄ cups milk, 2 tablespoons minced parsley, ¹/₂ teaspoon thyme leaves, ¹/₄ teaspoon rubbed sage, and ¹/₄ teaspoon pepper.

Broiled Salmon Béarnaise

TIME: about 1 hour—SERVINGS: 4

Béarnaise Sauce (see Index)

4 slices white bread

salad oil

4 small salmon steaks, each cut 1/2 inch thick (about 1 1/2 pounds)

salt

1 teaspoon lemon juice

1. Prepare Béarnaise Sauce.

2. Preheat broiler if manufacturer directs. Prepare toast for garnish: Using 3- to 3 1/4-inch round fluted cookie cutter, cut out a round from each bread slice; cut each round in half. Place bread on cookie sheet; toast in broiler. Remove cookie sheet from oven; set aside.

3. Lightly brush rack in broiling pan with salad oil. Place salmon steaks on rack; lightly sprinkle with salt and 1/2 teaspoon lemon juice. Broil 3 minutes. Turn salmon and sprinkle other side with salt and remaining lemon juice; broil 2 minutes longer.

4. To serve, arrange salmon steaks on warm platter. Garnish with toast. Pass Béarnaise Sauce in small bowl.

Grilled Trout with Summer-Vegetable Stuffing

TIME: about 1 hour—SERVINGS: 4

4 brook trout, bluefish, or other locally caught fish (about 3/4 pound each)

3/4 cup butter or margarine

3 tablespoons lemon juice

1 cup white-bread cubes (2 slices)

1 small zucchini (6 ounces), thinly sliced

1 small tomato, diced

1/4 pound mushrooms, thinly sliced

6 radishes, thinly sliced

1 teaspoon savory

3/4 teaspoon salt

1/8 teaspoon cracked pepper

1. Prepare outdoor grill for barbecuing.

2. Meanwhile, with vegetable peeler or fish scaler, remove scales from fish. With sharp knife, gut fish. Then cut three slashes on each side of fish. (Cutting slashes in thick part of fish will allow fish to cook faster and more evenly.) Rinse fish with running cold water; pat dry with paper towels.

3. In small metal-handled saucepan over low heat, heat butter or margarine and lemon juice until butter melts. Into medium bowl, measure 1/3 cup butter mixture. Add bread cubes and remaining ingredients; toss gently to mix well. Spoon one fourth of stuffing into each fish; pack mixture firmly; secure openings with small metal skewers.

4. Place fish in large flat wire barbecue basket (or wrap fish in heavy-duty foil). Cook fish on grill over medium heat about 5 minutes on each side or until fish flakes easily when tested with a fork and stuffing is heated through, brushing fish occasionally with some butter mixture. Serve fish with remaining butter mixture.

TO BROIL IN OVEN: About 30 minutes before serving, prepare fish, butter mixture, and stuffing as above. Preheat broiler if manufacturer directs. Place fish on rack in broiling pan; broil about 5 minutes on each side or until fish flakes easily when tested with a fork, basting fish occasionally with butter mixture, and serve as above.

Fish au Gratin

TIME: about 45 minutes—SERVINGS: 4

1 16-ounce package frozen cod, haddock, or flounder fillets

4 tablespoons butter or margarine

1 green onion, thinly sliced

1/3 cup all-purpose flour

1/4 teaspoon pepper

1 1/2 cups milk

1 4-ounce package shredded sharp Cheddar cheese (1 cup)

1. Remove frozen fish fillets from freezer; let stand at room temperature 15 minutes to thaw slightly.

2. Preheat oven to 450° F. With sharp knife, cut frozen fish crosswise into four pieces. Place fish in greased 10" by 6" baking dish; bake 25 minutes.

3. Meanwhile, in 2-quart saucepan over medium heat, melt butter or margarine; add green onion and cook until tender, stirring occasionally. Stir in flour and pepper until blended. Gradually stir in milk; cook over medium heat until thickened, stirring. (Sauce will be thick.) Remove from heat.

4. Reserve 2 tablespoons shredded cheese; stir remaining cheese into sauce until blended. Spoon cheese sauce over fish. Sprinkle with reserved cheese. Bake 3 to 4 minutes longer or until fish flakes easily when tested with a fork and cheese is melted.

Grilled Fish Packets

TIME: about 1 hour—SERVINGS: 4

1 16-ounce package frozen haddock, flounder, or cod fillets

1 medium tomato, diced

1 small cucumber, thinly sliced

4 tablespoons butter or margarine

2 tablespoons cooking or dry sherry

1/2 teaspoon salt

1/8 teaspoon pepper

1. Prepare outdoor grill for barbecuing.

2. Meanwhile, remove frozen fish fillets from freezer; let stand at room temperature 15 minutes to thaw slightly.

3. With sharp knife, cut frozen fish fillets crosswise into four pieces. Divide ingredients equally on four pieces double-thickness heavy-duty foil; wrap into four packets, being careful seam of foil is folded several times to seal in juices.

4. Place packets on grill over low heat; cook 20 minutes or until fish flakes easily when tested with a fork, turning packets occasionally with tongs.

TO BAKE IN OVEN: About 45 minutes before serving, thaw frozen fish fillets as above. Preheat oven to 450° F. In 10″ by 6″ baking dish in oven, melt butter or margarine. Cut fish into four pieces as above. Place fish in baking dish; top with tomato, cucumber, sherry, salt, and pepper. Cover and bake 25 to 30 minutes, until fish flakes easily when tested with a fork.

TO COOK IN MICROWAVE OVEN: About 25 minutes before serving, place frozen fish fillets in 10″ by 6″ microwave-safe baking dish. Cook on defrost 3 minutes to thaw slightly; remove fish from dish. Cut fish crosswise into four pieces. Place butter or margarine in same dish; cook on high 1 minute or until butter is melted. Place fish and remaining ingredients in melted butter or margarine as above. Cover dish loosely with waxed paper. Cook on high 10 to 12 minutes, until fish flakes easily when tested with a fork. Remove dish from oven and let stand 5 minutes to complete cooking.

Economical Fish-Chowder Pie

TIME: about 1 1/4 hours—SERVINGS: 4

4 bacon slices, cut into pieces

4 large carrots, sliced

3/4 pound small white onions

1 1/2 cups sliced celery

1/2 cup water

1 16-ounce package frozen flounder or ocean perch fillets, thawed

1/3 cup all-purpose flour

2 teaspoons salt

dash pepper

1 cup milk

1 4-ounce package refrigerated cheese-flavored dough for wieners

1. In 4-quart saucepan over medium heat, cook bacon until crisp. With slotted spoon, remove bacon to drain on paper towels; set aside.

2. Pour off all but 2 tablespoons drippings from saucepan; add carrots, onions, celery, and water; heat to boiling. Reduce heat to low; cover and simmer 15 minutes or until vegetables are fork-tender.

3. Preheat oven to 400° F. Meanwhile, cut fish into large chunks; pat dry with paper towels; set aside.

4. In small bowl, blend flour, salt, pepper, and milk until smooth; gradually stir into hot vegetable mixture and cook until mixture is thickened, stirring constantly. Gently stir in bacon and cut-up fish; pour into a 2-quart casserole. Bake, uncovered, 15 minutes.

5. Separate dough for wieners into five squares. With hands, roll each square into a 16-inch rope; pat ropes into 1/2-inch-thick strips. Remove casserole from oven; arrange strips on mixture to make a lattice top. Return to oven and bake, uncovered, 12 to 15 minutes longer, until golden.

Mediterranean Cod with Vegetables

TIME: about 1½ hours—SERVINGS: 8

2 16-ounce packages frozen cod or other fillets

²/₃ cup salad oil

3 garlic cloves, slivered

1 medium eggplant, cut up

3 medium onions, cut into wedges

2 green peppers, cut up

¼ teaspoon pepper

¾ cup water

salt

1 egg

2½ cups soft bread crumbs (5 white-bread slices)

2 tablespoons chopped fresh dill or 1 tablespoon dill weed

3 medium tomatoes, cut into wedges

1. Place unopened packages of frozen fish in large pan; add cold water to cover packages. Let stand until fillets are partially thawed, about 15 minutes.

2. In 12-inch skillet over medium-high heat, in ⅓ cup hot salad oil, cook garlic until golden; with slotted spoon, discard garlic. Add eggplant and onions; cook until vegetables are browned, stirring frequently, about 5 minutes. Stir in green peppers, pepper, water, and 1½ teaspoons salt; cover and cook 5 minutes longer, stirring occasionally. Remove cover; continue cooking until all the water has evaporated. Spoon vegetables into medium bowl; keep warm.

3. Meanwhile, bread fish: Cut each package of cod fillets crosswise into four pieces; sprinkle with 1 teaspoon salt. In pie plate with fork, beat egg. On waxed paper, combine bread crumbs and dill. Dip fish in egg; coat with bread-crumb mixture.

4. In same skillet over medium-high heat, heat remaining ⅓ cup salad oil; cook fish 10 minutes or until it flakes easily when tested with fork, turning fish once. Remove fish to warm large platter; keep warm while vegetables are heated.

5. Return vegetables to skillet; add tomatoes and cook, stirring frequently, until tomatoes are heated through. Remove vegetables to warm platter and arrange mixture next to fish.

Fish Fillets with Blue-Cheese Sauce

TIME: about 30 minutes—SERVINGS: 4

1 large lemon

1 pound fresh or 1 16-ounce package frozen (thawed) sole or flounder fillets

¼ cup all-purpose flour

¼ teaspoon salt

cracked pepper

butter or margarine

¼ cup crumbled blue or Gorgonzola cheese (about 2 ounces)

2 tablespoons water

1 tablespoon minced parsley

1. Cut lemon crosswise in half. From one half, squeeze 1 tablespoon juice; set aside. Slice remaining half for garnish later.

2. Cut fish fillets into serving pieces. On waxed paper, mix flour, salt, and ⅛ teaspoon pepper. Coat fish with flour mixture.

3. In 12-inch skillet over medium heat, melt 3 tablespoons butter or margarine; add fish; cook 2 to 3 minutes on each side, until fish flakes easily when tested with fork. With pancake turner, remove fish to warm platter; keep warm.

4. Meanwhile, in small saucepan over medium-low heat, into 3 tablespoons hot butter or margarine, stir blue cheese, water, ⅛ teaspoon pepper, and reserved lemon juice until cheese is melted and sauce is smooth. Stir in parsley; pour sauce over fish. Garnish with lemon slices.

Manhattan-style Fish Stew

TIME: about 40 minutes—SERVINGS: 4

1 16-ounce package frozen cod or haddock fillets

1 tablespoon salad oil

1 medium onion, chopped

1 28-ounce can tomatoes

2 medium potatoes, peeled and diced

1 teaspoon salt

½ teaspoon basil

¼ teaspoon pepper

¼ teaspoon sugar

1 10-ounce package frozen baby lima beans

1. Remove frozen fillets from freezer; let stand at room temperature 15 minutes to thaw slightly.

2. Meanwhile, in 4-quart saucepan over medium heat, in hot salad oil, cook onion until tender, stirring occasionally. Stir in tomatoes with their liquid and next 5 ingredients; over high heat, heat to boiling. Reduce heat to low; cover; simmer 20 minutes, stirring occasionally.

3. With sharp knife, cut frozen fish fillets into bite-size chunks; add fish and frozen baby lima beans to tomato mixture; over high heat, heat to boiling. Reduce heat to low; cover and simmer 5 minutes or until fish flakes easily when tested with a fork and vegetables are tender. Serve in bowls.

Lemony Salmon Casserole

TIME: about 1½ hours—SERVINGS: 4

1 16-ounce can salmon

1 10 ¾-ounce can condensed cream of celery soup

1 cup water

1½ cups regular long-grain rice

½ cup cooking or dry sherry

½ cup chopped onion

½ teaspoon salt

1 large lemon, halved

1. Preheat oven to 375° F. In 2½-quart casserole with fork, coarsely flake salmon with its liquid; add undiluted cream of celery soup, water, rice, sherry, onion, and salt. Squeeze juice from a lemon half into casserole; stir until well mixed. Cover and bake 45 minutes.

2. Meanwhile, thinly slice remaining lemon half. Remove casserole from oven; with spoon, stir salmon mixture and arrange lemon slices on top in a circle. Cover and continue baking 30 minutes or until rice is tender.

Salmon-Rice Mix

TIME: about 45 minutes—SERVINGS: 5

1 cup parboiled rice

3 eggs

1 medium cucumber

1 tablespoon butter or margarine

1 large onion, diced

1 7 ¾-ounce can salmon, drained and flaked

¼ cup milk

¼ cup sweet-pickle relish

1 teaspoon salt

¼ teaspoon cracked pepper

1. In 4-quart saucepan, prepare rice as label directs. Meanwhile, hard-cook eggs.

2. Reserve 1 egg yolk for garnish later; chop remaining hard-cooked eggs. Cut cucumber lengthwise in half; scoop out and discard seeds; dice cucumber; set aside.

3. In 1-quart saucepan over medium heat, melt butter or margarine; add onion and cook until tender, stirring occasionally. Stir onion into rice with chopped eggs, cucumber, salmon, and remaining ingredients.

4. To serve, spoon rice mixture onto platter. Coarsely shred reserved egg yolk; sprinkle on rice mixture for garnish.

Tuna-Rice Creole

TIME: about 45 minutes—SERVINGS: 4

½ cup regular long-grain rice

2 tablespoons butter or margarine

1 large celery stalk with leaves, chopped

1 small onion, diced

1 small garlic clove

1 16-ounce can stewed tomatoes

1 cup water

1 teaspoon brown sugar

¼ teaspoon salt

⅛ teaspoon pepper

1 6½- or 7-ounce can tuna, drained and coarsely flaked

celery leaves, for garnish (optional)

1. Prepare rice as label directs; set aside.

2. Meanwhile, in 10-inch skillet over medium heat, melt butter. Add celery, onion, and garlic; cook until tender. Discard garlic.

3. Preheat oven to 350° F. In 10″ by 6″ baking dish or 1½-quart shallow casserole, combine rice, onion mixture, stewed tomatoes, water, sugar, salt, and pepper. Gently stir in tuna.

4. Bake casserole, uncovered, 25 minutes or until hot. If you like, garnish with celery leaves.

Tuna-and-Macaroni Divan

TIME: about 1 hour—SERVINGS: 6

1 8-ounce package corkscrew macaroni

1 bunch broccoli

4 tablespoons butter or margarine

1/4 cup all-purpose flour

1 1/4 teaspoons salt

1/8 teaspoon pepper

1/8 teaspoon ground nutmeg

3 cups milk

2 tablespoons lemon juice

1 12 1/2- or 13-ounce can tuna, drained

lemon slices, for garnish

1. Cook macaroni as label directs; drain. Meanwhile, cut broccoli into spears. In covered 12-inch skillet over medium heat, in 1 inch boiling water, cook broccoli 10 minutes or until tender-crisp; drain. Preheat oven to 350° F.

2. Meanwhile, in 2-quart saucepan over medium heat, into hot butter or margarine, stir flour, salt, pepper, and nutmeg until blended. Gradually stir in milk, and cook until mixture is slightly thickened, stirring constantly. Stir in lemon juice.

3. In 12″ by 8″ baking pan, stir macaroni with tuna. Arrange broccoli on top, and pour on sauce. Bake, uncovered, 40 minutes or until hot and bubbly. Garnish with lemon slices.

Easy Tuna-Rice Casserole

TIME: about 1 hour—SERVINGS: 4

butter or margarine

1 small onion, diced

1 medium celery stalk, diced

1 10 3/4-ounce can condensed cream-of-celery soup

1 6 1/2- to 7-ounce can tuna, drained and flaked

2 cups water

1 cup regular long-grain rice

1 teaspoon salt

1/4 teaspoon pepper

10 round buttery crackers, coarsely crushed (1/2 cup)

1. Preheat oven to 375° F. In 10-inch skillet over medium heat, melt 2 tablespoons butter or margarine; add onion and celery, and cook until tender, stirring occasionally. Spoon mixture into 1 1/2-quart casserole. Stir in soup and next 5 ingredients.

2. Cover casserole; bake 45 minutes or until hot and rice is cooked, stirring occasionally.

3. Meanwhile, in same skillet over medium heat, melt 2 more tablespoons butter or margarine; add crushed crackers and cook until lightly browned, stirring frequently. Remove from oven; sprinkle with crackers.

Seafarer's Salad with Vinaigrette Dressing

TIME: about 30 minutes—SERVINGS: 4

1 8-ounce package seashell macaroni (2 1/4 cups)

3 tablespoons cider vinegar

1 tablespoon minced parsley

1/2 teaspoon prepared mustard

1/2 teaspoon salt

1/2 teaspoon sugar

1/8 teaspoon pepper

olive or salad oil

1 small head lettuce

1/2 pound feta cheese, cut into 1/2-inch cubes

1 7 3/4-ounce can salmon, drained and separated into bite-size chunks

1 7 1/4-ounce can pitted large ripe olives, drained

1 3 3/4-ounce can sardines in oil, drained

1 large tomato, cut into 1/2-inch pieces

1 medium onion, thinly sliced

1. Prepare seashell macaroni as label directs. Meanwhile, prepare dressing: In small bowl with fork or wire whisk, mix vinegar, parsley, mustard, salt, sugar, pepper, and 1/2 cup olive or salad oil. Pour into small cruet or pitcher.

2. Drain macaroni well. With rubber spatula, gently toss macaroni with 1 tablespoon oil.

3. Line large platter with lettuce leaves. Arrange macaroni mixture and remaining ingredients on lettuce. Pass dressing to serve with salad.

Fish-and-Broccoli Mousse with Shrimp Sauce

TIME: about 2¹/₂ hours—SERVINGS: 12

4 tablespoons butter or margarine

¹/₄ cup all-purpose flour

1 cup milk

1 16-ounce package frozen sole or flounder fillets, thawed and cut into chunks

7 eggs

1 small onion, cut in half

2 cups heavy or whipping cream

salt

vegetable cooking spray

1 10-ounce package frozen chopped broccoli

pepper

¹/₂ cup shredded Swiss cheese (2 ounces)

1 15¹/₂- or 16-ounce can salmon, drained

boiling water

Creamy Shrimp Sauce (see Index)

watercress, for garnish

1. In 1-quart saucepan over low heat, melt butter or margarine; stir in flour until blended. Gradually stir in milk; cook, stirring constantly, until sauce is thickened and smooth. Set sauce aside.

2. Prepare sole mousse: In blender at medium speed or in food processor with knife blade attached, blend sole, 3 eggs, half of onion, 1 cup heavy or whipping cream, 1 teaspoon salt, and half of sauce until smooth. Spray 8-cup ring mold with vegetable cooking spray. Pour sole mixture into mold.

3. Prepare broccoli mousse: Prepare frozen chopped broccoli as label directs; drain and squeeze dry. In blender at medium speed or in food processor with knife blade attached, blend broccoli, 1 egg, ¹/₄ cup heavy or whipping cream, ¹/₂ teaspoon salt, and ¹/₈ teaspoon pepper until smooth. Stir in cheese. Spoon broccoli mixture over sole mixture.

4. Prepare salmon mousse: In blender at medium speed or in food processor with knife blade attached, blend salmon, 3 eggs, ³/₄ cup heavy or whipping cream, ¹/₄ teaspoon salt, ¹/₈ teaspoon pepper, remaining half of onion, and remaining sauce until smooth. Spoon salmon mixture evenly over broccoli mixture.

5. Set ring mold in large roasting pan; place on oven rack. Fill roasting pan with boiling water to come halfway up side of ring mold. Cover and bake in 375° F. oven 2 hours or until knife inserted in center of mousse comes out clean. Remove ring mold from pan of water; let stand on wire rack 10 minutes to allow mixture to set for easier serving. Meanwhile, prepare Creamy Shrimp Sauce.

6. To serve, invert ring mold onto warm deep platter; spoon some shrimp sauce over mousse; garnish with watercress. Pass remaining shrimp sauce in bowl.

Seafood Newburg

TIME: about 1¹/₄ hours—SERVINGS: 10

Rich Biscuits (see Index)

1 16-ounce package frozen cod, flounder, or haddock fillets

1 pound medium shrimp or 1 12-ounce package frozen shelled and deveined shrimp, thawed and drained

butter or margarine

1 pound mushrooms, sliced

¹/₃ cup all-purpose flour

1 teaspoon salt

¹/₈ teaspoon pepper

4 cups half-and-half

1 cup milk

1 10-ounce package frozen peas

1 6-ounce package frozen Alaska King or Snow crabmeat, thawed

¹/₄ cup cooking or dry sherry

³/₄ cup shredded pasteurized process cheese spread (3 ounces)

2 4-ounce jars pimento, drained and cut into thin strips

paprika

1. Prepare Rich Biscuits; keep warm.

2. Let frozen fish stand at room temperature 15 minutes to thaw slightly; then cut into bite-size chunks. Meanwhile, if using fresh shrimp, shell and devein shrimp; set aside.

3. In 4-quart saucepan over medium-high heat, in 3 tablespoons hot butter or margarine, cook mushrooms until tender, stirring occasionally. With slotted spoon, remove mushrooms to bowl; set aside.

4. In same saucepan over medium heat, melt 4 more tablespoons butter or margarine. Stir in flour, salt, and pepper until blended; cook 1 minute. Gradually stir in half-and-half and milk until mixture is smooth. Add fish chunks, shrimp, frozen peas, crabmeat with its liquid, sherry, and mushrooms; cook, stirring frequently, until fish flakes easily when tested with a fork, shrimp are tender, and mixture is slightly thickened. Stir in cheese and pimento; cook until cheese is melted. Sprinkle lightly with paprika. Serve with biscuits.

Fish and Clams Provençale with Grilled Corn

TIME: about 1¼ hours—SERVINGS: 6

6 medium ears corn (with husks)

water

1 2-pound bluefish, whiting, or other locally caught fish, or substitute 1 16-ounce package frozen fish fillets

24 littleneck clams

butter or margarine

1 small onion, diced

1 garlic clove, minced

1 8-ounce can tomatoes

⅓ cup cooking or dry white wine

1 teaspoon salt

¼ teaspoon pepper

2 tablespoons minced parsley

1. Prepare outdoor grill for barbecuing.

2. Meanwhile, gently pull back husks halfway from corn; remove silk; rewrap corn with husks. In 6-quart saucepot or kettle, place corn and enough water to cover; let soak until briquettes are ready. (Soaking corn in water with husks will keep corn moist and tender for roasting on grill.)

3. While corn is soaking, if using fresh fish, with vegetable peeler or fish scaler, remove scales from fish. With sharp knife, remove head and gut fish. Then cut fish into 2-inch chunks; rinse under running cold water. (If using frozen fish, let stand at room temperature for 15 minutes to thaw slightly, then cut into eight chunks.) With stiff brush, scrub clams well under running cold water.

4. Remove corn from water; place corn on grill over medium heat. Grill corn about 30 minutes or until tender, turning often.

5. On same grill while corn is cooking, prepare fish dish: In all-metal 5-quart Dutch oven or saucepot, melt 2 tablespoons butter or margarine. Add onion and garlic; cook until tender, stirring occasionally. Add tomatoes with their liquid, wine, salt, pepper, and 2 cups water; heat to boiling. Add fish chunks and clams; heat to boiling; then cover Dutch oven and cook 10 minutes or until fish flakes easily when tested with a fork and clams open. Sprinkle with parsley. Serve fish and clams with broth in soup bowls. Serve corn on warm platter; pass butter or margarine to spread on corn.

TO COOK ON TOP OF RANGE: About 1 hour before serving, prepare fish and clams as above. In 5-quart Dutch oven or saucepot, cook as above over medium heat. Meanwhile, remove husks and silk from corn. In 6-quart Dutch oven or saucepot over medium heat, in 1 inch boiling water, heat corn to boiling. Reduce heat to medium; cover and cook 5 to 6 minutes, until corn is tender. Serve as above.

San Francisco Seafood Casserole

TIME: about 1 hour—SERVINGS: 6

1 pound mussels or 18 littleneck clams

½ pound medium shrimp

1 pound cod or flounder fillets or 1 16-ounce package frozen cod or flounder fillets

2 tablespoons salad oil

1 medium onion, diced

1 large garlic clove, minced

1 28-ounce can tomatoes

1 8-ounce bottle clam juice

1 6-ounce can tomato paste

¾ cup cooking or dry white wine

¾ teaspoon salt

½ teaspoon basil

¼ teaspoon pepper

chopped parsley, for garnish

1. With stiff brush, scrub mussels well under running cold water; remove beards. Shell and devein shrimp; cut fish into 2-inch chunks; set aside. (If frozen fish is used, let stand at room temperature about 15 minutes to thaw slightly, then cut into chunks.)

2. Preheat oven to 350° F. In 3-quart saucepan over medium heat, in hot salad oil, cook onion and garlic until tender, stirring occasionally. Stir in tomatoes with their liquid, clam juice, tomato paste, wine, salt, basil, and pepper; heat to boiling. Pour tomato mixture into 3-quart casserole; add fish chunks, mussels, and shrimp. Cover casserole and bake 20 to 25 minutes until fish flakes easily when tested with a fork, mussels open, and shrimp are tender. Sprinkle with parsley.

Curried Seafood Bake

TIME: about 1¼ hours—SERVINGS: 6

1 16-ounce package frozen flounder or
   sole fillets

1 12-ounce package frozen shelled and
   deveined shrimp or 1 pound large shrimp

¼ cup salad oil

¼ cup all-purpose flour

2 medium celery stalks, diced

1 medium green pepper, diced

1 medium onion, diced

1 tablespoon curry powder

1 28-ounce can tomatoes

¼ cup water

2½ teaspoons sugar

1½ teaspoons salt

1. Remove frozen fish fillets and frozen shrimp from freezer; let stand at room temperature 15 minutes to thaw slightly. If using fresh shrimp, shell and devein shrimp, leaving tail part on.

2. Meanwhile, in 3-quart saucepan over medium heat, into hot salad oil, stir flour; cook, stirring frequently, until flour is dark brown (mixture will be thick). Add celery, green pepper, and onion; cook until vegetables are lightly browned and tender, stirring occasionally. Stir in curry powder; cook 1 minute. Add tomatoes with their liquid, water, sugar, and salt; heat to boiling. Reduce heat to low; keep warm.

3. Preheat oven to 350° F. With sharp knife, cut frozen fish fillets into bite-size chunks.

4. Pour sauce into 2-quart casserole; arrange fish and shrimp in sauce. Bake casserole, uncovered, 25 to 30 minutes, until fish flakes easily when tested with a fork and shrimp are opaque and tender.

Butterflied Shrimp in Wine

TIME: about 45 minutes—SERVINGS: 4

½ cup water

⅓ cup dry vermouth

1 teaspoon instant chicken-flavor bouillon

¼ teaspoon salt

⅛ teaspoon pepper

1 pound large shrimp

1 egg

about ½ cup all-purpose flour

3 tablespoons butter or margarine

2 tablespoons salad oil

2 teaspoons minced parsley

lemon slices, for garnish

1. In measuring cup, mix water, vermouth, bouillon, salt, and pepper; set aside.

2. Butterfly shrimp: Remove shells from shrimp. With knife, cut each shrimp three fourths of the way through along center back; spread each shrimp open. Rinse under running cold water to remove vein. Pat shrimp dry with paper towels.

3. In pie plate with fork, beat egg. Onto waxed paper, measure flour. Dip shrimp in egg, then coat with flour.

4. In 12-inch skillet over medium heat, heat butter or margarine and salad oil until hot and bubbly. Cook shrimp, half at a time, until lightly browned on both sides (about 1 to 2 minutes on each side), removing shrimp to plate as they brown.

5. Return shrimp to skillet; stir in vermouth mixture. Over medium-high heat, heat to boiling; cook about 1 minute to blend flavors, stirring occasionally. Spoon shrimp and sauce into platter; sprinkle with parsley; garnish with lemon slices.

Bacon Broiled Scallops

TIME: about 20 minutes—SERVINGS: 8

12 bacon slices

24 sea scallops (about 1¾ pounds)

toothpicks

salt

seasoned pepper

watercress sprigs, for garnish

1 lemon, cut in 4 wedges, for garnish

1. Preheat broiler if manufacturer directs.

2. Cut each bacon slice crosswise in half; wrap each half around a scallop, securing with a toothpick.

3. On rack in broiling pan, place scallops side by side in one layer; broil, 3 inches from heat, 8 to 10 minutes, turning once.

4. Sprinkle lightly with salt and seasoned pepper; remove picks if serving as a main dish; transfer to platter. Garnish with watercress and lemon.

Curried Shrimp Salad

TIME: about 2 hours—SERVINGS: 6

2 pounds large shrimp

6 cups water

salt

1 small zucchini

½ cup mayonnaise

1 tablespoon lemon juice

2 teaspoons curry powder

lettuce leaves

1. Peel and devein shrimp. In 4-quart saucepan over high heat, heat water and 1 tablespoon salt to boiling. Add shrimp; heat to boiling, stirring occasionally. Cook 1 minute or until shrimp are tender; drain. Cover and refrigerate shrimp until chilled, at least 1 hour.

2. Cut zucchini crosswise into thin slices; cut slices into thin strips. In medium bowl with rubber spatula, mix mayonnaise, lemon juice, curry powder, and ½ teaspoon salt. Stir in shrimp and zucchini to coat with dressing. Serve on lettuce leaves.

Beans, Rice, and Pasta

Dutch-Oven Beans for a Crowd

TIME: about 3¹/₂ hours—SERVINGS: 12

1 16-ounce package dry pea (navy) beans

1 cup dry baby lima beans

1 cup dry red kidney beans

water

2 tablespoons salad oil

2 medium green peppers, cut into
   1-inch-wide strips

2 medium onions, diced

3 garlic cloves, minced

3 tablespoons brown sugar

4 teaspoons salt

¹/₂ teaspoon pepper

¹/₄ teaspoon ground cloves

1 28-ounce can tomatoes

1 12-ounce can tomato paste

1 1¹/₂-pound kielbasa (smoked Polish
   sausage), cut into 1¹/₂-inch chunks

1. Rinse beans in running cold water and discard any stones or shriveled beans. In 8-quart Dutch oven over high heat, heat beans and 12 cups water to boiling; cook 3 minutes. Remove Dutch oven from heat; cover and let stand 1 hour. Drain and rinse beans; set aside.

2. In same Dutch oven over medium-high heat, in hot salad oil, cook green peppers, onions, and garlic until tender, stirring occasionally. Return beans to Dutch oven; stir in brown sugar, salt, pepper, cloves, and 6 cups water; over high heat, heat to boiling. Reduce heat to low; cover and simmer 1 hour, stirring occasionally. Stir in tomatoes with their liquid, tomato paste, and kielbasa, stirring to mix well and break up tomatoes. Cover and simmer 30 minutes longer or until beans are tender. Skim off fat from liquid in Dutch oven.

Camper's Bean Stew

TIME: about 1 hour—SERVINGS: 8

3 16-ounce cans small white beans,
   drained

1 16-ounce package knackwurst, cut into
   1-inch pieces

1 8¹/₄-ounce can sliced carrots, drained

¹/₂ cup packed brown sugar

2 tablespoons prepared mustard

2 tablespoons catchup

2 tablespoons cider vinegar

1 teaspoon salt

1 teaspoon instant minced onion

¹/₄ teaspoon pepper

1. Prepare outdoor grill for barbecuing.

2. In all-metal 4-quart heavy saucepan, mix all ingredients.

3. Place saucepan on grill over medium heat; cover and cook 45 minutes to blend flavors, stirring occasionally.

TO COOK ON TOP OF RANGE: About 30 minutes before serving, in 4-quart saucepan over high heat, heat all ingredients to boiling. Reduce heat to low; cover and simmer 20 minutes, stirring occasionally.

Ranch-style Beans

TIME: about 3 hours—SERVINGS: 6

1 16-ounce package dry pinto beans

water

2 tablespoons salad oil

2 medium onions, sliced

2 garlic cloves, minced

1 10-ounce can whole green chilies,
  drained and cut into bite-size pieces

1 or 2 canned jalapeño chilies, diced

1 tablespoon salt

1 teaspoon sugar

1 teaspoon ground cumin

1 28-ounce can tomatoes

1/2 teaspoon oregano leaves

2 cups shredded Monterey Jack cheese
  (8 ounces)

1. Rinse beans in running cold water and discard any stones or shriveled beans. In 5-quart Dutch oven over high heat, heat beans and 8 cups water to boiling; cook 3 minutes. Remove Dutch oven from heat; cover and let stand 1 hour. Drain and rinse beans; set aside.

2. In same Dutch oven over medium heat, in hot salad oil, cook onions and garlic until tender, stirring occasionally. Add beans, chilies, salt, sugar, cumin, and 3 cups water; over high heat, heat to boiling. Reduce heat to low; cover and simmer 1 hour, stirring occasionally. Add tomatoes with their liquid, and oregano, stirring to mix well and break up tomatoes; over high heat, heat to boiling. Reduce heat to low; cover and simmer about 30 minutes longer or until beans are tender. Stir in half of the cheese and cook until cheese is melted, stirring occasionally.

3. Spoon bean mixture into large bowl; sprinkle with remaining cheese.

Cassoulet

TIME: about 4 hours—SERVINGS: 12

3 cups dry pea (navy) beans

water

1 4 1/2- to 5-pound fresh or frozen (thawed)
  duckling

1/2 pound salt pork, diced

1 pound hot Italian sausage links

1 5-inch square cheesecloth

4 parsley sprigs

1 celery stalk, cut into 1-inch pieces

1 bay leaf

2 garlic cloves

1/2 teaspoon thyme leaves

1/4 teaspoon whole cloves

6 large carrots, each cut into bite-size
  pieces

2 large onions, quartered

1 cup cooking or dry white wine

3/4 teaspoon salt

1/2 teaspoon pepper

1 8-ounce can tomato sauce

1. Rinse beans in running cold water and discard any stones or shriveled beans. In 8-quart Dutch oven over high heat, heat beans and 12 cups water to boiling; cook 3 minutes. Remove Dutch oven from heat; cover and let stand 1 hour. Drain and rinse beans; return beans to Dutch oven.

2. Meanwhile, rinse duckling, its giblets, and neck with running cold water. With sharp knife, cut off as much fatty skin as possible. With poultry shears, cut duckling and neck into 2-inch pieces. (Refrigerate giblets for soup another day.)

3. In 12-inch skillet over medium heat, cook salt pork until lightly browned. With slotted spoon, remove salt pork to large bowl; set aside. In drippings remaining in skillet, cook duckling pieces until browned on all sides; remove duckling to bowl with salt pork. Pour off drippings; reserve 2 tablespoons.

4. In same skillet over medium heat, heat sausages and 1/4 cup water to boiling. Reduce heat to low; cover; simmer 5 minutes. Remove cover; continue cooking, turning sausages frequently, until sausages are well browned. Remove sausages to paper towels to drain. Refrigerate.

5. In cheesecloth square, tie parsley, celery, bay leaf, garlic, thyme, and cloves; add to beans in Dutch oven. Stir in carrots, onions, wine, salt, pepper, salt pork, duckling, reserved drippings, and 7 1/2 cups water; over high heat, heat to boiling. Cover Dutch oven and bake in 350° F. oven 2 hours. Stir in tomato sauce and sausages; cover and bake 30 minutes longer or until beans and duckling are tender, stirring mixture occasionally.

6. To serve, discard spice bag. (Bean mixture will become very thick upon standing. Stir in enough water to make desired consistency and reheat if necessary.) Spoon each serving into soup bowl; serve with knife, fork, and spoon.

Island Pork and Beans

TIME: about 3¹/₂ hours—SERVINGS: 8

1 16-ounce package dry red kidney beans
water
1 pound ground pork
1 large onion, diced
2 tablespoons brown sugar
2 tablespoons Worcestershire
2¹/₂ teaspoons salt
1 teaspoon dry mustard
¹/₂ teaspoon pepper
1 8¹/₄-ounce can crushed pineapple
¹/₂ cup catchup

1. Rinse beans in running cold water and discard any stones or shriveled beans. In 8-quart Dutch oven over high heat, heat beans and 8 cups water to boiling; cook 3 minutes. Remove from heat; cover; let stand 1 hour. Drain and rinse beans.

2. In same Dutch oven over medium-high heat, cook pork and onion until pan juices evaporate and pork is browned, stirring often. Return beans to Dutch oven; add sugar, Worcestershire, salt, mustard, pepper, and 4 cups water; over high heat, heat to boiling. Reduce heat to low; cover and simmer 1¹/₄ hours.

3. Add pineapple with its liquid and catchup; over high heat, heat to boiling. Reduce heat to low; cover and simmer 15 minutes or until beans are tender.

Black Beans and Rice

TIME: about 4 hours—SERVINGS: 4

1 16-ounce package dry black beans
water
¹/₂ pound salt pork, diced
1 medium onion, diced
1 medium celery stalk, diced
1³/₄ teaspoons salt
¹/₄ teaspoon crushed red pepper
1¹/₂ cups regular long-grain rice
2 tablespoons chopped parsley, for garnish

1. Rinse beans in running cold water and discard any stones or shriveled beans. In 8-quart Dutch oven over high heat, heat beans and 8 cups water to boiling; cook 3 minutes. Remove Dutch oven from heat; cover and let stand 1 hour. Drain and rinse beans; set aside.

2. In same Dutch oven over medium heat, cook salt pork until lightly browned. Add onion and celery, and cook until vegetables are tender, stirring occasionally.

3. Return beans to Dutch oven; add salt, crushed red pepper, and 5¹/₂ cups water; over high heat, heat to boiling. Reduce heat to low; cover and simmer 2 hours or until beans are tender, stirring occasionally.

4. About 30 minutes before beans are done, prepare rice as label directs.

5. To serve, spoon bean mixture into deep dish. Arrange cooked rice around beans. Garnish with chopped parsley.

South-of-the-Border Casserole

TIME: about 1¹/₄ hours—SERVINGS: 6

3 tablespoons salad oil
8 6-inch packaged corn tortillas
¹/₂ pound ground beef
1 medium onion, diced
1 small garlic clove, minced
2 15¹/₂-ounce cans pinto beans
1 28-ounce can tomatoes
1 6-ounce can tomato paste
1 4-ounce can chopped green chilies, drained
2 teaspoons sugar
1 teaspoon salt
¹/₂ teaspoon oregano leaves
¹/₄ teaspoon pepper
1 cup coarsely shredded sharp Cheddar cheese

1. In 12-inch skillet over medium heat, in hot salad oil, fry 1 tortilla at a time, a few seconds on each side until soft and blistered. Remove tortilla to paper towels to drain. Cut tortillas into ¹/₂-inch strips.

2. In same skillet over medium-high heat, cook beef, onion, and garlic until pan juices evaporate and beef is browned, stirring occasionally. Remove from heat. Stir in pinto beans with their liquid, tomatoes with their liquid, and remaining ingredients except cheese.

3. Preheat oven to 350° F. In 13″ by 9″ baking dish, arrange one third of ground-beef mixture; top with one third of tortilla strips. Repeat layering, ending with tortilla strips. Sprinkle cheese on top. Bake 30 minutes or until hot.

Skillet Split-Pea Dinner

TIME: about 50 minutes—SERVINGS: 4

3 cups water

1 cup split peas

1 teaspoon salt

1/2 teaspoon basil

11/2 cups cubed cooked ham

1 medium green pepper, sliced into thin strips

1. In 10-inch skillet over medium-high heat, heat water, split peas, salt, and basil to boiling. Reduce heat to low; cover and simmer 35 minutes.

2. Add ham and green pepper; cover and cook 10 minutes longer or until peas are tender.

Vegetarian Casserole

TIME: about 11/2 hours—SERVINGS: 8

salad oil

1 medium eggplant, cut into 1-inch chunks

1 garlic clove, sliced

3 small zucchini, cut into 1/2-inch slices

3 medium onions, cut into 1/2-inch slices

1 15- to 20-ounce can white kidney (cannellini) beans

1 151/2- to 20-ounce can garbanzo beans

1 6-ounce can tomato paste

1/4 cup minced parsley

1 teaspoon Italian seasoning

1 teaspoon salt

1/4 teaspoon pepper

1 16-ounce package mozzarella cheese, cut into 8 slices

1. In 5-quart Dutch oven or saucepot over medium-high heat, in 1/2 cup hot salad oil, cook eggplant until lightly browned, stirring frequently, and adding more oil, if necessary. With slotted spoon, remove eggplant to paper towels to drain.

2. Preheat oven to 375° F. In same Dutch oven in 3 tablespoons more hot salad oil, cook garlic until lightly browned; discard garlic. Add zucchini and onions; cook over medium-high heat, stirring, until zucchini is browned.

3. Gently stir in eggplant, beans, and remaining ingredients except cheese. Spoon into 13" by 9" baking dish. Bake, uncovered, 35 minutes or until eggplant is fork-tender.

4. Arrange cheese slices on vegetables; bake 5 minutes longer or until melted.

Turkish Bean Salad

TIME: about 5 hours—SERVINGS: 10

1 16-ounce package dry Great Northern, navy, or pea beans

6 cups water

3 chicken-flavor bouillon cubes or envelopes

1 bay leaf

1 6-ounce can pitted ripe olives, drained and halved

2 large tomatoes, chopped

1/2 cup olive or salad oil

1/2 cup lemon juice

2 tablespoons crumbled dried mint or 1/3 cup chopped fresh mint

1 tablespoon salt

1 tablespoon sugar

1/4 teaspoon white pepper

mint leaves, for garnish

1. Rinse beans under running cold water, and discard any stones or shriveled beans.

2. In 8-quart Dutch oven over high heat, heat beans, water, bouillon, and bay leaf to boiling; boil 2 minutes. Remove from heat; cover and allow to stand 1 hour.

3. Over high heat, return beans to boiling. Reduce heat to low; cover and simmer beans 1 hour or until tender but firm, stirring occasionally. Drain beans; discard bay leaf.

4. In large bowl with rubber spatula, gently combine beans, olives, and remaining ingredients except mint leaves. Cover and refrigerate until well chilled.

5. To serve, spoon into salad dish, and garnish with mint leaves.

Tuna-and-Bean Salad

TIME: about 30 minutes—SERVINGS: 4

¹/₃ **cup cider vinegar**

¹/₄ **cup olive or salad oil**

1¹/₂ **teaspoons salt**

¹/₂ **teaspoon pepper**

1 **15¹/₂- to 20-ounce can garbanzo beans, drained**

1 **6¹/₂- to 7-ounce can tuna, drained and separated into chunks**

1 **small head red cabbage (about 1 pound), diced**

¹/₂ **cup pitted ripe olives, sliced**

¹/₄ **cup minced parsley**

¹/₂ **small head lettuce, separated into leaves**

1 **29-ounce can sliced cling peaches, drained**

1. In large bowl, mix vinegar, olive oil, salt, and pepper. Add garbanzo beans, tuna, red cabbage, olives, and parsley. With rubber spatula, toss gently to mix well.

2. On platter, arrange lettuce leaves. Spoon tuna salad on lettuce. Arrange sliced peaches on platter with salad.

No-Cook Bean Salad with Tuna

TIME: about 20 minutes or start early in day—SERVINGS: 6

¹/₂ **cup cider vinegar**

¹/₃ **cup olive oil**

2¹/₂ **teaspoons sugar**

³/₄ **teaspoon salt**

¹/₄ **teaspoon pepper**

2 **16- to 20-ounce cans white kidney beans (cannellini), drained**

1 **7¹/₄-ounce jar roasted sweet red peppers, drained and cut into thin strips**

1 **6¹/₂- to 7-ounce can tuna, drained and broken into large chunks**

¹/₄ **cup pitted ripe olives, each cut in half**

2 **tablespoons chopped parsley**

lettuce leaves

1. In large bowl with fork, mix first 5 ingredients. Gently stir in white kidney beans and remaining ingredients except lettuce.

2. Line bowl with lettuce leaves; top with bean mixture. Serve salad at room temperature, or cover and refrigerate to serve chilled later.

Rice with Peas

TIME: about 30 minutes—SERVINGS: 8

1¹/₄ **cups regular long-grain rice**

1 **10-ounce package frozen peas, thawed**

1 **tablespoon butter or margarine**

Prepare rice as label directs; when done, stir in peas and butter or margarine; heat through.

Herbed Orange Rice

TIME: about 45 minutes—SERVINGS: 6

4 tablespoons butter or margarine

1/3 cup chopped celery (with leaves)

2 tablespoons minced onion

1 1/2 cups water

1 tablespoon grated orange peel

1 cup orange juice

1 teaspoon salt

1/8 teaspoon thyme leaves

1 cup regular long-grain rice or 3/4 cup parboiled rice

1. In 2-quart saucepan over medium heat, in hot butter or margarine, cook celery and onion until tender, about 5 minutes.

2. Add water, grated orange peel, orange juice, salt, and thyme leaves. Heat to boiling; stir in rice. Reduce heat to low; cover and simmer mixture 15 to 20 minutes, until rice is tender and all liquid is absorbed. Fluff lightly with fork before serving.

Jasmine Rice

TIME: about 1 hour—SERVINGS: 8

3 cups water

3 jasmine or oolong tea bags

1 1/2 cups regular long-grain rice

4 tablespoons butter or margarine

1 1/2 teaspoons salt

celery leaves, for garnish

1. In 3-quart saucepan over high heat, heat water to boiling. Remove saucepan from heat; add tea bags; let steep 15 minutes. Discard tea bags.

2. Over high heat, heat tea in saucepan to boiling; add rice, butter or margarine, and salt. Reduce heat to low; cover and simmer 20 minutes or until rice is tender and all liquid is absorbed. Remove saucepan from heat.

3. If you like, divide rice into eight portions. Pack one portion of rice at a time into a 5-ounce timbale mold or small custard cup; unmold rice onto warm plate. (Or, use an ice-cream scoop.) Garnish each with a celery leaf.

Pork Fried Rice

TIME: about 2 1/2 hours or start early in day—SERVINGS: 6

1 1/2 cups regular long-grain rice (or 4 1/2 cups cold, cooked rice)

1 pound pork loin sirloin cutlets

1 tablespoon cooking or dry sherry

1 tablespoon soy sauce

1 teaspoon cornstarch

salt

2 eggs

1 10-ounce package frozen chopped spinach, thawed and squeezed dry

salad oil

1. Prepare rice as label directs; refrigerate rice until chilled.

2. About 30 minutes before serving, with sharp knife, cut pork loin sirloin cutlets into matchstick-thin strips. In small bowl, mix pork, sherry, soy sauce, cornstarch, and 1 1/4 teaspoons salt; set aside. In medium bowl with fork, beat eggs and 1/2 teaspoon salt; set aside. Mince spinach; set aside.

3. In 12-inch skillet over high heat, in 2 tablespoons hot salad oil, cook pork mixture until pork loses its pink color, about 3 to 4 minutes, stirring quickly and frequently. Spoon pork mixture into small bowl; keep warm.

4. In same skillet over high heat, in 2 more tablespoons hot salad oil, cook eggs, stirring quickly and constantly until eggs are the size of peas and leave side of pan. Reduce heat to low. Push eggs to one side of skillet. In same skillet, gently stir rice and 3 tablespoons salad oil until rice is well coated with oil. Add pork mixture and spinach; gently stir to mix ingredients in skillet; heat through.

Rice Supper Mold

TIME: about 1¹/₄ hours—SERVINGS: 6

1 **chicken-flavor bouillon cube or envelope**

water

butter or margarine

salt

pepper

1¹/₂ **cups regular long-grain rice**

1 **pound sweet Italian sausage links**

¹/₂ **pound medium mushrooms, thinly sliced**

1 **small onion, diced**

1 **cup milk**

1 **10-ounce package frozen peas, thawed**

1 **4-ounce package shredded Cheddar cheese (1 cup)**

2 **4- or 1 7-ounce jar diced pimento, drained**

3 **small zucchini, sliced (1 pound)**

1. In 4-quart saucepan over high heat, heat chicken-flavor bouillon, 3 cups water, 1 tablespoon butter or margarine, 1¹/₄ teaspoons salt, and ¹/₄ teaspoon pepper to boiling; stir in rice. Reduce heat to low; cover and simmer 20 minutes or until rice is tender and all liquid is absorbed.

2. Meanwhile, in 10-inch skillet over medium heat, heat sausages and ¹/₄ cup water to boiling. Reduce heat to low; cover and simmer 5 minutes. Remove cover and cook until sausages are well browned on all sides. Remove sausages to paper towels to drain. Cut sausages into ¹/₄-inch-thick slices.

3. In drippings remaining in skillet over medium heat, cook mushrooms and onion until tender, stirring occasionally. Gently stir vegetable mixture, sausages, milk, peas, cheese, and pimentos into rice.

4. Preheat oven to 350° F. Grease well 2¹/₂-quart oven-safe bowl. Spoon rice mixture into bowl, packing firmly. Cover bowl with foil; bake 30 minutes. Remove bowl from oven and let stand 5 minutes.

5. Meanwhile, in same skillet over medium heat, melt 3 tablespoons butter or margarine; add zucchini, ¹/₂ teaspoon salt, and ¹/₄ teaspoon pepper; cook over medium-high heat until zucchini is tender-crisp, stirring often.

6. To serve, with metal spatula, gently loosen rice mixture from bowl and invert onto warm large platter. Spoon zucchini around rice.

Vegetable Rice with Seafood Sauce

TIME: about 1 hour—SERVINGS: 8

1 **16-ounce package frozen cod, flounder, or haddock fillets**

butter or margarine

¹/₂ **pound mushrooms, sliced**

2 **medium carrots, thinly sliced**

1 **small onion, diced**

water

salt

1¹/₂ **cups regular long-grain rice**

1 **10-ounce package frozen peas, partially thawed**

dry or cooking sherry

¹/₄ **cup all-purpose flour**

¹/₈ **teaspoon white pepper**

1¹/₂ **cups milk**

1 **4-ounce package shredded Cheddar cheese (1 cup)**

1. Remove frozen fish fillets from freezer; let stand about 15 minutes to thaw slightly. Meanwhile, in 4-quart saucepan over medium heat, melt 3 tablespoons butter; add mushrooms, carrots, and onion, and cook until tender, stirring occasionally. With slotted spoon, remove vegetables to small bowl.

2. In same saucepan over high heat, heat 3 cups water and 1¹/₂ teaspoons salt to boiling; stir in rice. Reduce heat to low; cover and simmer 20 minutes or until rice is tender and all liquid is absorbed. Stir in peas and reserved vegetables; heat through; keep warm.

3. With knife, cut frozen fish fillets into bite-size chunks. In 3-quart saucepan over high heat, heat 1 cup water, 1 tablespoon sherry, and fish chunks to boiling. Reduce heat to low; cover and simmer about 5 minutes or until fish flakes easily when tested with a fork. With slotted spoon, remove fish to plate; reserve ¹/₂ cup fish-cooking liquid; wipe saucepan clean.

4. In same saucepan over low heat, melt 4 tablespoons butter; stir in flour, pepper, and ¹/₄ teaspoon salt. Gradually stir in milk and reserved fish-cooking liquid; cook, stirring constantly, until thickened and smooth. Stir in cheese and 2 tablespoons sherry; cook until cheese is melted, stirring constantly. Add fish; heat.

5. To serve, spoon rice mixture into deep platter; spoon fish mixture over rice.

Brown-Rice Cabbage Roll-ups

TIME: about 2¹/₂ hours—SERVINGS: 6

1 cup brown rice

1 medium head green cabbage (about 3 pounds)

water

1 8-ounce package mozzarella cheese, diced

2 eggs

2 15-ounce cans tomato sauce

salt

sugar

pepper

¹/₂ teaspoon basil

¹/₈ teaspoon fennel seeds

1 small eggplant (about ³/₄ pound), cut into bite-size chunks

1 medium zucchini (about ¹/₂ pound), cut into bite-size chunks

1. Prepare brown rice as label directs.

2. Meanwhile, discard tough green outer leaves from cabbage; with sharp knife, remove core. Fill 8-quart Dutch oven or saucepot three fourths full with water; heat to boiling. Place cabbage in water, cut side up. Using two large spoons, gently separate leaves as outer leaves soften slightly; remove 12 large leaves from cabbage and let drain in colander. Coarsely shred remaining cabbage; set aside. Trim rib of each reserved leaf very thin.

3. To brown rice, add cheese, eggs, ¹/₂ cup tomato sauce, 1 teaspoon salt, 1 teaspoon sugar, and ¹/₄ teaspoon pepper.

4. On center of each cabbage leaf, place about ¹/₃ cupful brown-rice mixture. Fold two sides of cabbage leaf toward center over rice, overlapping edges. From one narrow edge, roll jelly-roll fashion. Set cabbage rolls aside.

5. In same Dutch oven, mix shredded cabbage, 1¹/₂ cups water, basil, fennel, 4 teaspoons sugar, 1 teaspoon salt, ¹/₄ teaspoon pepper, and remaining tomato sauce. Place stuffed-cabbage rolls, seam side down, and eggplant in sauce; over high heat, heat mixture to boiling. Reduce heat to low; cover and simmer 25 minutes, stirring occasionally. Add zucchini; over high heat, heat to boiling. Reduce heat to low; cover and simmer 25 minutes longer or until cabbage rolls and vegetables are tender.

Summer-Garden Rice

TIME: about 45 minutes—SERVINGS: 4

2 tablespoons butter or margarine

1 small onion, diced

1 garlic clove, minced

1 chicken-flavor bouillon cube or envelope

water

salt

cracked pepper

1 cup regular long-grain rice

3 tablespoons salad oil

¹/₂ small bunch broccoli, cut into 2" by 1" pieces

2 large carrots, thinly sliced diagonally

2 medium yellow straightneck squash (8 ounces each), cut into matchstick-thin strips

1 cup half-and-half

1 tablespoon all-purpose flour

¹/₂ pound Monterey Jack cheese, shredded (2 cups)

2 medium tomatoes, diced

1. In 3-quart saucepan over medium heat, melt butter or margarine. Add onion and garlic; cook until tender, stirring occasionally. Stir in bouillon, 2 cups water, ¹/₂ teaspoon salt, and ¹/₈ teaspoon pepper; over high heat, heat to boiling. Stir in rice; reduce heat to low; cover and simmer 20 minutes or until rice is tender and all liquid is absorbed.

2. About 10 minutes before rice is done, in 12-inch skillet over medium-high heat, in hot salad oil, stir broccoli and carrots until well coated; add ¹/₄ cup water; cover and cook 3 minutes. Add yellow squash, ¹/₂ teaspoon salt, and ¹/₈ teaspoon pepper; cook, uncovered, until vegetables are tender-crisp, stirring frequently. Reduce heat to medium.

3. In cup, stir half-and-half and flour; gradually stir into liquid in skillet. Cook until mixture is slightly thickened, stirring constantly. Stir in 1¹/₂ cups shredded cheese until cheese is melted.

4. When rice is done, gently stir in tomatoes and remaining ¹/₂ cup shredded cheese, stirring until tomatoes are heated through and cheese is melted. Spoon rice mixture onto warm large platter; spoon vegetable mixture on rice.

Pork-and-Rice Medley

TIME: about 30 minutes—SERVINGS: 4

1²/₃ cups regular long-grain rice

1¹/₂ cups diced cooked pork

3 tablespoons soy sauce

1 10-ounce package frozen peas

boiling water

2 eggs

salt

salad oil

1 2-ounce jar diced pimento, drained

¹/₈ teaspoon pepper

1 green onion, thinly sliced

1. Prepare rice as label directs. Meanwhile, in medium bowl, mix pork with soy sauce; set aside. In another medium bowl, place frozen peas; cover with boiling water and let stand 5 minutes to "cook" peas; drain.

2. In small bowl with fork, beat eggs with ¹/₄ teaspoon salt. In 12-inch skillet over high heat, heat 2 tablespoons salad oil until very hot. Pour in egg mixture; cook, stirring quickly and constantly with spoon, until eggs are the size of peas and leave side of skillet. Push eggs to one side of skillet.

3. Reduce heat to medium. In same skillet, gently stir rice and 3 tablespoons salad oil until rice is well coated with oil. Stir pork mixture, peas, pimento, pepper, and ¹/₄ teaspoon salt into rice and eggs; heat. Spoon rice mixture into warm bowl; sprinkle with green onion.

Greek Rice Casserole

TIME: about 1 hour—SERVINGS: 8

1¹/₂ cups regular long-grain rice

1 pound ground beef

1 small onion, diced

1 small garlic clove, minced

1 16-ounce can tomatoes

¹/₂ teaspoon sugar

¹/₈ teaspoon pepper

¹/₈ teaspoon ground cinnamon

salt

4 eggs

2 cups milk

³/₄ cup grated Parmesan cheese (3 ounces)

4 tablespoons butter or margarine

¹/₄ cup all-purpose flour

1. Prepare rice as label directs. Grease 2-quart casserole.

2. Meanwhile, in 10-inch skillet over medium-high heat, cook ground beef, onion, and garlic until all pan juices evaporate and beef is well browned and onion is tender, stirring mixture occasionally. Add tomatoes with their liquid, sugar, pepper, cinnamon, and 1 teaspoon salt, stirring to mix well and break up tomatoes. Remove skillet from heat.

3. In medium bowl with fork or wire whisk, beat eggs, milk, and cheese until well mixed; set aside. In 2-quart saucepan over medium heat, melt butter or margarine. Stir in flour and ¹/₄ teaspoon salt until smooth; cook 1 minute. Gradually stir in egg mixture and cook until thickened and smooth, stirring constantly. (Do not boil, or custard will curdle.) Remove saucepan from heat.

4. Preheat oven to 350° F. Spoon half of rice into casserole; spoon meat mixture onto rice; top with remaining rice. Pour custard over rice. Bake 25 to 30 minutes, until custard is set.

Tomato Jambalaya

TIME: about 40 minutes—SERVINGS: 4

1 cup regular long-grain rice

2 tablespoons salad oil

1 medium onion, diced

1 medium green pepper, cut into thin strips

4 medium tomatoes (about 1¹/₂ pounds), cut into wedges

1 tablespoon brown sugar

¹/₂ teaspoon salt

¹/₄ teaspoon basil

¹/₈ teaspoon pepper

water

1 tablespoon all-purpose flour

2 6-ounce packages sliced cooked ham, diced

1. Prepare rice as label directs; keep warm.

2. Meanwhile, in 12-inch skillet over medium heat, in hot salad oil, cook onion and green pepper until tender, stirring occasionally. Add tomatoes, next 4 ingredients, and ¹/₄ cup water. Over high heat, heat to boiling. Reduce heat to low; cover and simmer 20 minutes, stirring occasionally.

3. In cup, mix 1 tablespoon water and flour; gradually stir into mixture in skillet; cook, stirring, until slightly thickened. Stir in ham; heat.

4. To serve, spoon rice into warm deep platter. Spoon tomato mixture over rice.

Cheesy Rice Salad

TIME: about 2 hours or start early in day—SERVINGS: 6

1 cup regular long-grain rice

$^1/_2$ cup mayonnaise

$^1/_3$ cup milk

2 tablespoons lemon juice

2 tablespoons olive or salad oil

2 teaspoons mild curry powder

1 teaspoon salt

$^1/_4$ pound Swiss or Edam cheese, cut into $^1/_2$-inch cubes

1 29- to 30-ounce can sliced cling peaches, drained and cut into bite-size pieces

1 $6^1/_2$- or 7-ounce can tuna, drained and flaked

2 large celery stalks, diced

lettuce leaves

1. Prepare rice as label directs. Cover and refrigerate until chilled.

2. About 30 minutes before serving, in large bowl, mix mayonnaise and next 5 ingredients. Stir in cooked rice, Swiss cheese, peaches, tuna, and celery.

3. Line platter with lettuce leaves. Spoon salad mixture on lettuce.

Sausage-and-Rice Skillet

TIME: about $1^1/_4$ hours—SERVINGS: 6

2 pounds hot Italian sausage links

water

2 medium onions, sliced

1 medium green pepper, cut into bite-size pieces

2 cups regular long-grain rice

$^1/_3$ cup catchup

$^1/_2$ teaspoon salt

1 teaspoon oregano leaves

$^1/_2$ teaspoon sugar

2 chicken-flavor bouillon cubes or envelopes

1. In 12-inch skillet over medium heat, heat sausages and $^1/_4$ cup water to boiling. Cover skillet and simmer sausages 5 minutes. Remove cover; cook until sausages are well browned. With slotted spoon, remove sausages to paper towels to drain.

2. In same skillet in drippings, cook onions and green pepper until tender. Spoon off drippings remaining in skillet. Return sausages to skillet; add rice, catchup, salt, oregano, sugar, bouillon, and $4^3/_4$ cups water; over high heat, heat to boiling. Reduce heat to low; cover and simmer 25 minutes or until rice is tender, stirring occasionally.

Fettucini Alfredo

TIME: about 30 minutes—SERVINGS: 8

1 8-ounce package fettucini noodles

4 tablespoons butter or margarine, melted

$^1/_4$ cup grated Parmesan cheese

2 tablespoons half-and-half

$^1/_4$ teaspoon salt

$^1/_8$ teaspoon pepper

1. Prepare noodles as label directs; drain noodles in colander, and keep hot.

2. Meanwhile, in warm serving dish, combine butter, cheese, half-and-half, salt, and pepper.

3. Toss hot noodles with cheese mixture to coat well. Serve immediately. Pass more grated cheese, if you like, to sprinkle over servings. Serve as an accompaniment.

Spaghetti with Herbed Tomatoes and Cheese

TIME: about 30 minutes—SERVINGS: 4

1 8-ounce package spaghetti
2 tablespoons olive or salad oil
1 small garlic clove, minced
3 medium tomatoes, diced
2 teaspoons basil
¹/₂ teaspoon salt
1 4-ounce package shredded mozzarella cheese (1 cup)
¹/₄ cup grated Parmesan cheese

1. In 6-quart saucepot, cook spaghetti as label directs.

2. Meanwhile, in 2-quart saucepan over medium heat, in hot olive oil, cook garlic until tender. Stir in tomatoes, basil, and salt; heat through, stirring occasionally.

3. Drain spaghetti. Return spaghetti to saucepot; toss gently with tomato mixture, mozzarella, and Parmesan cheese. Serve immediately.

Pasta with Chicken, Ham, and Zucchini

TIME: about 30 minutes—SERVINGS: 6

1 8-ounce package spaghetti
1 whole large chicken breast, boned and skinned
1 tablespoon cooking or dry sherry
2 teaspoons cornstarch
salt
salad oil
2 medium zucchini (1 pound), thinly sliced
1 4-ounce package sliced cooked ham, cut into ¹/₄-inch-wide strips
¹/₂ cup half-and-half
3 tablespoons butter or margarine
¹/₄ teaspoon pepper
2 tablespoons grated Parmesan cheese

1. In 6-quart saucepot, prepare spaghetti as label directs.

2. Meanwhile, cut chicken breast lengthwise in half. Then, with knife held in slanting position almost parallel to the cutting surface, slice across width of each half into ¹/₈-inch-thick slices. In medium bowl, mix chicken, sherry, cornstarch, and ¹/₄ teaspoon salt; set aside.

3. In 12-inch skillet over medium heat, in 1 tablespoon hot salad oil, cook zucchini and ¹/₄ teaspoon salt until zucchini is tender-crisp, stirring occasionally. With slotted spoon, remove zucchini to medium bowl.

4. In same skillet over medium-high heat, in 3 more tablespoons hot salad oil, cook chicken mixture until chicken loses its pink color, stirring frequently. Remove chicken to bowl with zucchini.

5. Drain spaghetti. Return spaghetti to saucepot; gently stir in chicken mixture, ham, half-and-half, butter or margarine, and pepper; heat through. Toss spaghetti mixture with Parmesan cheese; serve immediately. (Mixture becomes thick upon standing.)

Linguine with Clam Sauce Florentine

TIME: about 35 minutes—SERVINGS: 6

1 16-ounce package linguine
1 10-ounce package frozen chopped spinach
boiling water
2 10-ounce cans whole baby clams
¹/₄ cup olive or salad oil
4 tablespoons butter or margarine
1 small onion, minced
1 small garlic clove, minced
¹/₄ teaspoon salt
grated Parmesan cheese (optional)
freshly ground black pepper (optional)

1. Prepare linguine as label directs. Drain; keep warm.

2. Meanwhile, in medium bowl, place frozen spinach; cover with boiling water and let stand 10 minutes, breaking up spinach with fork. Drain.

3. Drain clams, reserving liquid; set aside. In 2-quart saucepan over medium heat, in hot olive oil and butter or margarine, cook onion and garlic until tender, stirring occasionally. Add salt and clam liquid; heat to boiling. Reduce heat to low; cover and simmer 10 minutes to blend flavors. Add clams and spinach; heat through, stirring occasionally.

4. Serve linguine with clam sauce. If you like, pass Parmesan cheese and black pepper to sprinkle over servings.

Fettucini Florentine

TIME: about 30 minutes—SERVINGS: 8

1 12-ounce package fettucini noodles

1 10-ounce package frozen chopped spinach

boiling water

3 tablespoons olive or salad oil

1 small onion, thinly sliced

1 15- or 16-ounce container ricotta cheese (2 cups)

1½ cups milk

1½ teaspoons salt

2 tablespoons slivered cooked ham

grated Parmesan cheese (optional)

freshly ground black pepper (optional)

1. In 6-quart saucepot, prepare fettucini as label directs; drain. Return fettucini to saucepot; cover and keep warm.

2. Meanwhile, place frozen chopped spinach in medium bowl; cover with boiling water, and let stand 5 minutes to thaw. Drain spinach well; squeeze dry. In 10-inch skillet over medium heat, in hot olive or salad oil, cook onion until tender, stirring occasionally. Add spinach and cook, stirring frequently, until mixture is heated through.

3. To fettucini in saucepot, add spinach mixture, ricotta cheese, milk, and salt; over low heat, heat through, gently tossing to mix well.

4. To serve, spoon fettucini mixture onto warm large platter; top with slivered ham. Pass grated Parmesan cheese and freshly ground black pepper, if you like, to sprinkle over each serving.

Creamy Fettucini with Salmon

TIME: about 30 minutes—SERVINGS: 4

½ 12-ounce package fettucini noodles

6 tablespoons butter or margarine

½ pound mushrooms, sliced

2 tablespoons minced onion

2 tablespoons all-purpose flour

2 cups milk

2 tablespoons cooking or dry sherry

¾ teaspoon salt

¼ teaspoon pepper

1 7¾-ounce can salmon, drained and separated into chunks

1. Prepare noodles as label directs; drain; keep warm.

2. Meanwhile, in 2-quart saucepan over medium heat, melt butter or margarine; add mushrooms and onion; cook until tender, stirring occasionally. Stir in flour until blended; cook 1 minute. Gradually stir in milk, sherry, salt, and pepper; cook until thickened and smooth, stirring constantly. Gently stir in salmon; heat through.

3. Arrange noodles on warm platter; top with salmon mixture.

Greek-style Macaroni

TIME: about 1½ hours—SERVINGS: 8

3 cups elbow macaroni (¾ 16-ounce package)

½ pound ground beef or lamb

1 small onion, chopped

1 garlic clove, minced

1 15-ounce can tomato sauce

2 teaspoons salt

¼ teaspoon pepper

¼ teaspoon ground cinnamon

Cheese Sauce (right)

1. Prepare macaroni as label directs; drain. Grease a 13″ by 9″ baking dish.

2. Meanwhile, in 10-inch skillet over medium-high heat, cook ground beef, onion, and garlic until meat is browned and onion is tender, about 10 minutes, stirring occasionally. Stir in tomato sauce, s ¹⁴, pepper, and cinnamon; heat to boiling.

3. Preheat oven to 350° F. Place half of macaroni in bottom of baking dish; pour meat sauce over macaroni; top with remaining macaroni. Prepare Cheese Sauce and pour over top of layered macaroni. Bake 30 minutes or until mixture is hot and bubbly.

Cheese Sauce: In bowl with fork, beat *2 eggs* and *¼ cup grated Parmesan cheese* until foamy; set aside. In 2-quart saucepan over low heat, melt *¼ cup butter* or margarine; stir in *¼ cup all-purpose flour, ¼ teaspoon salt,* and *¼ teaspoon ground nutmeg* until smooth; gradually stir in *2 cups milk,* and cook, stirring constantly, until mixture is thickened and smooth; remove from heat. Into egg mixture, stir small amount of hot sauce; slowly pour mixture back into sauce, stirring rapidly to prevent lumping.

Company Chicken Lasagna

TIME: about 2 hours—SERVINGS: 12

1 3- to 3½-pound broiler-fryer

2 celery stalks, each cut in half

1 carrot, cut in half

salt

pepper

water

butter or margarine

1½ pounds medium mushrooms, sliced

1 medium onion, diced

1 garlic clove, minced

2 15-ounce cans tomato sauce

1 16-ounce package lasagna noodles

1 cup all-purpose flour

3 cups milk

2 10-ounce packages frozen chopped broccoli, thawed and squeezed dry

1 cup grated Parmesan cheese

1 8-ounce package mozzarella cheese, sliced

1. Cook chicken: Rinse chicken, its giblets, and neck with running cold water. Place chicken, breast side down, in 5-quart saucepot or Dutch oven; add giblets, neck, celery, carrot, 1 teaspoon salt, ¼ teaspoon pepper, and 2 inches water; over high heat, heat to boiling. Reduce heat to low; cover and simmer 35 minutes or until chicken is fork-tender. Remove chicken to large bowl; refrigerate 30 minutes, until easy to handle. Reserve 2 cups broth. (Cover and refrigerate remaining broth and vegetables for soup another day.)

2. Meanwhile, prepare tomato sauce: In 2-quart saucepan over medium heat, melt 3 tablespoons butter or margarine; add mushrooms, onion, and garlic, and cook until tender, about 10 minutes. Stir in tomato sauce, ¼ teaspoon salt, and ¼ teaspoon pepper; remove saucepan from heat. When chicken is ready, discard skin and bones; dice meat and giblets.

3. Cook noodles as label directs.

4. While noodles are cooking, prepare broccoli mixture: In 3-quart saucepan over medium heat, melt 6 tablespoons butter or margarine. Stir in flour until smooth; cook 1 minute. Gradually stir in milk, reserved chicken broth, ½ teaspoon salt, and ½ teaspoon pepper, and cook, stirring constantly, until thickened and smooth. Add diced chicken and giblets, broccoli, and Parmesan cheese. Remove saucepan from heat.

5. Preheat oven to 375° F. In 14″ by 10″ roasting pan, evenly spread half of tomato sauce; top with a third of noodles, half of broccoli mixture, another third of noodles, and rest of the broccoli mixture; then top with rest of noodles, tomato sauce, and all mozzarella cheese slices. Cover pan with foil. Bake 35 to 40 minutes, until hot.

Danish Meatball-Noodle Casserole

TIME: about 1¼ hours—SERVINGS: 6

1 8-ounce package wide noodles

1 pound ground beef

1 small onion, grated

½ cup dried bread crumbs

⅛ teaspoon ground allspice

⅛ teaspoon pepper

1 egg

salt

3 tablespoons butter or margarine

¼ cup all-purpose flour

1 13¾- or 14½-ounce can beef broth

1¼ cups water

1 16-ounce jar red cabbage, drained

1. In 6-quart saucepot, prepare noodles as label directs; drain. Return noodles to saucepot; set aside. Meanwhile, in medium bowl, mix ground beef, onion, bread crumbs, allspice, pepper, egg, and ¾ teaspoon salt. Shape into 12 meatballs.

2. In 12-inch skillet over medium-high heat, in hot butter or margarine, cook meatballs until well browned on all sides. With slotted spoon, remove meatballs to large plate. Into drippings in skillet over medium heat, stir flour and ¼ teaspoon salt until blended; gradually stir in beef broth and water. Cook, stirring, until sauce is thickened. Remove 1 cup sauce; set aside.

3. Preheat oven to 350° F. Spoon red cabbage into 12″ by 8″ baking dish. Toss remaining sauce with noodles; spoon over cabbage. Place meatballs on top of noodles, pressing lightly into mixture; pour reserved sauce over meatballs. Cover dish with foil. Bake 30 minutes or until mixture is hot.

Tuna-sauced Noodle Pudding

TIME: about 1 hour—SERVINGS: 6

4 cups medium noodles

butter or margarine

2 tablespoons all-purpose flour

pepper

2¼ cups milk

1 8-ounce package pasteurized process cheese spread or cheese food, diced (1 cup)

2 eggs

¼ pound mushrooms, sliced

1 teaspoon grated onion

1 tablespoon cornstarch

½ teaspoon salt

¼ teaspoon paprika

1 3¼- or 3½-ounce can tuna, drained and flaked

1 tablespoon chopped parsley

1. Prepare noodles as label directs. Drain.

2. Meanwhile, in 3-quart saucepan over medium heat, melt 2 tablespoons butter or margarine. Stir in flour and ⅛ teaspoon pepper until blended. Gradually stir in 1¼ cups milk; cook over medium heat until thickened, stirring constantly. Remove saucepan from heat; stir in cheese until melted.

3. Preheat oven to 375° F. Grease 10″ by 6″ baking dish. Gently stir cooked noodles and eggs into cheese mixture. Spoon mixture into baking dish. Cover and bake 25 minutes or until knife inserted in center comes out clean.

4. While noodles are baking, prepare tuna sauce: In 1-quart saucepan over medium heat, cook mushrooms, onion, and 2 tablespoons butter or margarine until mushrooms are tender, stirring occasionally. In cup, stir cornstarch with remaining 1 cup milk; stir into saucepan with salt and paprika. Cook over medium heat until mixture thickens and boils, stirring constantly. Stir in tuna and parsley; heat through.

5. To serve, cut pudding into six pieces; pass sauce to spoon over each.

Chicken-and-Fettucini Bake

TIME: about 1 hour—SERVINGS: 6

1 12-ounce package spinach fettucini noodles

1½ cups milk

¼ cup grated Parmesan cheese

4 tablespoons butter or margarine, softened

½ teaspoon salt

⅛ teaspoon pepper

1 medium onion, grated

3 5- or 6¾-ounce cans boned chicken, flaked

1. In 6-quart saucepot, prepare fettucini as label directs; drain. Return fettucini to saucepot.

2. Preheat oven to 350° F. To fettucini in saucepot, add milk and next 5 ingredients; toss well. Gently stir in chicken.

3. Spoon fettucini mixture into 2-quart casserole. Cover casserole; bake 25 minutes or until hot, stirring once.

Lasagna Roll-ups

TIME: about 1¼ hours—SERVINGS: 6

½ 16-ounce package lasagna noodles (12 noodles)

1 tablespoon salad oil

1 10-ounce package frozen chopped broccoli, thawed and squeezed dry

2 tablespoons minced green onions

1 15- to 16-ounce container ricotta cheese (2 cups)

¼ cup grated Parmesan cheese

½ teaspoon salt

1 egg

1 21-ounce jar Italian cooking sauce

1 4-ounce package shredded mozzarella cheese (1 cup)

1. Cook lasagna noodles as label directs.

2. Meanwhile, in 2-quart saucepan over medium heat, in hot salad oil, cook broccoli and green onions until tender, about 5 minutes, stirring frequently. Remove saucepan from heat. Stir in ricotta cheese, Parmesan cheese, salt, and egg.

3. Preheat oven to 375° F. Drain noodles; place in single layer on waxed paper. Evenly spread some cheese mixture on each lasagna noodle. Roll up each noodle jelly-roll fashion.

4. Into 12″ by 8″ baking dish, spoon about three fourths of Italian cooking sauce. Arrange rolled noodles, seam side down, in sauce. Top with mozzarella cheese and remaining sauce. Cover dish loosely with foil; bake 30 minutes or until hot and bubbly and cheese is melted.

Cheese-filled Manicotti

TIME: about 1¼ hours—SERVINGS: 8

2 16-ounce containers ricotta cheese (4 cups)

1 8-ounce package mozzarella cheese, shredded

2 eggs

grated Romano cheese

chopped parsley

salt

pepper

1 8-ounce package manicotti shells

4 tablespoons butter or margarine

2 tablespoons all-purpose flour

2 cups milk

1. In large bowl, mix ricotta cheese, mozzarella cheese, eggs, ¼ cup grated Romano cheese, 2 tablespoons chopped parsley, ½ teaspoon salt, and ½ teaspoon pepper; set mixture aside.

2. Cook manicotti shells as label directs. Drain cooked manicotti immediately under running warm tap water to stop cooking (do not use cold water; it will cause shells to break); drain again.

3. Meanwhile, in 1-quart saucepan over medium heat, melt butter or margarine; stir in flour, ¼ teaspoon salt, and ¼ teaspoon pepper until blended. Gradually stir in milk; cook over medium heat until slightly thickened, stirring constantly. Stir in 3 tablespoons Romano cheese. Spoon one third of sauce into 13″ by 9″ baking dish.

4. Preheat oven to 375° F. Using decorating bag without tube, or with spoon, fill manicotti shells with cheese mixture. Arrange filled shells in baking dish over sauce in one layer. Spoon remaining sauce over manicotti. Bake 25 minutes or until mixture is hot and bubbly. If you like, garnish with some chopped parsley.

Tuna-and-Macaroni Toss

TIME: about 30 minutes—SERVINGS: 4

1 8-ounce package bow-tie macaroni

4 tablespoons butter or margarine

1 small onion, minced

2 tablespoons all-purpose flour

1½ cups milk

1 chicken-flavor bouillon cube or envelope

½ teaspoon salt

⅛ teaspoon pepper

1 6½- to 7-ounce can tuna, drained and flaked

1 2-ounce jar diced pimento, drained

1 tablespoon chopped parsley, for garnish

1. In a 5-quart saucepot, cook macaroni as label directs; drain. Return macaroni to saucepot; keep warm.

2. Meanwhile, in 2-quart saucepan over medium heat, melt butter or margarine; add onion and cook until tender, stirring occasionally. Stir in flour until blended; cook 1 minute. Gradually stir in milk, bouillon, salt, and pepper; cook until thickened and smooth, stirring constantly. Stir in tuna and pimentos; heat through.

3. Gently toss macaroni in saucepot with tuna mixture. Spoon mixture into warm bowl; garnish with parsley.

Ground Beef with Spaghetti Parmigiana

TIME: about 30 minutes—SERVINGS: 6

1 8-ounce package spaghetti

1 pound ground beef

1 medium onion, diced

1 12-ounce can vacuum-packed golden kernel corn with sweet peppers

1 8-ounce can tomato sauce

¼ cup water

½ teaspoon salt

¼ teaspoon pepper

¼ teaspoon sugar

⅛ teaspoon ground cinnamon

¼ cup grated Parmesan cheese

2 tablespoons butter or margarine

1. In 6-quart saucepot, prepare spaghetti as label directs.

2. Meanwhile, in 12-inch skillet over medium-high heat, cook ground beef and onion until all pan juices evaporate and meat is browned, stirring occasionally. Add corn and next 6 ingredients; heat through.

3. Drain spaghetti. Return spaghetti to saucepot; toss with Parmesan cheese and butter or margarine. Arrange spaghetti on warm platter. Spoon meat mixture onto platter with spaghetti.

Pasta with Northern Italian Meat Sauce

TIME: about 1 hour—SERVINGS: 6

2 tablespoons salad oil

2 medium carrots, finely chopped

1 celery stalk, finely chopped

1 small onion, finely chopped

3 cups finely chopped cooked beef top round roast

1 10¹/₂-ounce can condensed beef broth

1 6-ounce can tomato paste

1 cup water

¹/₃ cup cooking or dry red wine

1¹/₂ teaspoons brown sugar

1¹/₂ teaspoons salt

¹/₂ teaspoon cracked pepper

¹/₂ cup heavy or whipping cream

³/₄ 16-ounce package spaghetti

1 tablespoon minced parsley, for garnish

1 teaspoon grated lemon peel, for garnish

1. In 3-quart saucepan over medium heat, in hot salad oil, cook carrots, celery, and onion until very tender, stirring occasionally.

2. Stir in beef, beef broth, tomato paste, water, wine, sugar, salt, and pepper; over high heat, heat to boiling. Reduce heat to low; cover and simmer 30 minutes or until sauce is slightly thickened, stirring occasionally. Stir in heavy cream; simmer, uncovered, 5 minutes longer.

3. Meanwhile, in 6-quart saucepot, prepare spaghetti as label directs; drain.

4. Arrange spaghetti on warm platter; spoon sauce over spaghetti; sprinkle with parsley and lemon peel.

Eggplant Manicotti

TIME: about 1¹/₂ hours—SERVINGS: 6

1 8-ounce package manicotti shells

¹/₄ cup salad oil

1 large garlic clove, thinly sliced

1 medium eggplant (about 1 pound), chopped

¹/₂ cup chopped onion

¹/₂ cup water

1 29- or 32-ounce jar spaghetti sauce

¹/₂ pound Muenster cheese, shredded

1 cup ricotta cheese

³/₄ cup dried bread crumbs

2 eggs

¹/₂ teaspoon Italian seasoning

¹/₂ teaspoon salt

¹/₈ teaspoon pepper

1. Cook manicotti shells the minimum amount of time that label directs. Drain.

2. Meanwhile, in 12-inch skillet over medium heat, in hot oil, cook garlic until brown; remove and discard. In remaining oil in skillet, cook eggplant and onion 5 minutes, stirring. Add water; cover and cook 10 minutes or until vegetables are tender; remove from heat and cool eggplant mixture slightly.

3. Pour half of spaghetti sauce into 13″ by 9″ baking dish; sprinkle with half of Muenster cheese.

4. Preheat oven to 375° F. In medium bowl, stir ricotta cheese, bread crumbs, eggs, Italian seasoning, salt, and pepper until blended; stir in eggplant mixture. Fill decorating bag, without tube, with eggplant mixture, and fill each manicotti shell with about 2 heaping tablespoonfuls of mixture (or use a spoon to fill shells). Arrange filled manicotti shells in baking dish in a single layer.

5. Pour remaining spaghetti sauce over shells; sprinkle with remaining Muenster cheese. Cover dish with foil, and bake 20 minutes; remove foil and bake 10 minutes longer or until mixture is hot and bubbly.

Salmon-and-Pasta Bake

TIME: about 1¼ hours—SERVINGS: 6

½ 16-ounce package fusilli (twisted spaghetti) or spaghetti

2 hard-cooked eggs

4 tablespoons butter or margarine

1 medium green pepper, cut into thin strips

1 medium onion, diced

3 tablespoons all-purpose flour

3 cups milk

1¼ teaspoons salt

¼ teaspoon pepper

1 7¾-ounce can salmon, drained and flaked

1 2-ounce jar diced pimento, drained

1. Prepare fusilli in saucepot as label directs; drain. Return fusilli to saucepot.

2. Meanwhile, reserve 1 hard-cooked egg yolk for garnish later; coarsely chop remaining hard-cooked eggs; set aside. In 2-quart saucepan over medium heat, melt butter or margarine; add green pepper and onion, and cook until vegetables are tender, stirring occasionally. Stir in flour until blended. Gradually stir in milk, salt, and pepper; cook, stirring constantly, until mixture is slightly thickened and smooth. Stir in salmon, pimento, and chopped eggs.

3. Preheat oven to 350° F. Gently toss salmon mixture with fusilli in saucepot. Spoon mixture into 12″ by 8″ baking dish. Cover baking dish with foil and bake 25 minutes or until hot and bubbly.

4. To serve, coarsely shred reserved egg yolk; sprinkle on top of salmon mixture for garnish.

Quick Ham-Broccoli Tetrazzini

TIME: about 45 minutes—SERVINGS: 6

1 8-ounce package linguine or spaghetti

4 tablespoons butter or margarine

1 medium onion, diced

¼ pound mushrooms, thinly sliced

¼ cup all-purpose flour

3 cups milk

½ teaspoon salt

¼ teaspoon coarsely ground black pepper

1 10-ounce package frozen chopped broccoli

2 cups diced cooked ham

1. In 6-quart saucepot, cook linguine as label directs; drain well. Return linguine to saucepot; cover and keep warm.

2. Meanwhile, in 2-quart saucepan over medium heat, melt butter or margarine; add onion and mushrooms, and cook until onion is tender, stirring occasionally. Stir in flour until blended. Gradually stir in milk, salt, and pepper; cook, stirring constantly, until mixture is slightly thickened. Stir in broccoli and ham, separating broccoli with fork; heat mixture to boiling.

3. Stir ham mixture into linguine; gently toss to mix well and heat through.

Hearty Manicotti

TIME: about 2½ hours—SERVINGS: 8

water

1 pound sweet Italian sausage links

1 pound ground beef

1 medium onion, chopped

2 16-ounce cans tomato puree

1 6-ounce can tomato paste

1 teaspoon sugar

½ teaspoon pepper

basil

salt

1 8-ounce package manicotti shells

4 cups ricotta cheese

1 8-ounce package mozzarella cheese, diced

2 tablespoons chopped parsley

grated Parmesan cheese

1. In covered 5-quart Dutch oven over medium heat, in ¼ cup water, cook sausage links 5 minutes. Uncover; brown well and drain on paper towels.

2. Spoon fat from Dutch oven; over medium heat, brown ground beef and onion well; stir in tomato puree, tomato paste, sugar, pepper, 1 teaspoon basil, 1 teaspoon salt, and 1 cup water; simmer, covered, 45 minutes.

3. Cut sausage into bite-size pieces; add to mixture; cook 15 minutes, stirring occasionally. Meanwhile, cook manicotti as label directs; drain in colander. Preheat oven to 375° F.

4. In large bowl, combine ricotta and mozzarella cheeses, parsley, ¾ teaspoon basil, and ½ teaspoon salt; stuff into shells.

5. Spoon half of meat sauce into 13″ by 9″ baking dish. Place half of shells over sauce in one layer. Spoon remaining sauce except ¾ cup over shells; top with remaining shells in one layer. Spoon reserved meat sauce over top. Sprinkle with Parmesan. Bake 30 minutes.

Franks and Spaghetti

TIME: about 30 minutes—SERVINGS: 5

$^3/_4$ **16-ounce package spaghetti**

1 **16-ounce package frankfurters, each sliced lengthwise into 4 wedges**

1 **16-ounce can tomatoes**

1 **6- or 7-ounce can tomato paste**

$1^1/_2$ **teaspoons brown sugar**

$^1/_2$ **teaspoon salt**

$^1/_4$ **teaspoon Italian herb seasoning**

$^1/_8$ **teaspoon pepper**

1. In large saucepot, prepare spaghetti as label directs; drain. Set aside.

2. Meanwhile, in 12-inch skillet over medium-low heat, cook frankfurters until lightly browned and curled. Add tomatoes with their liquid, tomato paste, brown sugar, salt, Italian herb seasoning, and pepper; over medium-high heat, heat mixture to boiling, stirring to break up tomatoes. Reduce heat to low; cover skillet and simmer 5 to 10 minutes to blend flavors.

3. To serve, gently toss spaghetti with frankfurter mixture.

Macaroni Bolognese

TIME: about $1^1/_2$ hours—SERVINGS: 6

1 **8-ounce package large shell macaroni**

3 **tablespoons olive or salad oil**

1 **small onion, finely chopped**

1 **small carrot, finely chopped**

1 **celery stalk, finely chopped**

1 **small garlic clove, minced**

1 **pound ground beef**

$^1/_2$ **pound chicken livers, diced**

1 **28-ounce can tomatoes**

1 **6-ounce can tomato paste**

$^1/_2$ **cup water**

3 **tablespoons cooking or dry red wine**

$1^1/_4$ **teaspoons salt**

$^1/_2$ **teaspoon basil**

$^1/_4$ **teaspoon pepper**

grated Parmesan cheese (optional)

1. Prepare shell macaroni as label directs; drain. Spoon macaroni into $2^1/_2$-quart casserole.

2. Meanwhile, in 12-inch skillet over medium heat, in hot olive or salad oil, cook onion, carrot, celery, and garlic until vegetables are very tender, stirring occasionally. With slotted spoon, remove vegetables to small bowl.

3. In drippings remaining in skillet over medium-high heat, cook ground beef 5 minutes, stirring occasionally. Add chicken livers; cook until chicken livers lose their pink color, all pan juices evaporate, and ground beef is well browned, stirring frequently.

4. Preheat oven to 350° F. Return vegetables to skillet; stir in tomatoes with their liquid, tomato paste, water, wine, salt, basil, and pepper; over high heat, heat to boiling. Pour meat sauce over macaroni in casserole; stir gently to mix. Cover casserole and bake 45 minutes or until hot and bubbly. If you like, serve with grated Parmesan cheese.

Tuna-stuffed Shells

TIME: about $1^1/_2$ hours—SERVINGS: 8

1 **12-ounce package jumbo shell macaroni**

1 **$6^1/_2$- or 7-ounce can tuna**

6 **slices white bread, cut into $^1/_4$-inch cubes**

1 **cup minced celery**

$^3/_4$ **cup milk**

$^1/_2$ **cup California walnuts, finely chopped**

$^1/_4$ **cup minced onion**

1 **teaspoon salt**

4 **teaspoons lemon juice**

$^1/_4$ **teaspoon coarsely ground pepper**

1 **tablespoon brown sugar**

1 **32-ounce jar marinara sauce**

1. Prepare shell macaroni as label directs; drain well. Meanwhile, preheat oven to 350° F. In large bowl with fork, mix all ingredients except macaroni, brown sugar, and marinara sauce. Stuff a tablespoonful of tuna mixture into each shell.

2. Stir brown sugar into marinara sauce. Spoon half of sauce into 13″ by 9″ baking dish. Arrange stuffed shell macaroni over sauce in one layer; top with remaining sauce. Cover dish with foil; bake 40 minutes or until heated.

Eggs and Cheese

Chicken-Spinach Quiche

TIME: about 1¹/₂ hours—SERVINGS: 6

piecrust mix for one 9-inch piecrust

butter or margarine

1 green onion, minced

2 cups half-and-half

1 teaspoon salt

¹/₈ teaspoon pepper

3 eggs

¹/₄ pound Swiss cheese, shredded (1 cup)

1 10-ounce package frozen chopped spinach or kale, thawed and squeezed dry

1 5- to 6³/₄-ounce can chunk chicken, drained and flaked

1. Prepare piecrust mix as label directs; use to line 9-inch pie plate. Spread crust with 1 tablespoon softened butter or margarine.

2. Preheat oven to 425° F. In 1-quart saucepan over medium heat, melt 2 tablespoons butter or margarine; add green onion and cook until tender, stirring occasionally. Remove saucepan from heat; set aside.

3. In medium bowl with wire whisk or fork, mix half-and-half, salt, pepper, and eggs; stir in cheese, spinach, chicken, and green-onion mixture; pour into piecrust. Bake 15 minutes; turn oven control to 300° F.; bake 30 or 40 minutes longer, until knife inserted in center comes out clean.

No-Crust Zucchini Quiche

TIME: about 40 minutes—SERVINGS: 6

2 medium zucchini, coarsely shredded (6 cups)

8 ounces Swiss cheese, coarsely shredded (2 cups)

4 eggs

1 cup buttermilk-baking mix

¹/₄ cup salad oil

¹/₂ teaspoon salt

¹/₄ teaspoon Italian seasoning

1. Preheat oven to 400° F. Grease a 9-inch pie plate.

2. In large bowl with fork, mix all ingredients. Pour mixture into prepared pie plate. Bake 30 to 35 minutes, until golden brown and knife inserted in center comes out clean.

Best Quiche

TIME: about 1³/₄ hours—SERVINGS: 6

piecrust mix for one 9-inch piecrust

1 tablespoon butter or margarine, softened

12 slices bacon

¹/₄ pound Swiss, Gruyère, or Havarti cheese, shredded (1 cup)

4 eggs

2 cups heavy or whipping cream

¹/₄ teaspoon salt

¹/₈ teaspoon ground red pepper

parsley sprigs, for garnish

1. Prepare piecrust mix as label directs; use to line 9-inch pie plate. Spread piecrust with butter or margarine.

2. In 12-inch skillet over medium-low heat, cook bacon slices, half at a time, until browned; drain on paper towels. While still warm, roll 6 slices, one at a time, to form "roses"; keep warm. Crumble remaining slices; sprinkle, with cheese, on piecrust.

3. Preheat oven to 425° F. In medium bowl with fork, beat eggs, cream, salt, and pepper; pour into piecrust. Bake 15 minutes; turn oven control to 300° F.; bake 40 minutes longer or until knife inserted in center comes out clean. Garnish with bacon "roses" and parsley.

TO DO AHEAD: Early in day, prepare piecrust as in step 1; cover with plastic wrap; refrigerate. Cook only 6 slices of bacon and crumble; refrigerate; omit bacon "roses" for garnish. Then prepare filling as in step 3; cover and refrigerate.

About 1¹/₄ hours before serving, preheat oven to 425° F. Assemble quiche as above. Bake 15 minutes; turn oven control to 300° F. and bake 50 minutes longer; test for doneness as above.

TO FREEZE AND USE WITHIN ONE MONTH: Prepare piecrust, 6 slices bacon, and filling as above; omit bacon "roses." Sprinkle cheese and crumbled bacon on piecrust. Pour filling into piecrust. Carefully place unbaked quiche in freezer, making sure quiche is level. When quiche is frozen, freezer-wrap and return to freezer.

To bake the frozen quiche, preheat oven to 325° F. Unwrap quiche and bake 1 hour and 10 minutes or until knife inserted in center comes out clean.

Italian Cheese-and-Ham Pie

TIME: about 5 hours or start early in day—SERVINGS: 10

1 16-ounce container creamed cottage cheese (2 cups)

1 15- or 16-ounce container ricotta cheese (2 cups)

2 cups diced cooked ham (³/₄ pound)

²/₃ cup grated Parmesan cheese

3 eggs

2 teaspoons Italian seasoning

¹/₂ teaspoon salt

¹/₄ teaspoon pepper

piecrust mix for two 2-crust 9-inch pies

1 egg yolk, slightly beaten

1. In medium bowl, mix creamed cottage cheese and next 7 ingredients; set aside.

2. Prepare piecrust mix as label directs. With hands, shape two thirds of pastry into large ball; shape remaining pastry into another ball.

3. On lightly floured surface with lightly floured rolling pin, roll large ball onto 16-inch circle about ¹/₈ inch thick. Fold circle into fourths and carefully lift into 10-inch springform pan; unfold. With fingers, lightly press pastry onto bottom and sides of pan; trim edge of pastry to make it even with rim of pan. Brush pastry with some beaten egg yolk.

4. Spoon cheese mixture into pastry-lined pan; fold edge of pastry over filling; brush pastry with some beaten egg yolk. Preheat oven to 375° F.

5. Roll remaining pastry ball into a 10-inch circle. With knife, cut design in pastry. Place pastry circle over filling in pan, pressing lightly around edges to seal; brush top with remaining egg yolk.

6. Bake pie 1 hour or until knife inserted in center comes out clean. Cool pie in refrigerator.

7. To serve, carefully remove side of springform pan. With a sharp knife, cut pie into wedges.

Crusty Ham-Swiss Bake

TIME: about 1 hour—SERVINGS: 8

piecrust mix for one 9-inch piecrust

1 16-ounce can or package sauerkraut, well drained

1/4 cup minced parsley

1 16-ounce package Swiss cheese slices

1 8-ounce package sliced cooked ham

1/3 cup bottled creamy Russian dressing

8 large lettuce leaves

1. Prepare piecrust mix as label directs. On lightly floured surface with lightly floured rolling pin, roll pastry into 9" by 9" square; use to line 8" by 8" baking dish.

2. Preheat oven to 425° F. In medium bowl, toss sauerkraut with parsley. In pastry-lined baking dish, arrange one fourth of Swiss cheese, overlapping slices; top with one third of sliced ham, one third of sauerkraut mixture, and one third of Russian dressing. Repeat layering, ending with cheese.

3. Cover dish with foil, and bake 35 minutes or until crust is golden. Cut pie into 8 pieces. Serve immediately on lettuce leaves.

Cheese Soufflé

TIME: about 40 minutes—SERVINGS: 2

2 tablespoons butter or margarine

2 tablespoons all-purpose flour

1/8 teaspoon salt

1/8 teaspoon ground red pepper

3/4 cup milk

1/2 4-ounce package shredded Cheddar cheese (1/2 cup)

3 eggs, separated

1. In 2-quart saucepan over medium heat, melt butter or margarine; stir in flour, salt, and ground red pepper until smooth; cook 1 minute. Gradually stir in milk; cook, stirring constantly, until thickened and smooth. Add cheese; cook just until cheese melts. Remove saucepan from heat.

2. Preheat oven to 325° F. In small bowl with fork, beat egg yolks slightly. Into egg yolks, beat small amount of hot cheese mixture. Gradually stir warm egg-yolk mixture into cheese mixture in pan until blended, stirring rapidly to prevent lumping; set aside.

3. In small bowl with mixer at high speed, beat egg whites until stiff peaks form. With rubber spatula or wire whisk, gently fold cheese mixture into beaten egg whites. Pour mixture into 1-quart soufflé dish. With back of spoon, about 1 inch from edge of dish, make 1-inch indentation all around in cheese mixture. (This makes a top-hat effect when soufflé is done.)

4. Bake soufflé 30 minutes, until puffy and golden brown and knife inserted under top hat comes out clean. Serve immediately.

Egg-and-Spinach Soufflé

TIME: about 45 minutes—SERVINGS: 2

5 eggs

2 tablespoons butter or margarine

2 tablespoons all-purpose flour

3/4 teaspoon salt

1/2 cup milk

1 10-ounce package frozen chopped spinach, thawed and well drained

1 tablespoon grated onion

1. Preheat oven to 325° F. Separate 3 eggs; set aside. In 1-quart saucepan over medium heat, into hot butter or margarine, stir flour and salt until blended. Slowly stir in milk; cook, stirring, until thickened. Stir in spinach, onion, then 3 egg yolks.

2. In medium bowl with mixer at high speed, beat 3 egg whites until stiff. Fold in spinach mixture.

3. Spoon mixture into two 12-ounce individual shallow casseroles. With spoon, make an indentation in center of each. Break one egg into each indentation. Bake about 20 minutes or until soufflé is puffy and lightly browned. Serve immediately.

Corn Soufflé

TIME: about 50 minutes—SERVINGS: 4

about 3 large ears corn, husked

3 tablespoons butter or margarine

1/4 cup all-purpose flour

1 teaspoon sugar

3/4 teaspoon salt

1/8 teaspoon ground red pepper

3/4 cup milk

1 4-ounce package shredded Cheddar
cheese (1 cup)

5 eggs, separated

1. With sharp knife, cut kernels from corn to make 1 1/2 cups kernels. In blender at high speed, blend corn kernels until pureed; set aside.

2. In 2-quart saucepan over medium heat, melt butter or margarine; stir in flour, sugar, salt, and ground red pepper until smooth; cook 1 minute. Gradually stir in milk and pureed corn; cook, stirring constantly, until mixture is thickened. Add cheese; cook just until cheese melts. Remove saucepan from heat.

3. Preheat oven to 325° F. Grease and flour bottom and side of 2-quart soufflé dish.

4. In small bowl with fork, beat egg yolks slightly. Into egg yolks, beat small amount of hot corn mixture. Gradually stir warm egg-yolk mixture into corn mixture in saucepan until blended, stirring rapidly to prevent lumping; set aside.

5. In large bowl with mixer at high speed, beat egg whites until stiff peaks form. With rubber spatula or wire whisk, gently fold corn mixture into beaten egg whites. Pour mixture into prepared soufflé dish. With back of spoon, about 1 inch from edge of dish, make 1-inch indentation all around soufflé mixture. (This makes a top-hat effect when soufflé is done.) Bake soufflé 50 minutes or until puffy and golden brown and knife inserted under top hat comes out clean. Serve immediately as a main dish.

Autumn Ham Omelet

TIME: about 40 minutes—SERVINGS: 2

1 medium red cooking apple

1 small potato

butter or margarine

2 teaspoons brown sugar

salt

3/4 cup diced cooked ham

1 tablespoon coarsely chopped parsley

3 eggs, separated

2 tablespoons water

1/4 cup sour cream

1 tablespoon milk

parsley sprigs, for garnish

1. Cut apple into six wedges; cut each wedge crosswise into thin slices. Cut potato into quarters; cut each crosswise into thin slices. In 2-quart saucepan over medium heat, melt 3 tablespoons butter or margarine; add apple and potato slices, brown sugar, and 1/8 teaspoon salt; cook until tender, stirring occasionally. Stir in ham and chopped parsley; keep warm.

2. Meanwhile, preheat oven to 350° F. In large bowl with mixer at high speed, beat egg whites until stiff peaks form. In small bowl with same beaters and with mixer at high speed, beat egg yolks, water, and 1/4 teaspoon salt until very thick. Fold egg-yolk mixture into beaten egg whites.

3. In 10-inch oven-safe skillet over medium-low heat, melt 1 tablespoon butter or margarine; add egg mixture and cook until top is puffy and bottom is golden when gently lifted with a pancake turner, about 5 minutes.

4. Place skillet in oven. Bake until top of omelet is golden and springs back when lightly touched with finger, about 10 minutes. Meanwhile, in small bowl, stir sour cream with milk until blended.

5. To serve, loosen side and bottom of omelet from skillet; spoon ham mixture over half of omelet; fold omelet over mixture. Tip skillet; with pancake turner, slide omelet onto warm platter. Garnish with parsley sprigs. Pass sour-cream mixture to serve over omelet.

Omelet Primavera

TIME: about 40 minutes—SERVINGS: 4

8 eggs, separated

water

salt

thyme leaves

pepper

butter or margarine

1 pound asparagus, cut diagonally into
1½-inch pieces

½ pound small mushrooms, each cut into
quarters

2 medium onions, thinly sliced

1 8-ounce can tomatoes

¼ teaspoon sugar

1 teaspoon cornstarch

1. Preheat oven to 350° F. In large bowl with mixer at high speed, beat egg whites until stiff peaks form. In small bowl with mixer at high speed, beat egg yolks, ¼ cup water, ½ teaspoon salt, ½ teaspoon thyme, and ⅛ teaspoon pepper until very thick. Fold egg-yolk mixture into beaten egg whites.

2. In 12-inch oven-safe skillet over medium-low heat, melt 2 tablespoons butter or margarine; add egg mixture and cook until top is puffy and bottom is golden when gently lifted with a pancake turner, about 5 minutes.

3. Place skillet in oven. Bake until top of omelet is golden and springs back when lightly touched with finger, about 10 minutes.

4. Meanwhile, in 10-inch skillet over medium heat, melt 2 tablespoons butter or margarine; add asparagus, mushrooms, onions, ¾ teaspoon salt, ½ teaspoon thyme, and ⅛ teaspoon pepper, and cook until vegetables are tender-crisp, about 5 minutes, stirring frequently. Stir in tomatoes with their liquid and sugar. In cup, stir cornstarch and 1 tablespoon water until blended; stir into vegetable mixture. Cook over medium heat until slightly thickened, stirring constantly.

5. To serve, loosen side and bottom of omelet from skillet; spoon half of vegetable mixture over half of omelet; fold omelet over vegetables. Tip skillet; with pancake turner, slide omelet onto warm platter. Spoon remaining vegetable mixture around omelet.

Egg Brunch Puffs

TIME: about 1 hour—SERVINGS: 6

4 eggs

2 cups milk

1½ cups all-purpose flour

2 teaspoons sugar

½ teaspoon salt

1 8-ounce package sliced salami, coarsely
chopped

1. Preheat oven to 375° F. Grease six 10-ounce custard cups; set in jelly-roll pan for easier handling.

2. In large bowl with wire whisk or fork, beat eggs lightly; add milk, flour, sugar, and salt; beat until well blended. Stir in salami.

3. Fill each cup three quarters full with mixture. Bake 45 minutes or until toothpick inserted into center comes out clean. Serve in cups immediately (puffs will fall upon standing).

Baked Eggs and Rice

TIME: about 1 hour—SERVINGS: 6

2 tablespoons butter or margarine

1 medium onion, chopped

2 cups packaged precooked rice

2 cups boiling water

1 envelope chicken-flavor bouillon

salt

seasoned pepper

1 16-ounce can tomatoes

1 9-ounce package frozen Italian green
beans, thawed

1 4-ounce package shredded Cheddar
cheese (1 cup)

6 eggs

1. In 1-quart saucepan over medium heat, melt butter or margarine; add onion and cook until tender, stirring occasionally. Remove from heat.

2. Preheat oven to 375° F. Into 12″ by 8″ baking dish, measure rice, boiling water, bouillon, 1 teaspoon salt, and ¼ teaspoon seasoned pepper; mix well. Stir in onion mixture, tomatoes with their liquid, green beans, and cheese.

3. With spoon, make six indentations in rice mixture. One at a time, break eggs into saucer and slip into indentations. Cover baking dish with foil; bake 30 minutes or until eggs are just set or of desired doneness.

4. To serve, fluff rice with fork; sprinkle eggs lightly with ¼ teaspoon salt and ¼ teaspoon seasoned pepper.

Egg-and-Mushroom Casserole

TIME: about 50 minutes—SERVINGS: 4

5 hard-cooked eggs

1 2¹/₂- to 4-ounce can sliced mushrooms

milk

3 tablespoons butter or margarine

2 tablespoons all-purpose flour

¹/₄ teaspoon salt

¹/₄ teaspoon onion salt

¹/₂ cup minced celery

¹/₂ cup packaged stuffing mix

¹/₂ cup grated American cheese food

1. Slice eggs into 10″ by 6″ baking dish. Drain juice from mushrooms into measuring cup; add milk to make 1 cup.

2. Preheat oven to 375° F. Into 2-quart saucepan over medium heat, in hot butter or margarine, stir flour, salt, and onion salt until blended. Gradually stir in milk mixture; cook, stirring constantly, until sauce is thickened. Add mushrooms and celery; pour over eggs. Scatter stuffing, mixed with cheese, over top. Bake, uncovered, 20 minutes, or until bubbly.

Noodle-Cottage-Cheese Bake

TIME: about 1¹/₄ hours—SERVINGS: 6

1 8-ounce package wide noodles

1 8-ounce package sliced bacon, cut into 1-inch pieces

4 green onions, chopped

3 8-ounce containers creamed cottage cheese (3 cups)

1¹/₂ 8-ounce containers sour cream (1¹/₂ cups)

³/₄ teaspoon salt

3 eggs

2 slices white bread

1. Prepare noodles as label directs; drain.

2. Meanwhile, in 12-inch skillet over medium-low heat, cook bacon until browned; remove to paper towels to drain. Spoon off all but 1 tablespoon drippings from skillet. Add green onions; cook until tender, stirring occasionally. Remove skillet from heat.

3. Preheat oven to 350° F. Grease 12″ by 8″ baking dish. Into large bowl, press cottage cheese through fine sieve. Stir in sour cream, salt, and eggs until blended. Gently toss noodles, bacon, and green onions with cottage-cheese mixture; spoon into baking dish. Tear bread into small pieces; sprinkle over top of noodle mixture; bake, uncovered, 30 minutes or until hot. Cut into 6 pieces.

Fresh-Vegetable Crepes

TIME: about 1 hour—SERVINGS: 4

3 medium zucchini (about 6 ounces each)

2 medium yellow straightneck squash (about 6 ounces each)

1 medium red or green pepper

1 medium onion

6 eggs

water

salad oil

1 teaspoon salt

¹/₂ teaspoon oregano leaves

¹/₈ teaspoon pepper

1 8-ounce package Longhorn cheese, shredded

1. Slice zucchini and yellow squash lengthwise in half; cut each half crosswise into ¹/₄-inch slices. Cut pepper into thin strips. Dice onion.

2. In medium bowl with fork, beat eggs and ¹/₃ cup water until well blended. In 6- or 7-inch crepe pan over medium heat, heat 1 teaspoon salad oil, tilting pan to grease side. Pour ¹/₄ cup egg mixture into skillet, tilting to make a thin crepe. When top of crepe is set and underside is delicately browned, run spatula around side and bottom to loosen; slide crepe onto plate. Repeat to make seven more; keep warm.

3. In 12-inch skillet over medium heat, in ¹/₄ cup hot salad oil, cook onion until tender and lightly browned, stirring occasionally. Add zucchini, yellow squash, red pepper, salt, oregano, pepper, and ¹/₂ cup water; cook until all vegetables are tender, about 20 minutes, stirring frequently. Remove skillet from heat; stir in cheese until blended.

4. To serve, spread a heaping ¹/₃ cupful vegetable mixture onto center of each crepe; fold two sides of crepe over filling to make roll. Arrange filled crepes on warm platter. Serve as a main dish.

Cheese-and-Beer Bake

TIME: about 30 minutes—SERVINGS: 6

1 8- or 12-ounce long loaf Italian bread

1 pound Monterey Jack cheese

1¼ cups beer

1 tablespoon sesame seeds

1. Preheat oven to 400° F. Cut bread into 18 slices. Place slices on large cookie sheet; toast in oven for 10 to 12 minutes until browned.

2. Meanwhile, grease 13″ by 9″ baking dish. Cut cheese into 18 slices. Sprinkle each slice of bread with about 1 tablespoon beer. Arrange bread and cheese in dish lengthwise in two rows, alternating bread and cheese slices and overlapping slightly; sprinkle with sesame seeds.

3. Bake 15 minutes or until cheese is melted.

Party Pizza

TIME: about 1 hour—SERVINGS: 6

1 13¾-ounce package hot-roll mix

1 cup water

3 tablespoons salad oil

½ pound mushrooms, sliced

2 medium green peppers, diced

1 small onion, diced

1 12¾- to 14-ounce jar pizza sauce

1 large tomato, diced

1 8-ounce package mozzarella cheese, sliced

¼ pound Swiss cheese, shredded (1 cup)

½ cup grated Parmesan cheese

6 pitted ripe olives, sliced

⅛ teaspoon crushed red pepper (optional)

1. Prepare hot-roll mix as label directs for pizza, but use 1 cup water; omit egg; do not knead dough. Grease 15½″ by 10½″ jelly-roll pan. With greased hands, pat dough evenly onto bottom and up sides of pan; let dough rise in pan 15 minutes.

2. Meanwhile, in 12-inch skillet over medium heat, in hot salad oil, cook mushrooms, green peppers, and onion until vegetables are tender-crisp, stirring occasionally.

3. Preheat oven to 425° F. Spread pizza sauce evenly over dough; top with green-pepper mixture and diced tomato. Tuck mozzarella cheese slices over and under vegetables; sprinkle pizza with shredded Swiss cheese, grated Parmesan cheese, sliced olives, and crushed red pepper. Bake pizza on bottom rack of oven 20 to 30 minutes or until hot and bubbly and crust is browned and crisp.

Spinach-and-Cheese Dumplings

TIME: about 1 hour—SERVINGS: 6

1 15- to 16-ounce container ricotta cheese (2 cups)

1 10-ounce package frozen chopped spinach, thawed and squeezed dry

½ cup grated Parmesan cheese

½ teaspoon salt

1 egg

1 small garlic clove, minced

all-purpose flour

water

Cheese Sauce (right)

1. In large bowl, mix first 6 ingredients and ¾ cup flour.

2. Onto waxed paper, measure 2 tablespoons flour. With floured hands, shape spinach mixture into 1-inch balls; gently roll balls in flour to coat lightly.

3. Meanwhile, fill 5-quart saucepot half full with water; over high heat, heat to boiling. Carefully add spinach balls, half at a time, to boiling water; cook 10 minutes or until slightly puffed and set. With slotted spoon, remove spinach balls to paper towels to drain.

4. Prepare Cheese Sauce.

5. Preheat broiler if manufacturer directs. Into 12″ by 8″ baking dish, spoon small amount of Cheese Sauce; arrange spinach balls in sauce; spoon remaining sauce over and around balls. About 7 to 9 inches from source of heat (or at 450° F.), broil 10 to 15 minutes, until hot and bubbly.

Cheese Sauce: In 2-quart saucepan over medium heat, melt *2 tablespoons butter* or margarine; stir in *2 tablespoons all-purpose flour, ⅛ teaspoon salt*, and *⅛ teaspoon ground red pepper;* cook 1 minute. Gradually stir in *2 cups milk;* cook until sauce is slightly thickened and smooth, stirring. Add *½ cup shredded Swiss cheese;* cook until cheese melts, stirring.

Baked Cheese Fondue

TIME: about 2 hours—SERVINGS: 4

4 slices white bread

butter or margarine, softened

1 cup shredded or slivered American
   cheese

4 eggs

2 cups milk

1 teaspoon salt

$1/2$ teaspoon dry mustard

1. Spread bread lightly with butter or margarine; cut into 1-inch squares. In greased $1^1/2$-quart casserole, arrange half of squares; top with half of cheese; repeat. In medium bowl with wire whisk or hand beater, beat eggs with rest of ingredients; pour over cheese.

2. Set casserole in shallow baking pan on oven rack; fill pan with hot water to come halfway up side of casserole. Bake in 350° F. oven, uncovered, 1 hour and 20 minutes or until cheese mixture is puffed and golden. Serve at once.

Ranchero Casserole

TIME: about $1^1/2$ hours—SERVINGS: 6

$3/4$ pound ground beef

1 small onion, diced

1 tablespoon chili powder

1 15- to 16-ounce can tomato sauce

1 4-ounce can chopped green chilies,
   drained

$1/2$ cup water

$1^1/2$ teaspoons sugar

1 teaspoon salt

8 6-inch packaged corn tortillas

salad oil

1 15- to 16-ounce container ricotta cheese

1 egg

1 4-ounce package shredded sharp
   Cheddar cheese (1 cup)

$1/2$ cup shredded lettuce

10 large pitted ripe olives, sliced

1 small tomato, diced

1. In 3-quart saucepan over high heat, cook ground beef and onion until all pan juices evaporate and meat is well browned, stirring occasionally. Stir in chili powder; cook 1 minute. Stir in tomato sauce, green chilies, water, sugar, and salt; heat to boiling and stir to loosen brown bits on bottom of saucepan. Reduce heat to low; cover and simmer 20 minutes, stirring occasionally.

2. Meanwhile, slice tortillas into $1/2$-inch strips. In 10-inch skillet over medium-high heat, in $1/4$ inch hot salad oil, fry several tortilla strips at a time, a few seconds, until golden. With slotted spoon, remove tortillas to paper towels to drain.

3. Preheat oven to 350° F. In medium bowl, mix ricotta cheese with egg. Into 12″ by 8″ baking dish, spoon half of meat sauce. Top with half of Cheddar cheese and half of ricotta mixture. Arrange all tortilla strips on ricotta mixture in baking dish; top with remaining ricotta mixture, then remaining meat sauce. Sprinkle with remaining Cheddar. Bake casserole, uncovered, 30 minutes or until heated through.

4. To serve, top casserole with lettuce, olives, and tomato.

Condiments and Sauces

Curried Cucumber Pickles

YIELD: about 8 pints

10 **large cucumbers (about 6¹/₂ pounds)**

³/₄ **cup salt**

water

about 8 1-pint canning jars and caps

4 **cups cider vinegar**

1²/₃ **cups sugar**

¹/₂ **cup all-purpose flour**

¹/₄ **cup curry powder**

2 **teaspoons turmeric**

¹/₂ **teaspoon cracked pepper**

1. On day before canning, cut cucumbers lengthwise in half; cut halves crosswise into ¹/₂-inch-thick slices. Into 10-quart enamel, stainless steel, or glass container, measure salt and 3¹/₂ quarts water; stir until salt dissolves. Add cucumbers; cover and let stand in cool place 12 to 18 hours.

2. On canning day, prepare jars and caps for processing. Check jars to be sure they have no nicks, cracks, or sharp edges that will prevent an airtight seal or cause breakage. Wash jars, lids, and screw bands (or caps and rubber rings) in hot soapy water; rinse well. Leave jars and lids in hot water until ready to use. Wet rubber rings before using.

3. Drain cucumbers; rinse with running cold water; drain thoroughly. In 8-quart saucepot or Dutch oven, mix vinegar, sugar, flour, curry powder, turmeric, pepper, and ³/₄ cup water until smooth. Cook over medium heat until mixture thickens slightly and boils, stirring. Add cucumbers; over high heat, heat to boiling. Reduce heat to medium; cook 15 minutes, stirring often.

4. With slotted spoon, spoon hot vegetables into hot jars to ¹/₄ inch from top of jar. Immediately ladle hot vinegar mixture over cucumbers in jar to ¹/₄ inch from top of jar. (Keep mixture simmering while filling jars.) With small spatula, carefully remove any air bubbles between cucumbers and jar. Close jars as manufacturer directs.

5. Place jars on rack in canner half filled with boiling water, far enough apart so that water can circulate freely; add additional boiling water if needed so that water level is 1 to 2 inches above tops of jars (do not pour water directly on jars). Over high heat, heat to boiling. Cover canner; reduce heat to medium; boil gently 15 minutes. With jar lifter or tongs, remove jars from canner; set jars, several inches apart, on wire racks. Complete seal on jars with glass or zinc caps as manufacturer directs. Do not tighten screw bands. Cool at least 12 hours.

6. Now, test seal: Press lid at center; if center is down and stays down, jar is sealed. Turn jars with glass or zinc caps and rubber rings partly over; if no leakage, jars are sealed. Refrigerate unsealed jars; use within one month. Store sealed jars in cool, dry place; use within one year.

Dill Pickles

YIELD: about 20 pickles

about 20 small cucumbers, each about 3 to
  3¹/₂ inches long (about 4¹/₄ pounds)

4 medium garlic cloves

1 medium bunch fresh dill (about 16 large
  sprigs)

¹/₄ cup mixed pickling spice

2 teaspoons dill seeds

¹/₄ teaspoon crushed red pepper

2 quarts water

¹/₂ cup white vinegar

¹/₂ cup pure granulated or pickling salt

2 tablespoons sugar

1. Wash cucumbers thoroughly to remove any sand and grit; drain.

2. With flat side of knife, crush garlic cloves slightly. In bottom of 2-gallon crock or wide-mouth jar, place 2 garlic cloves, half of fresh dill, half of mixed pickling spice, half of dill seeds, and half of crushed red pepper. Pack cucumbers into crock to 3 inches from top of crock. Add remaining garlic, pickling spice, dill seeds, and crushed red pepper. Top with layer of remaining fresh dill.

3. In large bowl, mix water, vinegar, salt (pure granulated or pickling salt should be used if at all possible; uniodized salt can be used, but additives in the salt that prevent caking may make the brine cloudy; iodized table salt should not be used because it may darken pickles), and sugar until salt and sugar dissolve. Pour saltwater brine into jar to completely cover cucumbers. Cover cucumbers with clean heavy plate or something similar to hold cucumbers under brine. Place crock on stainproof surface or plate (brine may overflow as pickles ferment). Keep cucumbers at about 70° F. Let cucumbers ferment about 3 to 5 days for half sour, about 6 to 8 days for very sour. Check pickles every day, and remove any scum that forms over the top. (The development of some cloudiness in the brine is also typical.)

4. When pickles have reached the degree of sourness you like, they can be stored in the refrigerator to use up within one month. To store in the refrigerator, remove pickles from crock, reserving brine. Pack pickles in jars. Strain brine and pour over pickles to completely cover. (Do not leave pickles at room temperature after fermentation is complete or they may spoil.)

Pepper-Pear Relish

YIELD: about 5 pints

10 large pears (5 pounds), peeled, cored,
  and cut into ¹/₂-inch chunks

5 medium red peppers, diced

5 medium green peppers, diced

2 cups cider vinegar

2 cups packed dark-brown sugar

2 tablespoons salt

2 tablespoons minced peeled ginger root

1 tablespoon mustard seeds

about 5 1-pint canning jars and caps

1. In 8-quart Dutch oven or heavy saucepot over high heat, heat all relish ingredients to boiling, stirring occasionally. Reduce heat to low; cover and simmer 40 minutes, stirring occasionally. Remove cover and simmer 30 minutes longer or until relish is thickened, stirring frequently.

2. Meanwhile, prepare jars and caps for processing. Check jars to be sure they have no nicks, cracks, or sharp edges that will prevent an airtight seal or cause breakage. Wash jars, lids, and screw bands (or caps and rubber rings) in hot soapy water; rinse well. Leave jars and lids in hot water until ready to use. Wet rubber rings before using to make them more pliable.

3. Immediately ladle hot relish mixture into hot jars to within ¹/₄ inch of top of jar. (Keep mixture simmering while filling jars.) Close jars as directed by manufacturer.

4. Place jars on rack in canner half filled with boiling water, far enough apart so that water can circulate freely. Add additional boiling water if needed so that water level is 1 to 2 inches above tops of jars (do not pour water directly on jars). Over high heat, heat to boiling. Cover canner; reduce heat to medium; boil gently 20 minutes. With jar lifter or tongs, remove jars from canner; set jars, several inches apart, on wire rack. Complete seal on jars with glass or zinc caps as manufacturer directs. Do not tighten screw bands. Cool at least 12 hours.

5. Now, test seal: Press lid at center; if center is down and stays down, jar is sealed. Turn jars with glass or zinc caps and rubber rings partly over; if no leakage, jars are sealed. Store unsealed jars in refrigerator to use within one month. Store sealed jars in cool, dark, dry place to use within one year.

Tangy Onion Relish

TIME: about 4 hours or start up to 2 weeks ahead—YIELD: about 3 cups

6 medium onions (about 2 pounds), diced

1 medium red pepper, diced

1/2 cup packed brown sugar

1/2 cup apple juice

1/3 cup white-wine vinegar

1 tablespoon salt

1 tablespoon prepared horseradish

1 tablespoon salad oil

2 1/2 teaspoons prepared mustard

In 3-quart saucepan over medium-high heat, heat all ingredients to boiling. Reduce heat to low; simmer, uncovered, 20 minutes, stirring occasionally. Spoon relish into medium bowl; cover and refrigerate until well chilled, about 3 hours or up to 2 weeks. Serve with hamburgers, frankfurters, broiled steaks, or chicken.

Tomato-Apple Chutney

YIELD: about 11 half-pints

preserved ginger in syrup

12 medium, firm tomatoes (about 4 pounds), peeled and cut into quarters

5 large green cooking apples (about 2 pounds), peeled and diced

1 medium onion, diced

1 garlic clove, minced

1 16-ounce package light-brown sugar (2 1/4 cups)

1 cup dark seedless raisins, chopped

1 cup cider vinegar

4 teaspoons salt

1/2 teaspoon ground cinnamon

1/4 teaspoon ground red pepper

about 11 1/2-pint canning jars and caps

1. Mince enough preserved ginger to make 1/4 cup. In 8-quart Dutch oven or heavy saucepot over medium-high heat, heat ginger and all remaining chutney ingredients to boiling, stirring frequently. Reduce heat to medium-low; simmer, uncovered, until chutney is very thick, about 1 1/2 hours, stirring mixture occasionally.

2. Meanwhile, prepare jars and caps for processing. Check jars to be sure they have no nicks, cracks, or sharp edges that will prevent an airtight seal or cause breakage. Wash jars, lids, and screw bands (or caps and rubber rings) in hot soapy water; rinse well. Leave jars and lids in hot water until ready to use. Wet rubber rings before using, to make them more pliable.

3. Immediately ladle hot chutney mixture into hot jars to within 1/4 inch of top of jar. (Keep mixture simmering while filling jars.) Close jars as manufacturer directs.

4. Place jars on rack in canner half filled with boiling water far enough apart so that water can circulate freely. Add additional boiling water if needed so that water level is 1 to 2 inches above tops of jars (do not pour water directly on jars). Over high heat, heat to boiling. Cover canner; reduce heat to medium; boil gently 10 minutes. With jar lifter or tongs, remove jars from canner; set jars, several inches apart, on wire racks. Complete seal on jars with glass or zinc caps as manufacturer directs. Do not tighten screw bands. Cool at least 12 hours.

5. Now, test seal: Press lid at center; if center is down and stays down, jar is sealed. Turn jars with glass or zinc caps and rubber rings partly over; if no leakage, jars are sealed. Store unsealed jars in refrigerator to use within one month. Store sealed jars in cool, dark, dry place to use within one year.

Cranberry Chutney

TIME: about 4 hours or start up to 1 week ahead—YIELD: about 6 cups

2 12-ounce packages fresh or frozen cranberries

1 medium red cooking apple, diced

2¹/₂ cups packed brown sugar

¹/₂ cup diced pitted prunes

¹/₂ cup water

¹/₂ cup cider vinegar

¹/₄ cup minced preserved ginger

1 tablespoon grated orange peel

2 teaspoons salt

1 teaspoon ground allspice

In 5-quart saucepot or Dutch oven over medium-high heat, heat all ingredients to boiling, stirring occasionally. Reduce heat to low; cover and simmer until thickened, about 15 minutes, stirring occasionally. Spoon chutney into large bowl; cover and refrigerate to use up within one week.

Green-Tomato-Lemon Marmalade

YIELD: 8 half-pints

2 medium lemons

water

5 pounds green tomatoes, thinly sliced

5 cups sugar

1 cup packed light-brown sugar

1 tablespoon salt

about 8 ¹/₂-pint canning jars and caps

1. With vegetable peeler, cut peel from lemons; then with sharp knife, cut peel into very thin strips. In 1-quart saucepan over high heat, heat lemon peel and 1 inch water to boiling. Reduce heat to medium; cook 10 minutes. Drain; discard water.

2. Meanwhile, trim off as much white membrane from lemons as possible; discard membrane. Cut lemons into thin slices; remove seeds.

3. In 8-quart Dutch oven or heavy saucepot over high heat, heat lemon peel, lemon slices, tomatoes, and all remaining marmalade ingredients to boiling, stirring frequently. Reduce heat to medium; cook, uncovered, until marmalade is very thick, about 50 minutes, stirring occasionally.

4. Meanwhile, prepare jars and caps for processing. Check jars to be sure they have no nicks, cracks, or sharp edges that will prevent an airtight seal or cause breakage. Wash jars, lids, and screw bands (or caps and rubber rings) in hot soapy water; rinse well. Leave jars and lids in hot water until ready to use. Wet rubber rings before using to make them more pliable.

5. With metal spoon, skim off foam. Immediately ladle hot marmalade mixture into hot jars to ¹/₄ inch from top of jar. (Keep mixture simmering while filling jars.) Close jars as manufacturer directs.

6. Place jars on rack in canner half filled with boiling water, far enough apart so that water can circulate freely. Add additional boiling water if needed so that water level is 1 to 2 inches above tops of jars (do not pour water directly on jars). Over high heat, heat to boiling. Cover canner; reduce heat to medium; boil gently 15 minutes. With jar lifter or tongs, remove jars from canner; set jars, several inches apart, on wire racks. Complete seals on jars with glass or zinc caps and rubber rings as manufacturer directs. Do not tighten screw bands. Cool at least 12 hours.

7. Now, test seal: Press lid at center; if center is down and stays down, jar is sealed. Turn jars with glass or zinc caps and rubber rings partly over; if no leakage, jars are sealed. Store unsealed jars in refrigerator to use within one month. Store sealed jars in cool, dark, dry place to use within one year.

Spicy Country Barbecue Sauce

TIME: about 15 minutes—YIELD: about $1^2/3$ cups

2 tablespoons salad oil
1 medium onion, diced
1 8-ounce can tomato sauce
$1/2$ cup packed brown sugar
$1/4$ cup white vinegar
1 tablespoon Worcestershire
4 teaspoons chili powder
2 teaspoons salt
$1/4$ teaspoon dry mustard

1. In 1-quart saucepan over medium heat, in hot salad oil, cook onion until tender, about 5 minutes, stirring occasionally.

2. Add remaining ingredients; heat to boiling, stirring constantly. Use to baste spareribs, beef, or lamb during grilling. Serve remainder with meat.

Zesty Mustard Barbecue Sauce

TIME: about 5 minutes—YIELD: about $1/2$ cup

$1/4$ cup red-wine vinegar
2 tablespoons prepared mustard
1 tablespoon meat-extract paste
2 teaspoons coarsely ground black pepper
$1/4$ teaspoon salt

In small bowl, mix all ingredients. Use to baste steaks and hamburgers during grilling.

Spicy Horseradish Barbecue Sauce

TIME: about 5 minutes—YIELD: about $1/2$ cup

$1/4$ cup catchup
2 tablespoons cider vinegar
1 tablespoon Worcestershire
2 teaspoons prepared horseradish
$1^1/2$ teaspoons prepared mustard
$1/4$ teaspoon hot-pepper sauce

In small bowl, mix all ingredients. Use to baste steak and hamburgers during grilling.

Caper Barbecue Sauce

TIME: about 5 minutes—YIELD: about $1/2$ cup

$1/4$ cup drained capers
$1/4$ cup mayonnaise
2 tablespoons cooking or dry white wine
2 tablespoons prepared mustard

In blender at medium speed or in food processor with knife blade attached, blend all ingredients until smooth. Use to baste steaks, hamburgers, or fish during grilling.

Tangy Beer Barbecue Sauce

TIME: about 5 minutes—YIELD: about $3/4$ cup

$1/3$ cup chili sauce
$1/4$ cup beer
1 tablespoon soy sauce
1 tablespoon salad oil
$1/2$ teaspoon sugar
$1/2$ teaspoon salt
$1/2$ teaspoon grated onion
$1/4$ teaspoon dry mustard
$1/8$ teaspoon hot-pepper sauce

In medium bowl, mix all ingredients. Use to baste steaks, hamburgers, or kabobs during grilling.

Lemony Barbecue Sauce

TIME: about 5 minutes—YIELD: about $1/2$ cup

$1/3$ cup lemonade-flavor drink mix

$1/3$ cup dark molasses

2 teaspoons salt

$1/8$ teaspoon pepper

In small bowl, mix all ingredients. Use to baste pork during grilling.

Peanut-Ginger Barbecue Sauce

TIME: about 5 minutes—YIELD: about 1 cup

$3/4$ cup packed light-brown sugar

$1/3$ cup red-wine vinegar

3 tablespoons soy sauce

1 tablespoon creamy peanut butter

$1^1/4$ teaspoons ground ginger or
  1 tablespoon minced fresh ginger root

$3/4$ teaspoon salt

In small bowl, mix all ingredients. Use to baste pork during grilling.

Piquant Plum Barbecue Sauce

TIME: about 5 minutes—YIELD: about 1 cup

1 17-ounce can purple plums, drained and pitted

2 tablespoons brown sugar

2 tablespoons chili sauce

1 tablespoon soy sauce

$1^1/2$ teaspoons lemon juice

$1/2$ teaspoon salt

$1/2$ teaspoon prepared mustard

In blender at medium speed or in food processor with knife blade attached, blend all ingredients. Use to baste pork during grilling.

Cranberry-Honey Barbecue Sauce

TIME: about 5 minutes—YIELD: about 1 cup

1 8-ounce can whole-berry cranberry sauce

3 tablespoons honey

1 tablespoon salad oil

1 tablespoon red-wine vinegar

$1^1/2$ teaspoons salt

$1/2$ teaspoon ground cinnamon

In small bowl, mix all ingredients. Use to baste pork during grilling.

Buttery Rosemary Barbecue Sauce

TIME: about 10 minutes—YIELD: about $1/3$ cup

1 teaspoon rosemary

4 tablespoons butter or margarine

1 tablespoon lemon juice

$3/4$ teaspoon salt

$1/8$ teaspoon pepper

In mortar with pestle, crush the rosemary. In small saucepan over low heat, heat all ingredients until butter is melted. Use to baste chicken during grilling.

Fiery Chili Barbecue Sauce

TIME: about 5 minutes—YIELD: about $1^1/_2$ cups

1 8-ounce can stewed tomatoes

2 (or more) pickled jalapeño chilies, minced

2 tablespoons brown sugar

2 tablespoons salad oil

1 teaspoon salt

1 teaspoon Worcestershire

$^1/_8$ teaspoon garlic powder

In small bowl, mix all ingredients. Use to baste chicken or pork during grilling.

Soy Barbecue Sauce

TIME: about 5 minutes—YIELD: about $^3/_4$ cup

$^1/_4$ cup minced green onions

$^1/_3$ cup soy sauce

2 tablespoons cooking or dry white wine

2 tablespoons catchup

1 tablespoon salad oil

1 teaspoon Worcestershire

In small bowl with back of spoon, mash slightly the green onions. Stir in remaining ingredients. Use to baste chicken or pork during grilling.

East Indies Barbecue Sauce

TIME: about 5 minutes—YIELD: about $^1/_3$ cup

$^1/_4$ cup lemon juice

2 tablespoons salad oil

$1^1/_2$ teaspoons salt

$1^1/_2$ teaspoons turmeric

1 teaspoon ground cardamom

1 teaspoon ground ginger

$^3/_4$ teaspoon sugar

1 small garlic clove, minced

In small bowl, mix all ingredients. Use to baste chicken, beef, or lamb during grilling.

Best Big-Batch Tomato Sauce

TIME: about $3^1/_2$ hours—YIELD: about 9 pints

$^1/_4$ cup salad oil

3 medium onions, thinly sliced

3 large carrots, thinly sliced

2 medium green peppers, diced

2 medium garlic cloves, minced

12 pounds tomatoes, peeled and diced

1 12-ounce can tomato paste

$^1/_4$ cup packed brown sugar

2 tablespoons salt

2 teaspoons oregano leaves

$1^1/_2$ teaspoons basil

$^1/_2$ teaspoon pepper

In 8-quart Dutch oven over medium heat, in hot salad oil, cook onions, carrots, green peppers, and garlic until tender, stirring occasionally. Add tomatoes and remaining ingredients; over high heat, heat to boiling. Reduce heat to medium-low; partially cover Dutch oven and cook 2 hours, stirring occasionally. (One pint is enough to serve over *one 8-ounce package spaghetti*, cooked, as four accompaniment servings. Or use sauce in Swiss steak, pizza, lasagna, or eggplant Parmigiana.)

TO FREEZE AND USE UP TO 1 YEAR LATER: Spoon sauce into nine 1-pint freezerproof wide-mouthed containers or freezer-weight plastic bags, leaving at least 1 inch space at top of container. Close container; label and freeze. Reheat frozen sauce with a little water to avoid scorching.

Bordelaise Sauce

TIME: about 25 minutes—YIELD: about $1\frac{1}{3}$ cups

2 tablespoons butter or margarine

2 tablespoons all-purpose flour

1 tablespoon minced onion

1 tablespoon minced parsley

1 bay leaf

$\frac{1}{4}$ teaspoon thyme leaves

$\frac{1}{4}$ teaspoon salt

$\frac{1}{8}$ teaspoon coarsely ground or cracked black pepper

1 $10\frac{1}{2}$-ounce can condensed beef broth (bouillon), undiluted

$\frac{1}{4}$ cup dry red wine

1. In heavy 1-quart saucepan over low heat, in hot butter or margarine, cook the flour until it is just lightly browned, stirring often.

2. Stir in minced onion, parsley, bay leaf, thyme leaves, salt, and coarsely ground pepper.

3. Slowly add undiluted beef broth and red wine. Stir the mixture to blend together well. Increase the heat to medium-high.

4. Cook, stirring constantly, until the mixture thickens. Discard bay leaf. Serve hot over roast or broiled beef.

Béarnaise Sauce

TIME: about 15 minutes—YIELD: about 1 cup

$\frac{1}{4}$ cup white-wine vinegar

1 tablespoon minced green onion

$1\frac{1}{2}$ teaspoons tarragon

$\frac{1}{4}$ teaspoon coarsely ground black pepper

2 egg yolks

$\frac{3}{4}$ cup butter or margarine

1 tablespoon chopped parsley

1. In double-boiler top, combine wine vinegar, green onion, tarragon, and pepper. Over high heat, heat to boiling. Boil about 3 minutes or until vinegar is reduced to about 1 tablespoon.

2. Place double-boiler top over double-boiler bottom with hot, *not boiling*, water. Add egg yolks and cook, beating constantly with wire whisk until slightly thickened. Add butter or margarine, a tablespoon at a time, beating constantly with wire whisk until butter is melted and mixture is thickened. Stir in parsley. Keep sauce warm over hot, *not boiling*, water.

Caper Mayonnaise

TIME: about 5 minutes—YIELD: about $1\frac{1}{2}$ cups

1 cup mayonnaise

$\frac{1}{3}$ cup milk

3 tablespoons catchup

1 tablespoon capers, minced

In small bowl with wire whisk or fork, mix all ingredients. Cover and refrigerate. Serve with cold poached fish.

Radish Mayonnaise

TIME: about 5 minutes—YIELD: about $2\frac{3}{4}$ cups

1 6-ounce package radishes, minced

2 cups mayonnaise

$\frac{1}{3}$ cup milk

In medium bowl, mix all ingredients. Cover and refrigerate. Serve with cold sliced poultry or meat.

Parmesan-Cheese Sauce

TIME: about 15 minutes—YIELD: about $3\frac{1}{2}$ cups

4 tablespoons butter or margarine

$\frac{1}{4}$ cup all-purpose flour

$1\frac{1}{2}$ cups half-and-half

$1\frac{1}{2}$ cups water

2 chicken-flavor bouillon cubes

$\frac{1}{2}$ cup grated Parmesan cheese

1. In 2-quart saucepan over medium heat, into hot butter, stir flour until well blended.

2. Gradually stir in half-and-half, water, and chicken bouillon cubes. Cook, stirring constantly, until sauce is thickened. Stir in the grated Parmesan cheese and heat just until melted. Serve with baked or poached fish or pasta.

Cheddar-Cheese Sauce

TIME: about 15 minutes—YIELD: about 1 cup

1 tablespoon butter or margarine

1 tablespoon all-purpose flour

$^1/_8$ teaspoon salt

dash ground red pepper

$^3/_4$ cup milk

$^1/_3$ cup shredded Cheddar cheese

In 1-quart saucepan over low heat, melt butter; stir in flour, salt, and ground red pepper until blended. Gradually stir in milk; cook, stirring constantly, until sauce is thickened and smooth. Stir in cheese until blended. Serve on cooked vegetables, poached eggs, or poached or broiled fish.

Peppery Blue-Cheese Sauce

TIME: about 15 minutes—YIELD: about 1 cup

1 tablespoon butter or margarine

1 tablespoon all-purpose flour

$^3/_4$ cup milk

$^1/_2$ cup crumbled blue cheese

$^1/_2$ teaspoon salt

$^1/_4$ teaspoon coarsely ground pepper

1. In 1-quart saucepan over medium heat, into hot butter or margarine, stir flour until blended. Gradually stir in milk and cook, stirring constantly, until mixture is thickened.

2. Remove mixture from heat; stir in cheese and remaining ingredients. Serve hot over grilled steak, lamb or beef patties, or lamb chops.

Creamy Shrimp Sauce

TIME: about 20 minutes—YIELD: about $2^3/_4$ cups

1 8-ounce package frozen shelled and deveined shrimp

3 tablespoons butter or margarine

3 tablespoons all-purpose flour

$^3/_4$ teaspoon salt

$^1/_8$ teaspoon pepper

1 cup heavy or whipping cream

$^3/_4$ cup milk

$^1/_4$ cup dry vermouth

1. In 2-quart saucepan over high heat, in 1 inch boiling water, heat shrimp to boiling. With slotted spoon, remove shrimp to small bowl; discard water.

2. In the same saucepan over low heat, melt butter; stir in flour, salt, and pepper until blended. Gradually stir in cream, milk, and vermouth. Over medium heat, cook, stirring constantly, until mixture is thickened and smooth. Stir in shrimp; heat through. Serve on poached or broiled fish.

Creamy Mushroom Gravy

TIME: about 15 minutes—YIELD: about $2^1/_2$ cups

3 tablespoons butter or margarine

$^1/_2$ pound mushrooms, thinly sliced

1 green onion, sliced

2 tablespoons all-purpose flour

$^1/_4$ teaspoon salt

$^1/_8$ teaspoon pepper

2 cups milk

1 chicken-flavor bouillon cube or envelope

In 3-quart saucepan over medium heat, melt butter. Add mushrooms and green onion, and cook until vegetables are tender, stirring occasionally. Stir in flour, salt, and pepper. Gradually stir in milk and bouillon cube; cook, stirring frequently, until mixture thickens. Serve on broiled or roast poultry.

Sandwiches

Barbecued Beef Heros for Two

TIME: about 30 minutes—SERVINGS: 2

½ pound cooked beef top round roast

1 tablespoon salad oil

1 small onion, diced

1 small garlic clove, minced

1 8-ounce can tomato sauce

⅓ cup water

2 teaspoons brown sugar

1 teaspoon vinegar

½ teaspoon salt

½ teaspoon chili powder

1 6- to 7-inch-long hard roll

green onions (optional)

pickles (optional)

1. Cut beef top round roast into very thin slices; set aside.

2. In 2-quart saucepan over medium heat, in hot salad oil, cook onion and garlic until tender, stirring occasionally. Stir in tomato sauce, water, brown sugar, vinegar, salt, and chili powder; over high heat, heat to boiling. Reduce heat to low; cover; simmer 15 minutes, stirring occasionally. Add meat; heat.

3. To serve, split roll horizontally. Arrange mixture on bottom half; replace top. Cut sandwich crosswise in half. If you like, serve with green onions and pickles.

Turkey Burgers

TIME: about 25 minutes—SERVINGS: 2

1 cup diced cooked turkey

½ cup dried bread crumbs

1 tablespoon water

1 teaspoon grated onion

½ teaspoon salt

⅛ teaspoon pepper

1 egg

butter or margarine

2 sesame-seed hamburger buns

lettuce leaves

whole-berry cranberry sauce

1. In small bowl with fork, mix first 7 ingredients and 1 tablespoon softened butter. Shape mixture into two 3½-inch round patties.

2. In 10-inch skillet over medium heat, melt 1 tablespoon butter; add patties and cook about 10 minutes or until golden, turning once.

3. Slice each bun horizontally in half. Serve patties in buns with lettuce and cranberry sauce.

Mozzarella Loaf

TIME: about 40 minutes—SERVINGS: 6

1 long loaf Italian bread with sesame seeds

1 16-ounce package mozzarella cheese

1/2 cup olives for salad

1 1/2 teaspoons oregano

1. Preheat oven to 400° F. Cut bread crosswise into 1-inch slices, being careful not to cut through bottom crust. Cut cheese into 1/4-inch slices. Place cheese and olives between bread slices.

2. Place bread on cookie sheet, and bake about 15 minutes or until cheese is melted. Sprinkle loaf with oregano. With a sharp knife, divide loaf into slices by cutting through bottom crust. Serve immediately.

Pork-and-Pepper Sandwich

TIME: about 20 minutes—SERVINGS: 2

1 large green pepper

1 medium onion

2 tablespoons salad oil

1 cup thinly sliced cooked pork (6 ounces)

2 tablespoons catchup

1 tablespoon soy sauce

1/4 teaspoon Worcestershire

2 English muffins, split in halves

1. Thinly slice green pepper and onion. In 10-inch skillet over medium-high heat, in hot salad oil, cook green pepper and onion until tender-crisp and lightly browned. Reduce heat to low. Add sliced pork, catchup, soy sauce, and Worcestershire; heat through, stirring frequently.

2. To serve, toast English muffin halves. Arrange mixture in muffins.

Open-faced Reubens

TIME: about 30 minutes—SERVINGS: 2

1/2 8-ounce can sauerkraut, drained

1 small carrot, shredded

2 slices rye bread

1 3-ounce package sliced corned beef or about 1/4 pound sliced cooked corned beef

1/4 cup bottled creamy Russian dressing

1/2 8-ounce package Swiss-cheese slices

2 tablespoons butter or margarine

1. In small bowl, toss sauerkraut and carrot. On bread slices, arrange corned beef, then Russian dressing, Swiss cheese, and sauerkraut mixture.

2. In 10-inch skillet over low heat, in melted butter or margarine, arrange Reubens, bread side down. Cover skillet and cook until bread is browned and cheese is melted, about 5 minutes.

Ham-and-Swiss Buns

TIME: about 30 minutes—SERVINGS: 4

1 8-ounce package refrigerated crescent dinner rolls

1 4-ounce package sliced cooked ham

1/2 8-ounce package sliced Swiss cheese

2 teaspoons prepared mustard

1 egg, slightly beaten

carrot sticks (optional)

potato chips (optional)

1. Preheat oven to 375° F. On floured surface, separate dough from the crescent dinner rolls into four rectangles. Gently pinch diagonal perforations together on each rectangle. With lightly floured rolling pin, roll each rectangle into 7" by 5" rectangle.

2. Arrange ham and cheese slices on dough rectangles, cutting ham and cheese to fit and leaving 1/2-inch rim of dough all around. Spread filling with mustard. Brush rim of dough with some egg. Fold dough and filling over so 5-inch sides meet.

3. With fork, firmly press edges together to seal. Place on cookie sheet; brush with remaining egg. Bake 12 to 15 minutes until browned. If you like, serve with carrot sticks and potato chips.

Summer Tuna Cakes

TIME: about 30 minutes—SERVINGS: 2

1 medium zucchini

1 6¹/₂- or 7-ounce can tuna, drained and flaked

1¹/₂ cups white-bread cubes (3 slices)

1 egg

2 teaspoons grated onion

1 teaspoon lemon juice

¹/₄ teaspoon salt

¹/₄ teaspoon pepper

2 tablespoons salad oil

2 slices whole-wheat bread

about 3 tablespoons mayonnaise

2 large lettuce leaves

1 small tomato, sliced

1. Finely shred zucchini; pat dry with paper towels. In medium bowl, mix zucchini with next 7 ingredients. With hands, shape the zucchini mixture into two 3-inch round patties.

2. In 10-inch skillet over medium heat, in hot salad oil, cook patties until browned on both sides, about 8 to 10 minutes.

3. Toast whole-wheat slices. For each serving, on plate, cut each whole-wheat toast slice diagonally in half; spread with some mayonnaise; top with a lettuce leaf, half of tomato slices, and a tuna patty. Top each sandwich with a dollop of mayonnaise.

Western-Omelet Heros

TIME: about 30 minutes—SERVINGS: 4

3 tablespoons butter or margarine

1 small onion, minced

8 eggs

2 tablespoons water

¹/₄ teaspoon salt

¹/₈ teaspoon pepper

1 4-ounce package sliced cooked ham, diced

4 8-inch-long hero rolls

bottled creamy Russian dressing

lettuce leaves

1 7¹/₂-ounce jar roasted sweet red peppers

1. In 12-inch skillet over medium heat, melt butter or margarine; add onion and cook until tender, stirring occasionally.

2. Meanwhile, in medium bowl with fork, beat eggs, water, salt, and pepper. Add egg mixture and ham to onion mixture in skillet. Reduce heat to medium-low; cook until eggs are set around edge; with metal spatula, gently lift edge as it sets, tilting skillet to allow uncooked portion to run under egg mixture. Shake skillet occasionally to keep egg mixture moving freely in pan. When egg mixture is set, increase heat slightly to brown bottom of eggs. With metal spatula, cut egg mixture in four portions.

3. Cut each roll horizontally in half but not all the way through. Spread cut surface of each roll with some Russian dressing; top with lettuce leaves and a portion of egg mixture, then with one fourth of roasted red peppers.

Curried Beef in Pita

TIME: 3 hours—SERVINGS: 6

Pita (see Index)

1 pound lean ground beef

¹/₂ cup chopped onion

1 medium apple, chopped

¹/₄ cup dark seedless raisins

1¹/₄ teaspoons salt

1 teaspoon curry powder

1 8-ounce container plain yogurt

1. Prepare Pita.

2. About 30 minutes before serving, prepare curried beef: In 10-inch skillet over medium-high heat, cook ground beef and onion until meat is browned and onion is tender; spoon off any excess fat. Add apple, raisins, salt, and curry. Reduce heat to low; cover and simmer 5 minutes or until apple is tender-crisp.

3. Cut each piece of pita bread in half to make two "pockets." Fill each half with about ¹/₃ cup of beef mixture. Pass the plain yogurt separately to spoon into each sandwich. Makes 12 sandwiches.

Barbecued Pork Sandwiches

TIME: about 3 1/2 hours—SERVINGS: 10

2 1/2 pounds pork shoulder blade roast, boneless, cut into 1 1/2-inch chunks

2 medium onions, chopped

2 medium green peppers, chopped

1 6-ounce can tomato paste

1/2 cup packed brown sugar

1/2 cup water

1/4 cup cider vinegar

3 tablespoons chili powder

2 teaspoons salt

1 teaspoon dry mustard

2 teaspoons Worcestershire

10 6-inch-long hard rolls

lettuce leaves

1 large tomato, diced

1. In 5-quart Dutch oven, combine first 11 ingredients. Over high heat, heat to boiling. Reduce heat to low; cover and simmer about 3 hours or until pork is *very* tender, stirring occasionally.

2. Skim off any fat. With wire whisk, stir mixture until meat is shredded.

3. To serve, cut each roll horizontally in half. Line rolls with lettuce; fill with pork mixture. Sprinkle with tomato.

Tacos

TIME: about 1 3/4 hours—SERVINGS: 12

Corn Tortillas (see Index) or 12 packaged taco shells

salad oil

2 pounds ground beef

2 medium onions, chopped

2 teaspoons oregano

2 teaspoons salt

1 teaspoon pepper

2 garlic cloves, minced

8 medium tomatoes, chopped

shredded lettuce

2 cups shredded Cheddar cheese

hot-pepper sauce

1. Prepare Corn Tortillas if using homemade taco shells. In 10-inch skillet over medium heat, in about 1/2 inch hot salad oil, fry a tortilla just until it softens. With tongs, fold in half, holding it open about an inch. Fry one side crisp; turn and fry the other side. Drain on paper towels. Repeat with rest of tortillas.

2. About 30 minutes before serving, prepare beef filling: In 10-inch skillet over medium-high heat, brown ground beef and onions; spoon off any excess fat. Add oregano, salt, pepper, garlic, and half the chopped tomatoes; heat until piping hot.

3. Stuff each shell with 2 or 3 tablespoons filling; top with shredded lettuce, Cheddar cheese, hot-pepper sauce, and remaining tomatoes.

Deviled Pork Patties

TIME: about 1 hour—SERVINGS: 4

1 pound ground pork

2 medium carrots, finely shredded (about 1 cup)

1 egg

2 tablespoons chili sauce

2 tablespoons prepared mustard

1/2 teaspoon salt

1/4 teaspoon pepper

4 hamburger buns, split

4 lettuce leaves

bread-and-butter pickles

1. Prepare outdoor grill for barbecuing.

2. In medium bowl, mix first 7 ingredients. Shape mixture firmly into four 1-inch-thick patties.

3. Place patties on grill over medium heat; cook about 20 minutes or until well done, carefully turning patties occasionally. During last 2 to 3 minutes of cooking patties, toast hamburger buns on grill, cut side down, until golden. Serve pork patties in toasted buns with lettuce leaves and pickles.

TO BROIL IN OVEN: About 45 minutes before serving, preheat broiler if manufacturer directs. Prepare pork patties as above. Place patties on rack in broiling pan; broil 20 minutes, turning once. Remove broiling pan from oven; keep patties warm. Arrange buns, cut side up, on cookie sheet. Broil 2 to 3 minutes until golden. Serve as above.

Canadian-Bacon Buns

TIME: about 15 minutes—SERVINGS: 6

1 16-ounce package Canadian-bacon slices

6 hamburger buns

butter or margarine, softened

Preheat broiler if manufacturer directs. In 10-inch skillet over medium-high heat, fry bacon just until heated. Meanwhile, split buns and spread with butter or margarine; broil until golden brown. To serve: Place two or three slices bacon in each bun; cut in half. Serve hot.

Cheese Sandwiches with Anchovy Sauce

TIME: about 30 minutes—SERVINGS: 4

butter or margarine

1/4 2-ounce can anchovy fillets, drained

2 tablespoons minced parsley

1 1/2 teaspoons lemon juice

1/2 pound Fontina or Port du Salut cheese, thinly sliced

8 slices white bread

2 eggs

2 tablespoons milk

1. Prepare anchovy sauce: In 1-quart saucepan over low heat, melt 3 tablespoons butter or margarine. Add anchovies, parsley, and lemon juice; heat through, mashing anchovies with fork. Keep warm.

2. Arrange cheese on 4 bread slices; top with remaining bread.

3. In 12-inch skillet over medium heat, melt 1 tablespoon butter or margarine. In pie plate with fork, beat eggs and milk. Dip sandwiches, one at a time, into egg mixture to coat on all sides. Place sandwiches in skillet; cover and cook over medium heat until golden on both sides and cheese is melted, about 6 minutes, turning once.

4. To serve, cut each sandwich diagonally in half; top with some anchovy sauce.

Corned-Beef-and-Egg Brunch Biscuits

TIME: about 30 minutes—SERVINGS: 5

6 eggs

1/2 teaspoon salt

1/8 teaspoon pepper

2 tablespoons butter or margarine

1 cup diced cooked corned beef

1 10-ounce package refrigerated flaky biscuits

celery sticks

1. In medium bowl with wire whisk or fork, beat eggs, salt, and pepper until blended. In 10-inch skillet over medium heat, melt butter or margarine; pour in egg mixture and cook until set but still very moist, stirring occasionally. Stir in corned beef; remove skillet from heat.

2. Preheat oven to 375° F. Grease large cookie sheet. On lightly floured surface with floured rolling pin, roll each biscuit into 5-inch oval. Arrange half of biscuits on cookie sheet. Spoon egg mixture onto center of biscuits on cookie sheet. Top with remaining biscuits. With fork, firmly press edges together to seal, moistening edges with water if necessary. Cut two diagonal slashes on top of each biscuit. Bake 12 to 15 minutes until lightly browned. Serve with celery sticks.

Breads

Pecan Loaf

TIME: about 3 hours or start a day ahead—YIELD: 1 loaf

1 8-ounce package cream cheese, softened

1¼ cups sugar

1 cup butter or margarine, softened

1 teaspoon grated orange peel

½ teaspoon orange extract

4 eggs

2 cups all-purpose flour

¾ cup pecans, finely chopped

2 teaspoons double-acting baking powder

½ teaspoon salt

1. Preheat oven to 325° F. Grease and flour 9" by 5" loaf pan.

2. Into large bowl, measure first 6 ingredients. With mixer at medium speed, beat ingredients until light and fluffy, about 5 minutes, constantly scraping bowl with rubber spatula. Reduce speed to low; add flour and remaining ingredients; beat just until blended, occasionally scraping bowl.

3. Pour batter into pan. Bake 1 hour and 10 minutes or until toothpick inserted in center of loaf comes out clean. Cool loaf in pan on wire rack 10 minutes; remove from pan. Cool loaf completely on rack.

Zucchini Bread

TIME: about 2 hours or start up to 3 days ahead—YIELD: 2 loaves

3 cups all-purpose flour

1½ cups sugar

1 cup California walnuts, chopped

4½ teaspoons double-acting baking powder

1 teaspoon salt

4 eggs

⅔ cup salad oil

2 cups grated zucchini

2 teaspoons grated lemon peel

1. Preheat oven to 350° F. Grease two 8½" by 4½" loaf pans. In large bowl with fork, mix flour, sugar, walnuts, baking powder, and salt.

2. In medium bowl with fork, beat eggs slightly; stir in salad oil, zucchini, and lemon peel.

3. Stir liquid mixture into flour mixture just until flour is moistened; spread evenly in pans.

4. Bake bread 1 hour. Cool in pans on wire racks 10 minutes; remove from pans. Serve warm or cold.

Poppy-Seed Poticas

TIME: about 6 hours or start early in day—YIELD: 2 loaves

½ cup sugar

2 teaspoons grated lemon peel

½ teaspoon salt

1 package active dry yeast

3½ to 4 cups all-purpose flour

1 cup milk

½ cup butter or margarine

1 egg

Poppy-Seed Filling (right)

1 egg yolk, beaten

1. In large bowl, combine sugar, lemon peel, salt, yeast, and 1 cup flour. In 1-quart saucepan over low heat, heat milk and butter until very warm (120° to 130° F.). (Butter does not need to melt.)

2. With mixer at low speed, beat liquid into dry ingredients; beat until just mixed. Increase speed to medium; beat 2 minutes, occasionally scraping bowl with rubber spatula. Beat in egg and 1 cup flour or enough to make thick batter; beat 2 minutes more, occasionally scraping bowl. With spoon, stir in enough additional flour (about 1½ cups) to make soft dough.

3. On lightly floured surface, knead dough until smooth and elastic, about 5 minutes. Shape into ball; place in greased large bowl, turning to grease top. Cover; let rise until doubled, about 1 hour.

4. Punch down dough. Turn onto lightly floured surface; cut in half; cover; let rest 15 minutes.

5. Grease two cookie sheets. With lightly floured rolling pin, roll one dough half into 18″ by 12″ rectangle. Spread half of filling on dough, to within ½ inch of sides. From 18-inch edge, tightly roll dough jelly-roll fashion; pinch ends to seal. Arrange dough in flat coil, seam side down, on a cookie sheet. Repeat with remaining dough. Cover with towel; let rise until doubled, about 1½ hours.

6. Preheat oven to 350° F. Brush loaves with beaten yolk. Bake 25 to 30 minutes, until loaves sound hollow when tapped. Remove to wire racks to cool.

Poppy-Seed Filling: In medium bowl, *combine one 12-ounce can poppy-seed cake-and-pastry filling, ½ cup finely chopped California walnuts, 1 tablespoon grated lemon peel,* and *1 teaspoon ground cinnamon;* set aside. In small bowl with mixer at high speed, beat *1 egg white* until soft peaks form; fold into poppy-seed mixture.

Irish Soda Bread

TIME: about 5 hours or start early in day—YIELD: 1 loaf

4 cups all-purpose flour

3 tablespoons sugar

1 tablespoon double-acting baking powder

1 teaspoon salt

¾ teaspoon baking soda

6 tablespoons butter or margarine

1½ cups dark seedless raisins

1 tablespoon caraway seeds

2 eggs

1½ cups buttermilk

1. Preheat oven to 350° F. Grease 2-quart round casserole. In large bowl with fork, mix flour and next 4 ingredients. With pastry blender, cut in butter until mixture resembles coarse crumbs; stir in raisins and caraway seeds.

2. In small bowl with fork, beat eggs slightly; remove 1 tablespoon and reserve. Stir buttermilk into remaining egg; stir into flour mixture just until flour is moistened (dough will be sticky).

3. Turn dough onto well-floured surface; knead about 10 strokes to mix thoroughly. Shape into a ball; place in casserole. In center of ball, cut 4-inch cross ¼ inch deep. Brush dough with reserved egg.

4. Bake about 1 hour and 20 minutes. Cool in casserole on wire rack 10 minutes; remove from casserole and cool completely on rack.

Corn Tortillas

TIME: about 45 minutes—YIELD: 12 tortillas

2 cups instant corn masa (specially treated, finely ground corn sold in Mexican and gourmet-food stores)

1/2 teaspoon salt

about 1 cup warm water

1. In medium bowl with fork, stir together instant corn masa and salt. Gradually add water to corn-masa mixture, mixing lightly with fork until dough is just moist enough to hold together. If necessary, add a little more water, a tablespoon at a time.

2. With hands, gather dough into a ball; knead a few times in bowl until smooth.

3. Divide the dough into 12 pieces; then, with hands, shape each piece into a small ball. Keep dough covered with plastic wrap while you are shaping tortillas.

4. To shape: Flatten one ball to about 1/4-inch thickness; place between sheets of waxed paper. With rolling pin, roll into 6-inch circle. Leave in paper until all are rolled.

5. Remove top sheet of paper and invert the tortilla onto hot, ungreased 8-inch skillet or griddle over medium heat. Carefully peel off bottom sheet. Cook about 30 seconds or until edge of tortilla curls up.

6. Turn; press gently with pancake turner until bubbles form in tortilla (this will make a lighter tortilla). Turn again; cook 1 minute longer or until bottom of tortilla has small brown specks.

7. Remove to foil and wrap to keep warm, stacking tortillas as each is made.

Sesame Thins

TIME: about 1 hour or start up to 1 week ahead—YIELD: 30 crisp breads

1³/₄ cups all-purpose flour

1/2 cup cornmeal

2 tablespoons sugar

1/2 teaspoon baking soda

1/2 teaspoon salt

1/2 cup butter or margarine, softened

1/2 cup water

2 tablespoons vinegar

2 tablespoons sesame seeds

1. Into large bowl, measure flour, cornmeal, sugar, baking soda, and salt. With pastry blender or two knives used scissor fashion, cut 1/4 cup butter or margarine into flour mixture just until mixture resembles coarse crumbs. Stir in water and vinegar. With hands, knead flour mixture until well blended.

2. Preheat oven to 375° F. Divide dough into 30 small balls. On lightly floured surface, with floured rolling pin, roll five balls, each into 4¹/₂-inch paper-thin circle (edges may be ragged). With pancake turner, place circles 1 inch apart on ungreased cookie sheet.

3. In small saucepan over low heat, melt remaining 1/4 cup butter or margarine. With pastry brush, lightly brush each dough circle with some butter or margarine; sprinkle with some sesame seeds. With pancake turner, firmly press sesame seeds into dough. Bake 8 to 10 minutes, until lightly browned. With pancake turner, remove to wire rack to cool. Repeat with remaining dough.

4. Cool completely on wire rack. Store in tightly covered container.

Crunchy Onion Twists

TIME: about 45 minutes or start a day ahead—YIELD: 8 dozen onion twists

1¼ cups all-purpose flour
½ cup yellow cornmeal
1 teaspoon salt
¼ cup shortening
⅓ cup instant minced onions
cold water

1. In medium bowl, mix flour, cornmeal, and salt. With pastry blender or two knives used scissor fashion, cut in shortening until mixture resembles coarse crumbs. With fork, stir in onions and ⅓ cup water. With hands, shape dough into a ball. (If mixture is too dry, add more water, a teaspoon at a time, until moist enough to hold together.)

2. Preheat oven to 425° F. On lightly floured surface with lightly floured rolling pin, roll half of pastry into 12″ by 10″ rectangle. With knife, cut dough into 5″ by ½″ strips. Remove each strip; holding ends, make twist by turning ends in opposite directions. Arrange twists on cookie sheet; press ends to sheet to prevent uncurling.

3. Bake twists 6 to 8 minutes, until golden. Remove twists to wire racks to cool. Repeat with remaining dough. Store in tightly covered container. Serve as bread sticks.

Rich Biscuits

TIME: about 30 minutes—YIELD: about 10 biscuits

2 cups all-purpose flour
1 tablespoon double-acting baking powder
1 teaspoon salt
⅓ cup shortening
⅔ cup milk
1 egg

1. Preheat oven to 450° F. In medium bowl with fork, mix flour, baking powder, and salt. With pastry blender or two knives used scissor fashion, cut in shortening until mixture resembles coarse crumbs. With fork, stir in milk just until mixture forms soft dough and leaves side of bowl.

2. On lightly floured surface with lightly floured hands, knead dough 10 times. Pat dough into ½-inch-thick circle. With floured 3-inch flower-shaped cookie cutter (or, use 3-inch round cookie cutter), cut out as many biscuits as possible. Place biscuits, about ½ inch apart, on large cookie sheet. Press dough trimmings together; pat and cut as above until all dough is used. In cup with fork, beat egg. Brush biscuits with beaten egg. Bake 10 to 12 minutes, until golden.

Apple-Molasses Muffins

TIME: about 1 hour or start a day ahead—YIELD: 18 muffins

4 cups all-purpose flour
¾ cup molasses
½ cup packed brown sugar
½ cup butter or margarine, softened
⅓ cup milk
2 teaspoons baking soda
2 teaspoons ground cinnamon
1 teaspoon ground allspice
1 teaspoon salt
2 eggs
3 large red cooking apples (1¾ pounds), peeled and diced
¾ cup California walnuts, chopped

1. Grease and flour eighteen 3-inch muffin-pan cups; set aside.

2. Preheat oven to 375° F. Into large bowl, measure all ingredients except apples and walnuts; with mixer at low speed, beat until blended, constantly scraping bowl. Stir in apples and walnuts.

3. Spoon batter into muffin-pan cups to come almost to the top of each cup. Bake 25 minutes or until toothpick inserted in center of muffin comes out clean. Cool muffins in pans on wire racks 10 minutes; remove from pans. Serve muffins warm. Or, to serve later, cool muffins on wire racks; wrap muffins in single layer with foil. Just before serving, reheat wrapped muffins in preheated 375° F. oven 10 minutes or until warm.

Cranberry-Almond Muffins

TIME: about 45 minutes or start early in day

YIELD: 12 large or 24 small muffins

3 cups all-purpose flour

1/2 cup sugar

2 teaspoons double-acting baking powder

1 teaspoon baking soda

1/4 teaspoon salt

1 16-ounce container sour cream (2 cups)

1/3 cup milk

1/4 cup salad oil

1/2 teaspoon almond extract

2 eggs

1 1/2 cups fresh or frozen cranberries, coarsely chopped

2 tablespoons sliced blanched almonds

1. Grease and flour twelve 3-inch or twenty-four 2 1/2-inch muffin-pan cups; set aside.

2. Preheat oven to 375° F. In large bowl with fork, mix first 5 ingredients. In medium bowl with fork, beat sour cream, milk, salad oil, almond extract, and eggs until blended. Stir sour cream mixture into flour mixture just until flour is moistened. (Batter will be lumpy.) With rubber spatula, gently fold in cranberries.

3. Spoon batter into muffin-pan cups; sprinkle with sliced almonds. Bake large muffins 30 minutes or until toothpick inserted in center of muffin comes out clean; bake small muffins 25 minutes. Immediately remove from pans. Serve muffins warm, or cool on wire rack to serve later.

Zucchini-Oatmeal Muffins

TIME: about 45 minutes or start early in day

YIELD: 12 large or 18 small muffins

2 1/2 cups all-purpose flour

1 1/2 cups sugar

1 cup pecans, chopped

1/2 cup quick-cooking oats, uncooked

1 tablespoon double-acting baking powder

1 teaspoon salt

1 teaspoon ground cinnamon

4 eggs

1 medium zucchini (10 ounces), finely shredded

3/4 cup salad oil

1. Grease twelve 3-inch or eighteen 2 1/2-inch muffin-pan cups.

2. Preheat oven to 400° F. Into large bowl, measure first 7 ingredients. In medium bowl with fork, beat eggs slightly; stir in zucchini and oil. Stir mixture all at once into flour mixture just until flour is moistened. (Batter will be lumpy.)

3. Spoon batter into muffin-pan cups. Bake large muffins 25 minutes or until toothpick inserted in center of muffin comes out clean; bake small muffins 20 minutes. Remove muffins from pans. Serve muffins warm, or cool on wire rack to serve later.

Giant Popovers

TIME: about 1 1/2 hours—YIELD: 8 popovers

6 eggs

2 cups milk

6 tablespoons butter or margarine, melted

2 cups all-purpose flour

1 teaspoon salt

butter curls or balls

1. Preheat oven to 375° F. Grease eight deep 7-ounce pottery custard cups. Set greased custard cups in jelly-roll pan for easier handling.

2. In large bowl with mixer at low speed, beat eggs until frothy; beat in milk and butter. At low speed, beat flour and salt into egg mixture.

3. Pour batter into prepared custard cups. Bake 1 hour; make slit in each to let out steam; bake 10 minutes more. Immediately remove from cups. Serve hot with butter curls or balls.

Party Dinner Rolls

TIME: about 4$^{1}/_{2}$ hours or start up to 3 days ahead — YIELD: 30 rolls

$^{1}/_{2}$ **cup sugar**

2 teaspoons salt

2 packages active dry yeast

about 6 cups all-purpose flour

2 cups water

$^{1}/_{2}$ **cup butter or margarine**

2 eggs

salad oil

1. In large bowl, combine sugar, salt, yeast, and 2$^{1}/_{4}$ cups flour. In 1-quart saucepan over low heat, heat water and butter or margarine until very warm (120° to 130° F). (Butter or margarine does not need to melt completely.) With mixer at low speed, gradually beat liquid into dry ingredients just until blended. Increase speed to medium; beat 2 minutes, occasionally scraping bowl with rubber spatula. Gradually beat in 1 egg and 1$^{1}/_{4}$ cups flour to make a thick batter; continue beating 2 minutes, scraping bowl often. With wooden spoon, stir in 2 cups flour to make a soft dough.

2. Turn dough onto well-floured surface, and knead until smooth and elastic, about 10 minutes, working in more flour while kneading (about $^{1}/_{4}$ to $^{1}/_{2}$ cup). Shape dough into a ball and place in greased large bowl, turning dough over so that top is greased. Cover and let rise in warm place (80° to 85° F.), away from draft, until doubled, about 1$^{1}/_{2}$ hours. (Dough is doubled when two fingers pressed lightly into dough leave a dent.)

3. Punch down dough. Turn dough over; brush with salad oil. Cover bowl tightly with plastic wrap and refrigerate, punching down dough occasionally, until ready to use. (Steps 1, 2, and 3 can be done up to 3 days ahead.)

4. About 2 hours before serving, remove dough from refrigerator. Grease two large cookie sheets. Cut dough into 30 pieces. On lightly floured surface, with lightly floured hands, shape half of dough pieces into ovals; shape remaining dough pieces into balls. Place rolls on cookie sheets. Cover and let rise in warm place until doubled, about 1 hour. (Dough is doubled when one finger very lightly pressed against dough leaves a dent.)

5. Preheat oven to 400° F. With razor, cut lengthwise slash along top of each oval roll; cut a cross on top of each round roll. In cup with fork, beat remaining egg. With pastry brush, brush rolls with egg. Bake rolls 15 minutes or until golden. Remove rolls from cookie sheets; cool on wire racks.

Old-fashioned Rolls

TIME: about 3$^{1}/_{2}$ hours or start early in day — YIELD: 24 rolls

$^{1}/_{3}$ **cup sugar**

1$^{1}/_{2}$ **teaspoons salt**

2 packages active dry yeast

4$^{1}/_{2}$ **to 5$^{1}/_{2}$ cups all-purpose flour**

1 cup milk

4 tablespoons butter or margarine

2 eggs

Egg Glaze (right)

1. In large bowl, combine sugar, salt, yeast, and 1$^{1}/_{2}$ cups flour. In 1-quart saucepan, heat milk and butter until very warm (120° to 130° F). With mixer at low speed, gradually beat liquid into dry ingredients. At medium speed, beat 2 minutes, occasionally scraping bowl with a rubber spatula. Beat in eggs and about $^{1}/_{2}$ cup flour to make a thick batter; continue beating 2 minutes. Stir in flour (2 to 2$^{1}/_{2}$ cups) to make a soft dough.

2. On lightly floured surface, knead dough until smooth and elastic, about 10 minutes. Shape dough into ball. Place in greased large bowl, turning dough over so that top is greased. Cover; let rise in warm place until doubled, about 1 hour.

3. Punch down dough. Transfer to lightly floured surface; cut in half; cover; let rest 15 minutes.

4. Cut each half into 12 pieces; shape into balls. Place 2 inches apart on greased cookie sheets. Cover; let rise until doubled, about 30 minutes.

5. Preheat oven to 400° F. Brush with Egg Glaze. Bake 10 minutes or until golden. Cool slightly on wire racks. Serve warm.

Egg Glaze: In small bowl with fork, beat *1 egg* with *1 tablespoon milk*.

Sour-Cream Rolls

TIME: about 2¹/₂ hours or start a day ahead—YIELD: about 2 dozen rolls

¹/₄ cup sugar

2 teaspoons salt

1 package active dry yeast

about 4³/₄ cups all-purpose flour

¹/₃ cup water

1 16-ounce container sour cream (2 cups)

1 egg, beaten

1. In large bowl, combine sugar, salt, yeast, and 1 cup flour. In 1-quart saucepan over low heat, heat water until very warm (120° to 130° F.). With mixer at low speed, gradually beat water into dry ingredients just until blended. Increase speed to medium; beat 2 minutes, occasionally scraping bowl with rubber spatula. Beat in sour cream and 1 cup flour to make a thick batter; continue beating 2 minutes, scraping bowl often. With wooden spoon, stir in 2 cups flour to make a soft dough.

2. Turn dough onto lightly floured surface, and knead until smooth and elastic, about 10 minutes, working in more flour while kneading (about ¹/₂ to ³/₄ cup). Shape dough into a ball and place in greased large bowl, turning dough over so that top is greased. Cover and let rise in warm place (80° to 85° F.) away from draft, until doubled, about 1¹/₂ hours. (Dough is doubled when two fingers pressed lightly into dough leave a dent.)

3. Punch down dough and turn onto lightly floured surface. Cover dough with bowl and let rest 15 minutes for easier shaping. Meanwhile, grease large cookie sheets.

4. Preheat oven to 400° F. With floured rolling pin, roll dough ¹/₂ inch thick. Using 3-inch round cookie cutter, cut dough into circles; reserve trimmings. With pancake turner, place circles on cookie sheets, 1 inch apart. With pastry brush, brush circles with some beaten egg. Fold each circle almost in half; with tip of spoon, firmly press together to seal. Brush tops with beaten egg. Reroll trimmings, and cut and shape as above until all dough is used.

5. Bake 15 minutes or until lightly browned. Serve rolls warm. Or, to serve later, cool rolls on wire racks; wrap rolls in single layer with foil. Just before serving, reheat wrapped rolls in preheated 400° F. oven 10 minutes or until warm.

Holiday Bubble Loaf

TIME: about 4 hours or start up to 2 days ahead—YIELD: 1 loaf

3 tablespoons sugar

2 teaspoons salt

1 package active dry yeast

about 6 cups all-purpose flour

2 cups water

butter or margarine

1 teaspoon thyme leaves

1. In large bowl, combine sugar, salt, yeast, and 2 cups flour. In 1-quart saucepan over low heat, heat water and 3 tablespoons butter or margarine until very warm (120° to 130° F.). (Butter or margarine does not need to melt completely.) With mixer at low speed, gradually beat liquid into dry ingredients just until blended. Increase speed to medium; beat 2 minutes, occasionally scraping bowl with rubber spatula. Beat in ³/₄ cup flour to make a thick batter; continue beating 2 minutes, scraping bowl often. With wooden spoon, stir in 2¹/₂ cups flour to make a soft dough.

2. Turn dough onto well-floured surface and knead until smooth and elastic, about 10 minutes, working in more flour while kneading (about ³/₄ cup). Shape dough into a ball and place in greased large bowl, turning dough over so that top is greased. Cover and let rise in warm place (80° to 85° F.), away from draft, until doubled, about 1 hour. (Dough is doubled when two fingers pressed lightly into dough leave a dent.)

3. Punch down dough and turn onto lightly floured surface. Cover dough with bowl and let rest for 15 minutes for easier shaping.

4. Meanwhile, in small skillet over medium heat, melt 4 tablespoons butter or margarine; set aside. Grease 10-inch tube pan.

5. Cut dough in half; cut each half into 16 pieces. Shape each piece into a ball by tucking ends under. Place half of balls in tube pan; brush with half of melted butter or margarine; sprinkle with half of thyme leaves. Repeat with remaining balls, melted butter, and thyme leaves.

6. Cover with towel and let rise in warm place until doubled, about 1 hour.

(Dough is doubled when one finger very lightly pressed against dough leaves a dent.)

7. Preheat oven to 350° F. Bake 30 to 35 minutes, until loaf sounds hollow when lightly tapped with fingers. Cool loaf in pan on wire rack 10 minutes; remove loaf from pan; serve warm. Or, cool loaf on wire rack; wrap with foil. Just before serving, heat loaf in 350° F. oven 10 to 15 minutes to heat through.

8. To serve, let each person pull off his own serving of bread.

Greek Christmas Bread

TIME: about 4 hours or start day ahead—YIELD: 2 loaves

1 cup sugar

1 1/2 teaspoons anise seeds, crushed

1 teaspoon salt

2 packages active dry yeast

about 7 3/4 cups all-purpose flour

2 cups milk

1 cup butter or margarine

3 eggs

16 candied red cherries

1. In large bowl, combine sugar, anise seeds, salt, yeast, and 2 cups flour. In 1-quart saucepan over low heat, heat milk and butter or margarine until very warm (120° to 130° F.). (Butter or margarine does not need to melt completely.) With mixer at low speed, gradually beat liquid into dry ingredients just until blended. Increase speed to medium; beat 2 minutes, occasionally scraping bowl with rubber spatula.

2. Reserve 1 egg white for brushing tops of loaves. Into mixture in large bowl, gradually beat egg yolk, remaining 2 eggs, and 2 cups flour to make a thick batter; continue beating 2 minutes, scraping bowl often. With wooden spoon, stir in 3 cups flour to make a soft dough.

3. Turn dough onto well-floured surface, and knead until smooth and elastic, about 10 minutes, working in more flour while kneading (about 3/4 cup). Shape dough into a ball and place in greased large bowl, turning dough over so that top is greased. Cover and let rise in warm place (80° to 85° F.), away from draft, until doubled, about 1 hour. (Dough is doubled when two fingers pressed lightly into dough leave dent.)

4. Punch down dough. Turn dough onto lightly floured surface; cover with bowl and let rest for 15 minutes for easier shaping. Meanwhile, grease two cookie sheets.

5. Prepare loaves: Cut dough in half; cut off and reserve 1/2 cup dough from each half. Shape each half into a 6-inch-round loaf; place loaves on cookie sheets. Roll one piece of reserved dough into two 12-inch-long ropes; cut a 3-inch-long slash into each end of the two ropes, as shown. Place ropes on top of loaf to make a cross; do not press down. Curl slashed ends of each rope; place a candied red cherry in each curl, as shown. Repeat with remaining reserved dough and second loaf. Cover loaves with towels; let rise in warm place until doubled, about 45 minutes. (Dough is doubled when one finger very lightly pressed against dough leaves a dent.)

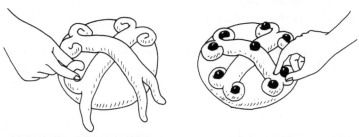

6. Preheat oven to 350° F. In cup with fork, beat reserved egg white. With pastry brush, brush loaves with egg white. Place cookie sheets with loaves on two oven racks; bake 15 minutes; switch cookie sheets between upper and lower racks so both loaves brown evenly; bake about 15 to 20 minutes longer until loaves sound hollow when lightly tapped with fingers. (If loaves start to brown too quickly, cover loosely with foil.) Remove loaves from cookie sheets and cool on wire racks.

Round Rye Bread

TIME: about 4¹/₂ hours or start early in day—YIELD: 2 loaves

4 cups all-purpose flour

2 cups rye flour

2 packages active dry yeast

1¹/₂ teaspoons salt

2 tablespoons caraway seeds

2 cups buttermilk

¹/₃ cup light molasses

butter or margarine

1. In medium bowl, combine all-purpose flour and rye flour. In large bowl, combine 2 cups flour mixture, yeast, salt, and caraway seeds. In 2-quart saucepan over low heat, heat buttermilk, molasses, and ¹/₃ cup butter or margarine until very warm (120° to 130° F.). (Butter or margarine does not need to melt, and mixture will appear curdled.)

2. With mixer at low speed, gradually beat liquid into dry ingredients. Increase speed to medium; beat mixture 2 minutes, occasionally scraping bowl with rubber spatula.

3. Gradually beat in ¹/₂ cup flour mixture or enough to make a thick batter; continue beating 2 minutes, occasionally scraping bowl with rubber spatula. With spoon, stir in enough additional flour mixture (about 2¹/₂ cups) to make a soft dough.

4. Turn dough onto well-floured surface and knead until smooth and elastic, about 10 minutes. Shape the dough into a ball and place it in a greased large bowl, turning dough over to grease top. Cover with towel; let rise in warm place (80° to 85° F.), away from draft, until doubled, about 1 hour. (Dough is doubled when two fingers pressed lightly into dough leave a dent.)

5. Punch down dough by pushing down the center with fist, then pushing edges of dough into center. Turn dough onto lightly floured surface; cut dough in half; cover with bowl and let rest for 15 minutes.

6. Grease large cookie sheet. Shape each dough half into a smooth round ball by pulling the sides of the dough underneath; place balls of dough on cookie sheet and flatten slightly. Cover with towel; let rise in warm place, away from draft, until the dough has doubled, about 1 hour.

7. Preheat oven to 350° F. Brush loaves with 2 tablespoons melted butter or margarine. Bake loaves 35 minutes or until loaves sound hollow when lightly tapped with fingers. Remove loaves from cookie sheet immediately so the bottoms don't become soggy, and leave them to cool completely on wire racks away from draft.

Cheddar Bread

TIME: about 4¹/₂ hours or start early in day—YIELD: 2 loaves

2 tablespoons sugar

2 teaspoons salt

2 packages active dry yeast

about 6¹/₂ cups all-purpose flour

2¹/₂ cups water

1 10-ounce package extra-sharp Cheddar cheese, shredded (2¹/₂ cups)

1. In large bowl, combine sugar, salt, yeast, and 2¹/₂ cups flour. In 1-quart saucepan over low heat, heat water until very warm (120° to 130° F.). With mixer at low speed, gradually beat water into dry ingredients just until blended. Increase speed to medium; beat 2 minutes, occasionally scraping bowl with rubber spatula. Gradually beat in cheese and ³/₄ cup flour to make a thick batter; continue beating 2 minutes, scraping bowl often. With wooden spoon, stir in 2¹/₂ cups flour to make a soft dough.

2. Turn dough onto well-floured surface and knead until smooth and elastic, about 10 minutes, working in more flour while kneading (about ³/₄ cup). Shape dough into a ball and place in greased large bowl, turning dough over so that top is greased. Cover and let rise in warm place (80° to 85° F.), away from draft, until doubled, about 1 hour. (Dough is doubled when two fingers pressed lightly into dough leave a dent.)

3. Punch down dough. Turn dough onto lightly floured surface. Cut dough in half; cover with bowl and let rest 15 minutes for easier shaping.

4. Grease two 9″ by 5″ loaf pans. On floured surface, with hands, pat one dough piece into an oval about 8 inches long and 5 inches wide. With hands, pick up ends of dough, gently stretching and shaking dough into a 15-inch-long and 5-inch-wide strip. Place strip on floured surface; fold ends

over so they overlap slightly in center; press ends lightly together. Then starting with a long edge, roll up dough, jelly-roll fashion, completely pressing out air as you roll; pinch edges together to seal. Place dough, seam side down, in loaf pan. Repeat with remaining dough. Cover with towel and let rise in warm place until doubled, about 1 hour. (Dough is doubled when one finger very lightly pressed against dough leaves a dent.)

5. Preheat oven to 375° F. Bake 40 minutes or until loaves sound hollow when lightly tapped with fingers. Remove loaves from pans and cool on wire racks.

Cheese-and-Raisin Coffee Braid

TIME: about 4¹/₂ hours or start early in day—YIELD: 1 coffee cake

¹/₂ cup sugar

¹/₂ teaspoon salt

2 packages active dry yeast

about 3¹/₂ cups all-purpose flour

6 tablespoons butter or margarine

²/₃ cup water

1 egg

Cheese-and-Raisin Filling (right)

1 egg white

1. In bowl, combine sugar, salt, yeast, and 1 cup flour. In saucepan, heat butter and water until very warm (120° to 130° F.). With mixer at low speed, beat liquid into dry ingredients. At medium speed, beat 2 minutes. Beat in egg and ³/₄ cup flour; beat 2 minutes. Stir in 1¹/₄ cups flour.

2. On floured surface, knead dough about 8 minutes, adding about ¹/₂ cup flour while kneading. Shape dough into ball; place in greased bowl, turning over to grease top. Cover; let rise in warm place (80° to 85° F.) until doubled, about 1 hour.

3. Meanwhile, prepare Cheese-and-Raisin Filling; refrigerate.

4. Punch dough down; turn onto floured surface; cover; let rest 15 minutes. Grease large cookie sheet.

5. With rolling pin, roll dough into 15″ by 12″ rectangle; spread filling in 4-inch strip lengthwise down center. Cut dough on both sides of filling crosswise into 1-inch strips, as shown. Place strips, at an angle across filling, alternating sides, for braided effect, as shown. Place braid on cookie sheet. Cover; let rise until doubled.

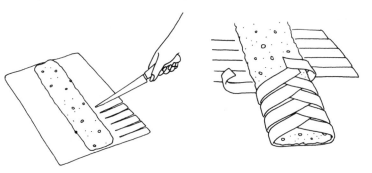

6. Preheat oven to 350° F. Beat egg white; use to brush braid. Bake 20 minutes or until browned. Cool 15 minutes.

Cheese-and-Raisin Filling: Into bowl, press *one 8-ounce container creamed cottage cheese* through fine sieve. With mixer at low speed, beat cottage cheese with *one 8-ounce package cream cheese,* softened, ¹/₂ *cup confectioners' sugar, 1 teaspoon grated lemon peel,* and *1 egg yolk* until smooth. Stir in ¹/₂ *cup dark seedless raisins.*

Colonial Oatmeal Bread

TIME: about 4 hours or start a day ahead—YIELD: 2 loaves

1 tablespoon salt

2 packages active dry yeast

4 cups whole-wheat flour

about 2³/₄ cups all-purpose flour

2¹/₄ cups water

¹/₂ cup honey

4 tablespoons butter or margarine

1 egg

1 cup quick-cooking oats, uncooked

1. In large bowl, combine salt, yeast, 2 cups whole-wheat flour, and 1 cup all-purpose flour. In 2-quart saucepan over low heat, heat water, honey, and butter or margarine until very warm (120° to 130° F.). (Butter or margarine does not need to melt completely.) With mixer at low speed, gradually beat liquid into dry ingredients just until blended. Increase speed to medium; beat 2 minutes, occasionally scraping bowl with rubber spatula. Gradually beat in egg and 1 cup whole-wheat flour to make a thick batter; continue beating 2 minutes, scraping bowl often. With wooden spoon, stir in oats, 1 cup whole-wheat flour, and 1 cup all-purpose flour to make a soft dough.

2. Lightly sprinkle work surface with all-purpose flour; turn dough onto surface and knead until smooth and elastic, about 10 minutes, working in more all-purpose flour while kneading (about ³/₄ cup). Shape dough into a ball and place in greased large bowl, turning dough over so that top is greased. Cover and let rise in warm place (80° to 85° F.) away from draft, until doubled, about 1 hour. (Dough is doubled when two fingers pressed lightly into dough leave a dent.)

3. Punch down dough. Turn dough onto lightly floured surface; cover with bowl and let dough rest 15 minutes for easier shaping.

4. Grease large cookie sheet. Cut dough in half; shape each half into a 7″ by 4″ oval, tapering ends slightly; place on cookie sheet. Cover with towel and let rise in warm place until doubled, about 1 hour. (Dough is doubled when one finger very lightly pressed against dough leaves a dent.)

5. Preheat oven to 350° F. With knife, cut three to five crisscross slashes across top of each loaf; lightly dust tops of loaves with some all-purpose flour. Bake 35 to 40 minutes, until loaves sound hollow when lightly tapped with fingers. Remove loaves from cookie sheet; cool on wire racks.

Pita (Pocket Bread)

TIME: about 3 hours or start early in day—YIELD: 6 pitas

1 teaspoon salt

¹/₄ teaspoon sugar

1 package active dry yeast

3¹/₂ to 3³/₄ cups all-purpose flour

1¹/₃ cups water

1 tablespoon salad oil

cornmeal

1. In large bowl, combine salt, sugar, yeast, and 1¹/₂ cups flour. In 1-quart saucepan over medium heat, heat water and salad oil until very warm (about 120° to 130° F.). With mixer at low speed, beat liquid into dry ingredients; beat until just mixed. Increase speed to medium; beat 2 minutes, occasionally scraping bowl. Stir in enough additional flour (about 2 cups) to make a soft dough.

2. On floured surface, knead dough until smooth and elastic, about 5 minutes, adding more flour as needed. Shape into ball; place in greased medium bowl, turning over to grease top. Cover; let rise in warm place, away from draft, until doubled, about 1 hour.

3. Punch down dough; turn onto floured surface. Cut dough into six pieces; cover; let rise 30 minutes. Lightly sprinkle three ungreased cookie sheets with cornmeal. On lightly floured surface with floured rolling pin, roll each piece of dough into a 7-inch circle. Place two circles on each cookie sheet. Cover with towel; let rise in warm place 45 minutes or until doubled in height.

4. Preheat oven to 475° F. Bake 8 to 10 minutes, until pitas are puffed and golden brown.

Desserts, Cookies, and Candies

Steamed Chocolate-Date Pudding
with Brandy-Custard Sauce

TIME: about 3 hours or start up to 2 weeks ahead—SERVINGS: 16

2 cups all-purpose flour

1¼ cups buttermilk

½ cup packed brown sugar

¼ cup cocoa

6 tablespoons butter or margarine, melted

1 teaspoon baking soda

1 teaspoon vanilla extract

¼ teaspoon salt

1 8-ounce package pitted dates, diced

1 cup pecans, coarsely chopped

Brandy-Custard Sauce (see Index)

1. Grease well 1½-quart steamed pudding or melon mold with lid, or mixing bowl. If using mixing bowl, cut foil 1 inch larger than top of bowl to use as lid; set aside.

2. In large bowl with spoon, mix first 8 ingredients just until blended. Stir in dates and pecans. Spoon batter into prepared mold; cover with lid. If using mixing bowl, cover bowl with foil; tie tightly with string.

3. Set mold on trivet in 12-quart saucepot. Pour in enough water to come halfway up side of mold; over high heat, heat to boiling. Reduce heat to low; cover and simmer 2½ to 3 hours, until toothpick inserted into center comes out clean.

4. About 30 minutes before pudding is done, prepare Brandy-Custard Sauce; keep warm.

5. When pudding is done, cool in mold on wire rack 5 minutes; loosen pudding and invert onto platter. Serve pudding with warm custard sauce.

TO DO AHEAD: Up to 2 weeks ahead, prepare pudding and steam as above. Cover and refrigerate. To serve, resteam pudding, covered, as directed above, for 1½ hours. Prepare Brandy-Custard Sauce. Serve as above.

Apricot-Almond Cream

TIME: about 40 minutes—SERVINGS: 6

1 3-ounce package apricot-flavor gelatin

1 cup boiling water

2 cups ice cubes

1 pint vanilla ice cream, cut into chunks

¾ teaspoon almond extract

1. In medium bowl, stir gelatin and boiling water until gelatin is completely dissolved. Add ice cubes, stirring often, until gelatin begins to thicken, about 4 minutes. Discard any undissolved ice.

2. In blender at medium speed, blend gelatin mixture with ice cream and almond extract about 30 seconds, just until mixed. Spoon apricot cream into six dessert glasses. Refrigerate about 25 minutes or until set.

169

Molded Chocolate Mousse

TIME: about 6 hours or start day ahead—SERVINGS: 16

1 cup sugar

2 envelopes unflavored gelatin

$\frac{1}{4}$ teaspoon salt

2 cups milk

1 6-ounce package semisweet-chocolate pieces

5 egg yolks

$\frac{3}{4}$ cup California walnuts, chopped

$\frac{1}{3}$ cup kirschwasser (white cherry brandy)

2 cups heavy or whipping cream

1. In 2-quart saucepan, stir sugar, gelatin, and salt until well mixed; gradually stir in milk. Cook over medium heat, stirring frequently, until gelatin is completely dissolved; add chocolate and stir constantly until chocolate is melted. Remove saucepan from heat.

2. In medium bowl with fork, beat egg yolks slightly; gradually beat in hot mixture. Refrigerate until mixture mounds slightly when dropped from spoon, about 45 minutes.

3. In small bowl, stir walnuts and kirschwasser.

4. In large bowl with mixer at medium speed, beat $1\frac{3}{4}$ cups cream until soft peaks form; gently fold in chocolate and nut mixtures. Pour mixture into 8-cup mold or bowl; refrigerate until set, about 4 hours.

5. To serve, in small bowl, whip remaining $\frac{1}{4}$ cup heavy cream until soft peaks form; use to garnish dessert.

Chestnut-Cream Mousse

TIME: about 5 hours or start day ahead—SERVINGS: 12

$1\frac{1}{2}$ pounds chestnuts

water

$2\frac{1}{2}$ cups milk

sugar

2 envelopes unflavored gelatin

$\frac{1}{2}$ teaspoon salt

4 egg whites, at room temperature

2 cups heavy or whipping cream

$\frac{1}{4}$ cup light corn syrup

1 teaspoon cocoa

1. In 3-quart saucepan over high heat, heat chestnuts and enough water to cover to boiling. Reduce heat to medium; cover and cook 15 minutes. Remove saucepan from heat. Immediately, with slotted spoon, remove 4 chestnuts from water. With kitchen shears, carefully cut each chestnut on flat side through shell; with fingers, peel off shell and skin, keeping chestnuts whole. (Chestnuts will be hard to peel when cool.) Repeat with 4 more chestnuts. Reserve whole peeled chestnuts for garnish.

2. Quickly remove remaining chestnuts, 3 or 4 at a time, from hot water to cutting board; cut each in half. With tip of small knife, scrape out chestnut meat from its shell into medium bowl. In food mill or in meat grinder using fine cutting disk, finely grind chestnuts. (Blender or food processor will make chestnuts too gummy.)

3. In 1-quart saucepan, mix $1\frac{1}{2}$ cups milk with $\frac{1}{3}$ cup sugar; sprinkle gelatin evenly over mixture; over medium-low heat, cook, stirring constantly, until gelatin is completely dissolved. In medium bowl, mix gelatin mixture, chestnuts, salt, and remaining 1 cup milk. Cover and refrigerate until mixture mounds when dropped from a spoon, about 45 minutes.

4. Meanwhile, prepare collar for $1\frac{1}{2}$-quart soufflé dish: Fold a 20-inch strip of waxed paper or foil lengthwise into 20″ by 6″ strip; wrap around outside of dish so collar stands 2 inches above rim. Secure with tape.

5. In small bowl with mixer at high speed, beat egg whites until soft peaks form. Beating at high speed, gradually sprinkle in $\frac{1}{4}$ cup sugar, beating until sugar is completely dissolved. (Whites should stand in stiff, glossy peaks.)

6. In large bowl with mixer at medium speed, beat heavy or whipping cream until stiff peaks form. With rubber spatula or wire whisk, fold chestnut mixture and egg whites into whipped cream until blended. Spoon mixture into soufflé dish; cover and refrigerate until set, about $2\frac{1}{2}$ hours.

7. Meanwhile, prepare garnish: In 1-quart saucepan over high heat, heat corn syrup to boiling. Reduce heat to medium; cook 2 minutes. Remove saucepan from heat. With fork, dip reserved whole chestnuts, one at a time, in corn syrup. Place coated chestnuts on wire rack to cool and allow coating to harden. Cover with waxed paper until serving time.

8. To serve, remove collar from soufflé dish. Sprinkle top of mousse with cocoa; garnish with whole chestnuts.

Espresso-Nut Mousse

TIME: about 5 hours or start day ahead—SERVINGS: 12

1¾ cups California walnuts

3 cups milk

sugar

instant espresso-coffee powder

2 envelopes unflavored gelatin

¼ teaspoon salt

4 egg whites, at room temperature

2 cups heavy or whipping cream

1. Reserve about 1 tablespoon walnuts for garnish. In blender at medium speed or in food processor with knife blade attached, finely grind walnuts, half at a time.

2. In 1-quart saucepan, mix 1½ cups milk, ½ cup sugar, and 3 tablespoons instant espresso-coffee powder; sprinkle gelatin evenly over mixture; over medium-low heat, cook, stirring constantly, until gelatin is completely dissolved. In medium bowl, mix gelatin mixture, walnuts, salt, and remaining 1½ cups milk. Cover and refrigerate until mixture mounds when dropped from a spoon, about 45 minutes.

3. Meanwhile, prepare collar for 1½-quart soufflé dish: Fold a 20-inch strip of waxed paper or foil lengthwise into a 20" by 6" strip; wrap around outside of dish so collar stands 2 inches above rim. Secure with tape.

4. In small bowl with mixer at high speed, beat egg whites until soft peaks form. Beating at high speed, gradually sprinkle in ¼ cup sugar, beating until sugar is completely dissolved. (Whites should stand in stiff, glossy peaks.)

5. In large bowl with mixer at medium speed, beat 1¾ cups heavy or whipping cream until stiff peaks form (reserve remaining ¼ cup cream for garnish). With rubber spatula or wire whisk, fold walnut mixture and egg whites into whipped cream until blended. Spoon mixture into soufflé dish; cover and refrigerate until set, about 2½ hours.

6. To serve, coarsely chop reserved walnuts. In small bowl with mixer at medium speed, beat reserved ¼ cup heavy cream with ½ teaspoon sugar until soft peaks form. Remove collar from soufflé dish. Garnish top of mousse with whipped cream and walnuts.

Frosty Lime Soufflé

TIME: about 5 hours or start early in day—SERVINGS: 8

1 envelope unflavored gelatin

½ teaspoon salt

sugar

4 eggs, separated

½ cup cold water

⅓ cup lime juice

grated peel of 1 lime

⅛ teaspoon green food color

1 cup heavy or whipping cream

1. In double boiler, stir gelatin with salt and ¼ cup sugar until well mixed.

2. In small bowl with wire whisk, beat egg yolks with cold water and lime juice until mixed; stir into gelatin mixture. Cook over hot, *not boiling,* water, stirring constantly, until mixture thickens and coats a spoon. Remove from heat; stir in 1 teaspoon of grated peel and the food color; pour into large bowl and cool to room temperature, stirring occasionally. Meanwhile, prepare collar for a 1-quart soufflé dish: Cut piece of 12-inch-wide foil to fit around dish, and overlap by 2 inches; fold in half lengthwise. Carefully wrap foil strip around outside of dish so that collar stands about 3 inches above rim. Fasten collar securely with a short piece of cellophane tape.

3. In small bowl with mixer at high speed, beat egg whites until soft peaks form; beating at high speed, gradually sprinkle in ½ cup sugar; beat until sugar is completely dissolved. Whites should stand in stiff peaks. Spoon into bowl with lime mixture.

4. In small bowl with mixer at medium speed, whip cream; gently fold with beaten egg whites into lime mixture. Pour into prepared soufflé dish; chill until firm, at least 3 hours. Carefully remove foil collar and garnish with remaining peel.

171

Banana Soufflé

TIME: about 1 hour—SERVINGS: 8

3 large bananas

1 tablespoon lemon juice

¹/₃ cup sugar

1 tablespoon cornstarch

¹/₂ teaspoon ground nutmeg

¹/₄ teaspoon grated lemon peel

¹/₈ teaspoon salt

³/₄ cup milk

3 large eggs, separated

2 tablespoons butter or margarine, melted

1¹/₂ teaspoons vanilla extract

1 cup heavy or whipping cream, whipped

1. Grease bottom of 1¹/₂-quart soufflé dish. Peel and slice bananas. In covered blender at medium speed, blend bananas and lemon juice until well mixed and creamy.

2. In 3-quart saucepan, mix sugar, cornstarch, nutmeg, lemon peel, and salt. Stir in milk until blended. Over medium heat, cook milk mixture until thickened, stirring constantly. Remove from heat.

3. Preheat oven to 375° F. In small bowl with fork, beat egg yolks well. Add a little of hot-milk mixture; mix together well. Mix egg-yolk mixture well with remaining hot-milk mixture. Stir in butter or margarine, vanilla extract, and banana mixture.

4. In small bowl with mixer at high speed, beat egg whites until stiff peaks form. Carefully fold into banana mixture; pour into soufflé dish. Bake 35 minutes or until golden brown. Serve immediately with whipped cream to spoon over the top.

Orange-Liqueur Soufflé

TIME: about 1¹/₄ hours—SERVINGS: 6

4 tablespoons butter or margarine

¹/₃ cup all-purpose flour

¹/₈ teaspoon salt

1¹/₂ cups milk

sugar

4 egg yolks

¹/₃ cup orange-flavor liqueur

1 tablespoon grated orange peel

6 egg whites, at room temperature

¹/₄ teaspoon cream of tartar

1 cup heavy or whipping cream

1. In 3-quart saucepan over low heat, melt butter or margarine. Stir in flour and salt until blended; gradually stir in milk; cook, stirring, until mixture is thickened. Remove saucepan from heat.

2. With wire whisk, beat 3 tablespoons sugar into milk mixture. Rapidly beat in egg yolks all at once until well mixed. Stir in liqueur and orange peel; set aside.

3. Preheat oven to 375° F. Grease 2-quart soufflé dish or round casserole with butter or margarine and lightly sprinkle with sugar.

4. In large bowl with mixer at high speed, beat egg whites and cream of tartar until stiff peaks form. With rubber spatula or wire whisk, gently fold egg-yolk mixture, one third at a time, into beaten egg whites.

5. Pour mixture into soufflé dish. With back of spoon, about 1 inch from edge of dish, make 1-inch indentation all around in soufflé mixture. (This makes a "top hat" effect when the soufflé is done.) Bake 30 to 35 minutes, until knife inserted under "top hat" comes out clean.

6. Meanwhile, in small bowl with mixer at medium speed, beat heavy or whipping cream until soft peaks form; cover and refrigerate.

7. When soufflé is done, serve immediately. Pass whipped cream in bowl to spoon onto each serving.

Chocolate Soufflé

TIME: about 2 hours—SERVINGS: 8

⅓ cup all-purpose flour

sugar

1½ cups milk

3 squares unsweetened chocolate, coarsely chopped or grated

6 eggs, separated

¼ teaspoon salt

2 teaspoons vanilla extract

1. In 2-quart saucepan, into flour and ¼ cup sugar, slowly stir milk. Cook over medium heat, stirring constantly, until the mixture thickens and starts to boil. Cook mixture 1 minute more. Remove pan from heat, and stir in chocolate until melted.

2. With wooden spoon, rapidly beat in egg yolks, all at once, beating until thoroughly blended; refrigerate to cool the mixture to lukewarm, stirring occasionally.

3. Grease 2-quart soufflé dish or round casserole with butter or margarine and lightly sprinkle dish with sugar. Preheat the oven to 375° F.

4. In large bowl with mixer at high speed, beat egg whites and salt to form soft peaks. With the mixer at high speed, gradually sprinkle in ¼ cup sugar; beat well until the sugar is completely dissolved. (The whites should stand in stiff, glossy peaks.)

5. With wire whisk or rubber spatula, gently fold chocolate mixture, one third at a time, and vanilla into egg whites, until blended. Pour mixture into soufflé dish.

6. With back of spoon, 1 inch from edge of dish, make 1-inch indentation all around soufflé. Bake 35 to 40 minutes, until knife inserted under "top hat" comes out clean.

Cantaloupe Sherbet

TIME: start early in day or up to 1 month ahead—SERVINGS: 16

1 small very ripe cantaloupe (1¾ pounds)

4 cups milk

2 envelopes unflavored gelatin

¾ cup light corn syrup

½ cup sugar

¾ teaspoon salt

3 drops yellow food color

1 drop red food color

1. With knife, cut cantaloupe in half. Remove and discard seeds and peel. Cut cantaloupe into chunks. In covered blender at medium speed or in food processor with knife blade attached, blend cantaloupe and 1 cup milk until smooth; set aside.

2. In 3-quart saucepan, sprinkle gelatin evenly over 1 cup milk. Cook over medium-low heat until gelatin is completely dissolved, stirring constantly. Remove saucepan from heat; stir in cantaloupe mixture, remaining milk, corn syrup, and remaining ingredients. (Mixture may have curdled appearance.) Pour mixture into 13" by 9" baking pan. Cover with foil and freeze until partially frozen, about 3 hours, stirring occasionally.

3. Spoon mixture into chilled large bowl; with mixer at medium speed, beat until smooth but still frozen; return mixture to pan. Cover and freeze until firm, about 3 hours.

4. To serve, let sherbet stand at room temperature 10 minutes for easier scooping. Makes 2 quarts.

Watermelon Ice

TIME: start early in day or up to 1 month ahead—SERVINGS: 10

½ small watermelon, peeled, seeded, and cut into 1-inch chunks (about 6 cups)

3 tablespoons confectioners' sugar

1 tablespoon lemon juice

¼ teaspoon salt

1. In covered blender at low speed, blend 1 cup watermelon chunks with confectioners' sugar, lemon juice, and salt until the mixture is smooth; add remaining watermelon chunks and blend a few seconds longer, until smooth. Pour into 9" by 9" baking pan; cover with foil or plastic wrap and freeze until partially frozen, about 2 hours.

2. Into chilled large bowl, spoon watermelon mixture. With mixer at high speed, beat until fluffy. Return mixture to baking pan and freeze until firm, about 1½ hours.

3. To serve, remove Watermelon Ice from freezer and let it stand at room temperature 10 minutes for easier scooping. Makes about 5 cups.

173

Pineapple Sherbet

TIME: start early in day or up to 1 month ahead—SERVINGS: 10

¾ cup sugar

½ cup water

1 large pineapple

3 tablespoons lemon juice

2 egg whites, at room temperature

1. In 1-quart saucepan over medium heat, heat sugar and water to boiling, stirring the mixture constantly. Remove saucepan from heat.

2. With sharp knife, cut crown and stem end off pineapple; cut off rind; remove eyes. Cut pineapple in half; remove core. Cut pineapple into small chunks.

3. In covered blender at medium speed, blend pineapple until smooth. Strain into large bowl; with spoon, press out all juice and discard fibers.

4. Stir sugar mixture and lemon juice into pineapple. In small bowl with mixer at high speed, beat egg whites until stiff. Fold beaten egg whites into pineapple mixture. Pour into 13″ by 9″ baking pan. Cover with foil and freeze until firm, 3 hours.

5. Spoon pineapple mixture into chilled large bowl; with mixer at low speed, beat until softened. Increase speed to medium and beat until fluffy but not melted; return to baking pan. Cover with foil. Freeze 2 hours, until partially frozen. Spoon into chilled large bowl and beat again as above. Return mixture to baking pan; cover again with foil and freeze until firm.

6. To serve, let sherbet stand at room temperature 10 minutes. Scoop into serving dishes. Makes about 5 cups.

Plum-Pudding Ice Cream

TIME: about 4½ hours or start up to 1 month ahead—SERVINGS: 32

4 quarts vanilla ice cream

1 6½-ounce container red candied cherries, diced

1 4-ounce container diced candied lemon or orange peel

1 4-ounce container candied pineapple slices, diced

1 cup dark seedless raisins

½ cup cider

1 teaspoon lemon extract

¾ teaspoon ground cinnamon

¾ teaspoon ground cloves

1. Remove vanilla ice cream from freezer; let stand at room temperature to soften slightly.

2. Meanwhile, in very large bowl combine red candied cherries and remaining ingredients; let stand 15 minutes, until all liquid is absorbed, stirring often.

3. Stir ice cream into fruit mixture until well mixed. Cover bowl and freeze until firm, about 4 hours.

4. To serve, with large ice-cream scoop, scoop ice cream into balls. Makes about 4 quarts.

Mincemeat Sundaes

TIME: about 30 minutes—SERVINGS: 4

1 pint vanilla ice cream

8 ladyfingers

2 small bananas

½ 28-ounce jar ready-to-use mincemeat

1. Remove ice cream from freezer; let stand at room temperature to soften slightly, about 10 minutes.

2. Meanwhile, split each ladyfinger horizontally in half; then cut each crosswise in half. Slice bananas into ¼-inch-thick slices. Arrange ladyfingers around side of each of four dessert dishes, allowing rounded end to extend just to rim of dish. Arrange banana slices inside ladyfingers.

3. Scoop a ball of ice cream into each dessert dish; top with mincemeat. Serve immediately.

Kiwi Sorbet

TIME: start early in day or up to 1 month ahead—SERVINGS: 9

2 cups water

1 cup sugar

6 or 7 ripe kiwi fruit, peeled and cut into
  ¹/₂-inch chunks

2 tablespoons lemon juice

¹/₄ teaspoon salt

1 kiwi fruit, for garnish

1. In 2-quart saucepan over medium heat, heat water and sugar to boiling; boil 5 minutes, stirring occasionally. Refrigerate sugar syrup until chilled, about 2 hours.

2. In blender at medium speed, blend kiwi fruit, lemon juice, and salt until smooth to make about 2 cups puree.

3. Stir kiwi fruit puree into cooled sugar syrup until mixed. Pour kiwi fruit mixture into 9″ by 9″ baking pan. Cover with foil or plastic wrap and freeze until firm, about 3¹/₂ hours, stirring occasionally.

4. To serve, let sorbet stand at room temperature 15 minutes to soften slightly. Spoon sorbet onto dessert dishes. If you like, garnish each serving with a slice of kiwi fruit. Makes about 4¹/₂ cups.

Brownie Baked Alaska

TIME: start early in day or up to 2 weeks ahead—SERVINGS: 16

1¹/₂ pints chocolate ice cream, slightly softened

1 pint vanilla ice cream, slightly softened

1 21- to 24-ounce can cherry-pie filling

1 15- to 15¹/₂-ounce package fudge brownie mix

4 egg whites, at room temperature

¹/₄ teaspoon salt

¹/₈ teaspoon cream of tartar

²/₃ cup sugar

1. Line chilled 1¹/₂-quart mixing bowl with plastic wrap. With back of large spoon, spread chocolate ice cream to line bowl, being sure ice cream comes to top of bowl. Freeze 30 minutes.

2. In medium bowl, stir vanilla ice cream with cherry-pie filling. Remove bowl with chocolate ice cream from freezer; spoon vanilla ice-cream mixture into center; cover and freeze until firm, about 5 hours.

3. Meanwhile, prepare brownie mix as label directs for cakelike brownies, but use 9-inch round cake pan and bake 30 minutes; cool.

4. Place brownie on sheet of foil; invert frozen ice cream on top; peel off plastic wrap. Wrap brownie ice-cream cake with foil and freeze.

5. About 20 minutes before serving, preheat oven to 500° F. Prepare meringue: In small bowl with mixer at high speed, beat egg whites, salt, and cream of tartar until soft peaks form. Gradually beat in sugar until completely dissolved. (Whites should stand in stiff, glossy peaks.)

6. Unwrap ice-cream cake; place on cookie sheet. Spread meringue over ice-cream cake, sealing to edge, down to cookie sheet. Bake 4 to 5 minutes, until meringue is lightly browned. Serve immediately.

Raspberry Baked-Alaska Pie

TIME: start early in day or up to 2 weeks ahead—SERVINGS: 12

18 ladyfingers, split

¹/₃ cup orange-flavor liqueur

1 10-ounce package frozen raspberries, slightly thawed

3 pints vanilla ice cream, slightly softened

4 egg whites, at room temperature

¹/₄ teaspoon salt

¹/₈ teaspoon cream of tartar

²/₃ cup sugar

1. Line 9-inch pie plate with about two thirds of ladyfingers, allowing ends to extend over rim; sprinkle with half of liqueur.

2. In medium bowl with potato masher, crush raspberries to make a paste consistency.

3. In large bowl, stir ice cream slightly. Spoon on berries; cut through mixture to create "ripple." Keeping ripples, spoon one half mixture into plate. Layer remaining ladyfingers on top; sprinkle with remaining liqueur. Spoon on remaining ice cream. Freeze until firm, 4 hours.

4. About 20 minutes before serving, preheat oven to 500° F. In large bowl with mixer at high speed, beat egg whites, salt, and cream of tartar until soft peaks form. Beat in sugar, 2 tablespoons at a time, beating at high speed until sugar is dissolved and whites stand in stiff peaks.

5. Quickly spread meringue over top of pie, sealing to edge; swirl up points. Bake 3 to 4 minutes, until light brown. Serve at once.

Frozen Almond Bonbons

TIME: start early in day or up to 2 weeks ahead—SERVINGS: 12

1 **pint vanilla ice cream**

1 **4¹/₂-ounce can whole blanched almonds, finely chopped**

1 **6-ounce package semisweet-chocolate pieces**

3 **tablespoons butter or margarine**

1 **tablespoon light corn syrup**

¹/₂ **teaspoon almond extract**

crystallized lilacs or violets, for garnish (available in specialty food stores or department-store food sections)

1. Place ice cream in refrigerator to soften slightly, about 30 minutes. Chill small cookie sheet in freezer. Meanwhile, in 10-inch skillet over medium heat, toast almonds until browned, stirring frequently. Remove skillet from heat. Cool; place toasted almonds on sheet of waxed paper.

2. Line chilled cookie sheet with waxed paper. Working quickly, with small ice-cream scoop or two spoons, scoop a ball of ice cream; roll in almonds; place on waxed-paper-lined cookie sheet. Repeat with remaining ice cream and almonds to make 12 ice-cream balls. Freeze until firm, about 1¹/₂ hours.

3. In double boiler over hot, *not boiling,* water, heat chocolate pieces, butter or margarine, corn syrup, and almond extract until chocolate is melted and mixture is smooth, stirring occasionally. Turn off heat, but leave top of double boiler over hot water in bottom of double boiler to keep the chocolate warm for easier dipping.

4. With two forks, quickly dip each ice-cream ball in chocolate mixture to coat completely; return to same cookie sheet; lightly press a crystallized lilac on top of each for garnish. Return to freezer; freeze until chocolate is firm, about 1 hour.

5. If not serving bonbons on same day, wrap with foil or plastic wrap to use within 2 weeks.

6. To serve, let bonbons stand at room temperature 10 minutes to soften slightly.

Melba-Fudge Bombe

TIME: start a day or up to 1 week ahead—SERVINGS: 10

4 **pints vanilla ice cream**

³/₄ **cup crushed almond macaroons**

²/₃ **cup sugar**

¹/₃ **cup cocoa**

¹/₃ **cup heavy or whipping cream**

3 **tablespoons butter or margarine**

³/₄ **teaspoon vanilla extract**

Raspberry Sauce (see Index)

Chocolate Curls, for garnish (right)

1. Remove ice cream from freezer; let stand in refrigerator until slightly softened, about 30 minutes. Chill deep, 2¹/₂-quart mold or bowl in freezer.

2. In large bowl, stir softened ice cream and crushed almond macaroons just until blended. Reserve about 2 cups ice-cream mixture; cover and freeze. With back of large spoon, spread remaining ice-cream mixture evenly to line inside of mold to within ¹/₂ inch from top of mold. Freeze about 1¹/₂ hours.

3. Meanwhile, prepare fudge filling: In 1-quart saucepan over medium heat, cook sugar, cocoa, heavy cream, and butter or margarine until mixture is smooth and boils, stirring frequently. Remove saucepan from heat; stir in vanilla. Cool fudge filling in refrigerator, about 30 minutes, stirring occasionally. Remove reserved ice-cream mixture from freezer; let stand in refrigerator until slightly softened, about 30 minutes.

4. Remove mold from freezer; spoon fudge filling into center; spoon reserved ice-cream mixture over fudge filling; cover and freeze until firm, about 8 hours or overnight.

5. About 1 hour before serving, prepare Raspberry Sauce; cover and refrigerate. Prepare Chocolate Curls.

6. To serve, invert bombe onto chilled platter. Spoon some Raspberry Sauce on and around bombe; pass remaining sauce to spoon over each serving. Garnish bombe with Chocolate Curls.

Chocolate Curls: *Remove paper from 2 squares semisweet chocolate.* Hold chocolate, 1 square at a time, between palms of hands, to soften slightly, about 5 minutes. With vegetable peeler, draw blade along smooth surface to make curls.

Rainbow Ice-Cream Torte

TIME: start early in day or up to 1 month ahead—SERVINGS: 16

2 pints chocolate ice cream

2 pints chocolate-chip-mint ice cream

2 pints strawberry ice cream

2 pints vanilla ice cream

2¹/₂ cups gingersnap crumbs

¹/₂ cup butter or margarine, melted

2 17-ounce cans pitted dark sweet cherries, drained

¹/₂ cup California walnuts, chopped

1. Soften ice cream in refrigerator about 30 minutes. Meanwhile, in 10-inch springform pan, combine gingersnap crumbs and butter or margarine. With hands, firmly press crumb mixture onto bottom of springform pan; chill in freezer 10 minutes or until firm.

2. On top of crumb mixture, evenly spread the chocolate ice cream, then the chocolate-chip-mint ice cream, drained sweet cherries, strawberry ice cream, and end with the vanilla ice cream. Sprinkle the top evenly with chopped California walnuts. Cover the torte and freeze until firm.

3. To serve, run knife or metal spatula, dipped in hot water, around edge of pan to loosen ice cream. Remove side of pan. Allow ice cream torte to stand at room temperature 10 minutes for easier slicing.

Rhubarb-Waffle Sundaes

TIME: about 30 minutes—SERVINGS: 4

³/₄ pound rhubarb, cut into 1-inch pieces (about 2 cups)

¹/₄ cup sugar

2 tablespoons water

¹/₂ teaspoon lemon juice

¹/₄ teaspoon salt

¹/₄ teaspoon ground ginger

¹/₂ 10- to 11-ounce package frozen waffles (4 waffles)

1 pint vanilla ice cream

1. Make rhubarb sauce: In 2-quart saucepan over medium heat, heat rhubarb, sugar, water, lemon juice, salt, and ginger to boiling. Reduce heat to low; cover and simmer 5 to 10 minutes, until rhubarb is tender.

2. Prepare frozen waffles as label directs; place each waffle on a dessert plate. With ice-cream scoop, scoop a ball of ice cream onto each waffle; spoon warm rhubarb sauce over ice cream and waffles.

Sacramento Fruit Bowl

TIME: start early in day—SERVINGS: 12

2 cups water

1¹/₂ cups sugar

3 tablespoons lemon juice

2 tablespoons anise seeds

¹/₂ teaspoon salt

1 small pineapple

1 small honeydew melon

1 small cantaloupe

2 oranges

2 nectarines or 4 apricots

2 purple plums

1 cup seedless green grapes

1 lime, sliced

1. In 2-quart saucepan over medium heat, cook water with sugar, lemon juice, anise seeds, and salt 15 minutes or until mixture becomes a light syrup. Chill syrup well.

2. Meanwhile, cut peel from pineapple, honeydew melon, cantaloupe, and oranges, and cut pulp from all into bite-size chunks. Cut nectarines or apricots and purple plums into halves and remove seeds; slice.

3. In large bowl, combine cut-up fruits with grapes and lime slices. Pour chilled syrup through strainer over fruits. Cover and refrigerate at least 4 hours to develop flavors, stirring the mixture frequently.

Almond-Cream Strawberries

TIME: about 40 minutes or start early in day—SERVINGS: 8

2 **pints large strawberries**

1 **3¹/₂- to 3³/₄-ounce package vanilla-flavor instant pudding and pie filling**

1 **cup milk**

1 **cup heavy or whipping cream, whipped**

1 **teaspoon almond extract**

1. Cut stem ends off strawberries. Cut a deep "X" in top of each strawberry; gently spread apart strawberry to make "petals"; set aside.

2. Prepare instant pudding as label directs, but use only 1 cup milk. With wire whisk or rubber spatula, gently fold whipped cream and almond extract into prepared instant pudding.

3. Spoon cream mixture into decorating bag with large writing tube. Pipe cream into strawberries. Refrigerate strawberries if not serving right away.

Papayas with Lemon Cream

TIME: about 1 hour—SERVINGS: 6

3 **medium papayas**

1 **cup heavy or whipping cream**

2 **egg yolks**

¹/₃ **cup sugar**

3 **tablespoons lemon juice**

¹/₈ **teaspoon salt**

lemon slices, for garnish

1. Cut each papaya in half lengthwise and scoop out seeds. In small bowl with mixer at medium speed, beat the heavy cream until stiff peaks form.

2. In another small bowl with mixer at high speed, beat egg yolks, sugar, lemon juice, and salt until sugar dissolves. Gently fold mixture into whipped cream.

3. Spoon mixture into center of each papaya. Refrigerate until cream is slightly set, about 30 minutes.

4. To serve, garnish papaya halves with lemon slices made into twists.

Rhubarb Crumble

TIME: about 50 minutes—SERVINGS: 6

1¹/₂ **pounds rhubarb, cut into 1-inch pieces (about 4 cups)**

¹/₄ **cup water**

1 **teaspoon lemon juice**

sugar

1¹/₄ **cups all-purpose flour**

¹/₂ **cup butter or margarine**

half-and-half or vanilla ice cream

1. In 4-quart saucepan over medium heat, heat rhubarb, water, lemon juice, and ¹/₂ cup sugar to boiling. Reduce heat to low; cover and simmer 10 minutes or until rhubarb is tender. Pour mixture into 8″ by 8″ baking dish. Preheat oven to 425° F.

2. In medium bowl with fork, stir flour and ¹/₄ cup sugar. With pastry blender or two knives used scissor fashion, cut butter or margarine into flour mixture until mixture resembles coarse crumbs.

3. Sprinkle flour mixture over rhubarb. Bake 25 minutes or until crumbs are golden. Serve warm with half-and-half or ice cream.

Banana-Coconut Betty

TIME: about 40 minutes—SERVINGS: 6

1 **large lemon**

4 **tablespoons butter or margarine**

3 **cups lightly packed fresh bread cubes**

¹/₃ **cup sugar**

¹/₂ **teaspoon ground nutmeg**

¹/₂ **teaspoon ground cinnamon**

4 **medium bananas, thinly sliced**

¹/₄ **cup water**

¹/₂ **cup shredded coconut**

half-and-half

1. Preheat oven to 375° F. Grease 1¹/₂-quart casserole. Grate 1 tablespoon peel and squeeze 2 tablespoons juice from lemon.

2. In 2-quart saucepan, melt butter or margarine; add bread cubes and toss to coat evenly. In small bowl, stir lemon peel, sugar, nutmeg, and cinnamon.

3. Place one third of bread cubes in even layer in casserole; cover with half of bananas; sprinkle with half of sugar mixture. Repeat layering once. (Bread cubes will be left over.)

4. In cup, mix lemon juice with water; pour over mixture. Toss remaining bread cubes with coconut; sprinkle over mixture. Cover and bake 25 minutes; uncover and bake 5 minutes longer or until coconut is golden. Serve warm with half-and-half.

Spiced Pears

TIME: about 5 hours or start day ahead—SERVINGS: 4

4 small pears

3 cups apple juice

1/4 cup packed light-brown sugar

1 tablespoon grated lemon peel

6 3-inch-long cinnamon sticks

6 whole cloves

Chocolate Sauce (right)

1/2 pint vanilla ice cream, softened

1. Peel pears. With apple corer, remove cores from bottom of pears, but do not remove stems.

2. In 2-quart saucepan over medium heat, heat pears, apple juice, and next 4 ingredients to boiling. Reduce heat to low; cover and simmer 30 minutes or until pears are tender, turning pears occasionally. Spoon pears and their liquid into bowl; cover and refrigerate until well chilled and to blend flavors, about 4 hours, turning pears occasionally.

3. About 10 minutes before serving, prepare Chocolate Sauce. Remove pears from cooking liquid; refrigerate remaining liquid to serve as beverage another day. In each of four chilled dessert dishes, place 1/4 cup ice cream; arrange a pear on top of ice cream; drizzle Chocolate Sauce over top of pear. Serve immediately.

Chocolate Sauce: In 1-cup glass measuring cup, place *1 square semisweet chocolate* and *1 tablespoon corn syrup.* In 1-quart saucepan over low heat, in 1/2 inch hot, *not boiling,* water, place cup; heat until chocolate is melted, stirring frequently.

Winter Fruit Cobbler

TIME: about 30 minutes—SERVINGS: 6

1 29- or 30-ounce can sliced or halved pears in heavy syrup

1/2 16-ounce package fresh or frozen cranberries (2 cups)

1/2 cup sugar

1 tablespoon cornstarch

1/4 teaspoon ground cinnamon

1/2 11-ounce package refrigerated heat-and-serve biscuits (6 biscuits)

1 cup heavy or whipping cream

1. Drain and reserve 1 cup syrup from pears. Cut pears into bite-size chunks; set aside.

2. In 10-inch skillet, combine cranberries, sugar, cornstarch, cinnamon, and reserved pear syrup. Over medium-high heat, heat mixture to boiling, stirring frequently. Reduce heat to low; simmer 10 minutes or until cranberries pop, stirring occasionally. Gently stir pear chunks into cranberry mixture; arrange biscuits on top. Cover and cook 10 to 12 minutes longer, until biscuits are heated through. Pass cream in small pitcher to pour over each serving.

Honey-Pear Bake

TIME: about 40 minutes—SERVINGS: 6

1 16-ounce can sliced pears

1 cup buttermilk-baking mix

1/3 cup milk

3 tablespoons honey

2 tablespoons butter or margarine, softened

1/2 teaspoon vanilla extract

1 egg

1/4 cup California walnuts, chopped

1. Preheat oven to 350° F. Grease 9-inch pie plate; set aside.

2. Drain pears well; pat dry with paper towels; dice; set aside.

3. Into small bowl, measure baking mix and next 5 ingredients. With mixer at low speed, beat ingredients just until blended, constantly scraping bowl with rubber spatula. Increase speed to medium; beat 2 minutes, occasionally scraping bowl. Fold pears and walnuts into baking-mix mixture. Spread batter in pie plate. Bake 25 to 30 minutes, until toothpick inserted in center comes out clean.

Quick Strawberry Shortcakes

TIME: about 20 minutes—SERVINGS: 6

1 **pint strawberries**

2 **tablespoons sugar**

½ **11-ounce package refrigerated heat-and-serve biscuits (6 biscuits)**

½ **4-ounce container frozen whipped topping, thawed**

1. Reserve six whole strawberries. Wash and hull remaining strawberries; place in medium bowl. Sprinkle strawberries in bowl with sugar; with potato masher, mash slightly; set aside.

2. Prepare biscuits as label directs. Split each biscuit in half. On each of six dessert plates, place two biscuit halves. Top with some mashed strawberry mixture and whipped topping. Garnish with a reserved whole strawberry.

Cherry Cobbler

TIME: about 45 minutes—SERVINGS: 6

1 **pound sweet cherries**

1 **cup water**

2 **tablespoons cornstarch**

1 **teaspoon grated lemon peel**

¼ **teaspoon ground cinnamon**

sugar

salt

⅓ **cup all-purpose flour**

½ **teaspoon double-acting baking powder**

1 **tablespoon salad oil**

1 **egg**

¾ **cup heavy or whipping cream**

1. Reserve 6 cherries with stems for garnish. Remove any stems from remaining cherries; using a cherry pitter, remove pits. (Or, with sharp knife, cut each cherry in half and remove pit.)

2. In 2-quart saucepan, stir water and cornstarch until blended; add pitted cherries, lemon peel, cinnamon, ¼ to ⅓ cup sugar (sweetness of cherries varies), and ¼ teaspoon salt. Over medium heat, cook until cherries are soft and mixture thickens and boils, about 5 minutes, stirring frequently. Spoon cherry mixture into six 6-ounce custard cups or ramekins.

3. Preheat oven to 375° F. In small bowl with spoon, mix flour, baking powder, salad oil, egg, ¼ cup sugar, and ⅛ teaspoon salt just until blended. Spoon batter on top of cherry mixture. Bake 15 minutes or until topping is golden.

4. To serve, garnish top of each cobbler with a reserved cherry. Pass heavy or whipping cream to serve over dessert.

Cheese-Pear Strudel

TIME: about 2 hours or start early in day—SERVINGS: 12

1 **16-ounce can sliced pears**

½ **8-ounce container creamed cottage cheese (½ cup)**

1 **8-ounce package cream cheese, softened**

2 **egg yolks**

¾ **teaspoon vanilla extract**

⅛ **teaspoon salt**

confectioners' sugar

⅓ **pound phyllo (also called strudel leaves, available in Greek pastry shops or most supermarket frozen-food sections)**

6 **tablespoons butter or margarine, melted**

about ⅓ cup dried bread crumbs

1. Drain pears well; pat dry with paper towels; dice. Set aside. Into large bowl, press cottage cheese through fine sieve. With mixer at low speed, beat cottage cheese with cream cheese, egg yolks, vanilla, salt, and ½ cup confectioners' sugar until smooth. Gently stir in pears; set aside.

2. Cut two 24-inch lengths of waxed paper; overlap two long sides about 2 inches to make a sheet 24″ by 22″. Fasten with cellophane tape.

3. On waxed paper, overlap a few sheets of phyllo to make a 16″ by 12″ rectangle, brushing phyllo where they overlap with some melted butter or margarine. Then brush entire phyllo rectangle with melted butter or margarine; sprinkle with scant tablespoon of bread crumbs. Repeat, brushing each layer with butter or margarine and sprinkling with bread crumbs.

4. Preheat oven to 375° F. Starting along one short side of phyllo, evenly spoon cheese mixture to about 1 inch from edges to cover about half of phyllo rectangle. From cheese-mixture side, roll phyllo jelly-roll fashion.

5. Place roll on cookie sheet seam side down. Brush with remaining melted butter or margarine. Bake 35 minutes or until golden. For easier slicing, cool strudel on cookie sheet on wire rack 30 minutes.

6. To serve, sprinkle strudel with confectioners' sugar; slice. Serve warm or cold.

Swan Cream Puffs

TIME: about 2¼ hours or start early in day—SERVINGS: 8

1 cup water

½ cup butter or margarine

¼ teaspoon salt

1 cup all-purpose flour

4 eggs

Almond-Cream Filling (right)

1. Grease large cookie sheet. In 2-quart saucepan over medium heat, heat water, butter or margarine, and salt until butter melts and mixture boils. Remove saucepan from heat. Add flour all at once; with wooden spoon, vigorously stir until mixture leaves side of pan and forms a ball.

2. Add eggs, one at a time, beating well with wooden spoon after each addition.

3. Preheat oven to 375° F. Spoon ½ cupful batter into decorating bag with large writing tube (about ½ inch in diameter). On prepared cookie sheet, pipe eight 3-inch-long "question marks" for swans' necks, making a small dollop at the beginning of each for head.

4. Drop remaining batter, using a large spoon and pushing off with rubber spatula, onto cookie sheet into eight large mounds, 2 inches apart. With moistened finger, gently smooth batter to round slightly. Bake 20 minutes or until necks are golden. Remove necks to wire rack to cool. Continue baking remaining cream puffs 45 to 50 minutes longer, until golden; remove to racks to cool.

5. When cream puffs are cool, prepare Almond-Cream Filling. Cut off top third of cream puffs (swans' bodies); set aside. Spoon some cream mixture into each swan's body. Cut reserved top pieces of swans' bodies in half; set into cream for wings. Insert swans' necks into cream. Refrigerate.

Almond-Cream Filling: In small bowl with mixer at medium speed, beat *1 cup heavy or whipping cream* until soft peaks form; set aside. Prepare *one 3½- to 3¾-ounce package vanilla-flavor instant pudding and pie filling* as label directs, but use only *1¼ cups milk*. With rubber spatula, gently fold whipped cream and *½ teaspoon almond extract* into prepared vanilla pudding.

 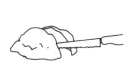 

Petite Cream Puffs

TIME: about 1¾ hours or start early in day

YIELD: about 2 dozen cream puffs

½ cup water

4 tablespoons butter or margarine

⅛ teaspoon salt

½ cup all-purpose flour

2 eggs

Cream Filling (right)

about 24 medium strawberries (1 pint)

1. Preheat oven to 375° F. Grease large cookie sheet. In 2-quart saucepan over medium heat, heat water, butter or margarine, and salt until butter melts and mixture boils. Remove saucepan from heat.

2. Into very hot butter mixture, with spoon, vigorously stir flour all at once until mixture forms ball and leaves side of pan. Add eggs, one at a time, beating well after each addition, until smooth. Drop batter, by rounded teaspoonfuls, onto cookie sheet, making small mounds, 1½ inches apart. Bake 25 to 30 minutes, until golden; cool on wire rack, about 30 minutes.

3. When puffs are cool, cut each horizontally in half. Prepare Cream Filling. Fill each puff bottom with some Cream Filling; invert cream-puff top on cream; top with more cream and a strawberry. Refrigerate.

Cream Filling: In small bowl with mixer at medium speed, beat *1½ cups heavy or whipping cream, 2 tablespoons confectioners' sugar,* and *2 tablespoons orange-flavor liqueur* until stiff peaks form.

Streusel-Cheese Bars

TIME: about 4¹/₂ hours or start early in day—SERVINGS: 36

¹/₃ cup sugar

¹/₂ teaspoon salt

1 package active dry yeast

about 3¹/₄ cups all-purpose flour

²/₃ cup water

6 tablespoons butter or margarine

1 egg

Cream-Cheese Filling (right)

Streusel-Nut Topping (right)

1. In large bowl, combine sugar, salt, yeast, and 1 cup flour. In 1-quart saucepan over low heat, heat water and butter or margarine until very warm (120° to 130° F.). (Butter or margarine does not need to melt completely.) With mixer at low speed, gradually beat liquid into dry ingredients just until blended. Increase speed to medium; beat 2 minutes, occasionally scraping bowl with rubber spatula. Gradually beat in egg and ³/₄ cup flour to make a thick batter; continue beating 2 minutes, scraping bowl often. With wooden spoon, stir in 1 cup flour to make a soft dough.

2. Turn dough onto well-floured surface and knead until smooth and elastic, about 8 minutes, working in more flour while kneading (about ¹/₂ cup). Shape dough into a ball and place in greased medium bowl, turning dough over so that top is greased. Cover and let rise in warm place (80° to 85° F.), away from draft, until doubled, about 1 hour. (Dough is doubled when two fingers pressed lightly into dough leave a dent.)

3. Punch down dough. Turn dough onto lightly floured surface; cover with bowl and let dough rest for 15 minutes for easier shaping.

4. Meanwhile, prepare Cream-Cheese Filling and Streusel-Nut Topping; set aside.

5. Preheat oven to 375° F. Grease 15¹/₂" by 10¹/₂" jelly-roll pan. Pat dough evenly into pan. Spread Cream-Cheese Filling over dough; then sprinkle with Streusel-Nut Topping. Bake 25 minutes or until toothpick inserted in center comes out clean. Cool in pan on wire rack. With sharp knife, cut into 36 bars.

Cream-Cheese Filling: In small bowl with mixer at low speed, beat *two 8-ounce packages cream cheese, softened, 2 eggs, ¹/₂ cup sugar, 1 teaspoon grated lemon peel,* and *1 teaspoon vanilla extract* until smooth.

Streusel-Nut Topping: In medium bowl with fork, stir *1 cup all-purpose flour, ¹/₄ cup packed brown sugar,* and *³/₄ teaspoon ground cinnamon.* With pastry blender or two knives used scissor fashion, cut *¹/₂ cup butter* or margarine into flour mixture until mixture resembles large crumbs; stir in *1 cup California walnuts,* coarsely chopped.

Apple Turnovers

TIME: about 5 hours or start early in day—SERVINGS: 8

2 cups all-purpose flour

1 teaspoon salt

1 cup butter or margarine

¹/₂ cup iced water

2 apples, peeled, cored, and sliced

¹/₂ cup sugar

1 tablespoon cornstarch

1 teaspoon lemon juice

¹/₄ teaspoon ground cinnamon

1 egg

water

¹/₂ cup confectioners' sugar

1. In medium bowl with pastry blender, combine flour and salt. Cut in ¹/₂ cup butter until mixture resembles coarse crumbs. Sprinkle with iced water. With fork, mix well. Shape dough into a ball; with lightly floured rolling pin on lightly floured surface, roll into an 18" by 8" rectangle. Cut ¹/₄ cup butter into thin slices. Starting at one of the 8-inch sides, place butter slices over one third of rectangle to within ¹/₂ inch of edges.

2. Fold unbuttered third of pastry over middle third; fold opposite end over to make an 8" by 6" rectangle. Roll dough into an 18" by 8" rectangle.

3. Slice remaining ¹/₄ cup butter; place slices on dough, and fold as in steps 1 and 2; wrap in plastic wrap. Chill 15 minutes. Roll folded dough into an 18" by 8" rectangle. Fold lengthwise then crosswise; wrap and chill 1 hour.

4. Prepare filling: In saucepan with spoon, mix apples, sugar, cornstarch, lemon juice, and cinnamon. Cook over low heat, stirring frequently, until apples are tender. Chill.

5. Preheat oven to 450° F. Cut dough crosswise in half; roll one half into a 12-inch square (keep rest chilled); cut into four 6-inch squares. In cup, beat egg with 1 tablespoon water. Brush mixture over squares. Spoon one eighth of apple mixture in center of each and fold in half; press edges to seal. Place on ungreased cookie sheet. Chill while preparing other half of pastry.

6. Brush turnovers with egg mixture. Cut a few slashes on each. Bake 20 minutes or until golden. Cool on rack.

7. In bowl, combine confectioners' sugar and 1 tablespoon water; drizzle over turnovers.

Almond-Cream Pie

TIME: start early in day or day ahead—SERVINGS: 10

1 3½-ounce can flaked coconut

½ cup graham-cracker crumbs

3 tablespoons butter or margarine, softened

4 eggs, separated

1 cup milk

¾ cup sugar

1 envelope unflavored gelatin

1 teaspoon almond extract

¼ teaspoon salt

1 cup heavy or whipping cream

1 tablespoon thinly sliced cranberries, for garnish

1. Preheat oven to 375° F. Spread coconut evenly in 15½" by 10½" jelly-roll pan. Bake 10 minutes or until lightly browned, stirring occasionally. Reserve ¼ cup toasted coconut for garnish. In 9-inch pie plate with hand, mix graham-cracker crumbs, butter or margarine, and remaining toasted coconut. Press mixture firmly on bottom and up side of pie plate, making a small rim. Bake 5 minutes or until golden brown. Cool.

2. In heavy 2-quart saucepan with wire whisk, beat egg yolks, milk, and sugar until well mixed. Sprinkle gelatin evenly over egg mixture. Cook over medium-low heat until gelatin is completely dissolved and mixture is thickened and coats a spoon, about 20 minutes (do not boil or mixture will curdle). Stir in almond extract. Refrigerate until chilled but not set, about 45 minutes.

3. In large bowl with mixer at high speed, beat egg whites and salt until stiff peaks form; set aside. In small bowl, using same beaters, with mixer at medium speed, beat heavy cream until stiff peaks form.

4. With wire whisk, gently fold egg-yolk mixture and whipped cream into egg-white mixture. Spoon into piecrust; refrigerate until set, about 3 hours.

5. To serve, garnish top of pie with reserved toasted coconut and sliced cranberries.

Country Cheese Pie

TIME: about 3 hours or start early in day—SERVINGS: 8

1¼ cups graham-cracker crumbs

¼ cup toasted coconut flakes

6 tablespoons butter or margarine, softened

1 cup water

1 envelope unflavored gelatin

1 16-ounce container creamed cottage cheese (2 cups)

1 8-ounce package cream cheese, softened

½ cup confectioners' sugar

¼ teaspoon salt

1 large lemon

⅓ cup apple jelly

1. In 9-inch pie plate, with hand, mix graham-cracker crumbs, coconut flakes, and butter or margarine. Press mixture firmly onto bottom and side of pie plate just to rim.

2. Measure water into small saucepan; evenly sprinkle gelatin over water. Cook over medium heat until gelatin is completely dissolved, stirring frequently. Remove from heat; set aside.

3. Into large bowl, press cottage cheese through fine sieve; add cream cheese, confectioners' sugar, salt, and gelatin mixture. With mixer at medium speed, beat cheese mixture until smooth. Pour mixture into crust; refrigerate until set, about 2 hours.

4. Cut lemon into very thin slices; cut each slice in half. Arrange lemon slices on cheese mixture. In small saucepan over low heat, melt apple jelly; brush over lemon slices. Refrigerate.

Holiday Pear-Peach Pie

TIME: about 3¹/₂ hours or start early in day—SERVINGS: 10

2 **29-ounce cans sliced pears**

1 **29- or 30-ounce can sliced cling peaches**

2 **tablespoons lemon juice**

¹/₂ **teaspoon ground cinnamon**

¹/₈ **teaspoon ground cloves**

all-purpose flour

salt

³/₄ **cup shortening**

5 **to 6 tablespoons cold water**

1 **pint vanilla ice cream, slightly softened (optional)**

1. Into sieve over large bowl, pour canned fruit to drain well. Pour off all but 2 tablespoons syrup. Into syrup in large bowl, add fruit slices, lemon juice, cinnamon, cloves, 2 tablespoons flour, and ¹/₄ teaspoon salt. With rubber spatula, toss gently to mix.

2. In medium bowl, stir 2 cups flour and 1 teaspoon salt. With pastry blender or two knives used scissor fashion, cut shortening into flour until mixture resembles coarse crumbs. Add water, a tablespoon at a time, mixing with fork until pastry holds together; shape pastry into two balls, one slightly larger.

3. On lightly floured surface with floured rolling pin, roll larger pastry ball into a circle about 2 inches larger than 9-inch pie plate. Line pie plate with pastry; with kitchen shears, trim pastry, leaving 1-inch overhang. Spoon fruit mixture into pie plate.

4. Preheat oven to 425° F. Roll remaining pastry ball into 12-inch circle; cut into ¹/₂-inch-wide strips. Place some strips about 1 inch apart across pie filling; do not seal ends. Fold every other strip back halfway from center. Place center cross strip on pie, and replace folded part of strips. Fold back alternate strips, and place second cross strip in place. Repeat to "weave" lattice. Trim strips; seal ends; make a fluted edge.

5. Bake pie 45 minutes or until fruit is heated through and crust is golden. Cool pie on wire rack. If you like, serve pie with ice cream.

Walnut Tarts

TIME: start early in day—SERVINGS: 12

Unbaked Tart Shells (right)

3 **eggs**

1 **cup dark corn syrup**

¹/₂ **cup sugar**

¹/₄ **cup butter or margarine, melted**

1 **teaspoon vanilla extract**

1 **cup coarsely chopped California walnuts**

whipped cream, for garnish

1. Prepare tart shells. Preheat oven to 350° F. In medium bowl with wire whisk, beat eggs well. Beat in next 4 ingredients until well blended.

2. Distribute chopped walnuts evenly among tart shells; carefully pour filling over walnuts. Place tarts on large cookie sheet for easier handling.

3. Bake 25 to 30 minutes. Cool 10 minutes; remove from pans and cool on wire rack. Serve topped with whipped cream.

Unbaked Tart Shells: In medium bowl with fork, mix *1¹/₂ cups all-purpose flour, 1 tablespoon sugar,* and *¹/₄ teaspoon salt.* With pastry blender or two knives used scissor fashion, cut in *¹/₃ cup shortening.* Sprinkle in *3 to 4 tablespoons cold water,* a tablespoon at a time, mixing lightly with fork after each addition, until pastry just holds together. Shape dough into ball; divide into 12 equal pieces; carefully shape each into a ball. On lightly floured surface with lightly floured rolling pin, roll each ball into circle, ¹/₈ inch thick and 5 inches in diameter. Press pastry circles into twelve 3¹/₄″ by 1¹/₄″ deep fluted tart pans. With knife, trim each pastry shell even with top of tart pan.

Pear-Almond Tart

TIME: about 3 hours or start early in day—SERVINGS: 10

Tart Shell (right)

2/3 cup blanched whole almonds

1 egg white

1 1/4 cups confectioners' sugar

almond extract

salt

1/4 cup sugar

3 tablespoons all-purpose flour

1 envelope unflavored gelatin

2 eggs

1 egg yolk

1 1/2 cups milk

1/2 cup heavy or whipping cream

1 29- to 30-ounce can pear halves, well drained

1/4 cup apricot preserves

1 teaspoon water

1. Prepare dough for Tart Shell.

2. While dough is chilling, prepare almond paste: In blender at medium speed or in food processor with knife blade attached, blend almonds, 1/3 cup at a time, until very finely ground and pastelike. (If using food processor, add egg white, confectioners' sugar, almond extract, and salt to ground almonds; blend to make a stiff dough.) In medium bowl with fork, mix ground almonds, egg white, confectioners' sugar, 1/2 teaspoon almond extract, and 1/8 teaspoon salt. With hands, knead to make a stiff dough. Cover with plastic wrap; refrigerate.

3. While tart shell is baking, prepare custard filling: In heavy 2-quart saucepan, stir sugar, flour, gelatin, and 1/4 teaspoon salt. In medium bowl with fork, beat eggs and egg yolk with milk; stir into sugar mixture. Cook over medium-low heat, stirring constantly, until gelatin is completely dissolved and mixture thickens and coats a spoon, about 15 minutes. (Do not boil or custard will curdle.) Remove saucepan from heat. Stir in 1/2 teaspoon almond extract. Refrigerate until custard mounds slightly when dropped from a spoon, about 1 hour, stirring occasionally.

4. When tart shell is cool, gently and firmly press almond paste onto bottom of tart shell.

5. In small bowl with mixer at medium speed, beat heavy or whipping cream until stiff peaks form. With rubber spatula or wire whisk, fold whipped cream into custard. Evenly spoon custard onto almond paste in tart shell. Arrange pear halves, cut side down, on custard.

6. In small saucepan over medium heat, heat apricot preserves and water until melted, stirring occasionally. Brush pear halves with melted preserves. Refrigerate tart 1 hour or until custard is completely set.

Tart Shell: Into medium bowl, measure *1 cup all-purpose flour, 3 tablespoons cold butter* or margarine, cut into 1/4-inch pieces, *1 tablespoon sugar,* and *1 tablespoon shortening.* With fingertips, blend mixture until it resembles coarse crumbs. Add *3 tablespoons iced water,* stirring with fork to mix well. Wrap and refrigerate dough 1 hour or until well chilled.

Preheat oven to 425° F. On well-floured surface with floured rolling pin, roll pastry into 1/8-inch-thick circle. Line 10-inch tart pan with removable bottom with pastry, gently pressing pastry to bottom and up side of pan; trim pastry edge. With fork, gently prick pastry in many places. Line pastry with foil; bake 10 minutes. Remove foil; again prick pastry with fork; bake 10 minutes longer or until pastry is browned. (If pastry puffs up again, prick with fork again.) Cool tart shell in pan on wire rack 20 minutes. Carefully remove side from pan and place tart shell on serving plate.

Grape-and-Kiwi-Fruit Tart

TIME: about 3 hours or start early in day—SERVINGS: 10

Tart Shell (right)

1/4 cup sugar

3 tablespoons all-purpose flour

1 envelope unflavored gelatin

1/4 teaspoon salt

2 eggs

1 egg yolk

1 1/2 cups milk

2 tablespoons almond-flavor liqueur or 1/2 teaspoon almond extract

about 1/2 pound green grapes

3 medium kiwi fruit, peeled and thinly sliced

1/2 cup heavy or whipping cream

2 tablespoons apple jelly

1. Prepare and bake Tart Shell.

2. While Tart Shell is baking, prepare custard filling: In heavy 2-quart saucepan stir sugar, flour, gelatin, and salt. In medium bowl with fork, beat eggs and egg yolk with milk; stir into sugar mixture. Cook over medium-low heat, stirring until gelatin is completely dissolved and mixture thickens and coats a spoon, about 15 minutes. (Do not boil, or custard will curdle.) Remove from heat. Stir in liqueur. Refrigerate until mixture mounds slightly when dropped from a spoon, about 1 hour, stirring occasionally.

3. Cut each grape lengthwise in half; remove seeds. Peel and thinly slice kiwi fruit. Set grapes and kiwi fruit aside.

4. In small bowl with mixer at medium speed, beat heavy or whipping cream until stiff peaks form. With rubber spatula or wire whisk, fold whipped cream into custard. Evenly spoon custard into cooled tart shell. Arrange grapes, cut side down, and kiwi fruit on custard.

5. In small saucepan over medium heat, melt apple jelly, stirring occasionally. Brush fruit with melted jelly. Refrigerate tart 1 hour or until custard is completely set.

Tart Shell: Into medium bowl, measure *1 1/2 cups all-purpose flour, 6 tablespoons cold butter* or margarine, cut into 1/4-inch pieces, and *1 tablespoon sugar*. With fingertips, blend mixture until it resembles coarse crumbs. Add *1/4 cup iced water*, stirring with fork to mix well. Wrap and refrigerate dough 1 hour or until well chilled.

Preheat oven to 425° F. On well-floured surface with well-floured rolling pin, roll pastry into a 1/8-inch-thick circle. Line 10-inch tart pan with removable bottom with pastry, gently pressing pastry to bottom and up side of pan; trim edge. With fork, gently prick pastry in many places. Bake 20 minutes or until browned. (If pastry puffs up, gently press to bottom of pan with spoon.)

In cup with fork, beat *1 egg white* until frothy. Quickly brush hot tart shell with beaten egg white. Cool tart shell in pan on wire rack. Carefully remove side from pan and place tart shell on serving plate.

Walnut-Pumpkin Pie

TIME: about 3 hours or start day ahead—SERVINGS: 10

piecrust mix for one 9-inch piecrust

1 16-ounce can pumpkin

1 13-ounce can evaporated milk

1/2 cup packed brown sugar

1/2 cup sugar

1 1/2 teaspoons ground cinnamon

1/2 teaspoon ground cloves

1/2 teaspoon ground ginger

1/2 teaspoon ground nutmeg

1/2 teaspoon salt

3 eggs

Walnut Topping (right)

Maple Whipped Cream (see Index)

1. Prepare piecrust mix as label directs for one 9-inch piecrust; shape mixture into a ball. On lightly floured surface with floured rolling pin, roll ball into a circle 2 inches larger all around than 9 1/2-inch deep-dish pie plate. Line pie plate with pastry; trim pastry edge, leaving 1-inch overhang. Fold overhang under; form high fluted edge.

2. Preheat oven to 400° F. In large bowl with mixer at medium speed, beat pumpkin with next 9 ingredients until well mixed. Place pastry-lined pie plate on oven rack; pour in pumpkin mixture. Bake pie 40 minutes. Meanwhile, prepare Walnut Topping.

3. Remove pie from oven; spoon Walnut Topping evenly over top of pie. Return pie to oven and bake 10 minutes longer or until knife inserted one inch from edge comes out clean. Cool pie completely on wire rack.

4. To serve, prepare Maple Whipped Cream. Garnish top of pie with some of whipped-cream mixture; pass remaining to serve with pie.

Walnut Topping: In 1-quart saucepan over low heat, melt *1 tablespoon butter* or margarine. Stir in *1 cup California walnuts*, chopped, and *1/4 cup packed brown sugar* until well mixed.

Cinnamon-Cream Pie

TIME: start early in day—SERVINGS: 8

1½ cups chocolate-wafer crumbs (about 30 wafers)

6 tablespoons butter or margarine, melted

3 eggs, separated

1¼ cups milk

sugar

½ teaspoon ground cinnamon

⅛ teaspoon salt

1 envelope unflavored gelatin

1 teaspoon vanilla extract

½ cup heavy or whipping cream

Chocolate Curls, for garnish (right)

1. In 9-inch pie plate with spoon, mix chocolate-wafer crumbs and butter or margarine. With back of spoon, evenly press crumb mixture onto bottom and side of pie plate.

2. In small, heavy saucepan with wire whisk or fork, mix egg yolks, milk, ¼ cup sugar, cinnamon, and salt; sprinkle gelatin over mixture. Cook over low heat, stirring constantly, until gelatin is completely dissolved and mixture is thickened and coats a spoon. Remove saucepan from heat; stir in vanilla.

3. Refrigerate until mixture mounds when dropped from spoon, about 40 minutes. With wire whisk or hand beater, beat mixture until smooth. In large bowl with mixer at high speed, beat egg whites until soft peaks form; beating at high speed, gradually sprinkle in ¼ cup sugar; beat until sugar is completely dissolved. (Whites should stand in stiff, glossy peaks.)

4. In small bowl, with same beaters and with mixer at medium speed, beat heavy or whipping cream until stiff peaks form. With wire whisk or rubber spatula, gently fold whipped cream and gelatin mixture into beaten egg whites. Spoon mixture into piecrust. Refrigerate until pie is set, about 5 hours. Garnish pie with Chocolate Curls.

Chocolate Curls: With heat of hands or in slightly warm oven, slightly soften *3 squares semisweet chocolate*. With vegetable peeler, draw blade along smooth surface of softened chocolate to make chocolate curls.

Deep-Dish Blueberry Pie

TIME: about 2 hours—SERVINGS: 8

CRUST:

1 cup all-purpose flour

½ teaspoon salt

⅓ cup shortening

2 to 3 tablespoons cold water

FILLING:

6 cups blueberries

⅔ cup sugar

¼ cup all-purpose flour

2 teaspoons lemon juice

½ teaspoon ground cinnamon

½ teaspoon grated lemon peel

¼ teaspoon ground nutmeg

⅛ teaspoon salt

1 tablespoon butter or margarine

1. Preheat oven to 425° F. Prepare Crust: In medium bowl with fork, lightly stir together flour and salt. With pastry blender or two knives used scissor fashion, cut in shortening until mixture resembles coarse crumbs.

2. Sprinkle cold water, a tablespoon at a time, mixing lightly with a fork after each addition until pastry just holds together. With hands, shape into a ball.

3. Prepare Filling: Toss together blueberries, sugar, flour, lemon juice, cinnamon, lemon peel, nutmeg, and salt. Place filling in 9½-inch deep-dish pie plate; dot with butter or margarine.

4. On lightly floured surface with floured rolling pin, roll pastry into a circle 2 inches larger all around than pie plate; place over filling; trim edges, leaving a 1-inch overhang; pinch to form a high edge and make a decorative edge. Cut a 4-inch "X" in center of crust; fold back points from center of "X" to make a square opening. Bake 50 minutes or until golden brown.

Rhubarb Cups

TIME: about 40 minutes—SERVINGS: 4

2 tablespoons water

1 teaspoon cornstarch

1 pound rhubarb, cut into 1/2-inch pieces (about 3 cups)

sugar

1 cup all-purpose flour

6 tablespoons butter or margarine, softened

1/8 teaspoon salt

1/2 cup heavy or whipping cream or milk

1. In 2-quart saucepan, stir water and cornstarch until blended; add rhubarb. Over medium heat, cook until rhubarb is tender and mixture is thickened, about 5 minutes, stirring frequently. During last minutes of cooking time, stir in 2 tablespoons sugar.

2. Meanwhile, in bowl, with hand, knead flour, butter or margarine, salt, and 1/3 cup sugar until well blended.

3. Preheat oven to 400° F. Reserve 1/4 cup dough. Gently press remaining dough onto bottom and up side of four 6-ounce custard cups. Fill custard cups with rhubarb mixture; sprinkle with reserved dough. Bake 15 minutes or until golden. Pass cream to serve over dessert.

Cheese-filled Crepes with Chocolate Sauce

TIME: about 3 1/2 hours—SERVINGS: 12

CREPES:

1 1/2 cups milk

2/3 cup all-purpose flour

1/2 teaspoon salt

3 eggs

about 6 tablespoons butter or margarine, melted

CHEESE FILLING:

1 15- to 16-ounce container ricotta cheese

1/2 cup sour cream

1/4 cup confectioners' sugar

2 teaspoons grated orange peel

3/4 cup peach preserves

CHOCOLATE SAUCE:

1/3 cup cocoa

1/3 cup sugar

1/4 cup milk

1/4 cup light corn syrup

3 tablespoons butter or margarine

1 tablespoon almond-flavor liqueur

1. Prepare Crepe batter: In medium bowl with wire whisk or fork, beat milk, flour, salt, eggs, and 2 tablespoons butter or margarine until well blended. Cover and refrigerate at least 2 hours.

2. Meanwhile, prepare Cheese Filling: In blender at medium speed, blend half of ricotta at a time until very smooth; spoon into medium bowl. Stir in remaining filling ingredients except preserves until blended. Cover and refrigerate until ready to use.

3. Cook Crepes: Brush bottoms of 7-inch crepe pan and 10-inch skillet with some melted butter or margarine. Over medium heat, heat pans. Pour scant 1/4 cup crepe batter into hot crepe pan, tipping pan to coat bottom. Cook until top of crepe is set and underside is lightly browned, about 2 minutes. With metal spatula, loosen crepe; invert crepe into hot skillet; cook other side, about 30 seconds. Slip crepe onto waxed paper. Meanwhile, start cooking another crepe. Stack crepes between waxed paper. Repeat making crepes until all batter is used. (You will have 12 crepes.)

4. Prepare Chocolate Sauce: In 1-quart saucepan over medium heat, heat all sauce ingredients except almond-flavor liqueur until mixture is smooth and boils, stirring frequently. Remove saucepan from heat; stir in liqueur. Set aside; keep warm.

5. Assemble Crepes: Spread 1 tablespoon peach preserves evenly over a crepe. Top with about 2 tablespoons Cheese Filling, spreading filling almost but not all the way to edge of crepe. Fold crepe into quarters; arrange on heat-safe platter. Repeat with remaining crepes, preserves, and filling. Cover platter with foil.

6. To serve, preheat oven to 350° F. Bake crepes until just heated through, about 10 minutes. Serve with Chocolate Sauce.

TO DO AHEAD: Early in day or day ahead, prepare crepes and filling as in steps 1 through 3. Wrap crepes well with plastic wrap or foil; refrigerate. About 45 minutes before serving, prepare Chocolate Sauce, and assemble crepes as in steps 4 and 5. Heat and serve as above.

Marble Swirl Pound Cake

TIME: about 4 hours or start day ahead—SERVINGS: 16

2 cups sugar

1 cup butter or margarine, softened

3½ cups cake flour

1 cup milk

1½ teaspoons double-acting baking powder

2 teaspoons vanilla extract

¼ teaspoon salt

4 eggs

¼ cup cocoa

1. Grease 10-inch tube pan; set aside.

2. In large bowl with mixer at low speed, beat sugar and butter or margarine until blended. Increase speed to high; beat until light and fluffy. Add flour and remaining ingredients except cocoa; at low speed, beat until well mixed, constantly scraping bowl with rubber spatula. Increase speed to high and beat batter 4 minutes longer, occasionally scraping bowl with rubber spatula.

3. Preheat oven to 350° F. Remove about 2½ cups batter to medium bowl. With wire whisk or fork, beat cocoa into batter in medium bowl until well blended. Alternately spoon vanilla and chocolate batters into prepared pan. With large spoon, cut and twist through batters to obtain marbled effect.

4. Bake 1 hour or until toothpick inserted in center of cake comes out clean. Cool cake in pan on wire rack 10 minutes. With spatula, loosen cake edge from pan. Remove cake from pan; cool completely on rack.

Chocolate Fantasy Cake

TIME: start early in day—SERVINGS: 12

CHOCOLATE CAKE:

6 tablespoons butter or margarine, softened

1¾ cups packed light-brown sugar

2 eggs

2 squares unsweetened chocolate, melted

1½ cups cake flour

⅓ cup milk

1½ teaspoons baking soda

1 teaspoon almond extract

¼ teaspoon salt

⅔ cup boiling water

CHOCOLATE COATING AND GARNISH:

waxed paper

1 12-ounce package semisweet-chocolate pieces

4 tablespoons butter or margarine

¼ cup light corn syrup

1 large strawberry

5 small lemon leaves or other nontoxic leaves

WHIPPED-CREAM FILLING:

¾ cup heavy or whipping cream

½ cup crème de cacao

confectioners' sugar

1. Prepare Chocolate Cake: Grease and flour two 8-inch round cake pans. Preheat oven to 350° F. In large bowl with mixer at high speed, beat butter or margarine, brown sugar, and eggs until light and fluffy, about 5 minutes, scraping bowl occasionally with rubber spatula. With mixer at low speed, beat in melted chocolate and next 5 ingredients; increase speed to medium; beat 1 minute. Gradually beat in water just until mixture is smooth (mixture will be thin). Pour batter into pans. Bake 35 minutes or until toothpick inserted in center of cake comes out clean. Cool cakes in pans on wire racks 10 minutes; remove from pans; cool completely.

2. Meanwhile, prepare Chocolate Coating: Cut waxed paper into three 12" by 8" rectangles; then cut each crosswise into four 8" by 3" strips. Place strips on three large cookie sheets; set aside.

3. In double boiler over hot, *not boiling,* water (or in heavy 1-quart saucepan over low heat), heat chocolate pieces, butter or margarine, and corn syrup until mixture is smooth, about 5 minutes. Remove double boiler from heat. Dip strawberry in chocolate to coat halfway; refrigerate. On each waxed-paper strip, with metal spatula, spread about 2 tablespoonfuls chocolate mixture. Spread remaining chocolate mixture on underside of lemon leaves. Refrigerate chocolate strips and leaves about 2 hours (chocolate should be firm).

4. Meanwhile, prepare Whipped-Cream Filling: In small bowl with mixer at medium speed, beat heavy or whipping cream and 2 tablespoons crème de cacao until stiff peaks form. Cover; refrigerate.

5. Assemble cake: Place 1 cake layer on cake plate; sprinkle with 3 tablespoons crème de cacao; spread with whipped-cream filling. Top with remaining cake layer; sprinkle with remaining 3 tablespoons crème de cacao.

6. Remove chocolate strips from refrigerator; let stand 3 to 5 minutes to soften slightly. Carefully place chocolate side of one strip vertically against side of cake, tucking end of strip under cake. Peel off paper; gently press chocolate onto side and top of cake. Repeat with remaining chocolate strips, overlapping slightly to completely cover cake.

7. Lightly dust top of cake with confectioners' sugar. Carefully peel off leaves from chocolate; arrange chocolate leaves on center of cake. Garnish with chocolate-covered strawberry.

Spicy Crumb Cake

TIME: about 2 hours or start day ahead—SERVINGS: 10

Crumb Topping (right)

1³/₄ **cups all-purpose flour**

1 **cup butter or margarine, softened**

¹/₂ **cup sugar**

¹/₄ **cup milk**

2 **teaspoons double-acting baking powder**

3 **eggs**

1 **tablespoon honey**

¹/₄ **teaspoon ground allspice**

¹/₄ **teaspoon ground cinnamon**

1. Prepare Crumb Topping; set aside. Grease and flour 9-inch springform pan.

2. Preheat oven to 350° F. In large bowl with mixer at low speed, beat flour and next 5 ingredients until just blended, constantly scraping bowl with rubber spatula. Continue beating 2 minutes, occasionally scraping bowl. (Do not overbeat or baked cake will be gummy.) Spoon batter into prepared pan.

3. In cup, mix honey, allspice, and cinnamon; drizzle over batter. With fork, swirl honey mixture just on top of batter; sprinkle with Crumb Topping. Bake cake 55 to 60 minutes, until toothpick inserted in center of cake comes out clean and Crumb Topping is golden brown. Cool cake in pan on wire rack 10 minutes. Remove cake from pan; serve cake warm. Or cool cake to serve later.

Crumb Topping: In medium bowl with fork, stir *¹/₂ cup all-purpose flour, ¹/₄ cup California walnuts,* finely chopped, and *2 tablespoons sugar.* With pastry blender or 2 knives used scissor fashion, cut *¹/₄ cup butter* or margarine into flour mixture until mixture resembles coarse crumbs.

Lane Cake

TIME: start early in day—SERVINGS: 16

8 **eggs, at room temperature**

2 **cups sugar**

2³/₄ **cups cake flour**

1 **cup milk**

1 **cup butter or margarine**

3 **teaspoons double-acting baking powder**

1 **teaspoon salt**

1 **teaspoon vanilla extract**

Filling (right)

Frosting (right)

1. Preheat oven to 375° F. Separate eggs, placing 6 whites in large bowl, 2 whites in small bowl, and all the yolks in 2-quart saucepan. Grease two 9-inch round cake pans; line bottoms of cake pans with waxed paper; grease paper.

2. In large bowl with mixer at high speed, beat egg whites until soft peaks form. Beating at high speed, sprinkle in 1 cup sugar, 2 tablespoons at a time. Beat until stiff peaks form.

3. In another large bowl with mixer at low speed, mix flour, next 5 ingredients, and 1 cup sugar. At medium speed, beat 4 minutes; fold in whites.

4. Pour into pans; bake 35 minutes. Cool in pans on wire racks 10 minutes; remove from pans; discard paper; cool. Prepare Filling. Cut each layer in half horizontally; assemble four-layer cake with filling. Prepare Frosting; frost cake.

Filling: Into 8 yolks, stir *1¹/₄ cups sugar* and *¹/₂ cup butter* or margarine. Over medium heat, cook, stirring, until slightly thickened, about 5 minutes. Stir in *one 4-ounce can shredded coconut, 1 cup pecan halves,* chopped, *1 cup candied red cherries,* chopped, *1 cup dark seedless raisins,* chopped, and *¹/₃ cup bourbon.*

Frosting: In 1-quart saucepan over medium heat, heat *1¹/₂ cups sugar, 1 tablespoon dark corn syrup, ¹/₃ cup water,* and *¹/₂ teaspoon salt* to boiling. Boil, without stirring, to 240° F. on candy thermometer. Remove from heat. With mixer at high speed, beat reserved 2 egg whites until soft peaks form. Pour syrup in thin stream into whites, beating constantly. Add *1 teaspoon vanilla extract,* and beat until very thick.

Raspberry-Banana Dream

TIME: start early in day or day ahead—SERVINGS: 12

6 eggs, separated, at room temperature

1/2 teaspoon cream of tartar

sugar

2 cups cake flour

1 cup water

1 tablespoon double-acting baking powder

1/2 teaspoon almond extract

1/4 teaspoon salt

1 10-ounce package frozen raspberries in quick-thaw pouch, thawed

1 4-ounce container frozen whipped topping, thawed

1 1/4 cups orange juice

2 ripe, medium bananas

lemon leaves, for garnish

1. In small bowl with mixer at high speed, beat egg whites and cream of tartar until soft peaks form. Beating at high speed, sprinkle in 1/3 cup sugar, 2 tablespoons at a time, beating well after each addition until sugar is completely dissolved. (Whites should stand in stiff, glossy peaks.) Set aside.

2. Preheat oven to 350° F. In large bowl with mixer at medium speed, beat egg yolks, flour, water, baking powder, almond extract, salt, and 1/4 cup sugar until light and fluffy, about 3 minutes, occasionally scraping bowl with rubber spatula. With wire whisk or rubber spatula, gently fold egg-white mixture into egg-yolk mixture just until blended. Pour batter into two ungreased 8-inch round cake pans. Bake 25 minutes or until top of cake springs back when lightly touched with finger. Cool cakes completely in pans on wire racks.

3. Drain raspberries, reserving syrup. Reserve 1 raspberry for garnish; cover and refrigerate. In medium bowl, fold remaining raspberries into whipped topping. In cup, mix raspberry syrup with orange juice. Thinly slice bananas.

4. With metal spatula, gently loosen cakes from pans. With serrated knife, cut each cake horizontally in half to form two layers. Gently press one cake layer into a 3-quart glass bowl. (If necessary, cut cake layers to fit bowl.) Sprinkle cake layer with one quarter of juice mixture; spread with one quarter of whipped-topping mixture; top with one third of banana slices, tucking some banana slices along side of bowl. Repeat layering, ending with whipped-topping mixture, pressing each layer gently but firmly. Cover and refrigerate at least 4 hours.

5. To serve, garnish top of dessert with lemon leaves and reserved raspberry.

Hungarian Cream Squares

TIME: about 4 hours or start day ahead—SERVINGS: 16

1 8-ounce package semisweet-chocolate squares

6 eggs, separated, at room temperature

sugar

1/3 cup all-purpose flour

1 1/2 cups heavy or whipping cream

1/3 cup cocoa

water

1. Preheat oven to 350° F. Grease two 8" by 8" baking pans. Finely grate 4 squares chocolate; set aside. In large bowl with mixer at high speed, beat egg whites until stiff peaks form.

2. In small bowl with same beaters and mixer at medium speed, beat egg yolks and 1/3 cup sugar until thick and lemon-colored; beat in flour and grated chocolate; continue beating about 2 minutes, scraping bowl occasionally.

3. With wire whisk or rubber spatula, fold yolk mixture into beaten egg whites. Pour batter into pans. Bake 15 minutes or until toothpick inserted in center comes out clean. Cool cakes in pans on wire racks 15 minutes. Loosen edges of cakes with spatula; invert onto racks; cool completely.

4. In large bowl with mixer at medium speed, beat heavy or whipping cream, cocoa, and 1/3 cup sugar until stiff peaks form. Spread whipped-cream mixture evenly on one cake layer; refrigerate 1 1/2 hours or until well chilled.

5. In double boiler over hot, *not boiling*, water, heat remaining chocolate squares and 2 tablespoons water until chocolate is melted, stirring constantly. Spread chocolate mixture evenly over remaining cake layer. Let stand few minutes to set; cut into 16 squares.

6. Place chocolate-covered squares side by side on top of cream-covered layer. With knife, cut dessert between squares through filling and bottom layer. Refrigerate dessert until serving.

Orange-Chiffon Cake

TIME: about 3^1/$_2$ hours or start early in day—SERVINGS: 16

1 cup egg whites, at room temperature

^{1}/$_2$ teaspoon cream of tartar

sugar

2^1/$_4$ cups cake flour

^{3}/$_4$ cup orange juice

^{1}/$_2$ cup salad oil

5 egg yolks

1 tablespoon double-acting baking powder

3 tablespoons grated orange peel

1 teaspoon salt

Fluffy Orange Frosting (right)

1. Preheat oven to 325° F. In large bowl with mixer at high speed, beat egg whites and cream of tartar until soft peaks form. At high speed, beat in ^{1}/$_2$ cup sugar, 2 tablespoons at a time, until dissolved and whites stand in stiff, glossy peaks. Do not scrape the bowl.

2. In another large bowl at low speed, beat 1 cup sugar and remaining ingredients except frosting.

3. With rubber spatula, gently fold mixture into beaten whites. Pour batter into ungreased 10-inch tube pan. Bake 1^1/$_4$ hours or until top springs back when lightly touched. Invert in pan on funnel; cool.

4. Prepare Fluffy Orange Frosting. Remove cake from pan; frost top and sides. Keep refrigerated.

Fluffy Orange Frosting: In 1-quart saucepan over medium heat, heat *one 12-ounce jar sweet orange marmalade* to boiling. In large bowl with mixer at high speed, beat *2 egg whites, ^{1}/$_2$ teaspoon vanilla extract, 10 drops yellow food color,* and *^{1}/$_8$ teaspoon salt* until soft peaks form. Slowly pour in hot marmalade, beating 6 to 8 minutes until peaks form again.

Chocolate-Mousse Cake

TIME: about 4 hours or start day ahead—SERVINGS: 16

1 18.5- to 18.75-ounce package devil's-food cake mix with pudding

orange-flavor liqueur

4 squares semisweet chocolate

5 tablespoons butter or margarine

3 eggs, separated, at room temperature

^{1}/$_8$ teaspoon salt

2 tablespoons sugar

Chocolate Glaze (right)

1. Preheat oven to 350° F. Grease and flour 10″ by 3″ springform pan. Prepare cake mix as label directs, but use 2 tablespoons less water and add ^{1}/$_4$ cup orange-flavor liqueur. Bake cake in prepared springform pan 45 minutes or until cake springs back when lightly touched with finger. Cool cake in pan on wire rack 10 minutes; then carefully remove side of pan; cool cake completely on wire rack.

2. Meanwhile, prepare chocolate mousse filling: In heavy 1-quart saucepan over low heat, heat chocolate and butter or margarine until melted and smooth, stirring occasionally. Remove saucepan from heat; cool 15 minutes. With wire whisk, beat in egg yolks until blended.

3. In small bowl with mixer at high speed, beat egg whites and salt until soft peaks form. Beating at high speed, gradually sprinkle in sugar, beating until sugar is completely dissolved. (Whites should stand in stiff, glossy peaks.) With rubber spatula or wire whisk, gently fold chocolate mixture into beaten egg whites. Cover and refrigerate until cooled and thick enough to spread, about 45 minutes.

4. Remove cake from cake-pan bottom. With serrated knife, cut cake horizontally into two layers. Place one cake layer on cake platter; spread with chocolate-mousse filling; top with remaining cake layer.

5. Prepare Chocolate Glaze. While glaze is still warm, with metal spatula, quickly spread three fourths of glaze over top and down side of cake. Refrigerate cake and remaining glaze until glaze on cake is set, about 15 minutes.

6. Spoon remaining glaze into decorating bag with small writing tube; use to pipe attractive design on top of cake.

Chocolate Glaze: In double boiler over hot, *not boiling,* water (or in heavy 1-quart saucepan over low heat), heat *9 squares semisweet chocolate, ^{1}/$_4$ cup milk, 3 tablespoons butter* or margarine, *3 tablespoons light corn syrup,* and *2 tablespoons orange-flavor liqueur* until chocolate is melted and mixture is smooth, stirring occasionally.

Raspberry-Strawberry-Cream Cake

TIME: start early in day or day ahead—SERVINGS: 16

1³/₄ cups cake flour

³/₄ cup milk

³/₄ cup butter or margarine, softened

1 tablespoon double-acting baking powder

³/₄ teaspoon salt

¹/₂ teaspoon baking soda

4 eggs

sugar

vanilla extract

Raspberry-Custard Filling (right)

about ¹/₄-pound piece whole citron (available in specialty food stores or department-store food sections)

2 pints strawberries

3¹/₂ cups heavy or whipping cream

1. Preheat oven to 375° F. Grease and flour two 9-inch round cake pans. Into large bowl, measure flour, milk, butter or margarine, baking powder, salt, baking soda, eggs, 1¹/₂ cups sugar, and 1 tablespoon vanilla. With mixer at low speed, beat just until mixed, constantly scraping bowl with rubber spatula. Increase speed to high; beat 4 minutes, occasionally scraping bowl.

2. Pour batter into pans. Bake 25 minutes or until toothpick inserted in center of cake comes out clean. Cool cake in pans on wire racks 10 minutes. Remove from pans; cool completely.

3. Meanwhile, prepare Raspberry Custard Filling.

4. Prepare citron leaves for garnish: Cut peel from whole citron; cut peel into 10 small leaves; cover and set aside. (Reserve remaining citron to use in fruitcake or sprinkle on ice cream another day.)

5. Reserve 6 large whole strawberries to garnish top of cake. Slice each remaining strawberry in half; set aside. With serrated knife, cut each cake horizontally in half to make two layers; set aside.

6. In large bowl with mixer at medium speed, beat heavy or whipping cream, 2 teaspoons sugar, and 1 teaspoon vanilla until stiff peaks form. Place one cake layer on cake platter; spread with about 1 cup whipped cream; arrange one third halved strawberries on top of cream. Top with second cake layer, pressing down gently but firmly. Spread raspberry-custard mixture over layer; top with third cake layer. Repeat with whipped cream and halved strawberries. Top with remaining cake layer.

7. Frost top and side of cake with one third of remaining whipped cream. Spoon remaining whipped cream into decorating bag with large star tube; use to decorate top and side of cake. Garnish top of cake with citron leaves and reserved whole strawberries, side of cake with remaining halved strawberries. Refrigerate until serving time.

Raspberry-Custard Filling: Drain *one 10-ounce package quick-thaw red raspberries*, reserving ¹/₂ cup juice; set aside. In heavy 2-quart saucepan, stir *4 teaspoons sugar, 4 teaspoons all-purpose flour, 1 envelope unflavored gelatin*, and *¹/₄ teaspoon salt*. In medium bowl with fork, beat *2 egg yolks* with *1 cup milk* and reserved raspberry juice until blended; stir into gelatin mixture. Cook over medium-low heat until gelatin is completely dissolved and mixture thickens and coats a spoon, stirring constantly, about 15 minutes. (Do not boil or custard will curdle.) Remove from heat; stir in raspberries. Refrigerate until mixture mounds slightly when dropped from a spoon, about 30 minutes to 1 hour, stirring occasionally.

In small bowl, with mixer at medium speed, beat *¹/₂ cup heavy or whipping cream* until stiff peaks form. With rubber spatula or wire whisk, fold whipped cream into custard. Cover and refrigerate until filling is firm enough to spread, about 20 minutes.

193

Maple-Crunch Squares

TIME: about 4 hours or start early in day—SERVINGS: 30

butter or margarine

³/₄ cup California walnuts, finely chopped

³/₄ cup packed light-brown sugar

³/₄ cup vanilla-wafer crumbs

1 cup cake flour

¹/₂ cup buttermilk, or substitute ¹/₂ cup milk mixed with 1¹/₂ teaspoons cider vinegar and allowed to stand a few minutes to "sour"

¹/₃ cup sugar

¹/₄ cup water

¹/₂ teaspoon baking soda

¹/₂ teaspoon salt

¹/₄ teaspoon double-acting baking powder

2 1-ounce packets premelted unsweetened chocolate flavor for baking or 2 squares unsweetened chocolate, melted

1 egg

1 cup heavy or whipping cream

1¹/₄ teaspoons maple extract

1 square semisweet chocolate, shaved, for garnish

1. In 13″ by 9″ baking pan in 350° F. oven, melt ¹/₂ cup butter or margarine; remove pan from oven. Reserve 1 tablespoon finely chopped walnuts for garnish. Into melted butter in pan, stir brown sugar, vanilla-wafer crumbs, and remaining walnuts until well blended. Pat mixture evenly on bottom of pan; set aside.

2. Into large bowl, measure flour, next 8 ingredients, and ¹/₄ cup softened butter or margarine. With mixer at low speed, beat ingredients until blended, constantly scraping bowl with rubber spatula. Increase speed to high; beat 3 minutes, occasionally scraping bowl.

3. Pour batter over crumb mixture in pan. Bake 20 minutes or until toothpick inserted into center of cake comes out clean. Cool cake in pan on wire rack 10 minutes. With spatula, loosen edge of cake from pan; invert cake onto wire rack to cool completely.

4. Cut cake into 30 squares. In small bowl with mixer at medium speed, beat heavy or whipping cream with maple extract until stiff peaks form. Spoon whipped cream into decorating bag with large rosette tube. With cake squares crumb side up, pipe a large rosette of whipped cream onto top of each. Sprinkle half of rosettes with reserved chopped walnuts, half with shaved semisweet chocolate.

Little Bee Cakes

TIME: about 4¹/₂ hours or start early in day—YIELD: 3 dozen cakes

¹/₂ cup sugar

¹/₂ teaspoon salt

1 package active dry yeast

about 3¹/₄ cups all-purpose flour

²/₃ cup water

6 tablespoons butter or margarine

1 egg

Almond-Coconut Topping (opposite)

Almond-Cream Filling (opposite)

1. In large bowl, combine sugar, salt, yeast, and 1 cup flour. In 1-quart saucepan over low heat, heat water and butter or margarine until very warm (120° to 130° F.). (Butter or margarine does not need to melt completely.) With mixer at low speed, gradually beat liquid into dry ingredients just until blended. Increase speed to medium; beat 2 minutes, occasionally scraping bowl with rubber spatula. Gradually beat in egg and ³/₄ cup flour to make a thick batter; continue beating 2 minutes, scraping bowl often. With wooden spoon, stir in 1 cup flour to make a soft dough.

2. Turn dough onto well-floured surface and knead until smooth and elastic, about 8 minutes, adding more flour while kneading (about ¹/₂ cup). Shape dough into a ball and place in greased medium bowl, turning dough over so that top is greased. Cover and let rise in warm place (80° to 85° F.), away from draft, until doubled, about 1 hour. (Dough is doubled when two fingers pressed lightly into dough leave a dent.)

3. Punch down dough. Turn dough onto lightly floured surface; cover with bowl and let dough rest for 15 minutes for easier shaping.

4. Grease two large cookie sheets. Cut dough into 36 equal pieces; shape into balls; place balls, 1 inch apart, on cookie sheets. Cover balls with towels and let rise in warm place until doubled, about 1 hour (when one finger very lightly pressed against dough leaves a dent).

5. Meanwhile, prepare Almond-Coconut Topping.

6. Preheat oven to 350° F. With fingers, gently press about 1 teaspoon Almond-Coconut Topping onto each dough ball. Bake 15 minutes or until golden. Remove buns from cookie sheets; cool completely on wire racks.

7. When buns are cool, with serrated knife, cut each horizontally in half.

Prepare Almond-Cream Filling. Spoon a heaping teaspoon onto each bottom; replace top.

Almond-Coconut Topping: In 2-quart saucepan, combine *one 4-ounce can slivered blanched almonds,* finely chopped, *1/2 cup honey, 1/3 cup flaked coconut, 1/4 cup packed light-brown sugar, 4 tablespoons butter* or *margarine, 1/4 teaspoon almond extract,* and *1/8 teaspoon salt.* Over medium heat, heat mixture to boiling, stirring constantly; cook 2 minutes. Do not cook longer or mixture will become hard. Remove saucepan from heat. Cover and refrigerate to cool, about 45 minutes. (Mixture will be thick.)

Almond-Cream Filling: In small bowl with mixer at medium speed, beat *1 cup heavy* or *whipping cream* until soft peaks form; set aside. Prepare *one 3 1/2- to 3 3/4-ounce package vanilla-flavor instant pudding and pie filling* as label directs, but use only *1 1/4 cups milk.* With rubber spatula, fold whipped cream and *1/2 teaspoon almond extract* into pudding.

Tiniest Cinnamon Tortes

TIME: start day ahead—SERVINGS: 18

1 **egg**

1 **cup sugar**

³/₄ **cup butter or margarine, softened**

1 **tablespoon ground cinnamon**

1¹/₃ **cups all-purpose flour**

2 **cups heavy or whipping cream**

¹/₃ **cup cocoa**

1 **square semisweet chocolate**

1. Tear nine sheets of waxed paper, each about 8 1/2 inches long. On one sheet, trace bottom of 8″ by 8″ baking pan. Evenly stack all sheets with pattern on top. With kitchen shears, cut out squares.

2. Into large bowl, measure egg, sugar, butter or margarine, cinnamon, and 1 cup flour. With mixer at low speed, beat ingredients until well mixed, constantly scraping bowl with rubber spatula. Increase speed to medium; beat 3 minutes or until mixture is light and fluffy, occasionally scraping bowl. With wooden spoon, stir in remaining flour to make a soft dough.

3. Preheat oven to 375° F. With damp cloth, moisten one large or two small cookie sheets. Place two waxed-paper squares on large cookie sheet or one on each small cookie sheet. With metal spatula, spread 1/4 cupful dough in a very thin layer on each square. Bake 8 minutes or until lightly browned around edges.

4. Remove cookie sheet to wire rack; cool 5 minutes. With pancake turner, carefully remove cookies still on waxed paper to wire rack to cool completely. (Allow cookie sheets to cool before spreading waxed-paper squares with more dough. The more cookie sheets you have, the faster you can bake the cookies.) Repeat until all dough is baked. Stack cooled cookies carefully on flat plate; cover with plastic wrap and store in cool, dry place.

5. Early in day, in large bowl with mixer at medium speed, beat heavy or whipping cream and cocoa until soft peaks form.

6. Carefully peel off waxed paper from one cookie; place on flat plate; spread with scant 1/2 cupful whipped-cream mixture. Repeat layering until all cookies are used, ending with whipped-cream mixture on top. Refrigerate at least 2 to 3 hours to soften cookie layers slightly for easier cutting.

7. Just before serving, cut dessert into 18 rectangles. Coarsely grate chocolate; sprinkle some on each rectangle.

Banana-Nut Cake

TIME: about 3 hours or start day ahead—SERVINGS: 12

1 **cup butter or margarine, softened**

1¹/₂ **cups sugar**

3¹/₂ **cups all-purpose flour**

1¹/₃ **cups mashed ripe bananas (about 2 large bananas)**

²/₃ **cup buttermilk**

1 **tablespoon double-acting baking powder**

1 **teaspoon baking soda**

¹/₂ **teaspoon ground cinnamon**

¹/₄ **teaspoon salt**

4 **eggs**

1 **cup California walnuts, chopped**

1. Grease 9-inch tube pan. In large bowl with mixer at medium speed, beat butter or margarine with 1 cup sugar until light and fluffy. Add 2 cups flour; at low speed, beat until well mixed. Spoon ¹/₂ cup flour mixture into small bowl; set aside.

2. Preheat oven to 350° F. To mixture remaining in large bowl, add mashed bananas, next 6 ingredients, remaining 1¹/₂ cups flour, and ¹/₂ cup sugar. Beat at low speed until well mixed, constantly scraping bowl with rubber spatula. Increase speed to medium; beat 2 minutes, scraping bowl occasionally. Stir in chopped walnuts.

3. Pour batter into tube pan. Sprinkle reserved flour mixture over batter. Bake 55 to 60 minutes, until toothpick inserted into center of cake comes out clean. Cool cake in pan on wire rack 10 minutes; remove from pan; cool completely on rack.

Mocha-Cream Roll

TIME: about 2 hours or start day ahead—SERVINGS: 10

5 **eggs, separated, at room temperature**

1 **cup confectioners' sugar**

¹/₈ **teaspoon salt**

cocoa

Mocha-Cream Filling (right)

Chocolate Icing (right)

Confectioners' Sugar Glaze (right)

1. Preheat oven to 400° F. Grease 15¹/₂" by 10¹/₂" jelly-roll pan; line bottom of pan with waxed paper; grease and flour paper.

2. In large bowl with mixer at high speed, beat egg whites until soft peaks form. Beating at high speed, gradually sprinkle in ¹/₂ cup confectioners' sugar, beating thoroughly after each addition. Continue beating until the egg whites stand in stiff, glossy peaks. Set mixture aside.

3. In small bowl with same beaters and with mixer at high speed, beat egg yolks until thick and lemon-colored. Reduce speed to low; beat in salt, ¹/₂ cup confectioners' sugar, and 3 tablespoons cocoa, occasionally scraping bowl with rubber spatula. With wire whisk or rubber spatula, gently fold yolk mixture into beaten whites just until the mixture is blended.

4. Spread batter evenly in pan, and bake 15 minutes or until top springs back when lightly touched with finger. Prepare a clean cloth towel by sprinkling it with cocoa.

5. When cake is done, with small spatula, immediately loosen edges from side of pan; invert cake onto prepared towel. Gently peel waxed paper from bottom of cake. Cut off crisp edges, if you like. Roll towel with cake from narrow end jelly-roll fashion. Cool completely, placing it seam side down on wire rack.

6. Meanwhile, prepare Mocha-Cream Filling. When cake is cool, unroll from towel. Evenly spread Mocha-Cream Filling on cake almost to edges. Starting at same narrow end, roll up cake without the towel this time. Place the cake, seam side down, on platter.

7. Prepare Chocolate Icing. Spread icing over top and down sides of roll.

8. Prepare Confectioners' Sugar Glaze; use to drizzle over top of the roll to make a decorative design. Keep the roll in the refrigerator until you are ready to serve it.

Mocha-Cream Filling: In medium bowl with mixer at medium speed, beat 1¹/₂ cups heavy or whipping cream, ¹/₂ cup cocoa, ¹/₄ cup confectioners' sugar, and 2 tablespoons coffee-flavor liqueur until stiff peaks form.

Chocolate Icing: In double boiler, over hot, not boiling, water, melt one-half 6-ounce package semisweet-chocolate pieces with 1 tablespoon butter or margarine; remove from heat; then beat in 1 tablespoon light corn syrup and 3 tablespoons milk until smooth.

Confectioners' Sugar Glaze: In small bowl, stir ¹/₂ cup confectioners' sugar and 2 to 3 teaspoons water until smooth.

Strawberry-Cream Nut Roll

TIME: about 3 hours or start early in day—SERVINGS: 12

6 eggs, separated, at room temperature

sugar

1 cup California walnuts, finely ground

1/4 cup dried bread crumbs

1/4 cup all-purpose flour

1/8 teaspoon salt

confectioners' sugar

1 pint strawberries

1 cup heavy or whipping cream

1 teaspoon vanilla extract

1. Grease 15 1/2″ by 10 1/2″ jelly-roll pan; line pan with waxed paper. In large bowl with mixer at high speed, beat egg whites until soft peaks form. Beating at high speed, gradually beat in 1/4 cup sugar, 2 tablespoons at a time, beating until each addition of sugar is completely dissolved. (Whites should stand in stiff, glossy peaks.)

2. Preheat oven to 375° F. In small bowl with mixer at medium speed, beat egg yolks and 1/2 cup sugar until thick and lemon-colored. With spoon, stir in walnuts, bread crumbs, flour, and salt. With wire whisk or rubber spatula, fold nut mixture into beaten egg whites. Spread batter evenly in jelly-roll pan; bake 15 minutes or until top of cake springs back when lightly touched with finger.

3. Sprinkle clean cloth towel with some confectioners' sugar. When cake is done, immediately invert onto prepared towel; carefully peel off waxed paper. Starting at a narrow end, roll cake with towel, jelly-roll fashion. Place cake, seam side down, on wire rack; cool completely, about 30 minutes.

4. Slice 6 large strawberries lengthwise in half; reserve for garnish. Thinly slice remaining strawberries; set aside. In small bowl with mixer at medium speed, beat heavy or whipping cream, vanilla, and 2 tablespoons sugar until stiff peaks form.

5. Gently unroll cooled cake. Spread top of cake evenly with whipped-cream mixture; top with sliced strawberries. Starting at same narrow end, reroll cake without towel. Place roll, seam side down, on platter. Lightly sprinkle roll with confectioners' sugar. Garnish top of roll with strawberry halves.

Almond-Cream Bombe

TIME: start day ahead—SERVINGS: 10

1 4-ounce can blanched whole almonds (about 3/4 cup)

1 10 3/4- or 12-ounce ready-to-serve frozen pound cake, thawed

1/4 cup almond-flavor liqueur

1/2 6-ounce package semisweet-chocolate pieces (1/2 cup)

2 cups heavy or whipping cream

2/3 cup confectioners' sugar

1/8 teaspoon salt

1. In 9″ by 9″ baking pan, toast the blanched whole almonds in 375° F. oven until golden, about 10 minutes, stirring occasionally; cool thoroughly. With a sharp knife, chop almonds coarsely.

2. Meanwhile, line 1 1/2-quart round-bottom bowl with plastic wrap; set aside. Cut pound cake into 1/4-inch-thick slices; cut each slice diagonally in half to make two triangles. Sprinkle with almond-flavor liqueur. Use triangles with top brown cake crust first to line bowl, with narrow points at bottom of bowl so that brown crusts form a pinwheel design. Complete lining bowl by placing more cake triangles around inside of bowl, making sure there are no spaces between triangles. Reserve any remaining cake triangles.

3. In heavy 1-quart saucepan over low heat, place chocolate pieces; stir occasionally until chocolate is melted; cool slightly.

4. In large bowl with mixer at medium speed, beat heavy or whipping cream, confectioners' sugar, and salt until the mixture stands in soft peaks. Fold in the toasted chopped almonds.

5. Spread two thirds whipped cream evenly to line the cake in bowl. Fold melted chocolate into remaining whipped-cream mixture; use to fill center of dessert. Top the dessert with the remaining cake triangles. Cover the dish with plastic wrap and leave in the refrigerator overnight.

6. To serve, remove top sheet of plastic wrap. Invert bowl onto chilled serving plate; remove and discard plastic wrap. With a sharp knife, carefully cut dessert into wedges.

Chocolate-Coffee Meringue Torte

TIME: start early in day—SERVINGS: 12

MERINGUE:

1 cup California walnuts, finely chopped

2 tablespoons cornstarch

1 cup sugar

5 egg whites, at room temperature

1/4 teaspoon cream of tartar

1/8 teaspoon salt

2 teaspoons vanilla extract

BUTTER CREAM:

1 1/2 cups butter or margarine

2 cups confectioners' sugar

5 egg yolks

2 squares unsweetened chocolate, melted and cooled

4 teaspoons instant espresso powder

1 tablespoon water

1. Prepare Meringue: In 10-inch skillet over medium heat, toast chopped walnuts until lightly browned, shaking skillet frequently. Remove skillet from heat. Reserve 1/2 cup nuts for decorating side of torte later. In small bowl, stir cornstarch, 1/4 cup sugar, and remaining nuts; set mixture aside.

2. Line two large cookie sheets with foil. Using 8-inch round plate as guide, outline two circles on foil on first cookie sheet and one circle on foil on second cookie sheet; set aside.

3. In large bowl with mixer at high speed, beat egg whites, cream of tartar, and salt until soft peaks form. Beating at high speed, gradually beat in remaining 3/4 cup sugar, 2 tablespoons at a time, beating well after each addition until sugar is completely dissolved. Add vanilla and continue beating until meringue stands in stiff, glossy peaks. With rubber spatula or wire whisk, gently fold nut mixture into meringue.

4. Preheat oven to 275° F. Spoon one third of meringue inside each tracing on cookie sheets. With metal spatula, evenly spread meringue within circles. Bake 1 hour or until meringues are golden. Cool meringues on cookie sheets 10 minutes. With metal spatula, carefully loosen and remove meringues to wire racks to cool completely.

5. Meanwhile, prepare Butter Cream: Cut butter into 1/4-inch-thick slices. In large bowl with mixer at high speed, beat butter or margarine and confectioners' sugar until smooth. Add egg yolks and continue beating until mixture is slightly thickened and creamy. Spoon half of butter cream into medium bowl; stir in melted chocolate until blended. In cup, dissolve instant espresso powder in water; stir into butter cream in large bowl.

6. To assemble torte: Place first meringue layer on flat cake plate; spread with half of coffee butter cream. Place second meringue layer on butter cream; spread with remaining coffee butter cream; top with remaining meringue layer. Spoon 3/4 cup chocolate butter cream into small decorating bag with small border or rosette tube; refrigerate. Spread remaining chocolate butter cream on side and top of torte. With hand, press reserved toasted nuts into butter cream on side of torte. Pipe chocolate butter cream in decorating bag to make a pretty design on top of torte. Refrigerate torte at least 4 hours.

Mixed-Nut Fruitcake

TIME: start early in day or up to 1 month ahead—YIELD: 1 fruitcake

2 6 1/2- to 8-ounce containers candied red cherries

1 12-ounce package pitted prunes

1 10-ounce container pitted dates

1 3 1/2- to 4-ounce container candied green cherries

1/2 cup cream sherry

2 12-ounce cans salted mixed nuts

1 6-ounce can pecans

1 1/2 cups all-purpose flour

1 cup sugar

1 teaspoon double-acting baking powder

6 eggs, slightly beaten

1. In very large bowl or 6-quart saucepot, combine first 5 ingredients; let stand 15 minutes or until almost all liquid is absorbed, stirring occasionally.

2. Meanwhile, line 10-inch tube pan with foil; press out wrinkles as much as possible so cake surface will come out smooth after baking.

3. Stir mixed nuts and pecans into fruit mixture in bowl. Remove 1 1/2 cups fruit mixture; set aside. Stir flour, sugar, and baking powder into fruit mixture in large bowl until well coated. Stir in eggs until well mixed.

4. Spoon batter into prepared pan, packing firmly to eliminate air pockets. Sprinkle reserved fruit mixture on top.

5. Cover pan loosely with foil. Bake in 300° F. oven 2 hours. Remove foil and bake 1/2 hour longer or until knife inserted into center of cake comes out clean.

6. Cool cake in pan on wire rack 30 minutes; remove from pan and carefully peel off foil. Cool cake completely on rack. Wrap fruitcake tightly with foil or plastic wrap. Refrigerate.

No-Bake Cheesecake

TIME: start early in day or day ahead—SERVINGS: 16

2 eggs, separated

1 cup milk

2 envelopes unflavored gelatin

1 cup sugar

¹/₄ teaspoon salt

1 teaspoon grated lemon peel

3 cups creamed cottage cheese

1 tablespoon lemon juice

1 teaspoon vanilla extract

1¹/₂ cups graham-cracker crumbs

¹/₃ cup melted butter or margarine

1 cup heavy or whipping cream

canned fruit, for garnish

1. In small bowl, beat egg yolks with milk until mixed; in 2-quart saucepan, stir gelatin with sugar and salt. Stir yolk mixture into gelatin mixture. Cook over medium heat, stirring, until mixture thickens and coats spoon. Remove from heat; add lemon peel; cool.

2. Into large bowl, press cottage cheese through sieve; add lemon juice and vanilla. Add gelatin mixture. Chill about 30 minutes, stirring, until mixture mounds when dropped from spoon.

3. Meanwhile, mix graham-cracker crumbs and melted butter or margarine; press half of crumb mixture on the bottom of 9-inch springform pan.

4. In small bowl with mixer at high speed, beat egg whites just until stiff peaks form; spoon onto gelatin mixture.

5. Beat cream until soft peaks form; spoon onto egg whites; fold egg whites and cream into gelatin mixture. Pour gelatin mixture into prepared springform pan.

6. Sprinkle top with remaining crumb mixture and refrigerate until firm.

7. To serve, remove side of pan and, with spatula, loosen cake from bottom. Slide onto plate. Garnish with fruit.

No-Bake Chocolate-Almond Cheesecake

TIME: start early in day or day ahead—SERVINGS: 16

CRUST:

1 cup crushed chocolate wafers (about 20 wafers)

4 tablespoons butter or margarine, softened

ALMOND-CHEESE LAYER:

1 envelope unflavored gelatin

¹/₂ cup water

1 cup heavy or whipping cream

¹/₂ cup confectioners' sugar

1 teaspoon almond extract

1 15- to 16-ounce container ricotta cheese (2 cups)

CHOCOLATE-CHEESE LAYER:

1 envelope unflavored gelatin

¹/₂ cup water

1 teaspoon instant coffee granules

4 squares semisweet chocolate

1 cup heavy or whipping cream

¹/₄ cup confectioners' sugar

1 15- to 16-ounce container ricotta cheese (2 cups)

¹/₂ cup sliced blanched almonds, for garnish

1. In 9″ by 3″ springform pan, with hand, mix chocolate wafers and butter or margarine; press onto bottom of pan; set aside.

2. Prepare Almond-Cheese Layer: In small saucepan, evenly sprinkle gelatin over water. Cook over medium heat until gelatin is completely dissolved, stirring frequently. Remove saucepan from heat; set aside.

3. In small bowl with mixer at medium speed, beat heavy or whipping cream, confectioners' sugar, and almond extract until stiff peaks form; set aside.

4. Into large bowl, press ricotta cheese through sieve; stir in gelatin mixture. With rubber spatula or wire whisk, fold in whipped-cream mixture. Spoon almond mixture evenly over crust in pan; set aside.

5. Prepare Chocolate-Cheese Layer: In same small saucepan, evenly sprinkle gelatin over water. Add instant coffee and chocolate; cook over low heat until gelatin is completely dissolved and chocolate is melted and blended, stirring frequently. Remove saucepan from heat; cool mixture slightly.

6. In small bowl with mixer at medium speed, beat heavy or whipping cream and confectioners' sugar until stiff peaks form.

7. Into large bowl, press ricotta cheese through sieve; stir in cooled chocolate mixture. With rubber spatula or wire whisk, fold in whipped-cream mixture. Spoon chocolate mixture evenly over almond layer in pan. Cover and refrigerate cheesecake 4 hours or overnight.

8. Meanwhile, in small skillet over medium heat, toast sliced almonds until lightly browned, shaking skillet frequently. Cool.

9. To serve, carefully remove side of pan from cheesecake; place cake on chilled plate. Garnish top of cheesecake with toasted almonds.

199

No-Bake Berry Cheesecake

TIME: *start early in day*—SERVINGS: 16

¹/₂ **10-ounce package shortbread cookies, finely crushed**

4 **tablespoons butter or margarine, softened**

1 **envelope unflavored gelatin**

water

2 **8-ounce packages cream cheese, softened**

¹/₂ **cup sugar**

2 **eggs, separated, at room temperature**

1¹/₂ **teaspoons lemon juice**

1 **teaspoon grated lemon peel**

¹/₂ **teaspoon vanilla extract**

2 **pints strawberries, hulled**

1 **pint blueberries**

1. In 10″ by 2″ springform pan, with hand, mix crushed cookies and butter or margarine; press onto bottom of pan; set aside.

2. In small bowl, mix gelatin with ¹/₄ cup cold water; let gelatin stand 5 minutes to soften. Add ³/₄ cup *very hot* tap water to mixture, and stir until gelatin is completely dissolved, about 3 minutes.

3. In large bowl with mixer at low speed, beat cream cheese, sugar, egg yolks, lemon juice, lemon peel, and vanilla until mixed; gradually beat in gelatin mixture. Increase speed to medium; beat until cheese mixture is very smooth, scraping bowl often with rubber spatula.

4. In small bowl with mixer at high speed, beat egg whites until stiff peaks form. With rubber spatula or wire whisk, fold egg whites into cheese mixture. Spoon mixture over crust in pan; cover pan with plastic wrap or foil, and refrigerate until firm, about 3 hours.

5. To serve, carefully remove side of pan from cheesecake. Arrange berries on cake.

Christmas-Wreath Cheesecake

TIME: *start early in day*—SERVINGS: 12

6 **tablespoons butter or margarine, softened**

all-purpose flour

sugar

3 **8-ounce packages cream cheese, softened**

3 **eggs**

¹/₄ **cup milk**

1 **tablespoon grated lemon peel**

¹/₄ **teaspoon salt**

Chocolate Leaves, for garnish (right)

other garnishes: 1 slice candied pineapple, about 6 dried apricot halves, 4 candied green cherries, and 12 cranberries

1. Preheat oven to 400° F. In small bowl with mixer at low speed, beat butter or margarine, ³/₄ cup flour, and 2 tablespoons sugar until well mixed. Press mixture onto bottom of 10″ by 2″ springform pan. Bake 10 minutes, or until crust is lightly browned. Cool on wire rack.

2. Turn oven control to 325° F. In large bowl with mixer at low speed, beat cream cheese just until smooth. Add eggs, milk, lemon peel, salt, ³/₄ cup sugar, and 2 tablespoons flour; beat 3 minutes longer, occasionally scraping bowl with rubber spatula.

3. Pour cream-cheese mixture into pan. Bake 45 minutes. Cool in pan on wire rack. Cover and refrigerate at least 4 hours or until well chilled.

4. Meanwhile, prepare Chocolate Leaves.

5. To serve, remove cake from pan. With small star-shaped canapé cutter, cut stars from candied pineapple and dried apricot halves; cut each candied green cherry in half. Arrange garnishes on cheesecake to resemble a wreath.

Chocolate Leaves: In double boiler over hot, *not boiling,* water (or in heavy 1-quart saucepan over low heat), heat *one-half 6-ounce package semisweet-chocolate pieces* (¹/₂ cup) and *2 teaspoons shortening* until chocolate is melted and smooth, about 5 minutes, stirring occasionally. With small metal spatula, spread a layer of chocolate mixture on underside of *10 medium lemon leaves.* (If other kinds of leaves are used, make sure that they are also nontoxic.) Place coated leaves, chocolate side up, on cookie sheet or plate; refrigerate at least 20 minutes or until chocolate is firm. Carefully peel off lemon leaves from chocolate. Refrigerate Chocolate Leaves until ready to use.

Raspberry Sauce

TIME: about 5 minutes—YIELD: about 1 cup

2 10-ounce packages quick-thaw frozen raspberries, thawed

1 tablespoon sugar

1 tablespoon cornstarch

1/2 teaspoon almond extract

In 2-quart saucepan, stir first 3 ingredients until blended. Over medium heat, cook mixture, stirring constantly, until sauce is thickened. Stir in almond extract. Serve over pound cake, ice cream, or peeled ripe or canned pears or peaches.

Chocolate Sauce

TIME: about 5 minutes—YIELD: about 2/3 cup

4 squares semisweet chocolate

1/4 cup corn syrup

In 1-quart saucepan over low heat, heat chocolate and corn syrup until chocolate is melted, stirring frequently. Serve over ice cream, dessert crepes, or baked bananas.

Orange-Fluff Sauce

TIME: about 3 hours or start early in day—YIELD: about 2 3/4 cups

1/2 cup sugar

1/2 cup frozen orange-juice concentrate, thawed

1/8 teaspoon salt

2 egg yolks

1 cup heavy or whipping cream, whipped

1. In 1-quart saucepan over low heat, cook sugar, undiluted juice concentrate, and salt, stirring constantly, until sugar dissolves; set aside.

2. In small bowl with mixer at high speed, beat egg yolks until light and fluffy; at medium speed, gradually beat in orange-juice mixture.

3. Return mixture to saucepan; over low heat, cook, stirring constantly, until the mixture is slightly thickened.

4. Cool, then fold in whipped cream. Refrigerate until well chilled. Serve over cut-up fruit, sliced pound cake.

Freezer Strawberry Topping

TIME: about 2 days or start up to 1 year ahead

YIELD: 6 8-ounce containers

1 quart fully ripened strawberries

4 cups sugar (about 1 3/4 pounds)

2 tablespoons orange juice

1 1 3/4-ounce package powdered fruit pectin

3/4 cup water

about 6 8-ounce freezer-safe containers

1. In large bowl with potato masher or slotted spoon, thoroughly crush berries, one layer at a time. Stir in sugar and orange juice until thoroughly mixed; let stand 10 minutes.

2. In 1-quart saucepan over medium heat, heat fruit pectin with water until boiling; boil 1 minute, stirring constantly. Stir pectin mixture into fruit; continue stirring 3 minutes to blend well (a few sugar crystals will remain).

3. Ladle mixture into containers to 1/2 inch from top; cover with lids. Let stand at room temperature for 24 hours or until set. Freeze to use within 1 year. For use within 3 weeks, store in refrigerator. Use to top angel cake or plain or toasted slices of pound cake; serve on rice pudding or ice cream; spoon over cheesecake; stir into plain yogurt.

Maple Whipped Cream

TIME: about 10 minutes—YIELD: about 2 1/4 cups

1 cup heavy or whipping cream

3 tablespoons maple syrup or maple-flavor syrup

1/2 teaspoon sugar

In small bowl with mixer at medium speed, beat all ingredients until stiff peaks form. Serve at once over ice-cream sundaes, gingerbread, or fresh berries.

Brandy-Custard Sauce

TIME: about 15 minutes—YIELD: about 2 cups

1 1/2 cups milk

1/4 cup sugar

1/8 teaspoon salt

3 egg yolks

2 tablespoons brandy or 1 teaspoon vanilla extract

In double boiler over hot, *not boiling,* water, or in heavy 2-quart saucepan with wire whisk, mix milk, sugar, salt, and egg yolks. Over medium-low heat, cook, stirring constantly, until mixture is slightly thickened and coats back of spoon. Remove saucepan from heat; stir in brandy or vanilla. Serve over warm apple pie, mincemeat pie, or rice pudding.

Molasses Ovals

TIME: about 3 hours or start up to 2 weeks ahead

YIELD: about 3 dozen cookies

2 1/2 cups all-purpose flour

1/2 cup sugar

1/2 cup shortening

1/2 cup molasses

1/4 cup water

1 1/2 teaspoons ground ginger

1 1/2 teaspoons ground cinnamon

1 teaspoon double-acting baking powder

3/4 teaspoon ground cloves

1/2 teaspoon baking soda

1/2 teaspoon salt

1 egg

1. Into large bowl, measure all ingredients. With mixer at low speed, beat ingredients until well blended, occasionally scraping bowl with rubber spatula. (Dough will be very sticky.) Cover bowl with plastic wrap; refrigerate 1 to 2 hours, until easy to handle.

2. Preheat oven to 350° F. With hands, roll 1 tablespoonful dough into 2 1/2-inch long oval; place on cookie sheet. Repeat with remaining dough, placing cookies 1 inch apart. Bake 10 minutes or until lightly browned. Remove cookies to wire racks to cool. Store cookies in tightly covered container to use up within 2 weeks.

Checkered Shortbread Cookies

TIME: about 3 1/2 hours or start up to 1 week ahead

YIELD: about 3 1/2 dozen cookies

3 cups all-purpose flour

1 1/4 cups butter or margarine, softened

1 cup confectioners' sugar

1 teaspoon vanilla extract

1/4 teaspoon salt

1/4 cup cocoa

1 egg white, slightly beaten

1. Into large bowl, measure first 5 ingredients. With hand, knead ingredients until well blended. Set aside half of dough. Knead cocoa into dough remaining in bowl.

2. Divide chocolate dough into five equal pieces. With hands, roll each piece into a 12-inch-long rope. Divide vanilla dough into five equal pieces; roll four of the pieces into 12-inch-long ropes. Reserve remaining piece of vanilla dough.

3. Brush all ropes with some egg white. On work surface, arrange three ropes side by side, starting with chocolate, and alternating colors; top with three more ropes of alternating colors, starting with vanilla; then top with remaining three ropes, starting with chocolate. Press ropes together gently to form one large roll.

4. On lightly floured surface with lightly floured rolling pin, roll out remaining vanilla dough into a 12″ by 7″ rectangle; press dough around roll, brushing roll with egg white. Cover and refrigerate about 2 hours, until firm enough to slice. (Dough can be refrigerated up to 1 week before baking.)

5. To bake, preheat oven to 375° F. Slice roll crosswise into 1/4-inch-thick slices. Place slices, 1 inch apart, on large cookie sheets. Bake 10 minutes or until lightly browned. With pancake turner, remove cookies to wire racks to cool. Store cookies in tightly covered container to use up within 1 week.

Peanut-Butter Kisses

TIME: about 2¹/₂ hours or start up to 2 weeks ahead

YIELD: about 4 dozen cookies

2¹/₂ **cups all-purpose flour**

1 **cup creamy peanut butter**

³/₄ **cup butter or margarine, softened**

¹/₂ **cup packed dark-brown sugar**

¹/₂ **teaspoon double-acting baking powder**

¹/₄ **teaspoon salt**

2 **eggs**

about 48 milk-chocolate kiss-type candies

1. Into large bowl, measure all ingredients except milk-chocolate kiss-type candies. With mixer at low speed, beat ingredients until well blended, occasionally scraping bowl with rubber spatula. Shape dough into a ball; wrap with plastic wrap. Refrigerate dough 1 hour or until easy to handle.

2. Preheat oven to 375° F. Shape dough into 1-inch balls. Place balls, 2 inches apart, on ungreased cookie sheets. With floured four-tined fork, press top of dough to make cross design.

3. Bake cookies 15 minutes or until cookies are golden; quickly press a milk-chocolate candy into center of each cookie. With pancake turner, carefully remove cookies to wire racks to cool. Store in tightly covered container to use up within 2 weeks.

All-Oatmeal Crunchies

TIME: about 2 hours or start up to 2 weeks ahead

YIELD: about 3 dozen cookies

³/₄ **cup butter or margarine, softened**

³/₄ **cup packed light-brown sugar**

1 **tablespoon grated lemon peel**

1 **teaspoon double-acting baking powder**

¹/₈ **teaspoon salt**

1 **egg**

3¹/₄ **cups quick-cooking oats, uncooked**

¹/₃ **cup blanched whole almonds, finely ground**

2 **egg yolks, slightly beaten**

1. Into large bowl, measure first 6 ingredients. With mixer at medium speed, beat ingredients until light and fluffy, occasionally scraping bowl with rubber spatula. With spoon, stir in oats and almonds; with hand, knead until mixture holds together.

2. Preheat oven to 350° F. Grease large cookie sheet. Between two sheets of waxed paper, roll half of dough ¹/₄ inch thick. With 2¹/₂-inch round cookie cutter, cut dough into as many cookies as possible.

3. Place cookies, 1 inch apart, on cookie sheet. Brush each cookie with some beaten egg yolk. Bake 12 minutes or until golden. With pancake turner, remove cookies to wire racks to cool. Repeat with remaining dough and reroll trimmings. Store cookies in tightly covered container to use up within 2 weeks.

Spice Cookies

TIME: start day ahead or up to 1 week ahead

YIELD: about 9 dozen cookies

sugar

3²/₃ **cups all-purpose flour**

1 **cup butter or margarine, softened**

2 **eggs**

1 **tablespoon milk**

1¹/₂ **teaspoons baking soda**

1¹/₂ **teaspoons ground cinnamon**

¹/₂ **teaspoon ground nutmeg**

¹/₄ **teaspoon ground cloves**

1 **cup dried currants**

1. Into large bowl, measure 1¹/₂ cups sugar and remaining ingredients except currants. With mixer at medium speed, beat ingredients until well mixed, occasionally scraping bowl with rubber spatula. Stir in currants. Cover; refrigerate overnight.

2. Preheat oven to 375° F. On lightly floured board, with floured rolling pin, roll dough as thin as possible; lightly sprinkle with sugar.

3. With pastry wheel or knife, cut dough into diamonds 2 inches in length. Place on ungreased cookie sheets.

4. Bake 8 minutes or until very lightly browned.

5. With pancake turner, remove cookies to wire racks and allow to cool completely. Store in tightly covered container to use up with 1 week.

Peanut-Butter Jumbles

TIME: about 1¹/₂ hours or start up to 2 weeks ahead

YIELD: about 4 dozen cookies

1 12-ounce package peanut-butter-
flavored chips (2 cups)

1 cup all-purpose flour

¹/₂ cup sugar

¹/₂ cup butter or margarine, softened

¹/₂ teaspoon salt

¹/₂ teaspoon baking soda

¹/₂ teaspoon ground cinnamon

¹/₂ teaspoon ground nutmeg

1 egg

¹/₂ cup California walnuts, finely chopped

1. Reserve 1 cup peanut-butter-flavored chips. In heavy small saucepan over low heat, melt remaining chips, stirring occasionally. Remove saucepan from heat.

2. Into large bowl, measure flour, sugar, butter or margarine, salt, baking soda, cinnamon, nutmeg, and egg. With mixer at low speed, beat ingredients until well blended. Gradually beat in melted chips. With spoon, stir in reserved chips and half of walnuts.

3. Preheat oven to 350° F. Drop dough by rounded teaspoonfuls 2 inches apart on ungreased cookie sheets. With fingers, flatten mounds slightly; sprinkle with some walnuts. Bake 12 minutes or until lightly browned. With pancake turner, remove cookies to wire rack to cool. Store in tightly covered container to use up within 2 weeks.

Jumbo Gingersnaps

TIME: about 1¹/₂ hours or start up to 1 month ahead—YIELD: 10 cookies

sugar

2¹/₄ cups all-purpose flour

³/₄ cup salad oil

¹/₄ cup dark molasses

¹/₄ cup maple syrup or maple-flavor syrup

2 teaspoons baking soda

1 teaspoon ground ginger

¹/₂ teaspoon ground cinnamon

¹/₂ teaspoon ground cardamom

¹/₄ teaspoon salt

1 egg

1. Into large bowl, measure ¹/₂ cup sugar and remaining ingredients. With mixer at low speed, beat ingredients until well blended, occasionally scraping bowl with rubber spatula.

2. Preheat oven to 350° F. Place 2 tablespoons sugar on waxed paper. Shape ¹/₄ cup dough into a ball; roll in sugar to coat evenly. Repeat with remaining dough to make 10 balls in all. Place balls, 3 inches apart, on ungreased cookie sheets. (Dough is very soft, and balls will flatten slightly.) Bake cookies 15 minutes. With pancake turner, remove cookies to wire racks to cool. Store cookies in tightly covered container to use up within 1 month.

Oatmeal Thins

TIME: about 1¹/₂ hours or start up to 3 weeks ahead

YIELD: about 4 dozen cookies

¹/₂ cup butter or margarine

1¹/₄ cups quick-cooking oats, uncooked

1 cup packed light-brown sugar

1¹/₂ teaspoons grated orange peel

¹/₈ teaspoon salt

1 egg

1. In 2-quart saucepan over low heat, melt butter or margarine. Stir in oats and remaining ingredients until blended. Remove saucepan from heat.

2. Preheat oven to 350° F. Grease and flour large cookie sheet. Drop mixture by rounded teaspoonfuls, 3 inches apart, on cookie sheet. Bake 8 minutes or until well browned around edges (centers will be lighter). Cool cookies slightly on cookie sheet, then with pancake turner, carefully loosen cookies and remove to wire rack to cool. Store in tightly covered container to use up within 3 weeks.

Sesame-Seed Pillows

TIME: about 2 hours or start up to 3 weeks ahead
YIELD: about 5$^{1}/_2$ dozen cookies

3 cups all-purpose flour

1 cup sugar

1 cup shortening

4 teaspoons vanilla extract

1 tablespoon double-acting baking powder

3 eggs

1 2$^{1}/_8$-ounce jar sesame seeds (about $^{1}/_2$ cup)

1. Into large bowl, measure all ingredients except sesame seeds. With mixer at low speed, beat ingredients until well blended, occasionally scraping bowl with rubber spatula.

2. Preheat oven to 350° F. Place sesame seeds on waxed paper. With hands, shape 2 teaspoons dough at a time into 2-inch-long ovals; roll ovals in sesame seeds. Place cookies 1 inch apart on ungreased cookie sheets. Bake 15 minutes or until cookies are very lightly browned. Remove cookies to wire racks to cool. Store cookies in tightly covered container to use up within 3 weeks.

Peanut-Butter "Ravioli" Cookies

TIME: about 4 hours or start up to 2 weeks ahead—YIELD: 50 cookies

3 cups all-purpose flour

1 cup sugar

$^{2}/_3$ cup shortening

2 teaspoons double-acting baking powder

1$^{1}/_2$ teaspoons vanilla extract

$^{1}/_4$ teaspoon salt

2 eggs

water

$^{3}/_4$ cup creamy or chunky peanut butter

$^{1}/_3$ cup confectioners' sugar

$^{1}/_4$ teaspoon ground cinnamon

2 egg yolks

$^{1}/_4$ cup peanuts, for garnish

1. Into large bowl, measure first 7 ingredients and 2 tablespoons water. With mixer at low speed, beat ingredients until well mixed, occasionally scraping bowl with rubber spatula. Shape dough into a ball; wrap with plastic wrap. Refrigerate dough 2 hours or until easy to handle.

2. Prepare filling: In small bowl with spoon, mix peanut butter, confectioners' sugar, and cinnamon; set aside.

3. Preheat oven to 350° F. Grease large cookie sheet. Cut cookie dough into four pieces. On lightly floured surface with lightly floured rolling pin, roll one piece of dough into 10″ by 10″ square, keeping remaining dough refrigerated. With dull edge of knife, lightly mark dough to indicate twenty-five 2″ by 2″ squares. Place a scant teaspoonful of peanut-butter filling in center of each square. On sheet of waxed paper, roll second dough piece into 11″ by 11″ square; invert dough over filling, and peel off waxed paper. With fingers, press around filling and along edges. With pastry wheel or knife, cut through dough around filling to make twenty-five 2″ by 2″ cookies; place on cookie sheet.

4. In cup with fork, beat egg yolks with 1 tablespoon water. Brush each cookie with some beaten egg-yolk mixture; top with a peanut. Bake 10 to 12 minutes, until golden. With pancake turner, remove cookies to wire racks to cool. Repeat with remaining dough, filling, and egg-yolk mixture. Store cookies in tightly covered container to use up within 2 weeks.

Old-fashioned Oatmeal Cookies

TIME: about 2 hours or start up to 2 weeks ahead
YIELD: about 3 dozen cookies

1 cup all-purpose flour

1 cup shortening

$^{3}/_4$ cup packed light-brown sugar

$^{1}/_2$ cup sugar

3 tablespoons water

1 teaspoon ground allspice

$^{3}/_4$ teaspoon vanilla extract

$^{1}/_2$ teaspoon salt

1 egg

3 cups quick-cooking oats, uncooked

$^{3}/_4$ cup California walnuts, chopped

$^{1}/_2$ cup dark seedless raisins

1. Grease large cookie sheet. In large bowl, measure first 9 ingredients. With mixer at low speed, beat ingredients until well blended, occasionally scraping bowl with rubber spatula. With spoon, stir in quick-cooking oats, walnuts, and raisins.

2. Preheat oven to 375° F. Drop dough by heaping tablespoonfuls, about 2 inches apart, onto cookie sheet. Bake 12 minutes or until golden. With metal spatula, carefully remove cookies to wire racks to cool. Repeat until all dough is used, greasing cookie sheet each time. Store in tightly covered containers to use within 2 weeks.

Coconut Rounds

TIME: about 1¼ hours or start up to 1 week ahead

YIELD: about 2 dozen cookies

1 cup all-purpose flour

¹/₂ cup butter or margarine, softened

¹/₄ cup sugar

1 teaspoon vanilla extract

¹/₄ teaspoon salt

water

1 egg white

¹/₂ cup flaked coconut

1. Into large bowl, measure first 5 ingredients and 1 tablespoon water. With mixer at low speed, beat ingredients until well blended, occasionally scraping bowl with rubber spatula. Shape mixture into ³/₄-inch balls.

2. Preheat oven to 350° F. In pie plate with fork, beat egg white and 1 tablespoon water. Place coconut on waxed paper. Dip balls in egg-white mixture, then roll in coconut to coat evenly. Place balls about 2 inches apart on large ungreased cookie sheet. Bake 15 minutes, until golden. With metal spatula, carefully remove cookies to wire racks to cool. Store in tightly covered container to use up within 1 week.

Filbert Cookie Rafts

TIME: about 1¹/₂ hours or up to 2 weeks ahead—YIELD: 32 cookies

¹/₂ cup filberts

sugar

1¹/₄ cups all-purpose flour

¹/₂ cup butter or margarine, softened

¹/₂ teaspoon vanilla extract

¹/₈ teaspoon salt

1. In blender at medium speed or in food processor with knife blade attached, blend filberts and 2 tablespoons sugar until nuts are very finely ground.

2. Into medium bowl, measure flour, butter or margarine, vanilla, salt, 2 tablespoons sugar, and ground filberts. With hands, knead ingredients until well blended and mixture holds together.

3. Preheat oven to 325° F. On sheet of waxed paper with floured rolling pin, roll out half of dough into a 6″ by 6″ square. Cut dough into sixteen 1¹/₂″ by 1¹/₂″ squares. With pancake turner, place cookies on ungreased cookie sheet. With dull edge of knife, mark each cookie with two or three parallel lines. (Be careful not to cut dough all the way through.)

4. Bake cookies 12 to 15 minutes, until lightly browned. With pancake turner, remove cookies to wire racks to cool. Repeat with remaining dough. Store in tightly covered container to use up within 2 weeks.

Fried Sesame Bows

TIME: about 1¹/₂ hours or start up to 1 month ahead

YIELD: about 9 dozen cookies

¹/₂ cup very hot tap water

1 package active dry yeast

2 cups all-purpose flour

3 tablespoons black or plain sesame seeds

3 tablespoons sugar

¹/₂ teaspoon salt

salad oil

1. In cup with spoon, stir water and yeast until yeast is dissolved. In medium bowl, measure flour, sesame seeds, sugar, salt, and 2 teaspoons salad oil. With hand, gradually knead in yeast mixture to make a soft dough, adding more cold water when kneading (about ¹/₄ cup).

2. Turn dough onto floured surface and knead until smooth and elastic, about 5 minutes.

3. On lightly floured surface, with lightly floured rolling pin, roll dough, one third at a time, until paper-thin. With knife, cut dough into 3″ by 1″ rectangles. Cut ³/₄-inch-long lengthwise slit in center of each rectangle; thread one end of rectangle through slit in center, and pull gently to make a bow tie.

4. In 4-quart saucepan or Dutch oven over medium heat, heat about ¹/₂ inch salad oil to 325° F. on deep-fat thermometer (or, heat oil in electric skillet set at 325° F.). Gently drop several dough pieces at a time into hot oil, and fry about 2 minutes or until golden. Drain cookies on paper towels; cool. Store cookies in tightly covered container to use up within 1 month.

Orange-Nut Pinwheels

TIME: about 3¹/₂ hours or start up to 2 weeks ahead

YIELD: about 4 dozen cookies

1 cup California walnuts, ground

¹/₂ cup orange marmalade

¹/₃ cup dark seedless raisins, finely chopped

¹/₂ teaspoon ground allspice

light-brown sugar

1³/₄ cups all-purpose flour

¹/₂ cup shortening

1 egg

1. In medium bowl, combine first 4 ingredients and 3 tablespoons light-brown sugar; set aside.

2. Into large bowl, measure flour, shortening, egg, and 1 cup packed light-brown sugar. With hands, knead ingredients until dough holds together.

3. On sheet of waxed paper, roll out half of dough into a 14″ by 6″ rectangle; spread with half of nut mixture. Starting with a 6-inch side, roll dough jelly-roll fashion. Wrap in waxed paper. Repeat with remaining dough and nut mixture. Refrigerate rolls 2 hours or until firm enough to slice. (Dough can be refrigerated up to 1 week before baking.)

4. To bake, preheat oven to 350° F. Grease large cookie sheets. With serrated knife, slice one roll of dough crosswise into ¹/₄-inch-thick slices. Place slices, 1 inch apart, on cookie sheet. Bake 10 minutes or until lightly browned. With pancake turner, remove cookies to wire racks to cool. Repeat with remaining roll. Store cookies in tightly covered container to use up within 2 weeks.

Almond-Ginger Crisps

TIME: about 1¹/₂ hours or start up to 1 month ahead

YIELD: about 5 dozen cookies

1 3¹/₂-ounce can sliced blanched almonds

1¹/₄ cups all-purpose flour

¹/₂ cup sugar

¹/₂ cup butter or margarine, softened

¹/₃ cup dark corn syrup

1 teaspoon ground ginger

1 teaspoon ground cinnamon

³/₄ teaspoon ground cloves

¹/₂ teaspoon salt

1. Reserve about 60 sliced almonds for garnish; finely chop remaining almonds.

2. Into large bowl, measure flour and remaining ingredients. With mixer at low speed, beat ingredients until well blended, occasionally scraping bowl with rubber spatula. With spoon, stir in chopped almonds.

3. Preheat oven to 350° F. Grease large cookie sheets. On lightly floured surface with lightly floured rolling pin, roll one third of dough ¹/₄ inch thick. With floured 2-inch flower-shaped cookie cutter, cut dough into as many cookies as possible.

4. Place cookies, 1 inch apart, on cookie sheet. Gently press a reserved almond into top of each cookie. Bake 10 minutes or until lightly browned. With pancake turner, remove cookies to wire racks to cool. Repeat with remaining dough and reroll trimmings. Store cookies in tightly covered container to use up within 1 month.

Walnut Refrigerator Cookies

TIME: about 3$1/2$ hours or start up to 2 weeks ahead

YIELD: about 6 dozen cookies

1$3/4$ cups California walnuts

2 cups all-purpose flour

1 cup butter or margarine, softened

$1/2$ cup sugar

$1/2$ cup packed light-brown sugar

1 teaspoon vanilla extract

$1/4$ teaspoon salt

$1/4$ teaspoon baking soda

1 egg

1. Finely chop 1 cup walnuts; reserve remaining walnuts for garnish later.

2. Into large bowl, measure flour and remaining ingredients except walnuts. With mixer at low speed, beat ingredients until well blended, occasionally scraping bowl with rubber spatula. With spoon, stir in chopped walnuts. With hands, on waxed paper, roll dough into three 5-inch-long rolls; wrap each in waxed paper. Refrigerate dough about 2 hours, until firm enough to slice. (Dough can be refrigerated up to 1 week before baking.)

3. To bake, preheat oven to 350° F. Grease large cookie sheet. Slice one roll of dough crosswise into $1/4$-inch-thick slices. Place slices, 1 inch apart, on cookie sheet. Press a reserved walnut into top of each cookie. Bake 8 to 10 minutes, until lightly browned. With pancake turner, remove cookies to wire racks to cool. Repeat with remaining dough and walnuts. Store cookies in tightly covered container to use up within 2 weeks.

Gumdrop Cookies

TIME: about 5 hours or start up to 2 weeks ahead

YIELD: about 3$1/2$ dozen cookies

2$1/2$ cups all-purpose flour

$3/4$ cup butter or margarine, softened

$2/3$ cup sugar

2 tablespoons milk

1 teaspoon double-acting baking powder

1 teaspoon almond extract

$1/2$ teaspoon salt

2 eggs

1 cup small gumdrops, thinly sliced

1. Into large bowl, measure all ingredients except gumdrops. With mixer at low speed, beat ingredients until well blended, occasionally scraping bowl with rubber spatula. Shape dough into a ball; wrap with plastic wrap and refrigerate 2 to 3 hours, until easy to handle.

2. Preheat oven to 350° F. Grease large cookie sheet. On lightly floured surface, with lightly floured rolling pin, roll one third of dough $1/4$ inch thick, keeping remaining dough refrigerated. With floured 3$1/2$-inch round fluted cookie cutter, cut dough into rounds. With pancake turner, place rounds on cookie sheet 1 inch apart. Decorate each cookie as desired with some gumdrops.

3. Bake 12 minutes or until lightly browned. With pancake turner, immediately remove cookies to wire racks to cool completely. Repeat with remaining dough and reroll trimmings. Store cookies in tightly covered container to use up within 2 weeks.

Meringue Drops

TIME: about 2 hours or start up to 1 week ahead

YIELD: about 2 dozen cookies

3 egg whites, at room temperature

$1/4$ teaspoon cream of tartar

$1/8$ teaspoon salt

$1/2$ cup sugar

1 teaspoon vanilla extract

1. Preheat oven to 200° F. Line two large cookie sheets with foil. In small bowl with mixer at high speed, beat egg whites, cream of tartar, and salt until soft peaks form. Beating at high speed, greadually beat in sugar, 2 tablespoons at a time, beating well after each addition until sugar is completely dissolved. Add vanilla extract and continue beating at high speed until meringue stands in stiff, glossy peaks.

2. Spoon meringue into decorating bag with medium writing tube. For each cookie, pipe some meringue onto foil in a continuous upward spiral, about 1 inch high, starting with a 1$3/4$-inch circle for base of cookie and narrowing meringue spiral to a point at the top. Space meringue cookies 1 inch apart on foil.

3. Bake 1 hour and 15 minutes or until set. Cool on cookie sheets on wire racks 10 minutes. With small spatula, carefully loosen and remove cookies from foil; cool completely on wire racks. Store in tightly covered container to use up within 1 week.

Parisian Hearts

TIME: about 3¹/₂ hours or start up to 2 days ahead

YIELD: about 14 cookies

1¹/₂ cups all-purpose flour

1 4¹/₂-ounce can blanched whole almonds, very finely ground

³/₄ cup butter or margarine, softened

¹/₂ teaspoon almond extract

¹/₈ teaspoon salt

1 egg

confectioners' sugar

4 teaspoons lemon juice

about 3 tablespoons raspberry preserves

1. Into large bowl, measure flour, ground almonds, butter or margarine, almond extract, salt, egg, and ¹/₂ cup confectioners' sugar. With mixer at low speed, beat ingredients until well blended, occasionally scraping bowl with rubber spatula. Shape dough into a ball; wrap with plastic wrap. Refrigerate dough 2 hours or until easy to handle.

2. Preheat oven to 375° F. Grease two large cookie sheets. On lightly floured surface with lightly floured rolling pin, roll half of dough ¹/₈ inch thick, keeping remaining dough refrigerated. With floured 3¹/₂-inch heart-shaped cookie cutter, cut dough into hearts. (Or, cut 3¹/₂-inch heart-shaped pattern from cardboard; use cardboard pattern and knife to cut out cookies.) With floured 1-inch round cookie cutter, cut out centers from half of hearts.

3. With pancake turner, place hearts ¹/₂ inch apart on cookie sheets. Bake 10 minutes or until golden. With pancake turner, immediately remove cookies to wire racks to cool. Repeat with remaining dough and trimmings.

4. To assemble cookies: In small bowl, stir lemon juice with ¹/₂ cup confectioners' sugar until smooth. Spread a thin layer of lemon icing on hearts without cut-out centers; top each with a heart with cut-out center, gently pressing hearts together. Fill cut-out centers with a heaping ¹/₄ teaspoonful of raspberry preserves. Sprinkle cookies lightly with confectioners' sugar. Store cookies in tightly covered container to use up within 2 days.

Pizzelles

TIME: about 1¹/₂ hours or start up to 3 weeks ahead

YIELD: about 8 dozen cookies

3¹/₂ cups all-purpose flour

1¹/₂ cups sugar

1 cup butter or margarine, melted

2 tablespoons vanilla or anise extract

4 teaspoons double-acting baking powder

6 eggs

1. Preheat 7-inch electric Pizzelle iron as manufacturer directs. Into large bowl, measure all ingredients. With mixer at low speed, beat ingredients until well blended, occasionally scraping bowl with rubber spatula.

2. Pour 2 tablespoonfuls batter at a time onto center of Pizzelle iron. Cover and bake as manufacturer directs (do not lift cover during baking). When done, lift cover and loosen Pizzelle with fork. Remove to wire rack to cool. (The 7-inch iron makes round cookies, each with four sections. When cookies are cool, break each into four pieces to serve.) Store cookies in tightly covered container to use up within 3 weeks. Makes about 2 dozen 7-inch Pizzelles.

NOTE: A Pizzelle iron is a special type of waffle iron that is available in electric and nonelectric models in various sizes. Be sure to follow the manufacturer's directions for the correct amount of batter for your iron. Pizzelle irons may be purchased in housewares departments of department stores, or write for catalogue to Kitchen Glamor, 26670 Grand River, Detroit, Michigan 48240.

Espresso Macaroons

TIME: about 1¹/₂ hours or start up to 2 days ahead

YIELD: about 3 dozen cookies

2 squares unsweetened chocolate

1 14-ounce can sweetened condensed milk

1 3¹/₂-ounce can flaked coconut

³/₄ cup California walnuts, coarsely chopped

2 teaspoons instant espresso-coffee powder

³/₄ teaspoon almond extract

¹/₄ teaspoon salt

1. In heavy 2-quart saucepan over low heat, heat chocolate until melted, stirring frequently. Remove saucepan from heat; stir in sweetened condensed milk and remaining ingredients until well mixed.

2. Preheat oven to 350° F. Grease two large cookie sheets. Drop mixture by tablespoonfuls, about 1 inch apart, onto cookie sheets. Bake 12 minutes. With pancake turner, remove cookies to wire racks to cool. Store cookies in tightly covered container to use up within 2 days.

Dutch Butter Cookies

TIME: about 3¹/₂ hours or start up to two weeks ahead

YIELD: about 6 dozen cookies

2¹/₂ cups all-purpose flour

1 cup sugar

1 cup butter, softened

1¹/₂ teaspoons double-acting baking powder

1 teaspoon vanilla extract

¹/₂ teaspoon salt

1 egg

1 egg yolk

2 tablespoons water

¹/₄ cup chopped candied ginger

1. Into large bowl, measure first 7 ingredients. With mixer at low speed, beat ingredients until well blended, occasionally scraping bowl with rubber spatula. With hands, on waxed paper, roll dough into three 6-inch-long rolls. Flatten each roll slightly to shape into a rectangular bar. Wrap each roll in waxed paper. Refrigerate dough 2 hours or until firm enough to slice. (Dough can be refrigerated up to 1 week before slicing.)

2. To bake, preheat oven to 350° F. Grease large cookie sheet. In cup with fork, beat egg yolk with water. Slice one roll of dough at a time crosswise into ¹/₄-inch-thick slices. Place slices, 1 inch apart, on cookie sheet. Brush each cookie with some egg-yolk mixture and press some candied ginger into top of each cookie. Bake 10 minutes or until lightly browned. With pancake turner, remove cookies to wire racks to cool. Store in tightly covered container to use up within 2 weeks.

Finnish Almond Cookies

TIME: about 1¹/₂ hours or start up to 2 weeks ahead

YIELD: 2¹/₂ dozen cookies

2 cups all-purpose flour

³/₄ cup butter or margarine, softened

1 teaspoon almond extract

sugar

1 egg, separated

²/₃ cup sliced blanched almonds

1. Into large bowl, measure flour, butter or margarine, almond extract, ¹/₄ cup sugar, and egg yolk. With hands, knead ingredients until well blended and mixture holds together. (Mixture will appear dry at first—if too dry, add about 1 tablespoon water while kneading.)

2. Preheat oven to 375° F. On lightly floured surface with lightly floured rolling pin, roll half of dough into a 10″ by 9″ rectangle. With pastry brush, brush dough with half of egg white; sprinkle with half of almonds and 1 tablespoon sugar.

3. Cut dough into fifteen 3″ by 2″ rectangles. With pancake turner, place cookies on ungreased cookie sheet. Bake 10 to 12 minutes, until lightly browned. With pancake turner, remove cookies to wire rack to cool. Repeat with remaining dough. Store cookies in tightly covered container to use up within 2 weeks.

Hungarian Filled Cookies

TIME: about 2¹/₂ hours or start up to 3 days ahead—YIELD: 3 dozen cookies

1¹/₃ cups all-purpose flour

²/₃ cup butter or margarine

²/₃ cup creamed cottage cheese

¹/₄ cup confectioners' sugar

³/₄ teaspoon vanilla extract

¹/₈ teaspoon salt

¹/₃ cup apricot preserves

¹/₃ cup California walnuts, finely chopped

¹/₃ cup light corn syrup

1. Into medium bowl, measure first 6 ingredients. With hand, knead ingredients until well blended. Shape dough into a ball; wrap with plastic wrap. Refrigerate dough 1 hour or until easy to handle.

2. Preheat oven to 375° F. Grease two large cookie sheets. On lightly floured surface with lightly floured rolling pin, roll one third of dough ¹/₈ inch thick, keeping remaining dough refrigerated. Using 10-inch plate as guide, with knife, cut dough into 10-inch round. Evenly spread dough round with one third of apricot preserves; sprinkle with one third of chopped walnuts.

3. Cut dough round into 12 wedges. Starting at curved edge, roll up each wedge jelly-roll fashion. Place cookies, point side down, 1¹/₂ inches apart on cookie sheet. Repeat with remaining dough, preserves, and walnuts. Bake 25 minutes or until golden. With pancake turner, remove cookies to wire racks to cool.

4. To glaze cookies: In small saucepan over medium heat, heat corn syrup to boiling; cook 2 minutes. Brush cooled cookies with some corn syrup; let stand 30 minutes to dry. Store in tightly covered container to use up within 3 days.

Confetti Christmas Trees

TIME: start early in day or up to 2 weeks ahead
YIELD: about 3 dozen cookies

1 small lemon

3 cups all-purpose flour

1 cup butter or margarine, softened

³/₄ cup sugar

1¹/₂ teaspoons vanilla extract

¹/₂ teaspoon double-acting baking powder

¹/₄ teaspoon salt

1 egg

1 1.5-ounce container confetti décors

1. From lemon, grate 1 teaspoon peel and squeeze 1 teaspoon juice. Place lemon peel and lemon juice in large bowl; add flour and remaining ingredients except décors. With mixer at low speed, beat ingredients until well blended, occasionally scraping bowl with rubber spatula. Shape dough into ball; wrap with plastic wrap. Refrigerate dough 2 to 3 hours, until easy to handle.

2. Preheat oven to 350° F. Grease large cookie sheet. On lightly floured surface with floured rolling pin, roll half of dough ¹/₄ inch thick, keeping remaining dough refrigerated. With floured 4¹/₂″ by 2¹/₄″ Christmas-tree cookie cutter, cut trees. With pancake turner, place trees on cookie sheet, 1 inch apart. Sprinkle each cookie lightly with confetti décors.

3. Bake cookies 8 to 10 minutes, until very lightly browned. With pancake turner, immediately remove cookies to wire racks to cool completely. Repeat with remaining dough and trimmings. Store cookies in tightly covered container to use up within 2 weeks.

Sugar Batons

TIME: about 1¹/₄ hours or start up to 1 week ahead
YIELD: about 5 dozen cookies

2¹/₂ cups all-purpose flour

1 cup butter or margarine, softened

1¹/₄ teaspoons vanilla extract

1 egg

sugar

1. Into large bowl, measure flour, butter or margarine, vanilla, egg, and ¹/₂ cup sugar. With mixer at low speed, beat ingredients until well blended, occasionally scraping bowl with rubber spatula.

2. Preheat oven to 400° F. Spoon half of dough into decorating bag with medium rosette tube. Pipe dough in 3-inch lengths about 1 inch apart onto ungreased cookie sheet. Sprinkle each cookie lightly with some sugar. Bake 6 to 8 minutes, until golden. With metal spatula, carefully remove cookies to wire racks to cool. Repeat until all dough is used. Store in tightly covered container to use up within 1 week.

Christmas Cards

TIME: about 5 hours or start up to 1 week ahead

YIELD: about 1 dozen cookies

3 cups all-purpose flour

1 cup butter or margarine, softened

³/₄ cup sugar

1 tablespoon grated orange peel

1 teaspoon orange extract

¹/₂ teaspoon double-acting baking powder

¹/₂ teaspoon salt

1 egg

1 egg yolk

1. Into large bowl, measure all ingredients, except egg yolk. With mixer at low speed, beat ingredients until well blended, occasionally scraping bowl with rubber spatula. Shape dough into a ball; wrap with plastic wrap. Refrigerate dough 2 to 3 hours, until easy to handle.

2. Preheat oven to 350° F. Grease large cookie sheet. On lightly floured surface with lightly floured rolling pin, roll half of dough ¹/₄ inch thick, keeping remaining dough refrigerated. Cut dough into 5″ by 3″ rectangles. With pancake turner, place rectangles on cookie sheet, 1 inch apart.

3. From remaining rolled-out dough, using 1¹/₄-inch star-shaped canapé cutter, cut out a star for each rectangle. Place star in upper left-hand corner of each rectangle. (Star will represent top of each card.) With floured hands, roll trimmings into ¹/₁₆-inch-thick ropes. Cut ropes into strips to form the word "NOEL" on each rectangle. Using skewer, mark holes around outer edge of each rectangle to form an attractive border.

4. In cup, beat egg yolk. Brush top of stars and letters with egg yolk. Bake cookies 10 to 12 minutes, until lightly browned. With pancake turner, remove cookies to wire racks to cool. Repeat with remaining dough and trimmings. Store in tightly covered container to use up within 1 week.

Frosted Snowmen

TIME: about 2¹/₂ hours or start up to 1 week ahead—YIELD: 3 dozen cookies

2 cups all-purpose flour

1 cup sugar

¹/₂ cup shortening

¹/₃ cup honey

1 teaspoon baking soda

³/₄ teaspoon salt

2 eggs

2 cups quick-cooking oats, uncooked

¹/₂ cup California walnuts, finely chopped

2 cups confectioners' sugar

¹/₄ teaspoon cream of tartar

2 egg whites

decorations: red or green sugar crystals, chocolate décors, cinnamon décors, silver décors

1. Into large bowl, measure first 7 ingredients. With mixer at low speed, beat ingredients until well blended, occasionally scraping bowl with rubber spatula. With spoon, stir in oats and walnuts.

2. Preheat oven to 375° F. With floured hands, shape mixture into thirty-six 1-inch balls and thirty-six ³/₄-inch balls. Place 1-inch balls 2¹/₂ inches apart on ungreased cookie sheets; then place ³/₄-inch balls ¹/₂ inch above 1-inch balls. (During baking, the large and small balls will join together to form snowman-like shapes.) Bake 10 to 12 minutes, until golden. With pancake turner, carefully remove cookies to wire racks to cool.

3. Prepare frosting: In medium bowl with mixer at low speed, beat confectioners' sugar, cream of tartar, and egg whites until blended. Increase speed to high, and beat 1 minute (mixture should be of easy spreading consistency).

4. Decorate snowmen: Dip top side of each snowman cookie into frosting to cover evenly. Place cookies frosted side up on wire racks. While frosting is still wet, quickly decorate each snowman as desired with sugar crystals, chocolate décors, cinnamon décors, and silver décors. Let frosting dry until firm, about 1 hour. Store in tightly covered container to use up within 1 week.

Snowflakes

TIME: about 4 hours or start up to 3 days ahead

YIELD: about 2 dozen cookies

1¹/₂ cups all-purpose flour

¹/₂ cup butter or margarine, softened

¹/₃ cup sugar

1 tablespoon water

1. Into large bowl, measure first 8 ingredients. With mixer at low speed, beat ingredients until well mixed, occasionally scraping bowl with rubber spatula. Shape dough into a ball; wrap with plastic wrap. Refrigerate dough 2 to 3 hours, until easy to handle.

1 teaspoon vanilla extract

¹/₂ teaspoon double-acting baking powder

¹/₄ teaspoon salt

1 egg

1 square semisweet chocolate, melted

2 tablespoons flaked coconut

2. Preheat oven to 350° F. Grease large cookie sheet. On lightly floured surface with lightly floured rolling pin, roll half of dough ¹/₈ inch thick, keeping remaining dough refrigerated. With floured 2³/₄" star-shaped cookie cutter, cut out 12 stars. With floured 2" star-shaped cookie cutter, cut out 12 stars. With pancake turner, place stars on cookie sheet, ¹/₂ inch apart. Bake 6 to 8 minutes, until lightly browned. With pancake turner, remove cookies to wire racks to cool. Repeat with remaining dough and trimmings, cutting out equal number of large and small stars.

3. To assemble cookies: With small metal spatula or artist's paint brush, lightly spread bottom of each small star with some melted chocolate. Immediately place small stars, chocolate side down, on top of large stars so that small star points are in between large star points. Then spread a small dab of chocolate on top center of each cookie; gently press some coconut on chocolate. Let chocolate dry. Store cookies in tightly covered container to use up within 3 days.

Sugar Horns

TIME: about 1¹/₂ hours or start up to 2 weeks ahead

YIELD: about 2 dozen cookies

¹/₂ cup all-purpose flour

¹/₂ cup sugar

4 tablespoons butter or margarine, softened

¹/₂ teaspoon vanilla extract

1 egg

1. Into large bowl, measure all ingredients. With mixer at low speed, beat ingredients until well blended, occasionally scraping bowl with rubber spatula.

2. Preheat oven to 425° F. Grease large cookie sheet. Drop a teaspoonful of dough on cookie sheet; with spoon or small metal spatula, spread dough into a 2¹/₂-inch round. Repeat to make four rounds (do not place more than four cookies on cookie sheet, because after baking, they must be shaped quickly before hardening). Bake about 4 minutes or until golden.

3. Remove cookie sheet from oven, and with pancake turner, quickly loosen and turn cookies over; one by one, roll each into a cone. (If cookies get too hard to roll, reheat in oven a minute to soften.) Cool cookies on wire racks. Repeat until all batter is used, greasing cookie sheet each time. Store cookies in tightly covered container to use up within 2 weeks.

Fruitcake Chews

TIME: about 1¹/₂ hours or start up to 2 weeks ahead

YIELD: about 3¹/₂ dozen cookies

1³/₄ cups all-purpose flour

³/₄ cup packed dark-brown sugar

¹/₂ cup shortening

¹/₄ cup milk

¹/₂ teaspoon double-acting baking powder

¹/₂ teaspoon salt

1 egg

orange-flavor liqueur

1¹/₂ cups pecan halves, coarsely chopped

1 6¹/₂-ounce container candied red cherries (1 cup), each cut in half

1 4-ounce container diced mixed candied fruit (¹/₂ cup)

1. Preheat oven to 400° F. Grease two large cookie sheets. Into large bowl, measure first 7 ingredients and 3 tablespoons orange-flavor liqueur. With mixer at low speed, beat ingredients until well blended, occasionally scraping bowl with rubber spatula. With wooden spoon, stir in pecans, candied red cherries, and mixed candied fruit.

2. Drop dough by heaping teaspoonfuls, 1¹/₂ inches apart, onto cookie sheets. Bake 12 minutes or until golden. With metal spatula, carefully remove cookies to wire racks to cool. Store in tightly covered container to use up within 2 weeks. If you like, brush cookies to be stored with some orange-flavor liqueur.

Valentine Sugar Cookies

TIME: about 4 hours or start up to 1 week ahead
YIELD: about 2¹/₂ dozen cookies

sugar

salt

2¹/₄ cups all-purpose flour

³/₄ cup butter or margarine, softened

1 tablespoon milk

2 teaspoons grated lemon peel

1¹/₂ teaspoons double-acting baking powder

1 egg

36 whole natural almonds

1. Into large bowl, measure ³/₄ cup sugar, ¹/₄ teaspoon salt, and remaining ingredients except almonds. With mixer at low speed, beat until well mixed, occasionally scraping bowl with rubber spatula. Shape mixture into a ball; wrap with plastic wrap; refrigerate 2 hours or until easy to handle.

2. Preheat oven to 350° F. Grease and flour two large cookie sheets. On floured surface with floured rolling pin, roll half of dough ¹/₈ inch thick, keeping remaining dough refrigerated. With floured 3¹/₂-inch heart-shaped cookie cutter, cut dough into hearts. (Or, cut 3¹/₂-inch heart-shaped pattern from cardboard; use cardboard pattern and knife to cut out cookies.) Place hearts, ¹/₂ inch apart, on cookie sheets. Using blunt end of wooden skewer, press holes around outer edge of each heart to form attractive border. Press an almond into center of each cookie.

3. In small bowl, mix ¹/₄ cup sugar with ¹/₄ teaspoon salt; sprinkle some on cookies. Bake 10 minutes or until golden; remove to wire racks to cool. Repeat with remaining dough and trimmings. Store cookies in tightly covered container.

Lemon Custard Bars

TIME: about 2 hours or start up to 3 days ahead—YIELD: 27 bars

1 3¹/₂-ounce can sliced blanched almonds

³/₄ cup butter or margarine, softened

¹/₂ cup confectioners' sugar

¹/₂ teaspoon lemon extract

all-purpose flour

salt

2 medium lemons

4 eggs

1¹/₄ cups sugar

1 teaspoon double-acting baking powder

1. Reserve ¹/₂ cup almonds. In covered blender at medium speed or in food processor with knife blade attached, blend remaining almonds until finely ground.

2. Preheat oven to 350° F. Into medium bowl, measure butter or margarine, confectioners' sugar, lemon extract, 1¹/₂ cups flour, and ¹/₈ teaspoon salt; add ground almonds. With hands, knead ingredients until blended. Pat mixture into bottom of 13″ by 9″ baking dish; bake 15 to 20 minutes until golden.

3. From lemons, grate 1 tablespoon peel and squeeze ¹/₃ cup juice.

4. Place peel and juice in small bowl; add eggs, sugar, baking powder, ¹/₄ cup flour, and ¹/₄ teaspoon salt. With mixer at medium speed, beat ingredients until well blended, about 1 minute, occasionally scraping bowl with rubber spatula. Pour egg mixture over baked layer; top with reserved almonds. Bake 25 minutes longer or until toothpick inserted in center comes out clean. Cool in pan on wire rack. Cut into 27 bars. Store bars in tightly covered container to use up within 3 days.

Chewy Butterscotch Brownies

TIME: about 1¹/₂ hours or start up to 1 week ahead—YIELD: 16 squares

³/₄ cup pecan halves

1 cup all-purpose flour

³/₄ cup packed light-brown sugar

¹/₂ cup flaked coconut

4 tablespoons butter or margarine, softened

1 teaspoon double-acting baking powder

1 teaspoon vanilla extract

¹/₄ teaspoon salt

1 egg

1. Reserve 16 pecan halves; chop remaining pecans.

2. Preheat oven to 350° F. Grease 8″ by 8″ baking pan. Into large bowl, measure chopped pecans, flour, and remaining ingredients. With mixer at low speed, beat ingredients until well blended, occasionally scraping bowl with rubber spatula. Pat brownie mixture into baking pan. Arrange reserved pecan halves on top of mixture so that when brownies are cut after cooking, pecans will be in the center of each of 16 squares. Bake 25 minutes or until toothpick inserted in center comes out clean. Cool brownies in pan on wire rack. Cut into 2″ by 2″ squares. Cover pan with foil or plastic wrap to use up within 1 week.

Whole-Wheat-Prune Bars

TIME: about 2¹/₂ hours or start up to 1 week ahead—YIELD: 28 bars

2¹/₄ cups whole-wheat flour
³/₄ cup packed brown sugar
¹/₂ cup butter or margarine, softened
¹/₄ cup water
1 teaspoon double-acting baking powder
2 eggs
¹/₂ cup firmly packed pitted prunes, diced

1. Into large bowl, measure first 5 ingredients and 1 egg. With mixer at low speed, beat ingredients until well blended. Gently stir in diced prunes. Shape dough into a ball; wrap with plastic wrap and refrigerate 1 hour or until easy to handle.

2. Preheat oven to 350° F. On lightly floured surface with lightly floured rolling pin, roll dough into a 14″ by 12″ rectangle. With pastry wheel or knife, cut dough into twenty-eight 3″ by 2″ rectangles.

3. With pancake turner, place cookies on ungreased cookie sheet, ¹/₂ inch apart. If you like, with dull edge of knife, mark each cookie with a design. In cup with fork, beat remaining egg slightly; brush each cookie with some beaten egg.

4. Bake cookies 25 minutes or until lightly browned. With pancake turner, remove cookies to wire racks to cool. Store cookies in tightly covered container to use up within 1 week.

Nutty Coconut Triangles

TIME: about 2 hours or start up to 1 week ahead—YIELD: 2 dozen triangles

¹/₂ cup butter or margarine, softened
all-purpose flour
light-brown sugar
2 eggs
1 teaspoon vanilla extract
¹/₂ teaspoon double-acting baking powder
¹/₄ teaspoon salt
1 3¹/₂-ounce can flaked coconut
1 cup pecan halves, chopped

1. Preheat oven to 375° F. In small bowl with mixer at low speed, beat butter or margarine, 1 cup all-purpose flour, and ¹/₂ cup packed light-brown sugar until well blended, occasionally scraping bowl with rubber spatula. With hand, evenly pat dough into 13″ by 9″ baking pan. Bake 15 minutes or until lightly browned.

2. Meanwhile, into large bowl, measure eggs, vanilla, baking powder, salt, ³/₄ cup packed light-brown sugar, and 3 tablespoons all-purpose flour. With mixer at medium speed, beat ingredients until well blended, occasionally scraping bowl with rubber spatula. With spoon, stir in coconut and pecans.

3. Evenly spread coconut mixture over baked layer in pan. Bake 20 to 25 minutes longer or until golden. Cool in pan on wire rack. When cool, cut into 24 triangle cookies. Store in tightly covered container to use up within 1 week.

Chocolate-Mint Bars

TIME: about 2 hours or start up to 1 week ahead—YIELD: 32 bars

1 cup butter or margarine
4 squares unsweetened chocolate
2 cups sugar
1 cup all-purpose flour
1 teaspoon vanilla extract
¹/₂ teaspoon salt
4 eggs
1 cup California walnuts, coarsely chopped
³/₄ cup confectioners' sugar
1 tablespoon water
¹/₄ teaspoon peppermint extract
green food color

1. Preheat oven to 350° F. Grease 13″ by 9″ baking pan. In small saucepan over very low heat, melt butter or margarine and chocolate, stirring occasionally.

2. Pour butter mixture into large bowl. Add sugar, flour, vanilla, salt, and eggs. With mixer at low speed, beat ingredients until blended, occasionally scraping bowl with rubber spatula. Stir in nuts. Pour chocolate mixture into pan. Bake 35 minutes or until toothpick inserted in center comes out clean. Cool in pan on wire rack.

3. In small bowl with spoon, mix confectioners' sugar, water, and peppermint extract until icing is smooth. Then stir in enough green food color to tint an attractive green color. Drizzle icing over cooled chocolate layer in pan. When icing is dry, cut into 32 bars. Cover and refrigerate to use up within 1 week.

Luscious Apricot Squares

TIME: about 3 hours or start early in day—YIELD: 16 squares

water

²/₃ cup dried apricots

¹/₂ cup butter or margarine, softened

¹/₄ cup sugar

all-purpose flour

1 cup packed light-brown sugar

2 eggs

¹/₂ cup California walnuts, chopped

¹/₂ teaspoon double-acting baking powder

¹/₂ teaspoon vanilla extract

¹/₄ teaspoon salt

confectioners' sugar

1. In covered 1-quart saucepan over low heat, in enough water to cover apricots, cook apricots 15 minutes; drain and finely chop.

2. Preheat oven to 350° F. Grease 8″ by 8″ baking pan. In large bowl with mixer at medium speed, beat butter, sugar, and 1 cup flour until well mixed and crumbly; pat into pan. Bake 25 minutes or just until layer is golden.

3. Meanwhile, in same bowl at medium speed, mix well apricots, brown sugar, ¹/₃ cup flour, and remaining ingredients except confectioners' sugar.

4. Pour over baked layer; bake 25 minutes longer.

5. Cool in pan; cut into squares. Sprinkle with confectioners' sugar.

Creamy Cheese Triangles

TIME: about 3 hours or start early in day—YIELD: 48 triangles

¹/₂ cup butter or margarine, softened

1¹/₂ cups all-purpose flour

¹/₂ cup packed brown sugar

³/₄ cup California walnuts, finely chopped

2 8-ounce packages cream cheese, softened

¹/₃ cup sugar

2 tablespoons grated orange peel

1 teaspoon orange extract

1 egg

1. Preheat oven to 350° F. Grease 12″ by 8″ baking pan; set aside.

2. In small bowl with mixer at low speed, beat butter or margarine, flour, and brown sugar until well blended, occasionally scraping bowl with rubber spatula. (Mixture will be crumbly.) Stir in walnuts. Reserve 1¹/₄ cups crumb mixture; evenly pat remaining mixture into bottom of baking pan. Bake 20 minutes or until lightly browned.

3. Meanwhile, in large bowl with mixer at medium speed, beat cream cheese, sugar, grated orange peel, orange extract, and egg until well blended, occasionally scraping bowl with rubber spatula. Evenly spread cream-cheese mixture over baked layer in pan. Sprinkle with reserved crumb mixture. Bake 30 minutes longer or until golden. Refrigerate until well chilled, at least 2 hours.

4. To serve, cut into 2″ by 2″ squares; cut squares into triangles.

Grandma's Candy Clusters

TIME: about 2 hours or start up to 1 week ahead

YIELD: about 3 dozen candies

2¹/₂ cups sugar

1 cup evaporated milk

¹/₄ cup light corn syrup

1 tablespoon butter or margarine

¹/₈ teaspoon baking soda

2¹/₂ cups California walnuts, coarsely chopped

2 teaspoons vanilla extract

1. In heavy 3-quart saucepan over medium heat, heat first 5 ingredients to boiling, stirring constantly, until sugar is dissolved. Set candy thermometer in place. Reduce heat to medium-low and continue cooking, stirring occasionally, until temperature reaches 240° F. or soft-ball stage (when small amount of mixture dropped into very cold water forms a soft ball that flattens on removal from water).

2. Remove from heat. Immediately, with spoon, stir in walnuts and vanilla; beat mixture until thick and creamy and it flows slightly when dropped from spoon.

3. Working quickly, drop mixture by scant tablespoonfuls onto waxed paper. Candies will become grainy if mixture is overbeaten and worked too slowly. Let stand about 30 minutes until cool before removing from paper. Store candy, tightly covered.

Best Chocolate Fudge

TIME: about 2¹/₂ hours or start up to 1 week ahead—YIELD: about 2 pounds

3 **cups sugar**

1 **cup milk**

3 **squares unsweetened chocolate**

2 **tablespoons light corn syrup**

¹/₂ **teaspoon salt**

3 **tablespoons butter or margarine**

1¹/₂ **teaspoons vanilla extract**

1 **cup pecans, coarsely chopped**

1. In 4-quart saucepan over medium heat, heat sugar, milk, chocolate, corn syrup, and salt to boiling, stirring frequently. Carefully set candy thermometer in place and cook, without stirring, until temperature on thermometer reaches 238° F. or soft-ball stage (when a small amount of chocolate mixture dropped into a bowl of very cold water forms a ball that flattens on removal from water), about 10 minutes. Remove saucepan from heat.

2. Cool chocolate mixture, without stirring, to 110° F., or until outside of saucepan is lukewarm. Meanwhile, lightly butter 8″ by 8″ baking pan.

3. When chocolate mixture is ready, add butter or margarine and vanilla extract. With wooden spoon, beat until mixture is thick and begins to lose its gloss, about 3 minutes. Quickly stir in chopped pecans; pour mixture into pan. Cool fudge in pan on wire rack; cut into about 1¹/₂-inch squares. Store fudge in tightly covered container. Makes 25 pieces.

Nutty Butterscotch Fudge

TIME: about 1¹/₂ hours or start up to 1 week ahead
YIELD: about 1¹/₄ pounds

1 **cup sugar**

¹/₄ **cup butter or margarine**

³/₄ **teaspoon salt**

1 **7¹/₂-ounce jar marshmallow cream**

1 **5.33-ounce can evaporated milk, undiluted**

1 **12-ounce package butterscotch-flavored pieces**

¹/₂ **teaspoon vanilla extract**

¹/₂ **cup salted peanuts, pecans, or cashews, chopped**

1. Grease 9″ by 9″ baking pan; set aside.

2. In heavy 3-quart saucepan, combine sugar, butter or margarine, salt, marshmallow cream, and evaporated milk. Over medium-high heat, heat to a rolling boil; cook 5 minutes, stirring.

3. Remove saucepan from heat. Quickly stir in butterscotch-flavored pieces and vanilla extract until butterscotch pieces are melted and well blended; stir in peanuts. Pour mixture into pan. Cool. Cut into 49 small squares with a sharp knife. Store fudge in tightly covered container.

Walnut Crunch

TIME: about 3¹/₂ hours or start early in day—YIELD: about 1¹/₂ pounds

1¹/₄ **cups sugar**

³/₄ **cup butter or margarine**

¹/₄ **cup water**

1¹/₂ **teaspoons salt**

1¹/₂ **cups California walnuts, coarsely chopped**

¹/₂ **teaspoon baking soda**

¹/₃ **cup semisweet-chocolate pieces, melted**

¹/₂ **cup California walnuts, finely chopped**

1. Butter 15¹/₂″ by 10¹/₂″ jelly-roll pan. In 2-quart saucepan over medium heat, heat sugar, butter or margarine, water, and salt to boiling, stirring often. Set candy thermometer in place, and continue cooking, stirring often, until temperature reaches 290° F., or until a small amount of mixture dropped into very cold water separates into threads that are hard but not brittle.

2. Remove mixture from heat; stir in coarsely chopped walnuts and baking soda; pour at once into pan. (Don't scrape saucepan; side may be sugary.)

3. Spread mixture with chocolate and sprinkle with walnuts; cool. With hands, snap candy into small pieces.

217

Nougats

TIME: start day ahead or up to 2 weeks ahead—YIELD: about 2¼ pounds

½ pound hard gum candy (not sugar-coated)

cornstarch

2 cups sugar

1½ cups light corn syrup

¼ cup water

¼ teaspoon salt

2 egg whites

1 teaspoon vanilla extract

¼ cup butter or margarine, softened

1 cup California walnuts, coarsely chopped

1. With kitchen shears, cut gum candy into small pieces; set aside. Grease 9″ by 9″ baking pan; sprinkle lightly with cornstarch. In 2-quart saucepan with candy thermometer in place, over medium-high heat, heat sugar, corn syrup, water, and salt to boiling, stirring constantly. Continue cooking, stirring occasionally, until temperature reaches 250° F., or hard-ball stage (when small amount of mixture dropped into very cold water forms a ball that is hard enough to hold its shape).

2. Meanwhile, in large bowl with mixer at high speed, beat egg whites until stiff peaks form. Beating at high speed, gradually pour about one fourth of hot syrup into egg whites. Continue beating while heating remaining syrup to 300° F. or hard-crack stage (when small amount of mixture dropped into very cold water separates into threads that are hard and brittle). Egg-white mixture should stand in stiff, glossy peaks; beat in vanilla extract.

3. With mixer at high speed, gradually beat remaining syrup into egg-white mixture, then beat in butter until blended. If mixture becomes too thick for the mixer to beat, continue beating with a wooden spoon.

4. With wooden spoon, stir in walnuts and gum candy; spoon evenly into baking pan. With pastry brush, lightly brush mixture with some cornstarch.

5. Let nougat cool in pan on wire rack for about 12 hours or overnight. Remove nougat from pan; with knife, cut into 1-inch squares, wiping knife as needed with damp cloth. To store, wrap each piece in plastic wrap.

Chocolate-dipped Fruit and Nuts

TIME: about 1½ hours or start early in day—YIELD: about 6 dozen candies

2 large oranges

2 pints large strawberries

1 cup salted peanuts

2 8-ounce packages semisweet-chocolate squares

1. Peel oranges and separate them into their sections; wrap sections with plastic wrap so fruits will not dry out. Rinse strawberries under running cold water but do not remove stems, being sure to pat berries completely dry with paper towels. Set fruit aside. (For dipping, fruit should be at room temperature.) In small bowl, place peanuts.

2. Into double-boiler top (not over water) grate semisweet-chocolate squares. Set candy thermometer in place; set aside. Heat water to boiling in double-boiler bottom; remove from heat. Place double-boiler top over hot water; melt chocolate, stirring chocolate constantly with rubber spatula, until temperature reaches 130° F.

3. Immediately discard hot water from double-boiler bottom and refill with cold water to come one third way up side of double boiler. Set top in place and cool chocolate, stirring constantly, until temperature reaches 83° F. on special 40° to 120° F. thermometer.

4. Remove double-boiler top and replace cold water in bottom with warm water (about 85° F.). This will keep chocolate at dipping consistency longer.

5. With fingers, hold one piece of fruit at a time and dip it into chocolate, leaving part of fruit uncovered. Shake off excess chocolate or gently scrape one side of fruit across rim of double boiler, being careful not to scrape too much chocolate from fruit; place on waxed paper.

6. Working quickly, stir peanuts into leftover chocolate in pan. Drop mixture by tablespoonfuls onto waxed paper. Let chocolate-covered fruit and peanut clusters stand until chocolate is set (about 10 minutes) before removing from waxed paper. Serve dipped fresh fruit same day. Store peanut clusters in covered container; use within 1 week.

Marzipan Apples

TIME: about $1^1/_2$ hours or start up to 1 week ahead

YIELD: about 20 candies

$1^1/_2$ **cups blanched whole almonds**

$1^1/_2$ **cups confectioners' sugar**

1 egg white

$1^1/_4$ **teaspoons almond extract**

$^1/_4$ **teaspoon salt**

green food color

red food color

water

about 20 whole cloves

1. In blender at medium speed or in food processor with knife blade attached, blend almonds, $^1/_2$ cup at a time, until very finely ground. (If using food processor, add confectioners' sugar, egg white, almond extract, salt, and green food color to ground almonds; blend to make a stiff paste.)

2. In medium bowl with fork, mix ground almonds, confectioners' sugar, egg white, almond extract, salt, and enough green food color to tint an attractive apple-green color. With hands, knead to make a stiff paste.

3. Shape 1 tablespoon dough into an apple (cover remaining dough with plastic wrap); repeat until all dough is used. Using a small artist's brush, tint apples with red food color diluted with water. Press stems from cloves part way into tops of apples. Let apples dry on wire rack, about 30 minutes.

Christmas Walnut Brittle

TIME: about 1 hour or start up to 1 week ahead—YIELD: about 1 pound

1 cup sugar

$^1/_2$ **cup light corn syrup**

$^1/_4$ **cup water**

$^1/_4$ **teaspoon salt**

1 cup California walnuts, coarsely chopped

1 tablespoon butter or margarine, softened

1 teaspoon baking soda

$^1/_3$ **cup diced mixed candied fruit**

1. Grease large cookie sheet. In heavy 2-quart saucepan over medium heat, heat sugar, corn syrup, water, and salt to boiling, stirring frequently until sugar is completely dissolved. Stir in chopped walnuts. Carefully set candy thermometer in place and continue cooking, stirring frequently, until temperature on candy thermometer reaches 300° F. or hard-crack stage (when a small amount of mixture dropped into a bowl of very cold water separates into hard and brittle threads), about 20 minutes.

2. Remove saucepan from heat; immediately stir in butter or margarine and baking soda; pour mixture at once onto cookie sheet. With two forks, lift and pull walnut mixture into a rectangle about 14″ by 12″. Sprinkle candied fruit over mixture. Place cookie sheet on wire rack; cool walnut brittle completely.

3. With hands, gently snap candy into small serving-size pieces. Store candy in tightly covered container to use within 1 week.

Wassail Bowl

TIME: about 30 minutes—YIELD: 32 ¹/₂-cup servings

2 quarts apple cider or apple juice

3 3¹/₂-inch-long cinnamon sticks

2 teaspoons whole cloves

2 teaspoons whole allspice

1 orange, for garnish

1 lemon, for garnish

whole cloves, for garnish

1 6-ounce can frozen orange-juice concentrate

1 6-ounce can frozen lemonade concentrate

1 750-milliliter bottle (⁴/₅ quart) dry white wine

4 cups water

³/₄ cup packed brown sugar

1. In 5-quart saucepot over high heat, heat apple cider, cinnamon, cloves, and allspice to boiling. Reduce heat to low; cover and simmer 15 minutes.

2. Meanwhile, slice orange and lemon. Place one lemon slice on each orange slice; secure in center with 1 or 2 whole cloves. Place orange-and-lemon-slice garnish in heat-safe punch bowl; set aside.

3. Add frozen orange-juice concentrate, lemonade concentrate, white wine, water, and brown sugar to cider mixture; over high heat, heat to boiling. Pour hot cider mixture over fruit slices in bowl. Makes 16 cups.

Orange-Cream Punch

TIME: about 2 hours or start early in day—YIELD: 16 ¹/₂-cup servings

3 large oranges

4 eggs, separated

¹/₄ cup sugar

¹/₄ cup orange-flavor liqueur

2 cups half-and-half

1 cup heavy or whipping cream

ground cinnamon, for garnish

1. Grate 1 teaspoon peel and squeeze juice from oranges (about 1 cup). Wrap peel with plastic wrap; reserve for garnish.

2. In large bowl with wire whisk, beat egg yolks and sugar until sugar is dissolved; beat in orange juice, orange-flavor liqueur, half-and-half, and heavy cream until well blended. Cover and refrigerate until well chilled.

3. About 20 minutes before serving, in small bowl with mixer at high speed, beat egg whites until soft peaks form. With rubber spatula or wire whisk, gently fold egg whites into yolk mixture just until blended.

4. Pour into 2-quart chilled punch bowl. Sprinkle cinnamon and reserved orange peel over punch. Makes 8 cups.

Espresso Eggnog

TIME: about 2 hours or start early in day—YIELD: 18 $^1/_2$-cup servings

1/4 cup instant espresso-coffee powder

1 cup boiling water

2 cups iced water

3 eggs, separated

1 cup coffee-flavor liqueur

1 pint coffee ice cream

2 cups half-and-half

grated chocolate, for garnish

1. In medium bowl, stir instant espresso-coffee powder with boiling water until dissolved. Add iced water; refrigerate until well chilled.

2. In small bowl with mixer at high speed, beat egg yolks until thick and lemon-colored, frequently scraping bowl with rubber spatula. Reduce speed to medium; gradually beat in coffee-flavor liqueur (egg yolks may curdle if liqueur is beaten in too quickly). Cover and refrigerate until well chilled.

3. About 30 minutes before serving, remove coffee ice cream from freezer; let stand at room temperature to soften slightly.

4. In large bowl with mixer at high speed, beat egg whites until soft peaks form.

5. In chilled 3-quart punch bowl, stir egg-yolk mixture, coffee ice cream, and half-and-half until blended. With rubber spatula or wire whisk, gently fold egg whites into yolk mixture just until blended. Lightly sprinkle grated chocolate over eggnog. Makes 9 cups.

Mocha Float

TIME: about 5 minutes—SERVINGS: 1

3/4 teaspoon quick chocolate-flavor milk mix

3/4 teaspoon instant-coffee powder

1/2 teaspoon sugar

club soda, chilled

2 small scoops chocolate-ripple ice cream

1. Into an 8-ounce glass, measure first 3 ingredients. Gradually add enough club soda to fill glass three quarters full; stir until sugar is dissolved.

2. Add ice cream; stir. Serve with spoon and straw.

Banana Milk Shakes

TIME: about 10 minutes—SERVINGS: 2

3/4 cup milk

1 large ripe banana

1 pint vanilla ice cream

1. In covered blender at high speed, blend ingredients until smooth.

2. Pour mixture into chilled 12-ounce glasses; serve with large straws. Makes 3 cups.

Sparkling Strawberry Punch

TIME: about 10 minutes—YIELD: 36 $^1/_2$-cup servings

2 10-ounce packages frozen sweetened strawberries, slightly thawed

1 6-ounce can frozen lemonade concentrate, slightly thawed

1 750-milliliter (4/5 quart) bottle rosé wine, chilled

2 28-ounce bottles ginger ale, chilled

1 28-ounce bottle club soda, chilled

2 trays ice cubes

1/4 cup sugar

orange slices, for garnish

1. In covered blender at high speed, blend strawberries and undiluted lemonade concentrate until they are thoroughly blended.

2. Pour strawberry mixture into a chilled large punch bowl. Add wine and remaining ingredients except orange slices; stir punch until sugar is completely dissolved.

3. To serve, garnish with orange slices. Makes 18 cups.

Best Lemonade

TIME: about 1 hour or start day ahead—YIELD: 16 1-cup servings

1½ cups sugar

1 tablespoon finely grated lemon peel

1½ cups very hot water

1½ cups lemon juice (about 8 to 10 large lemons)

ice cubes

cold water or club soda

1. Prepare syrup: In 1-quart jar with tight-fitting lid, shake sugar and lemon peel with hot water until sugar is dissolved. Add lemon juice, and refrigerate for at least 1 hour.

2. For each serving: Over ice cubes in 12-ounce glass, pour ¼ cup syrup. Stir in ¾ cup cold water or club soda. Makes 16 cups.

Best Iced Tea

TIME: about 15 minutes or start several hours ahead
YIELD: 8 1-cup servings

fresh cold water

3 tablespoons loose tea or 8 tea bags

ice cubes

sugar

lemon or lime slices or wedges

1. In 3-quart saucepan over high heat, heat 4 cups cold water to boiling. Remove saucepan from heat; immediately stir in loose tea or tea bags. Cover and let stand (steep) 5 minutes. Stir again; strain mixture (or remove tea bags and pour mixture) into pitcher holding an additional 4 cups cold water. Cover and let stand until serving time. (Don't refrigerate; tea may become cloudy. If it clouds, add a little boiling water until it clears.)

2. To serve, pour tea over ice cubes in 12-ounce glasses. Serve with sugar and lemon or lime slices or wedges. Makes 8 cups tea.

COLD-WATER METHOD: Start at least 4 hours ahead or the day before, if you like. Into large pitcher, measure 4 cups fresh cold water. Add 8 tea bags (remove tags); cover and refrigerate at least 4 hours. Serve as above. Makes four 1-cup servings.

FROST-RIMMED ICED TEA: Prepare iced tea as you wish. Then, about 15 minutes before serving, run the cut side of a lemon or lime wedge around rim of each glass to moisten; then invert moistened rim in saucer of sugar to coat well. Carefully fill each glass with ice and tea. Garnish with additional lemon or lime wedge.

Best Iced Coffee

ground coffee

ice cubes

cream (optional)

sugar (optional)

REGULAR COFFEE: Brew hot coffee, but use twice the amount of ground coffee as usual. Fill tall glasses with ice cubes and slowly pour in hot coffee. Serve with cream and sugar, if desired.

REGULAR COFFEE WITH COFFEE ICE CUBES: Brew coffee as usual; cool, then pour into ice-cube trays; freeze. At serving time, fill glasses with coffee cubes. Pour fresh-brewed regular-strength coffee over cubes. Serve with cream and sugar, if desired.

INSTANT COFFEE: In tall glass, dissolve *instant coffee* with a little *warm water.* (Use about twice as much instant coffee as you use for a cup.) Fill glass with ice cubes, then cold water; stir. Serve with cream and sugar, if desired.

Appendix

Favorite Menus

*Recipes for dishes marked by an asterisk can be found in the Index.

For the Family

Steak and Potatoes—SERVES 6
Broiled Chuck Steak
with Sautéed Vegetables*
Frozen Steak-fried Potatoes
Lettuce Wedges
with Bottled Coleslaw Dressing
Oatmeal Cookies and Apples

Soup-and-Sandwich Supper
SERVES 4
Minestrone Soup
Western-Omelet Heros*
Corn Chips
Bread-and-Butter Pickles
Chocolate-Chip Cookies

Chicken-and-Vegetable Delight
SERVES 4
Braised Chicken
with Julienne Vegetables*
Buttered Toasted English Muffins
Juicy-Ripe Papayas

Vegetarian Supper—SERVES 4
Stuffed Eggplant*
Alfalfa-Lettuce Salad
Toasted Whole-Wheat Pita Bread
Macaroons and Mixed Canned Fruit

"Chowder's On!"—SERVES 4
Frankfurter Chowder*
Avocado-Chicory Salad
Bread Sticks
French Apple Pie

Spaghetti-Night Special—SERVES 6
Ground Beef
with Spaghetti Parmigiana*
Broccoli Spears
Bakery Chocolate Cupcakes

Country Sausage Supper—SERVES 4
Knackwurst with Sweet-and-Sour
Cabbage*
Shoestring Potatoes
Hearty Rye Bread and Butter
Ice-Cream Sandwiches

Fish and Fries—SERVES 6
Frozen Fish Sticks
Frozen French Fries
Cucumbers with Dilled Yogurt Dressing*
Apricot-Almond Cream*

Soufflé for Two—SERVES 2
Cheese Soufflé*
Sautéed Snow Peas
Bakery Pumpernickel Rolls
Bakery Apple Pie

Stir-fried Steak—SERVES 4
Tangy Steak and Vegetables*
Rice
Hot Corn Bread
Fresh Fruit

Tuna-Salad Supper—SERVES 4
Tuna-and-Bean Salad*
Sliced Cling Peaches
French Bread Slices
Bakery Cannolis

Fish Stew—SERVES 4
Manhattan-style Fish Stew*
Spinach Salad with Green Onion
Cracked-Wheat Bread
Unsalted Butter
Ready-to-Serve Tapioca Pudding

Steak Special—SERVES 4
Cubed Steaks with Caper Sauce*
Buttered Baby Carrots
Romaine-and-Cucumber Salad
with Bottled Creamy Cucumber Dressing
Toast Points
Bakery Napoleons

Spring Omelet—SERVES 4
Omelet Primavera*
Shoestring Beets on Boston Lettuce
Crisp Dinner Rolls
Pineapple Wedges

For Company

Celebration Dinner—SERVES 2
Jumbo-Shrimp Appetizer*
Pan-fried Steaks with Wine Sauce*
Sautéed Cucumber Rounds
Endive-and-Watercress Salad
with Oil and-Vinegar Dressing
Bakery Croissants
Brie Cheese and Red Grapes
Instant Cappucino

Elegant Lamb Dinner—SERVES 4
Mushroom-stuffed Lamb Chops*
Grilled Tomato Wedges
Buttered Asparagus
Boiled Small Red Potatoes
Fresh Strawberries in Cream

Easy Chicken Dinner—SERVES 4
Sweet-and-Sour Chicken*
Buttered Broccoli Spears
Chow Mein Noodles
No-Bake Berry Cheesecake*

Burgers Continental—SERVES 6
Hamburgers Rémoulade*
Sesame Green Beans*
Hot Biscuits
Fontina Cheese and Orange Sections

Skillet Pork Supper—SERVES 4
Pork Chops with Sour-Cream Sauce*
Buttered Brussels Sprouts
Corkscrew Macaroni
Orange-Chiffon Cake*

Party Salad—SERVES 4
Seafarer's Salad with Vinaigrette
Dressing*
Whole-Wheat and Pumpernickel Breads
Rhubarb Cups*

Chicken-Liver Special—SERVES 4
Chicken Livers Marsala*
Buttered Parslied Noodles
Sliced Tomatoes and Cucumbers
with Vinaigrette Dressing
Marble Swirl Pound Cake*

Quick Quiche—SERVES 6
No-Crust-Zucchini Quiche*
Boston-Lettuce Salad*
Melba Toast
Banana-Nut Cake*

Elegant Pork Dinner—SERVES 4
Sherried Pork Tenderloin*
Frozen Mixed Italian Vegetables
Buttered Orzo
Italian Bread and Whipped Butter
Butter-Pecan Ice Cream

Easy Buffet—SERVES 6
Assorted Cold Meats and Cheese
Perfect Potato Salad*
Tomato Wedges
French Bread with Butter Balls
Honey-Pear Bake*

Pasta Favorite—SERVES 6
Linguine with Clam Sauce Florentine*
Sliced Tomatoes and Ripe Olives
on Lettuce with Bottled Italian Dressing
Sesame Bread Sticks
No-Bake Cheesecake*

Ham Steaks and Stuffing—SERVES 6
Pan-fried Ham Steaks
Buttered Italian Green Beans
Packaged Corn-Bread Stuffing
Banana-Coconut Betty*

Sunday Spaghetti—SERVES 6
Pasta with Chicken, Ham, and Zucchini*
Broiled Tomato Halves
with Crumb Topping
Bread Sticks
Quick Strawberry Shortcakes*
Espresso

Quick Pork Dinner—SERVES 4
Spicy Shredded Pork in Lettuce Cups*
Sautéed Cherry Tomatoes*
Hot Fluffy Rice
Deep-Dish Blueberry Pie*

Casseroles Italiano—SERVES 4
Baked Eggplant Casseroles*
Boston-Lettuce-and-Zucchini Salad
with Bottled French Dressing
Assorted Crackers
Canned Pear Halves
with Quick-Thaw Raspberries

Choice Chicken Dinner—SERVES 4
Elegant Stuffed Chicken Quarters*
Sautéed Cherry Tomatoes*
Pan-fried Potatoes*
Frosty Lime Soufflé*

Holiday Dinners

Candlelight Dinner—SERVES 12
Oyster Soup en Croute*
Turkey with Wild-Rice Stuffing*
Asparagus Mimosa*
Sugared Carrots*
Chocolate-Mousse Cake*
Strawberries

Party Roast Beef—SERVES 16
Favorite Rib Eye Roast*
Sautéed Mushrooms
Buttered Asparagus
Parslied Boiled Small Potatoes
Old-fashioned Rolls*
Unsalted Butter
Bibb-Lettuce-and-Watercress Salad
with Oil-and-Vinegar Dressing
Raspberry-Strawberry-Cream Cake*

Christmas Feast—SERVES 8 to 10
Christmas Goose with Glazed Oranges*
Buttered Petite Peas
Sugar-glazed Carrots
Spinach Salad with Crumbled Bacon
Colonial Oatmeal Bread*
Christmas-Wreath Cheesecake*

Colonial Turkey Dinner—SERVES 16
Succotash Chowder*
Roast Turkey
with Sausage-Cracker Stuffing*
Cranberry-Wine Mold*
Brown-Butter Potatoes and Rutabagas*
Green Beans with Bacon Bits
Relish Tray: Cabbage Salad,* Pickles,
Beets, Chow-Chow Pickles,
Cranberry Sauce
Sour-Cream Rolls*
Apple-Molasses Muffins*
Walnut-Pumpkin Pie*
Plum-Pudding Ice Cream*
Grandma's Candy Clusters*
Cider, Coffee, and Milk

Gala Turkey Buffet—SERVES 16
Wassail Bowl*
Creamed Turkey with Pastry Pillows*
Green-Vegetable Medley*
Cranberry-Pineapple Salad Mold*
Dessert Tray: Toasted Almonds,*
Brie Wedges, Cheddar Cheese,
Caraway Cheese
Red and Green Grapes, Apple Wedges
Steamed Chocolate-Date Pudding
with Brandy-Custard Sauce*

Festive Rock Cornish Hens
SERVES 4
Roast Cornish Hens
with Spinach Stuffing*
Green Beans Amandine
Sautéed Cherry Tomatoes*
Boston-Lettuce-and-Arugula Salad
Melba Toast
Grape-and-Kiwi-Fruit Tart*

Small Celebration—SERVES 4
Pork Loin Chops with Prune Stuffing*
Sautéed Red Cabbage
Buttered Green Beans
Tossed Three-Green Salad
Swiss and Cheddar Cheese
Fresh Fruit in Season

Do-Ahead Feast—SERVES 12
Salmon Pâté*
Party Turkey with Radish Mayonnaise*
Cranberry Chutney*
Tangy Winter Vegetables*
Parslied Potato Salad*
Holiday Bubble Loaf*
Chestnut-Cream Mousse*

Elegant Duckling—SERVES 4
Duckling with Raspberry Sauce*
Stir-fried Broccoli with Mushrooms
Pan-roasted Potato Chunks*
Tossed Green Salad with Hearts of Palm
Warm Pumpernickel Dinner Rolls
Butter
Cheese-Pear Strudel*

Calorie Watcher's Turkey Dinner
SERVES 12
Tomato-Curry Bisque*
Roast Turkey with Barley Stuffing*
Pan-roasted Sweet-Potato Chunks*
Celebration Vegetable Platter*
Raspberry-Banana Dream*
Tea with Lemon

Party Shrimp Dinner—SERVES 4
Butterflied Shrimp in Wine*
Hot Fluffy Rice
Sautéed Zucchini Slices
Endive Salad with Vinaigrette Dressing
Bread Sticks
Spiced Pears*

Turkey-Cutlet Dinner—SERVES 6
Cream-of-Squash Soup*
Turkey Cutlets Manhattan*
Broccoli Timbales*
Crisp Dinner Rolls with Butter Curls
Boston-Lettuce Salad*
Pear-Almond Tart*

How to Follow Our Recipes

Make it a habit to take these steps every time you try a new recipe:

Read the recipe before you begin. Be sure you understand all cooking terms used. Check how much time it will take to prepare the recipe, and allow yourself a few extra minutes in case you are interrupted.

Check the ingredient list. Make sure you have everything you need, in the amount called for. Assemble the ingredients.

Don't substitute key ingredients, unless the recipe suggests an alternate. That goes for product forms and package sizes, too. To take one example, some packaged pudding mixes come in both regular-size and family-size packages, and in both regular and instant forms. Using either the wrong size or the wrong kind of pudding in a recipe might result in a disaster!

Seasonings and spices *can* safely be varied. But it's a good idea to follow the recipe exactly the first time, to discover the family's tastes before making changes.

Check the utensils you'll need. Assemble items for measuring, mixing, cooking, and serving. Be sure pans are the right size (see "How to measure pans," below).

Do as much advance preparation as possible. Chop, cut, grate, melt, or otherwise prepare ingredients and have them ready before you start to mix. Grease and flour pans; turn the oven on at least 10 minutes before putting food in to bake, to allow it to preheat to the proper temperature.

Measure accurately. Our recipes are based on standard, consistent measurements. Use the proper measuring equipment and methods (see "Measuring Ingredients," below).

Mix carefully. Ingredients are combined in different ways (by folding, beating, stirring, etc.) to achieve different results. Be sure to take note of any specific mixing times or cautions given in the recipe.

Clean up as you work. Put empty bowls, used measuring equipment in the sink; throw away paper; sponge up spills. The less cluttered the work surface, the less chance of your making a mistake.

Cook or bake as directed. For best results, use the temperature specified in the recipe. Follow the time suggested too, but to be on the safe side, start checking for doneness before the end, since ovens and heating units vary.

Be careful about doubling or halving a recipe. Though some recipes can be increased or decreased successfully, many more cannot. For best results, make the recipe as given, and repeat it until the desired amount is obtained.

Measuring Ingredients

Using the correct measuring equipment. Accurate measurements are essential if you want the same good results each time you make a recipe. For dry ingredients, use a set of four graduated measuring cups, consisting of 1/4-, 1/3-, 1/2-, and 1-cup measures. For liquids, use a 1-cup liquid measuring cup that is also marked for smaller measurements. Two-cup and 4-cup liquid measuring cups are helpful for measuring larger amounts. A standard set of 1/4-, 1/2-, 1-teaspoon, and 1-tablespoon measuring spoons is used for both dry and liquid ingredients.

Measuring liquids. Always read the line on a measuring cup at eye level when checking the volume of liquid in a cup. With the liquid measure on a level surface, slowly pour the liquid into the cup until it reaches the desired line. If using measuring spoons, pour liquid just to the top of the spoon without letting it spill over.

Measuring sugar. Lightly spoon sugar into a graduated measuring cup, and level off with the straight edge of a knife or spatula.

For brown sugar, pack the sugar lightly into the cup with the back of a spoon, then level off; it will hold its shape when inverted from the cup.

Measuring flour. In the recipes in this book, all the flours are measured and used straight from the flour package or canister. Lightly spoon the flour into a graduated measuring cup or spoon; never pack flour down or shake or tap the side of the measuring cup. Then, quickly level off the surplus flour in the measuring cup with the straight edge of a small kitchen knife.

Measuring shortening. Liquid shortening, such as salad oil and melted butter or margarine, can be measured in the same way as liquids.

Measure shortening such as lard, vegetable shortening, even peanut butter, as follows: Pack in the shortening firmly, right to the top of the measuring spoon or graduated cup. Level off the shortening with the straight edge, not the flat side, of a knife or spatula.

Measuring butter or margarine. Each 1/4-pound stick of butter or margarine measures 1/2 cup; the wrapping is usually marked off in tablespoons for measuring smaller amounts. With a sharp knife, just cut off the number of tablespoons needed, following the guidelines on the wrapper. For butter or margarine not wrapped in this way, measure and level off as for solid shortening.

How to measure pans. Be sure your pans are the kind and size specified in the recipe. The size of some cookware is expressed in liquid measurement at its level full capacity. Measure top inside of bakeware for length, width, or diameter; measure perpendicular inside for depth. Sizes for skillets or frypans and griddles are stated as the top outside dimensions, exclusive of handles.

Equivalent Amounts

How many cups make a quart? Are three bananas enough to make one cup of mashed? For two tablespoons of grated orange peel, will you need more than one orange? How many cups are there in a pound of flour? These questions are answered below.

Equivalent measures

Dash	2 to 3 drops, or less than $^1/_8$ teaspoon	$^1/_2$ **cup**	8 tablespoons	**1 quart**	4 cups
		$^2/_3$ **cup**	10 tablespoons plus 2 teaspoons	**1 gallon**	4 quarts
1 tablespoon	3 teaspoons			**1 peck**	8 quarts
$^1/_4$ **cup**	4 tablespoons	**1 cup**	16 tablespoons	**1 bushel**	4 pecks
$^1/_3$ **cup**	5 tablespoons plus 1 teaspoon	**1 pint**	2 cups	**1 pound**	16 ounces

Food equivalents

Apples	1 pound	3 medium (3 cups sliced)	**Cheese**			
dried	1 pound	$4^1/_3$ cups (8 cups cooked)	blue	$^1/_4$ pound	1 cup crumbled	
Applesauce			Cheddar, Swiss	$^1/_4$ pound	1 cup shredded	
canned	16-ounce can	$1^3/_4$ cups	cottage	8 ounces	1 cup	
Apricots	1 pound	8 to 12 medium	cream	3 ounces	6 tablespoons	
canned	16-ounce can	8 to 12 whole; 12 to 20 halves	spread	5-ounce jar	$^1/_2$ cup	
dried	1 pound	3 cups (5 cups cooked)	**Chocolate**			
Bananas	1 pound	3 medium ($1^1/_3$ cups mashed)	unsweetened	1 ounce	1 square	
			semisweet pieces	6-ounce package	1 cup	
Beans			**Coconut**			
dry	1 pound	2 cups (5 to 7 cups cooked)	flaked	$3^1/_2$-ounce can	$1^1/_3$ cups	
green or wax	1 pound	3 cups ($2^1/_2$ cups cooked)	shredded	4-ounce can	$1^1/_3$ cups	
Berries	1 pint	$1^3/_4$ cups	**Cornmeal**	1 pound	3 to $3^1/_2$ cups	
Bread	1-pound loaf	14 to 20 slices		1 cup uncooked	4 to $4^1/_2$ cups cooked	
fresh	1 slice with crust	$^1/_2$ cup crumbs	**Corn syrup**	16 ounces	2 cups	
dried	1 slice grated	$^1/_4$ cup fine crumbs	**Cranberries**	1 pound	4 cups	
Broth, chicken or beef	1 cup	1 bouillon cube; 1 envelope bouillon; 1 teaspoon instant bouillon dissolved in 1 cup boiling water	**Cranberry sauce**	16-ounce can	$1^2/_3$ cups	
			Cream, heavy or whipping	1 cup	2 cups whipped cream	
Butter or margarine			**Cream, sour**	8 ounces	1 cup	
stick	$^1/_4$ pound	8 tablespoons ($^1/_2$ cup)	**Currants, dried**			
whipped	1 pound	3 cups		1 pound	$3^1/_4$ cups	
Cabbage	1 pound	$4^1/_2$ cups shredded	**Dates**	1 pound	$2^1/_2$ cups pitted	
Carrots	1 pound without tops	3 cups shredded; $2^1/_2$ cups diced	**Egg whites, large**	1 cup	8 to 10 whites	

Food equivalents (continued)

Egg yolks, large	1 cup	12 to 14 yolks
Figs, dried	1 pound	2²/₃ cups chopped
Flour	1 pound	
all-purpose		about 3¹/₂ cups
cake		about 4 cups
Gelatin		
unflavored	1 envelope	1 tablespoon
Graham crackers	14 squares	1 cup fine crumbs
Honey	1 pound	1¹/₃ cups
Lard	1 pound	2 cups
Lemon	1 medium	3 tablespoons juice, about 1 tablespoon grated peel
Lentils	1 pound	2¹/₄ cups (5 cups cooked)
Lime	1 medium	about 2 tablespoons juice
Macaroni		
elbow	4 ounces	1 to 1¹/₄ cups (2 to 2¹/₄ cups cooked)
Maple syrup	12 ounces	1¹/₂ cups
Milk		
evaporated	5¹/₃- or 6-ounce can	²/₃ cup
	13- or 14¹/₂-ounce can	1²/₃ cups
sweetened condensed	14-ounce can	1¹/₄ cups
Molasses	12 ounces	1¹/₂ cups
Mushrooms	1 pound	2 to 3 cups sliced
Noodles	1 pound	6 to 8 cups, uncooked
Nuts	1 pound	
ALMONDS		
in shell		1 to 1¹/₄ cups nutmeats
shelled		3 cups
BRAZIL NUTS		
in shell		1¹/₂ cups nutmeats
shelled		3¹/₄ cups
FILBERTS		
in shell		1¹/₂ cups nutmeats
shelled		3¹/₂ cups
PEANUTS		
in shell		2 to 2¹/₂ cups nutmeats
shelled		3 cups
PECANS		
in shell		2¹/₄ cups nutmeats
shelled		4 cups
WALNUTS		
in shell		2 cups nutmeats
shelled		4 cups

Oats		
uncooked	1 cup	1³/₄ cups cooked
Onion	1 large	³/₄ to 1 cup chopped
Orange	1 medium	¹/₃ to ¹/₂ cup juice 2 tablespoons grated peel
Peaches	1 pound	4 medium (2 cups sliced)
canned	16 ounces	6 to 10 halves 2 cups sliced
Pears	1 pound	4 medium (2 cups sliced)
canned	16 ounces	6 to 10 halves
Peas, split, dried	1 pound	2¹/₄ cups (5 cups cooked)
Pepper, green	1 large	1 cup diced
Pineapple	1 medium	2 cups cubed
canned	20 ounces	2¹/₂ cups crushed pineapple with liquid
		10 medium slices
		2¹/₂ cups chunks with liquid
Potatoes	1 pound	
white		3 medium (2¹/₄ cups diced, 1³/₄ cups mashed)
sweet		3 medium
Prunes, dried	1 pound	2¹/₄ cups pitted (4 to 4¹/₂ cups cooked)
Raisins	1 pound	3 cups, loosely packed
Rice	1 cup	
brown		3 to 4 cups cooked
parboiled		3 to 4 cups cooked
precooked		1 to 2 cups cooked
regular long-grain white		3 or more cups cooked
Salad oil	16 ounces	2 cups
Saltines	28 crackers	1 cup fine crumbs
Shortening, vegetable	1 pound	2¹/₃ cups
Spaghetti	1 pound	about 6¹/₂ cups cooked
Sugar	1 pound	
brown		2¹/₄ cups packed
confectioners'		4 to 4¹/₂ cups
granulated white		2¹/₄ to 2¹/₂ cups
Tomatoes	1 pound	3 medium (1¹/₂ cups cooked)
Vanilla wafers	22 wafers	1 cup fine crumbs
Yogurt	¹/₂ pint	1 cup

Index

Read Country Living and surround yourself with all the joys of country living at its very best…

SAVE over $900 from the single-copy cost.

Never before has it been so easy to bring that charming "country look" into your home…a hearty "country flavor" to your cooking and a little old-fashioned "country cheer" to your life.

If you consider yourself one who can appreciate living life to its fullest in the "old-fashioned…remember when" tradition—then welcome to Country Living, designed with your interests in mind.

With a subscription to Country Living you'll profit from and enjoy articles like these:

- Country in the City: A Charming Loft
- Simply Beautiful—7 Imaginative Flower Arrangements in Country-Style Containers
- Ceiling Fans: New Old-Time Energy Savers
- "Remember When" Home Cooking: A Treasury of Old-Fashioned Recipes

- Visit a Connecticut Herb Farm
- Buying Country Houses—What to Look For
- Decorating With Stencils
- New China and Linens For That Down Home Look
- Visit The Hancock Shaker Village

The subject matter is wide and the coverage is complete. Whether your interest lies in *decorating, crafts, cooking, collectibles, gardening, canning, travelling, real estate, remodelling*…Country Living has it all.

Country Living is certainly well deserving of your time and attention—and as soon as you read your first copy from cover to cover, we're confident you'll agree. To have the convenience of receiving Country Living right at your door, simply fill out the coupon, and send it to us, today! Your first copy will be on its way to you in 6 to 12 weeks. Look for it!